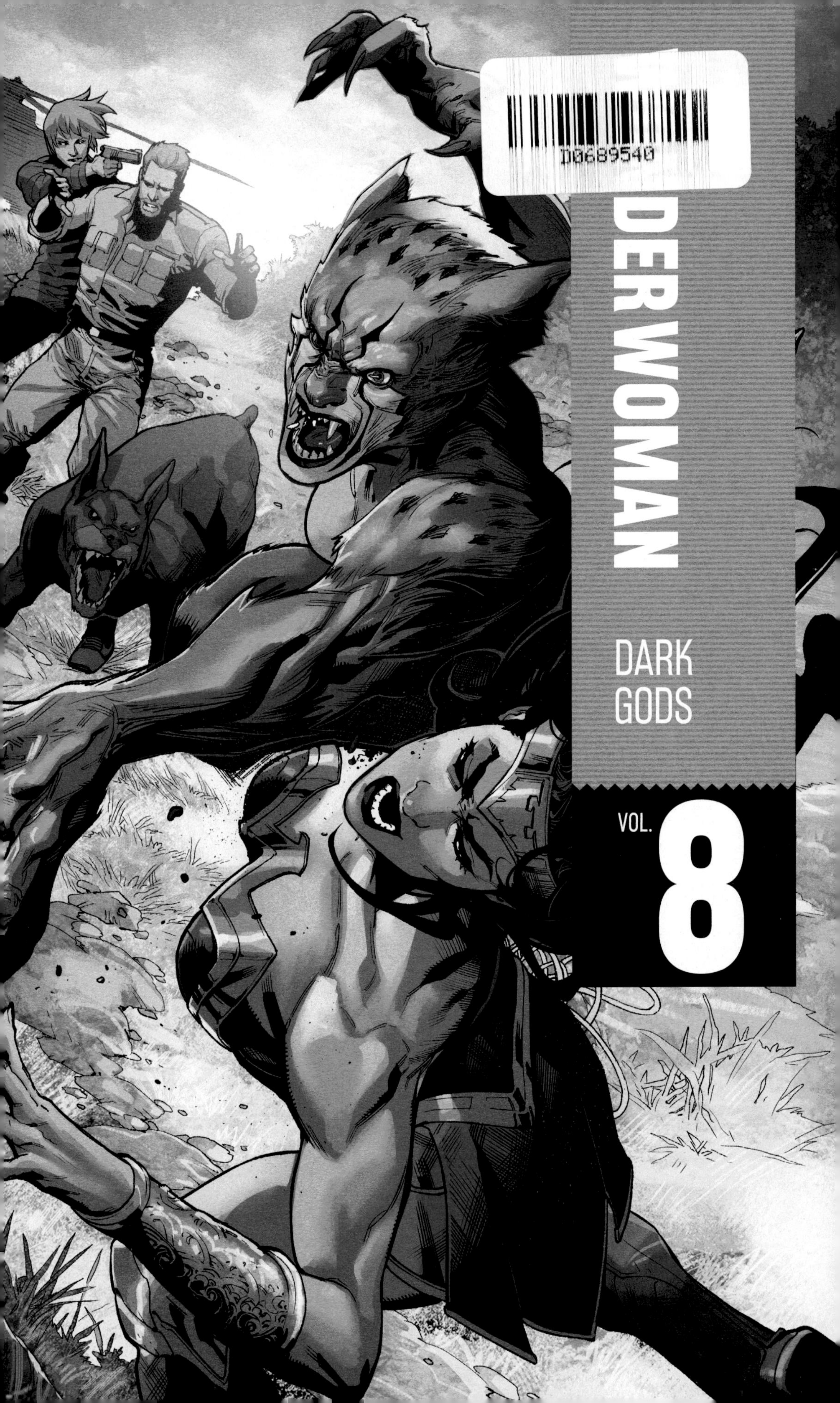
DER WOMAN
DARK GODS
VOL. 8

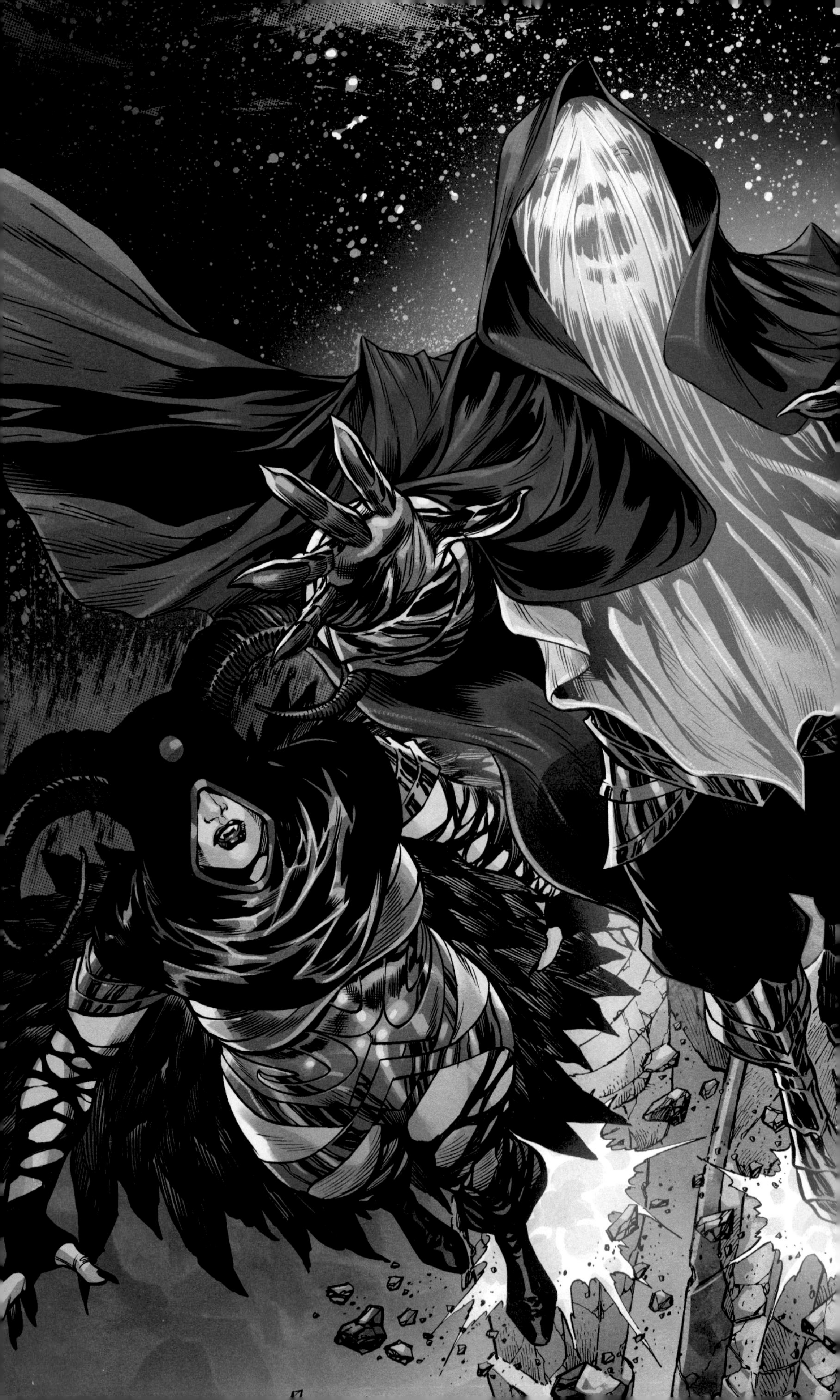

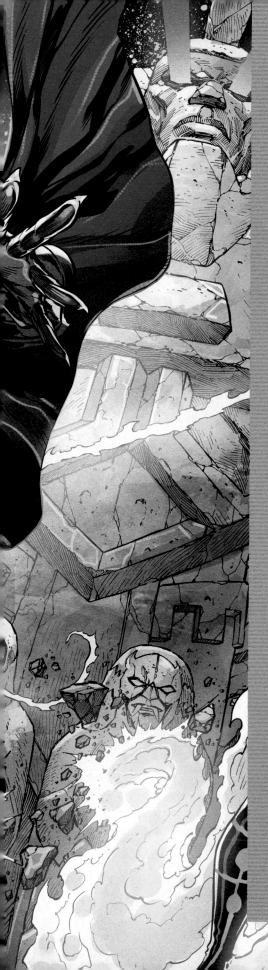

WONDER **WOMAN**
DARK GODS

writer
JAMES ROBINSON

artists
STEPHEN SEGOVIA
JESUS MERINO
MARC LAMING
FRAZER IRVING
J. CALAFIORE
ANDY OWENS
EMANUELA LUPACCHINO
RAY McCARTHY
RICK LEONARDI

colorists
ROMULO FAJARDO JR.
DAVID BARON
FRAZER IRVING
ALLEN PASSALAQUA
CHRIS SOTOMAYOR

letterer
SAIDA TEMOFONTE

collection cover artist
JENNY FRISON

VOL.
8

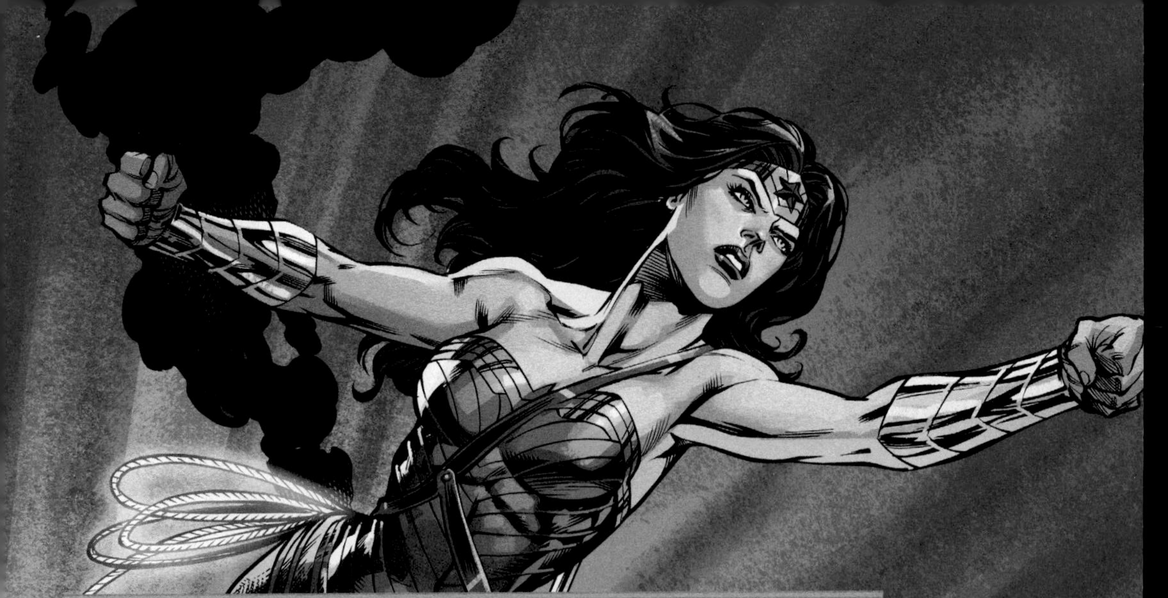

CHRIS CONROY Editor – Original Series
DAVE WIELGOSZ Assistant Editor – Original Series
JEB WOODARD Group Editor – Collected Editions
ROBIN WILDMAN Editor – Collected Edition
STEVE COOK Design Director – Books
MEGEN BELLERSEN Publication Design

BOB HARRAS Senior VP – Editor-in-Chief, DC Comics
PAT McCALLUM Executive Editor, DC Comics

DAN DiDIO Publisher
JIM LEE Publisher & Chief Creative Officer
AMIT DESAI Executive VP – Business & Marketing Strategy, Direct to Consumer & Global Franchise Management
BOBBIE CHASE VP & Executive Editor, Young Reader & Talent Development
MARK CHIARELLO Senior VP – Art, Design & Collected Editions
JOHN CUNNINGHAM Senior VP – Sales & Trade Marketing
BRIAR DARDEN VP – Business Affairs
ANNE DePIES Senior VP – Business Strategy, Finance & Administration
DON FALLETTI VP – Manufacturing Operations
LAWRENCE GANEM VP – Editorial Administration & Talent Relations
ALISON GILL Senior VP – Manufacturing & Operations
JASON GREENBERG VP – Business Strategy & Finance
HANK KANALZ Senior VP – Editorial Strategy & Administration
JAY KOGAN Senior VP – Legal Affairs
NICK J. NAPOLITANO VP – Manufacturing Administration
LISETTE OSTERLOH VP – Digital Marketing & Events
EDDIE SCANNELL VP – Consumer Marketing
COURTNEY SIMMONS Senior VP – Publicity & Communications
JIM (SKI) SOKOLOWSKI VP – Comic Book Specialty Sales & Trade Marketing
NANCY SPEARS VP – Mass, Book, Digital Sales & Trade Marketing
MICHELE R. WELLS VP – Content Strategy

WONDER WOMAN VOL. 8: DARK GODS

DC Comics, 2900 West Alameda Ave., Burbank, CA 91505
Printed by LSC Communications, Kendallville, IN, USA. 3/15/19. First Printing.
ISBN: 978-1-4012-8901-0

Library of Congress Cataloging-in-Publication Data is available.

PEFC Certified
This product is from sustainably managed forests and controlled sources
PEFC
PEFC/29-31-337
www.pefc.org

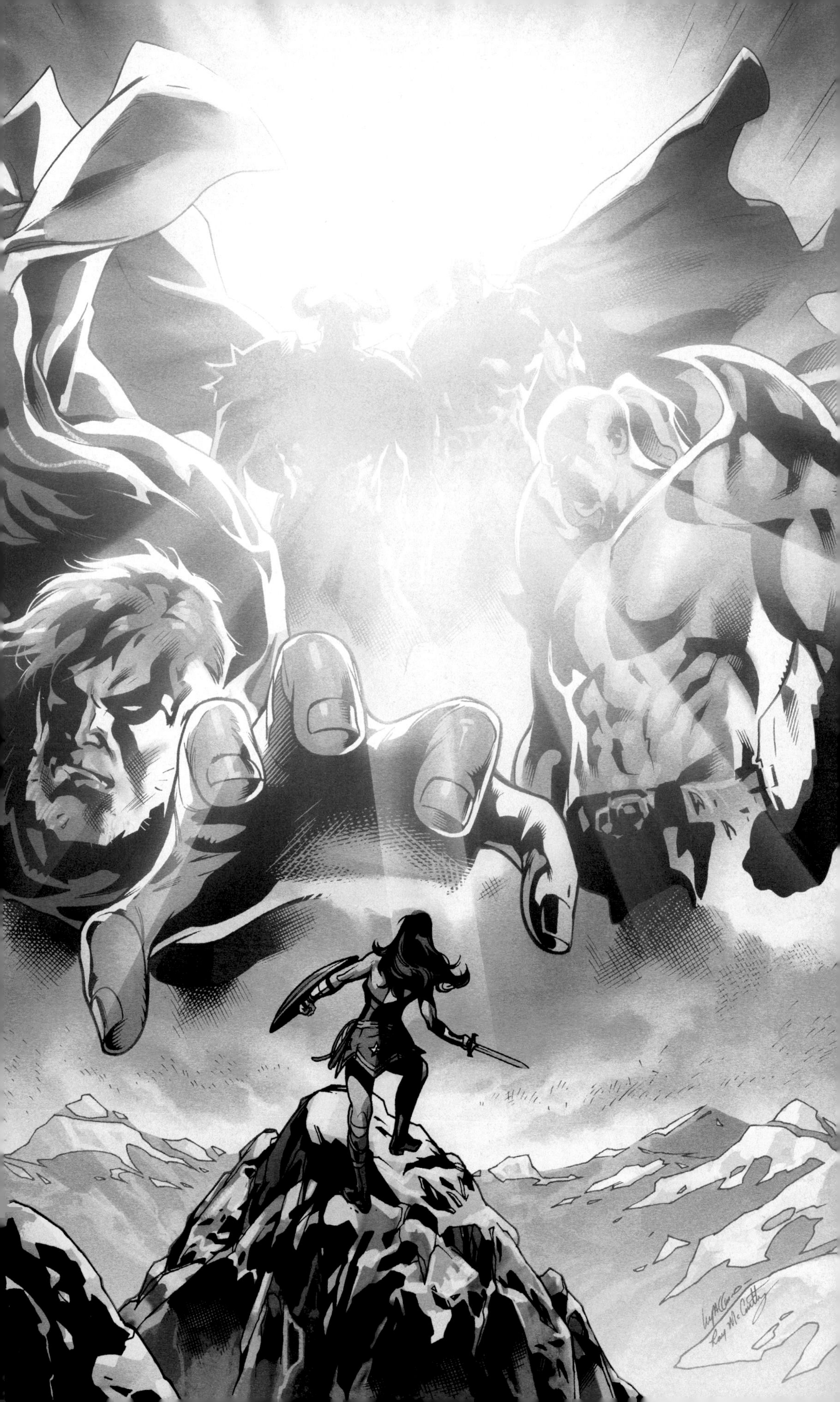

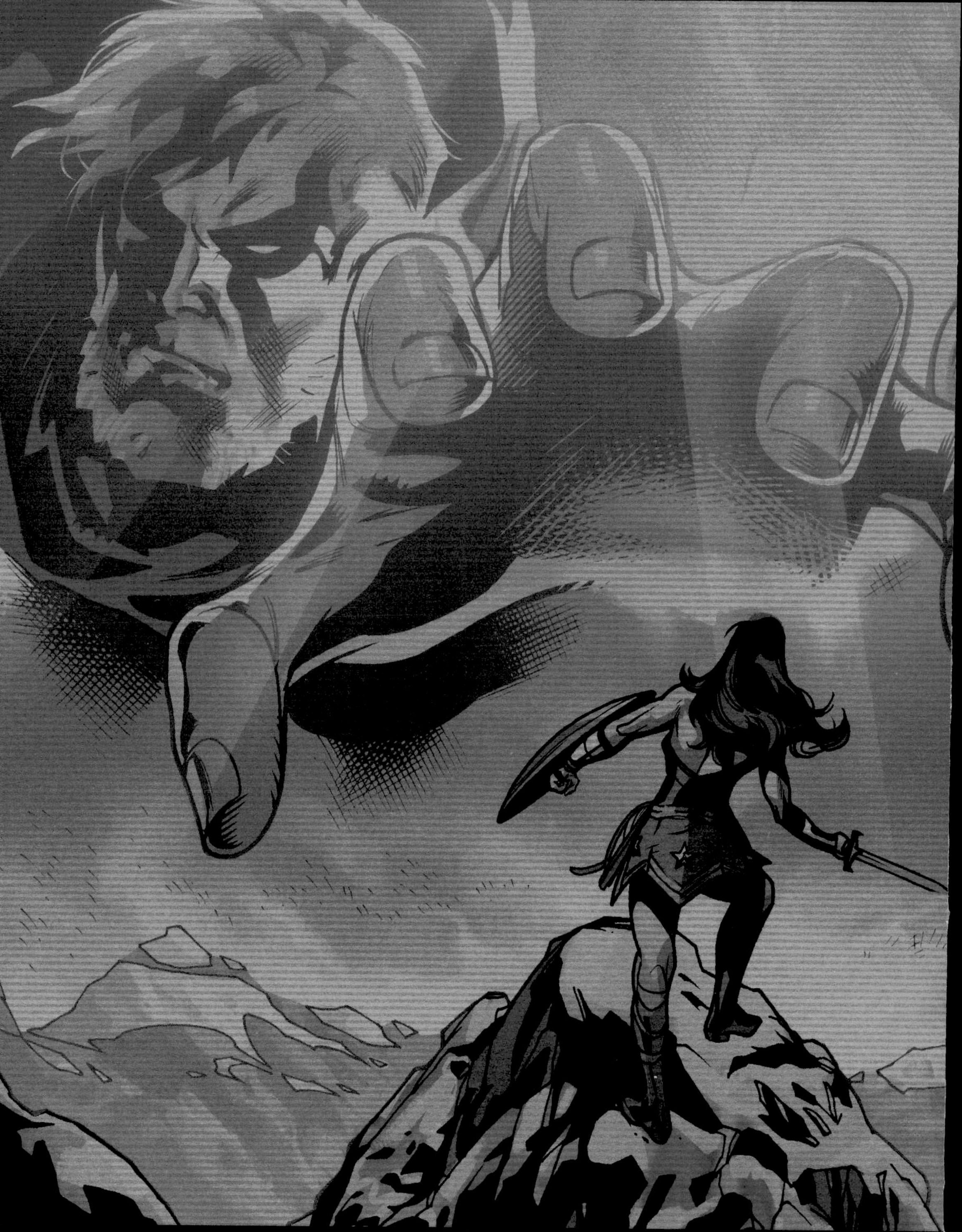

WONDER WOMAN

#46

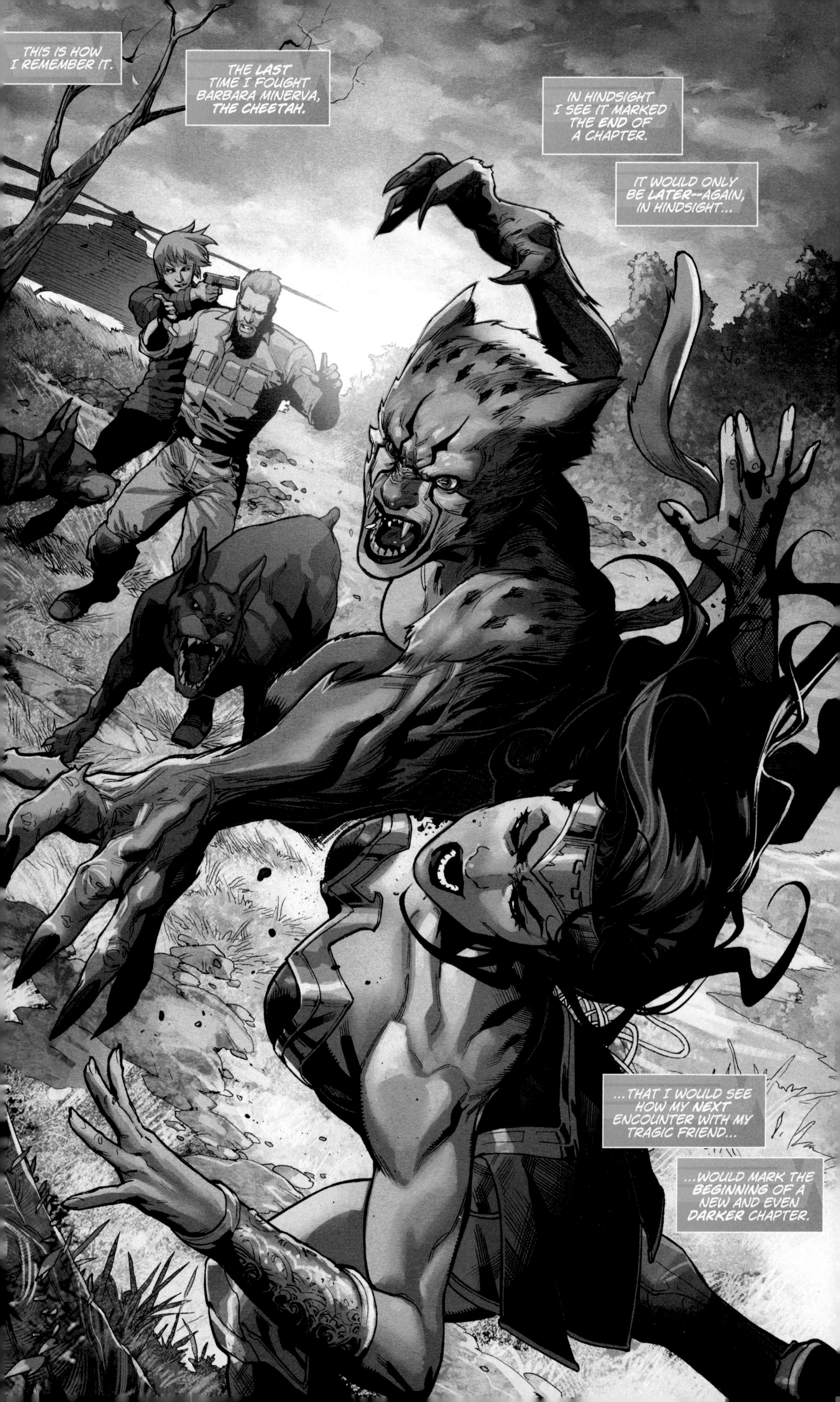
THIS IS HOW I REMEMBER IT.
THE LAST TIME I FOUGHT BARBARA MINERVA, THE CHEETAH.
IN HINDSIGHT I SEE IT MARKED THE END OF A CHAPTER.
IT WOULD ONLY BE LATER--AGAIN, IN HINDSIGHT...
...THAT I WOULD SEE HOW MY NEXT ENCOUNTER WITH MY TRAGIC FRIEND...
...WOULD MARK THE BEGINNING OF A NEW AND EVEN DARKER CHAPTER.

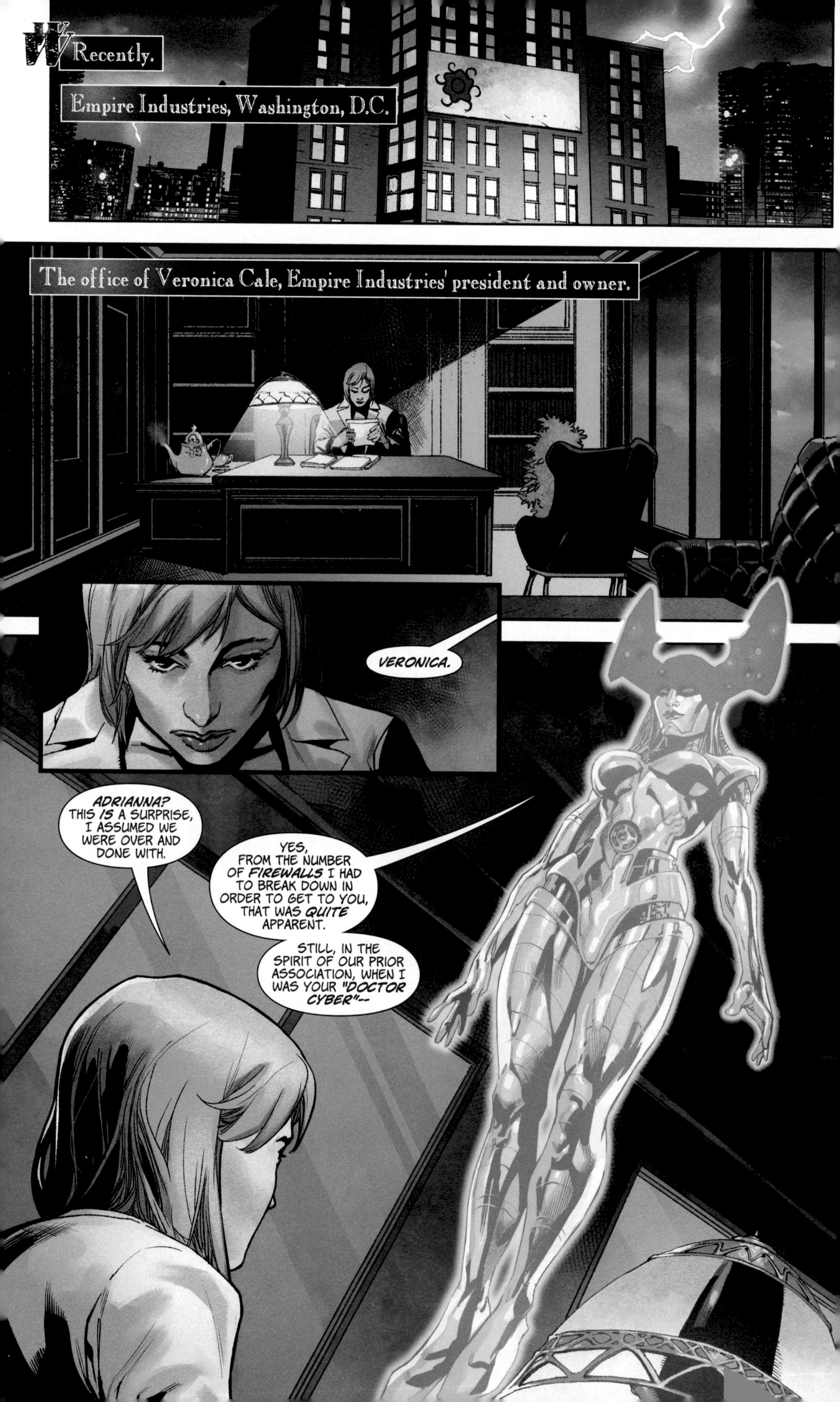
Recently.
Empire Industries, Washington, D.C.
The office of Veronica Cale, Empire Industries' president and owner.
VERONICA.
ADRIANNA? THIS IS A SURPRISE, I ASSUMED WE WERE OVER AND DONE WITH.
YES, FROM THE NUMBER OF FIREWALLS I HAD TO BREAK DOWN IN ORDER TO GET TO YOU, THAT WAS QUITE APPARENT.
STILL, IN THE SPIRIT OF OUR PRIOR ASSOCIATION, WHEN I WAS YOUR "DOCTOR CYBER"--

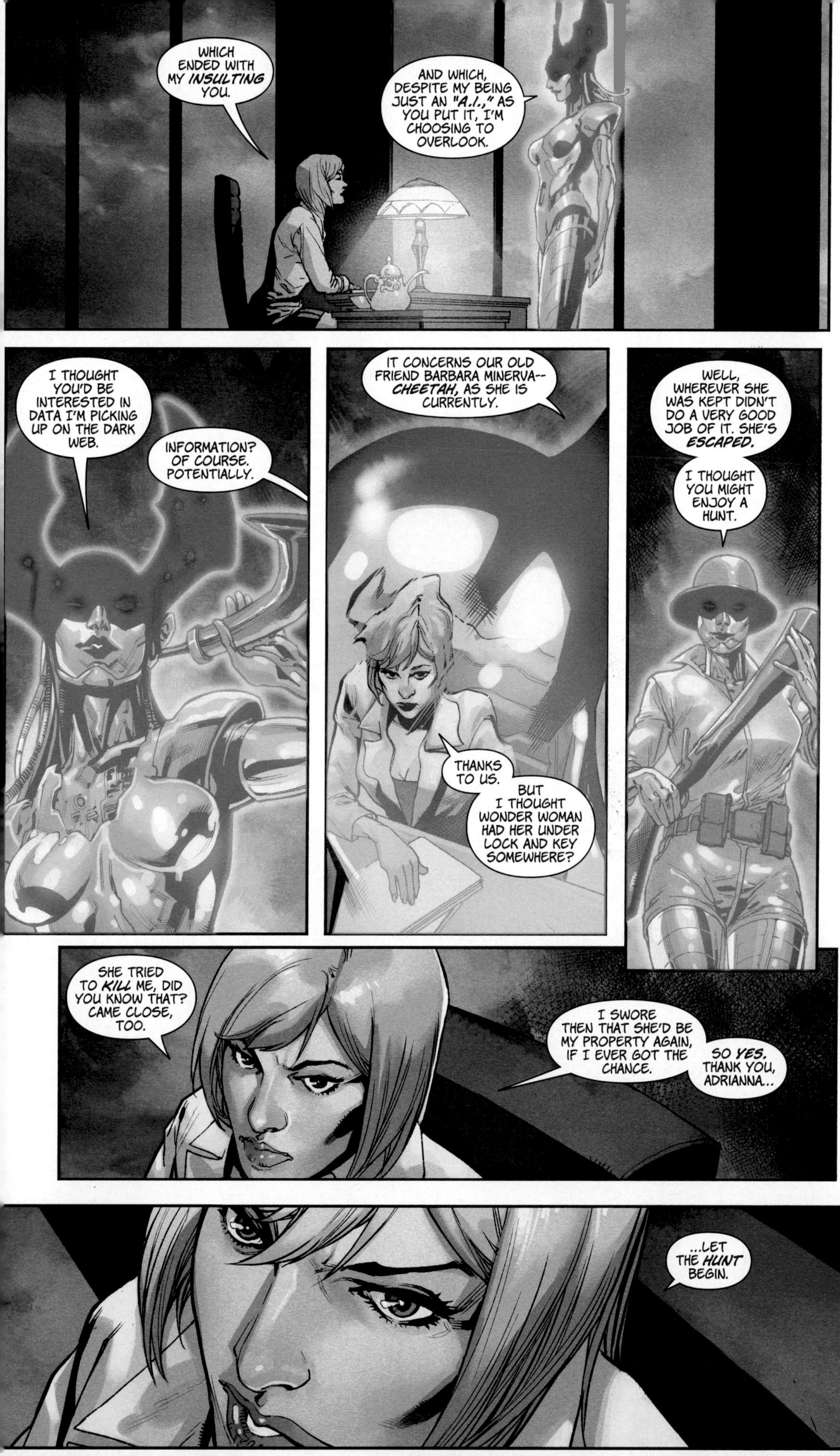
WHICH ENDED WITH MY *INSULTING* YOU.
AND WHICH, DESPITE MY BEING JUST AN *"A.I.,"* AS YOU PUT IT, I'M CHOOSING TO OVERLOOK.
I THOUGHT YOU'D BE INTERESTED IN DATA I'M PICKING UP ON THE DARK WEB.
INFORMATION? OF COURSE. POTENTIALLY.
IT CONCERNS OUR OLD FRIEND BARBARA MINERVA-- *CHEETAH,* AS SHE IS CURRENTLY.
THANKS TO US.
BUT I THOUGHT WONDER WOMAN HAD HER UNDER LOCK AND KEY SOMEWHERE?
WELL, WHEREVER SHE WAS KEPT DIDN'T DO A VERY GOOD JOB OF IT. SHE'S *ESCAPED.*
I THOUGHT YOU MIGHT ENJOY A HUNT.
SHE TRIED TO *KILL* ME, DID YOU KNOW THAT? CAME CLOSE, TOO.
I SWORE THEN THAT SHE'D BE MY PROPERTY AGAIN, IF I EVER GOT THE CHANCE.
SO *YES.* THANK YOU, ADRIANNA..
...LET THE *HUNT* BEGIN.

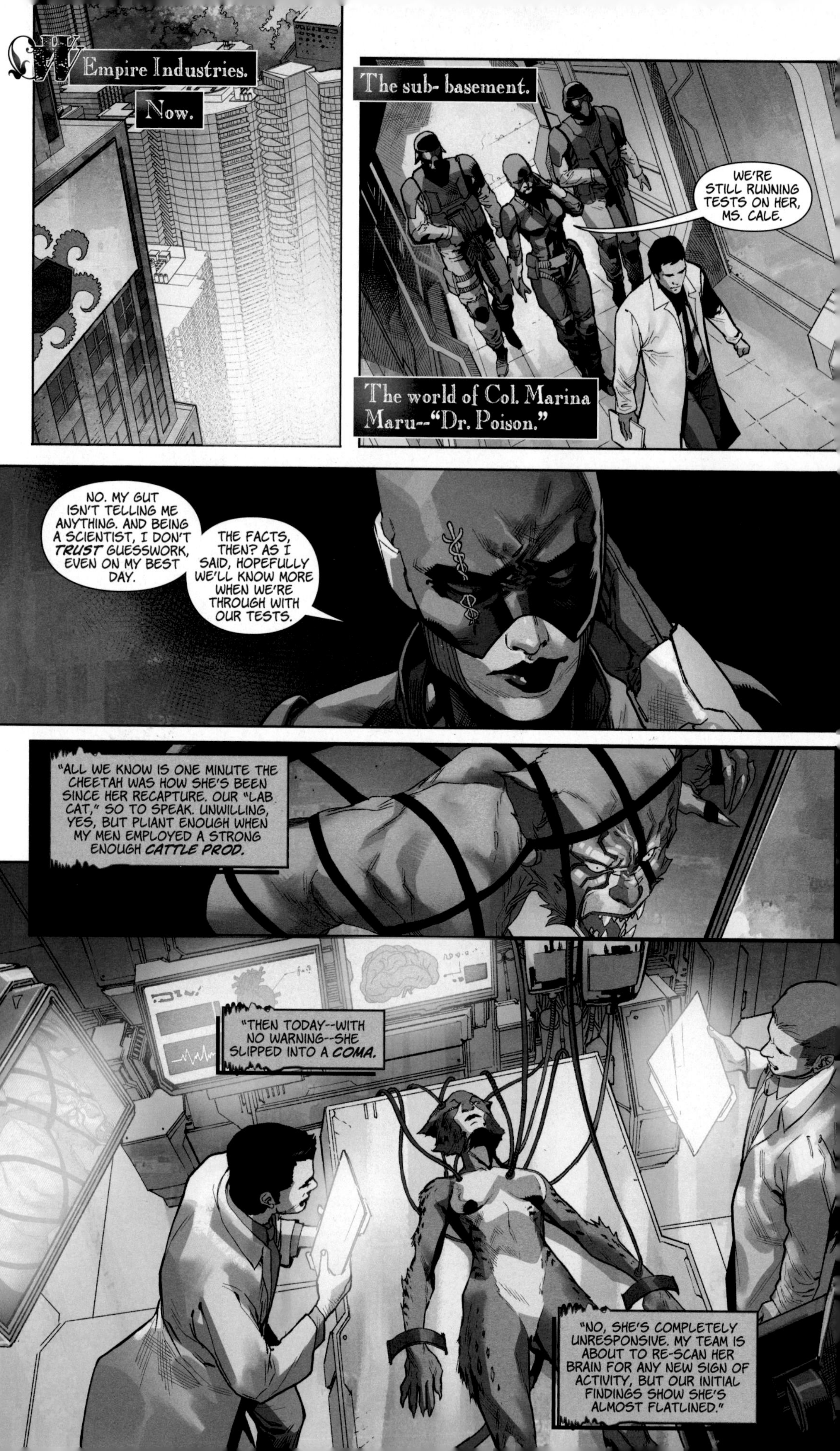

Empire Industries.
Now.
The sub- basement.
WE'RE STILL RUNNING TESTS ON HER, MS. CALE.
The world of Col. Marina Maru--"Dr. Poison."
NO. MY GUT ISN'T TELLING ME ANYTHING. AND BEING A SCIENTIST, I DON'T *TRUST* GUESSWORK, EVEN ON MY BEST DAY.
THE FACTS, THEN? AS I SAID, HOPEFULLY WE'LL KNOW MORE WHEN WE'RE THROUGH WITH OUR TESTS.
"ALL WE KNOW IS ONE MINUTE THE CHEETAH WAS HOW SHE'S BEEN SINCE HER RECAPTURE. OUR "LAB CAT," SO TO SPEAK. UNWILLING, YES, BUT PLIANT ENOUGH WHEN MY MEN EMPLOYED A STRONG ENOUGH *CATTLE PROD.*
"THEN TODAY--WITH NO WARNING--SHE SLIPPED INTO A *COMA.*
"NO, SHE'S COMPLETELY UNRESPONSIVE. MY TEAM IS ABOUT TO RE-SCAN HER BRAIN FOR ANY NEW SIGN OF ACTIVITY, BUT OUR INITIAL FINDINGS SHOW SHE'S ALMOST FLATLINED."

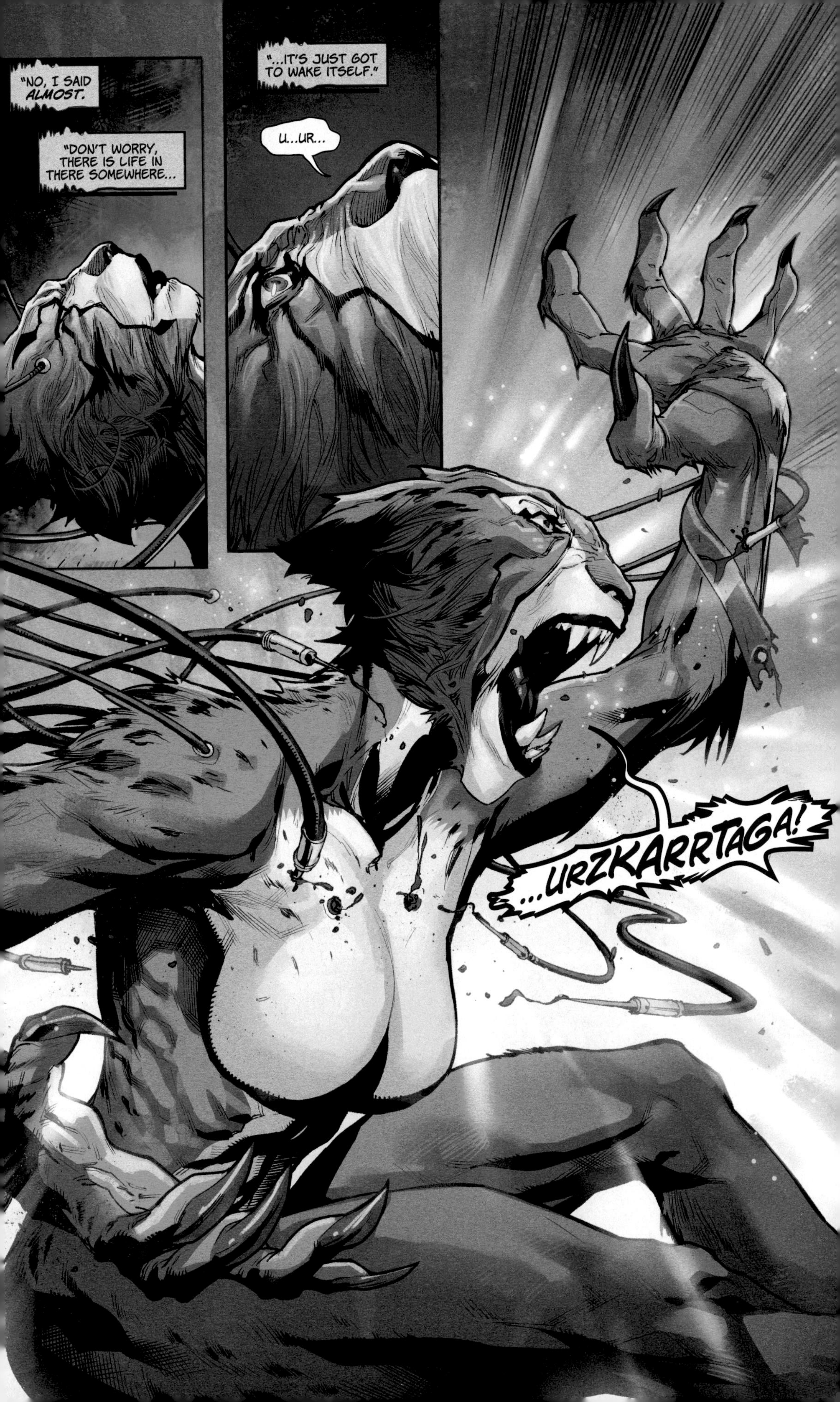
"NO, I SAID ALMOST.
"DON'T WORRY, THERE IS LIFE IN THERE SOMEWHERE...
"...IT'S JUST GOT TO WAKE ITSELF."
U...UR...
...URZKARRTAGA!

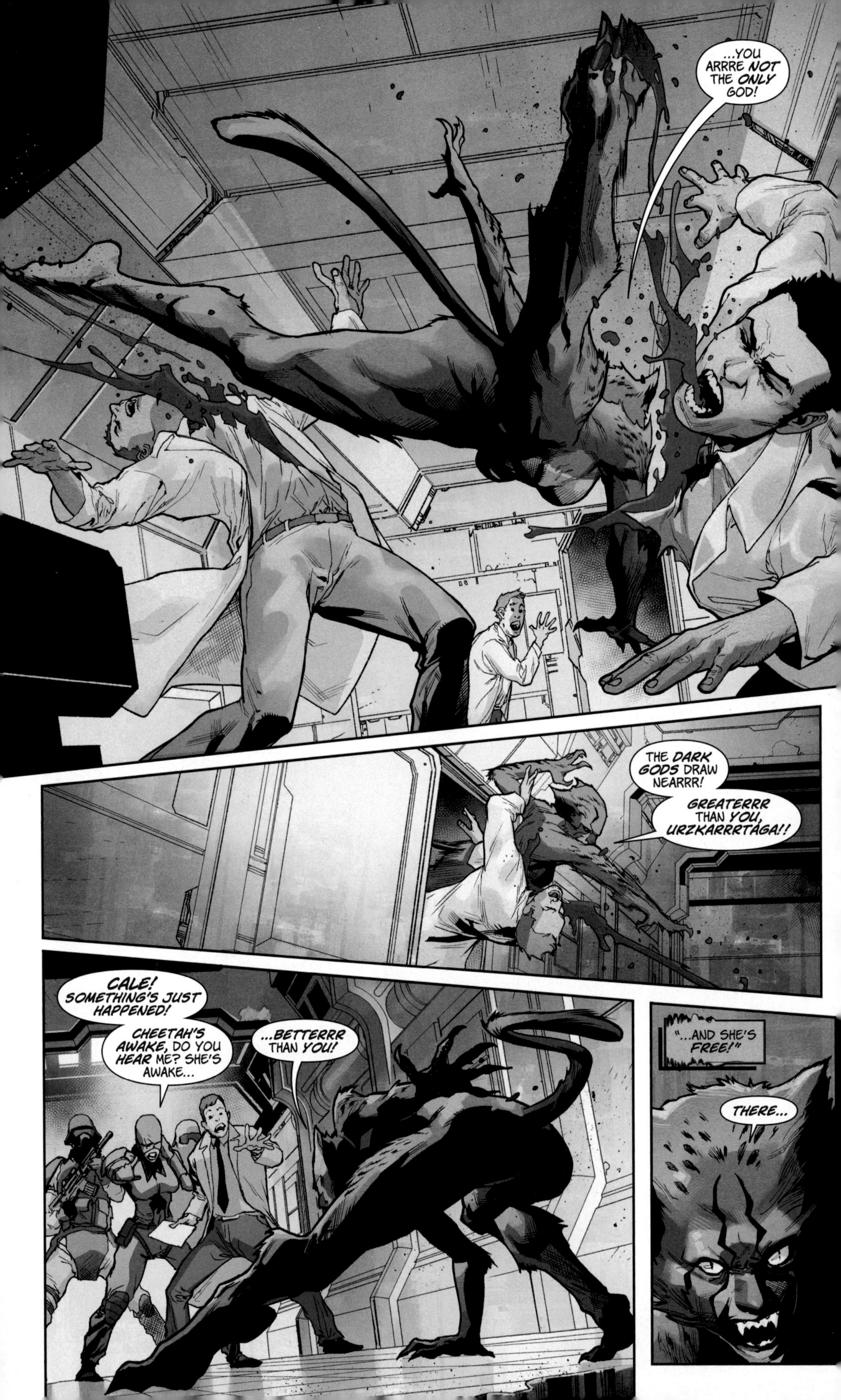
...YOU ARRRE NOT THE ONLY GOD!
THE DARK GODS DRAW NEARRR!
GREATERRR THAN YOU, URZKARRRTAGA!!
CALE! SOMETHING'S JUST HAPPENED!
CHEETAH'S AWAKE, DO YOU HEAR ME? SHE'S AWAKE...
...BETTERRR THAN YOU!
"...AND SHE'S FREE!"
THERE...

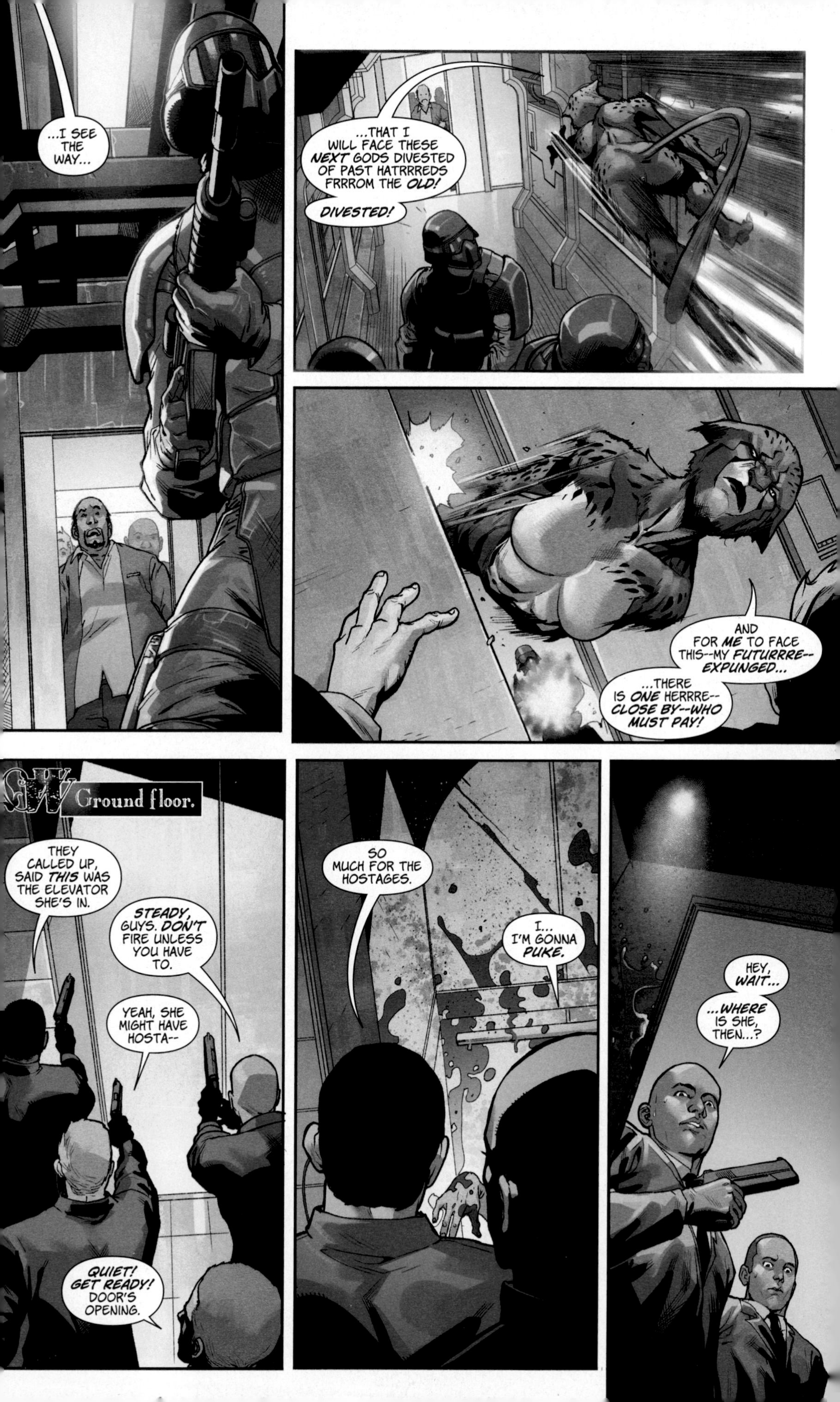

...I SEE THE WAY...
...THAT I WILL FACE THESE NEXT GODS DIVESTED OF PAST HATRRREDS FRRROM THE OLD!
DIVESTED!
AND FOR ME TO FACE THIS--MY FUTURRRE--EXPUNGED...
...THERE IS ONE HERRRE--CLOSE BY--WHO MUST PAY!
Ground floor.
THEY CALLED UP, SAID THIS WAS THE ELEVATOR SHE'S IN.
STEADY, GUYS. DON'T FIRE UNLESS YOU HAVE TO.
YEAH, SHE MIGHT HAVE HOSTA--
QUIET! GET READY! DOOR'S OPENING.
SO MUCH FOR THE HOSTAGES.
I... I'M GONNA PUKE.
HEY, WAIT...
...WHERE IS SHE, THEN...?

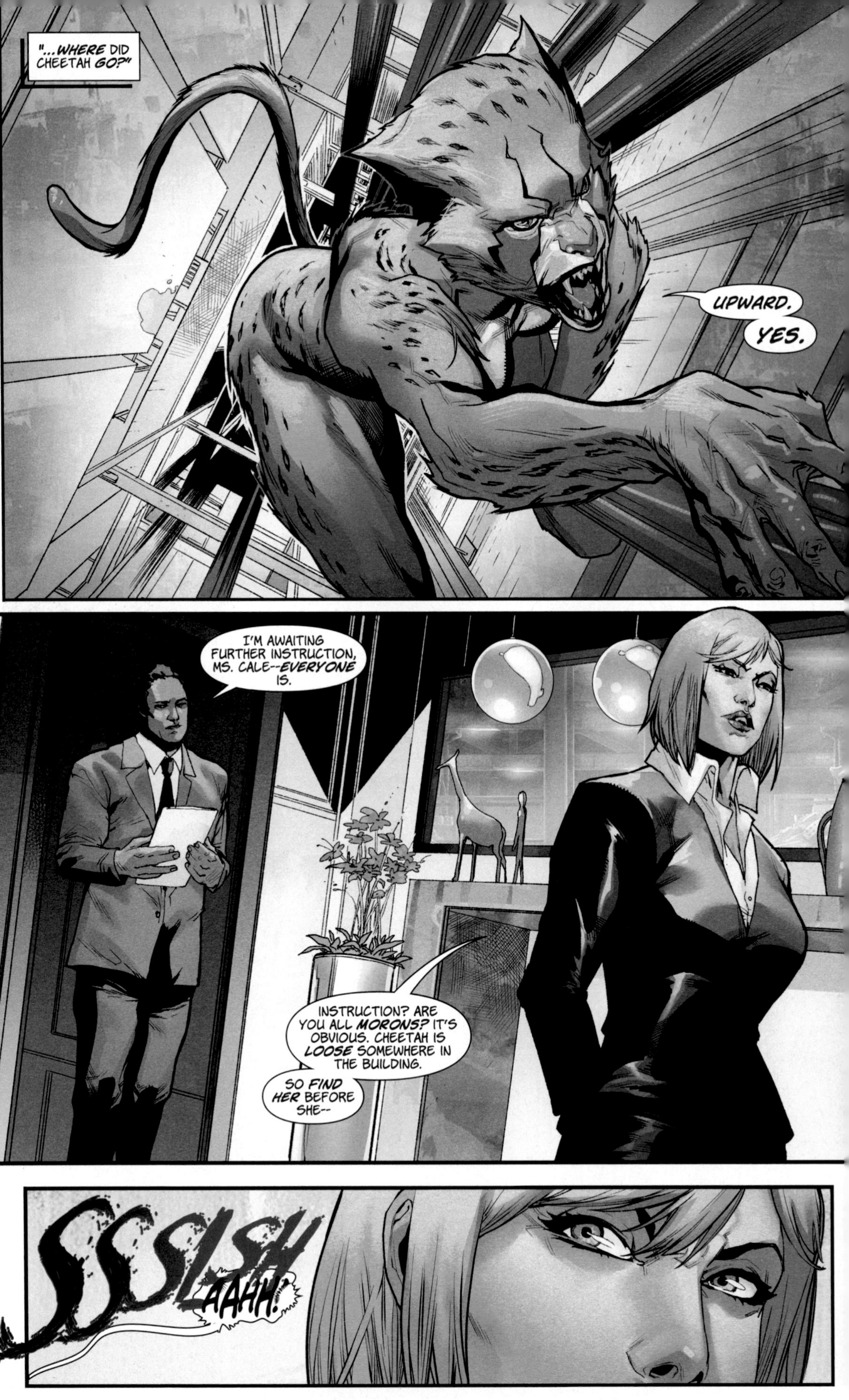
"...WHERE DID CHEETAH GO?"
UPWARD.
YES.
I'M AWAITING FURTHER INSTRUCTION, MS. CALE--EVERYONE IS.
INSTRUCTION? ARE YOU ALL MORONS? IT'S OBVIOUS. CHEETAH IS LOOSE SOMEWHERE IN THE BUILDING.
SO FIND HER BEFORE SHE--
SSSLISH
AAHH!

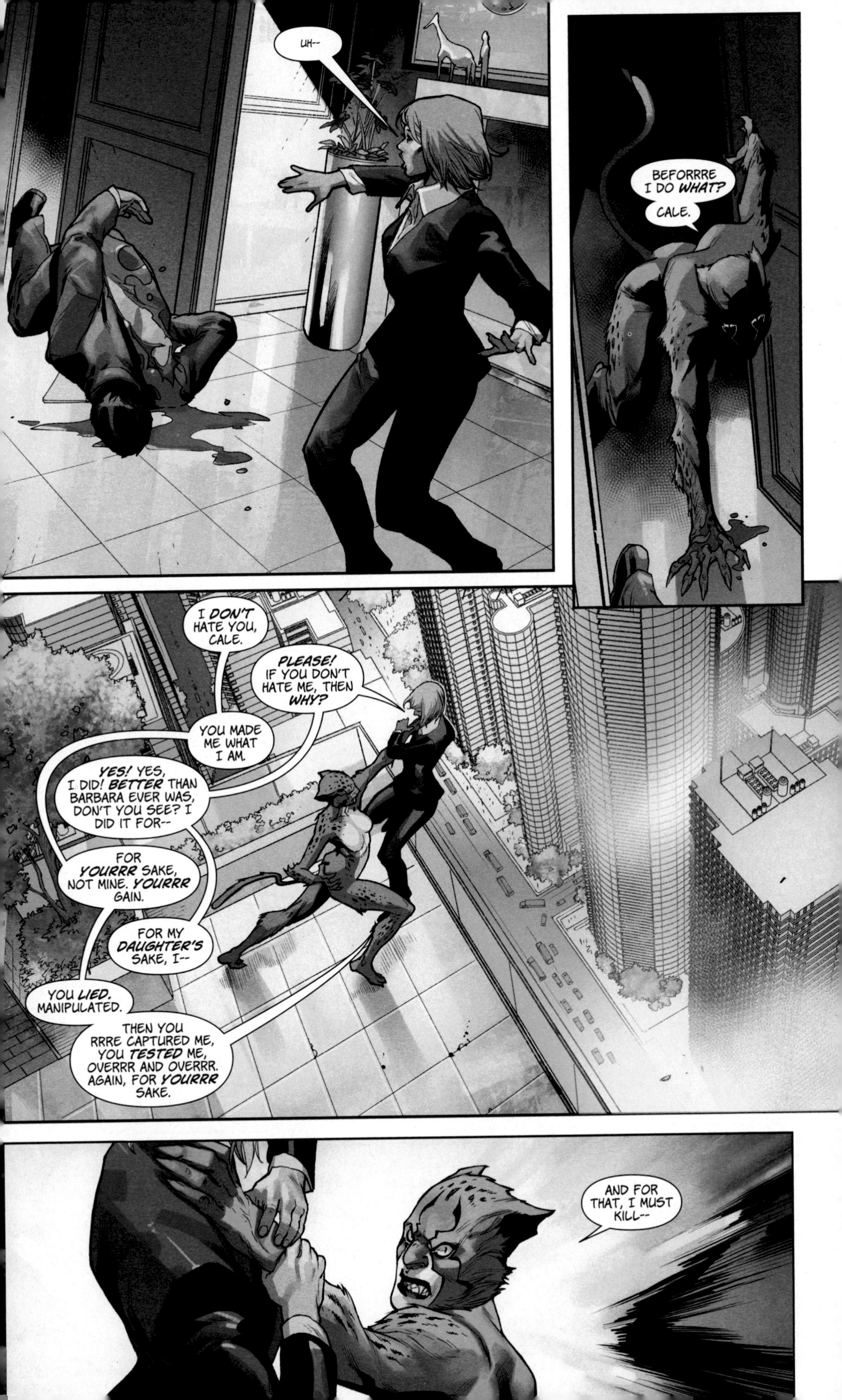

UH--
BEFORRRE I DO WHAT?
CALE.
I DON'T HATE YOU, CALE.
PLEASE! IF YOU DON'T HATE ME, THEN WHY?
YOU MADE ME WHAT I AM.
YES! YES, I DID! BETTER THAN BARBARA EVER WAS, DON'T YOU SEE? I DID IT FOR--
FOR YOURRR SAKE, NOT MINE. YOURRR GAIN.
FOR MY DAUGHTER'S SAKE, I--
YOU LIED. MANIPULATED.
THEN YOU RRRE CAPTURED ME, YOU TESTED ME, OVERRR AND OVERRR. AGAIN, FOR YOURRR SAKE.
AND FOR THAT, I MUST KILL--

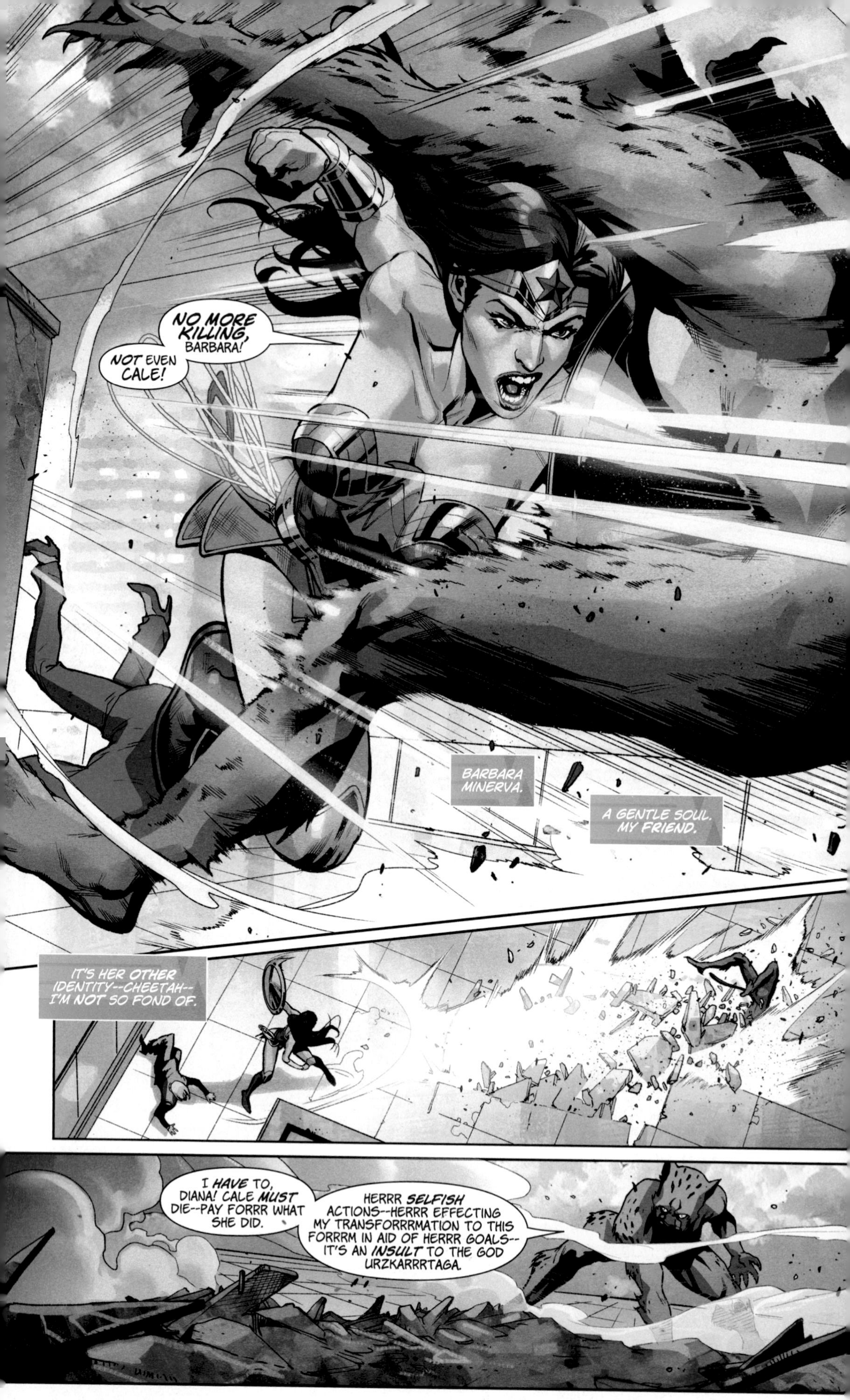

NO MORE KILLING, BARBARA!
NOT EVEN CALE!
BARBARA MINERVA.
A GENTLE SOUL. MY FRIEND.
IT'S HER OTHER IDENTITY--CHEETAH-- I'M NOT SO FOND OF.
I HAVE TO, DIANA! CALE MUST DIE--PAY FORRR WHAT SHE DID.
HERRR SELFISH ACTIONS--HERRR EFFECTING MY TRANSFORRRMATION TO THIS FORRRM IN AID OF HERRR GOALS-- IT'S AN INSULT TO THE GOD URZKARRRTAGA.

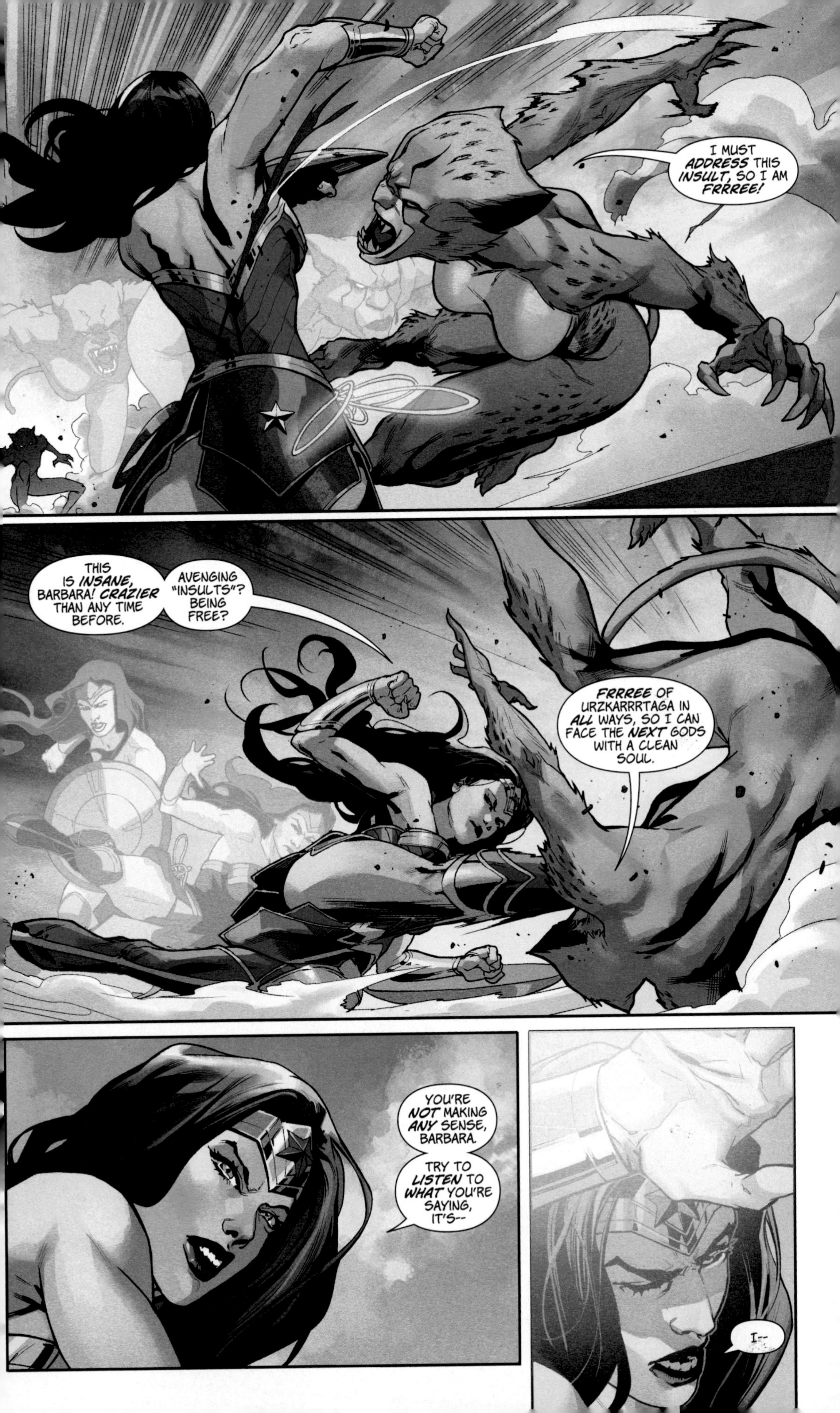
I MUST ADDRESS THIS INSULT, SO I AM FRRREE!
THIS IS INSANE, BARBARA! CRAZIER THAN ANY TIME BEFORE.
AVENGING "INSULTS"? BEING FREE?
FRRREE OF URZKARRRTAGA IN ALL WAYS, SO I CAN FACE THE NEXT GODS WITH A CLEAN SOUL.
YOU'RE NOT MAKING ANY SENSE, BARBARA.
TRY TO LISTEN TO WHAT YOU'RE SAYING, IT'S--
I--

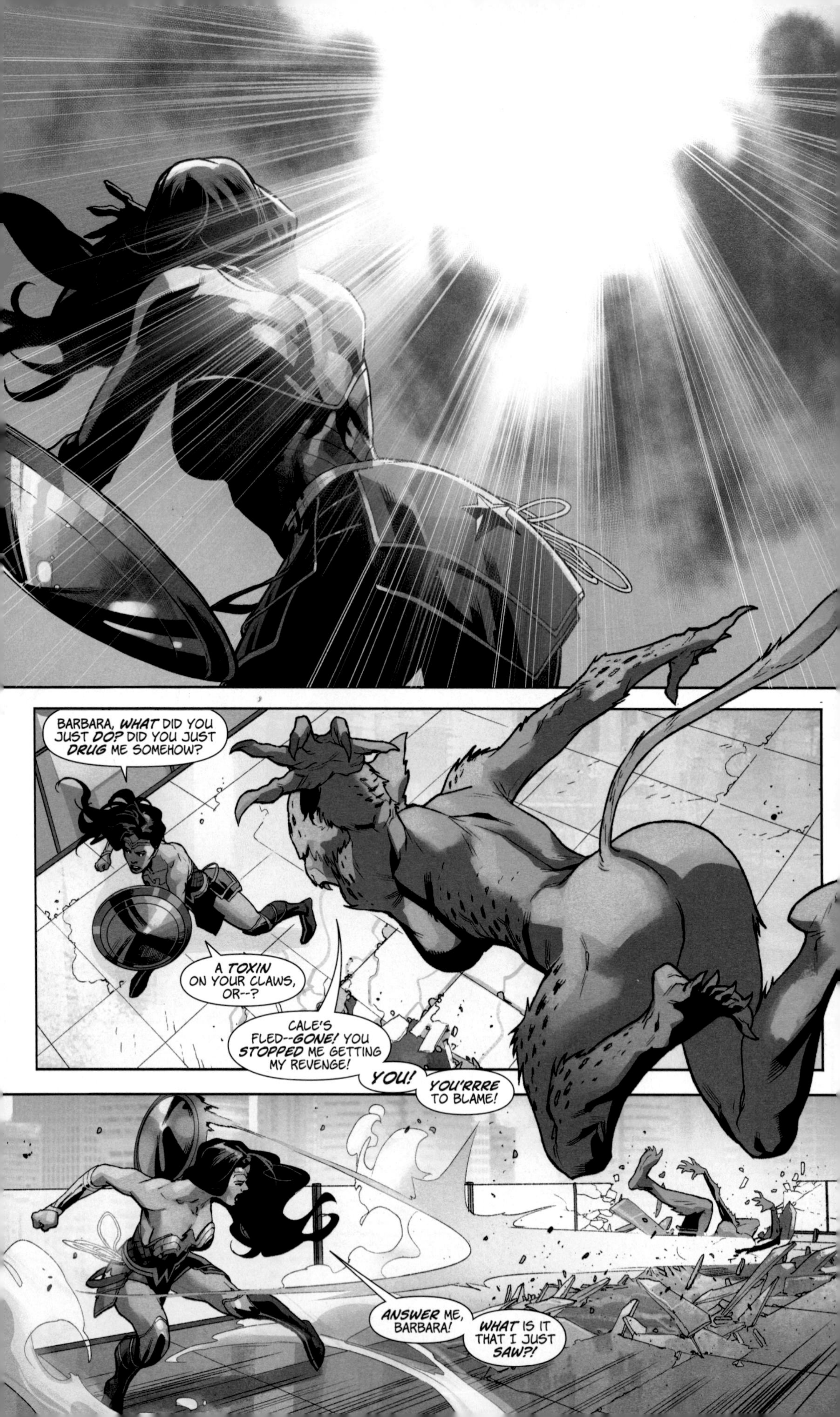
BARBARA, WHAT DID YOU JUST DO? DID YOU JUST DRUG ME SOMEHOW?
A TOXIN ON YOUR CLAWS, OR--?
CALE'S FLED--GONE! YOU STOPPED ME GETTING MY REVENGE!
YOU!
YOU'RRRE TO BLAME!
ANSWER ME, BARBARA!
WHAT IS IT THAT I JUST SAW?!

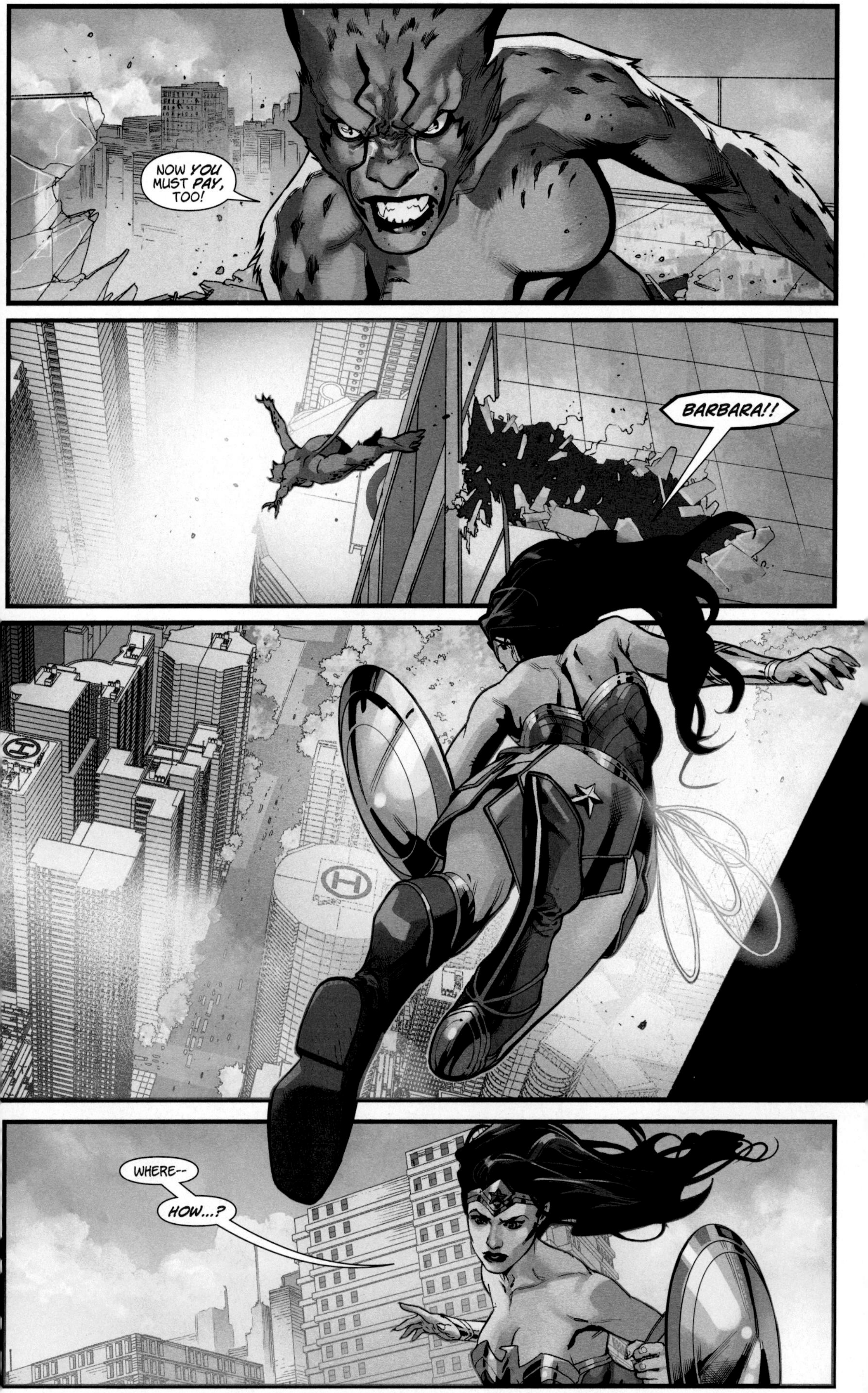
NOW YOU MUST PAY, TOO!
BARBARA!!
WHERE--
HOW...?

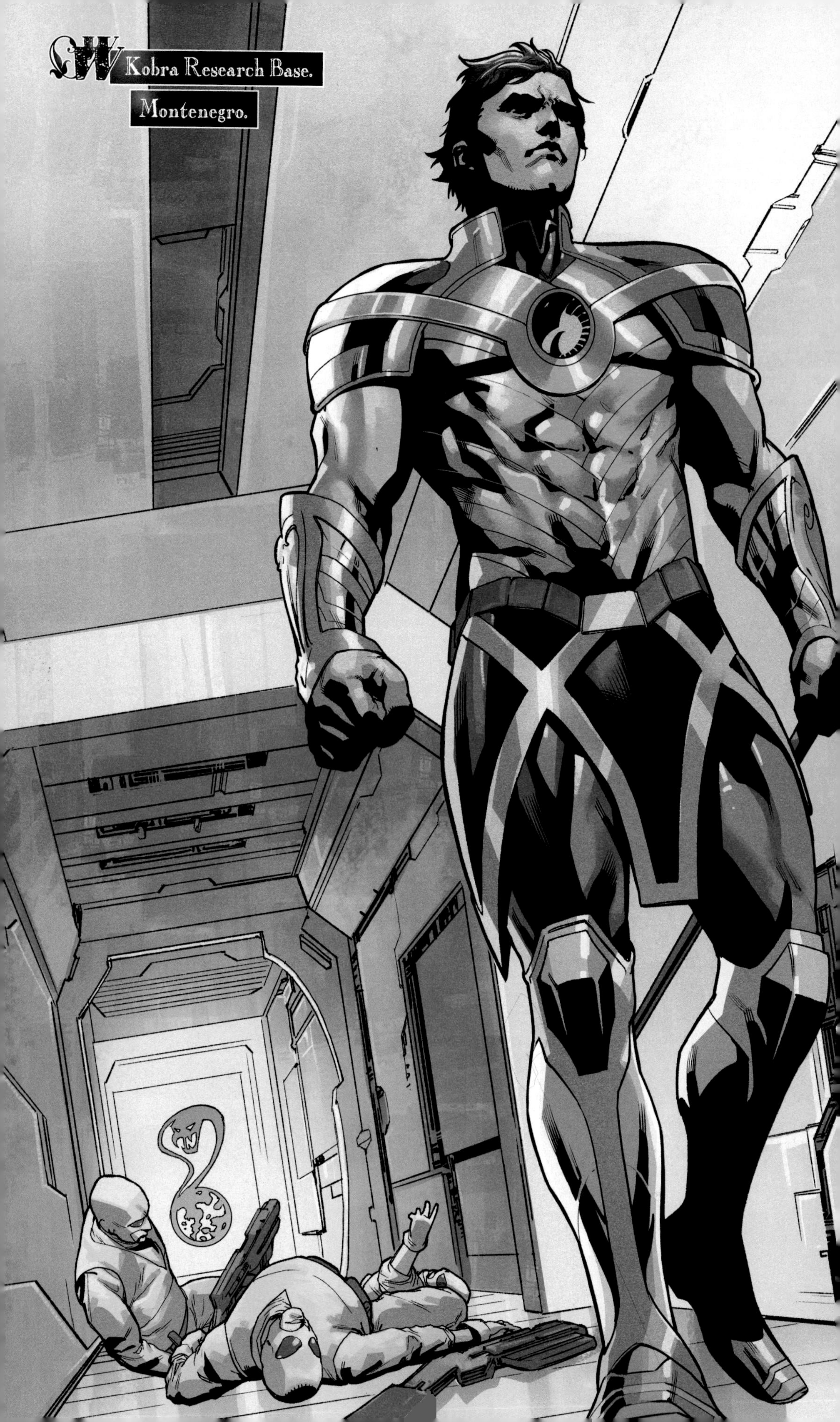
Kobra Research Base.
Montenegro.

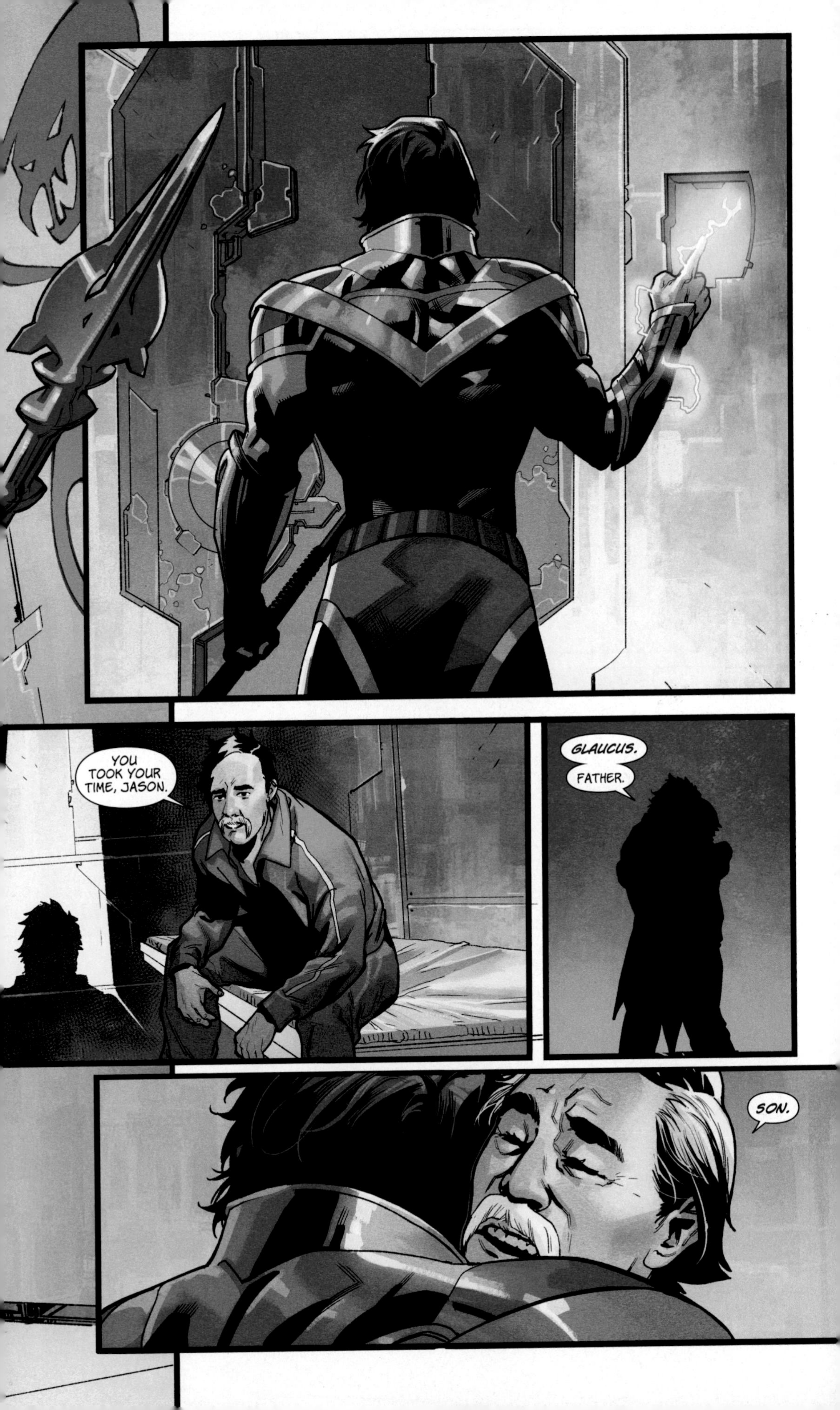
YOU TOOK YOUR TIME, JASON.
GLAUCUS.
FATHER.
SON.

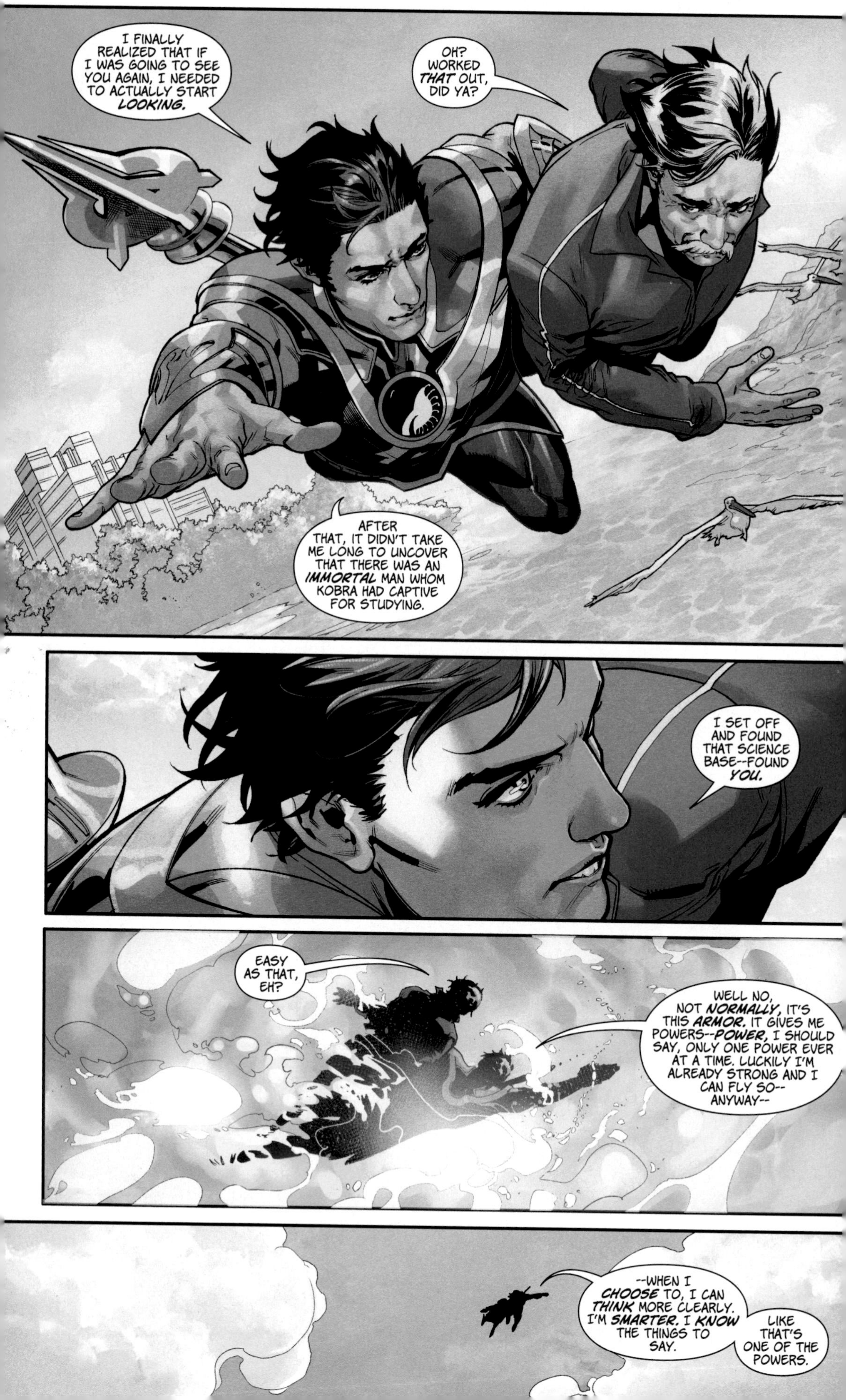
I FINALLY REALIZED THAT IF I WAS GOING TO SEE YOU AGAIN, I NEEDED TO ACTUALLY START LOOKING.
OH? WORKED THAT OUT, DID YA?
AFTER THAT, IT DIDN'T TAKE ME LONG TO UNCOVER THAT THERE WAS AN IMMORTAL MAN WHOM KOBRA HAD CAPTIVE FOR STUDYING.
I SET OFF AND FOUND THAT SCIENCE BASE--FOUND YOU.
EASY AS THAT, EH?
WELL NO, NOT NORMALLY, IT'S THIS ARMOR. IT GIVES ME POWERS--POWER, I SHOULD SAY, ONLY ONE POWER EVER AT A TIME. LUCKILY I'M ALREADY STRONG AND I CAN FLY SO-- ANYWAY--
--WHEN I CHOOSE TO, I CAN THINK MORE CLEARLY. I'M SMARTER. I KNOW THE THINGS TO SAY.
LIKE THAT'S ONE OF THE POWERS.

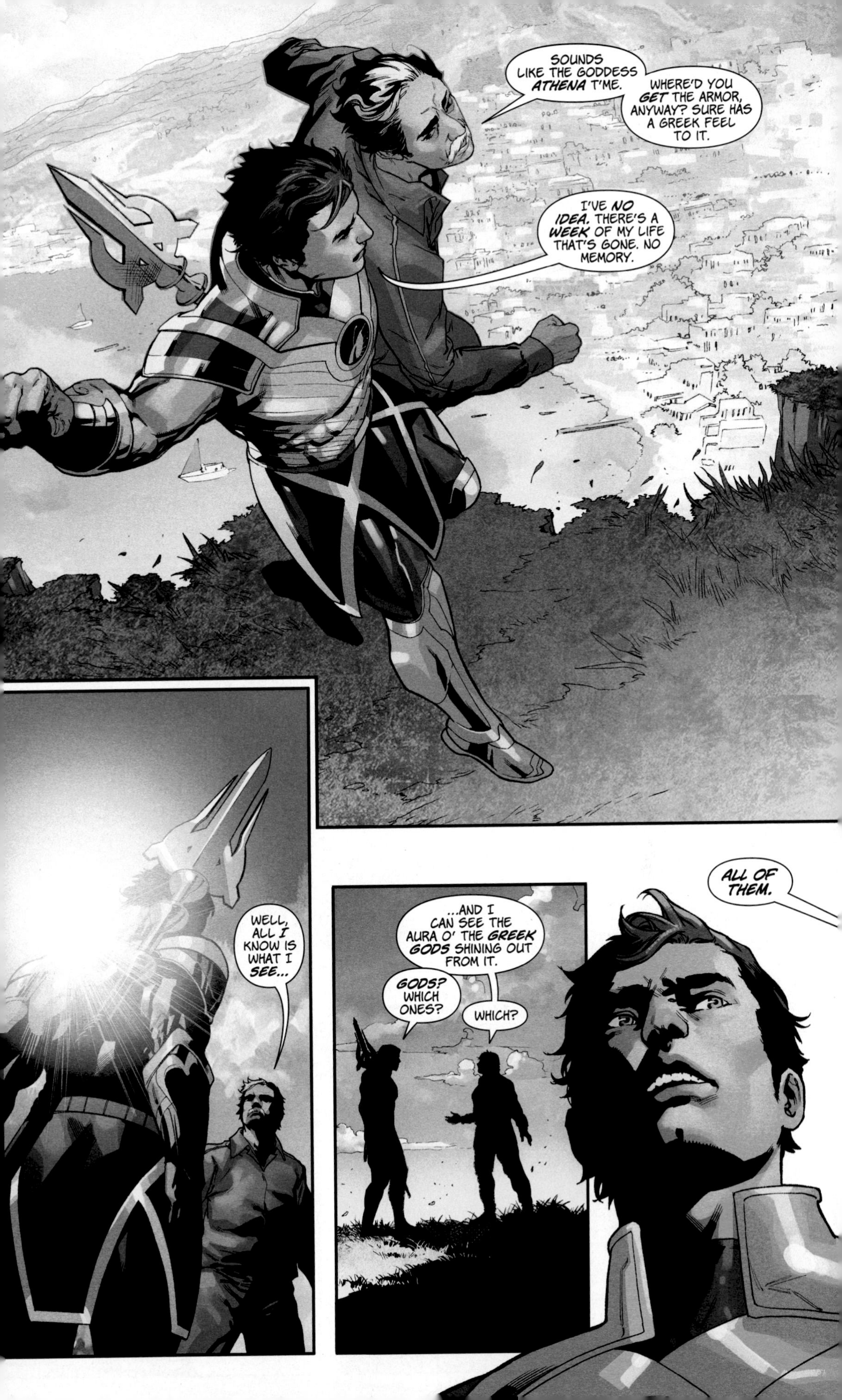
SOUNDS LIKE THE GODDESS ATHENA T'ME.
WHERE'D YOU GET THE ARMOR, ANYWAY? SURE HAS A GREEK FEEL TO IT.
I'VE NO IDEA. THERE'S A WEEK OF MY LIFE THAT'S GONE. NO MEMORY.
WELL, ALL I KNOW IS WHAT I SEE...
...AND I CAN SEE THE AURA O' THE GREEK GODS SHINING OUT FROM IT.
GODS? WHICH ONES?
WHICH?
ALL OF THEM.

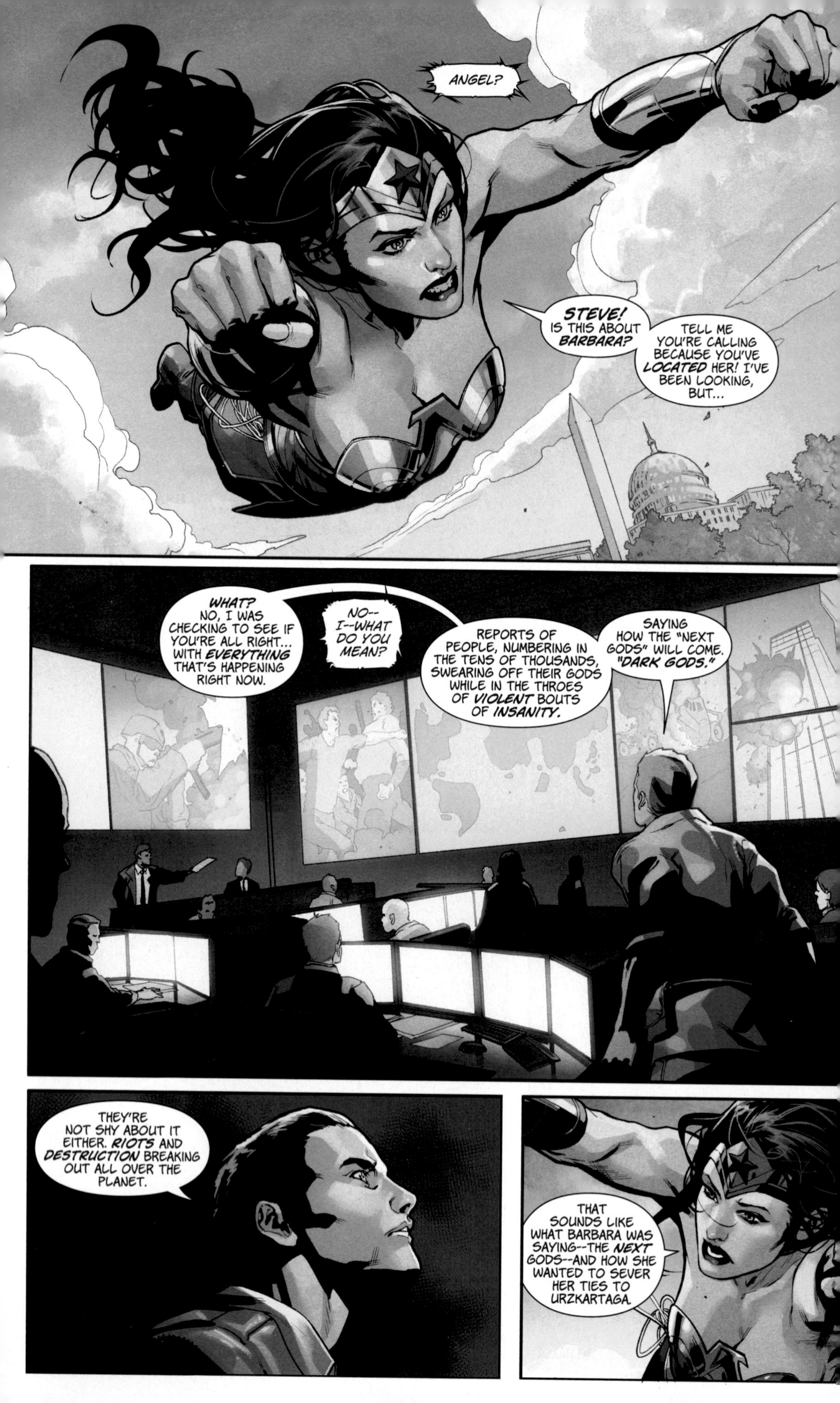

ANGEL?
STEVE! IS THIS ABOUT BARBARA?
TELL ME YOU'RE CALLING BECAUSE YOU'VE LOCATED HER! I'VE BEEN LOOKING, BUT...
WHAT? NO, I WAS CHECKING TO SEE IF YOU'RE ALL RIGHT... WITH EVERYTHING THAT'S HAPPENING RIGHT NOW.
NO-- I--WHAT DO YOU MEAN?
REPORTS OF PEOPLE, NUMBERING IN THE TENS OF THOUSANDS, SWEARING OFF THEIR GODS WHILE IN THE THROES OF VIOLENT BOUTS OF INSANITY.
SAYING HOW THE "NEXT GODS" WILL COME. "DARK GODS."
THEY'RE NOT SHY ABOUT IT EITHER. RIOTS AND DESTRUCTION BREAKING OUT ALL OVER THE PLANET.
THAT SOUNDS LIKE WHAT BARBARA WAS SAYING--THE NEXT GODS--AND HOW SHE WANTED TO SEVER HER TIES TO URZKARTAGA.

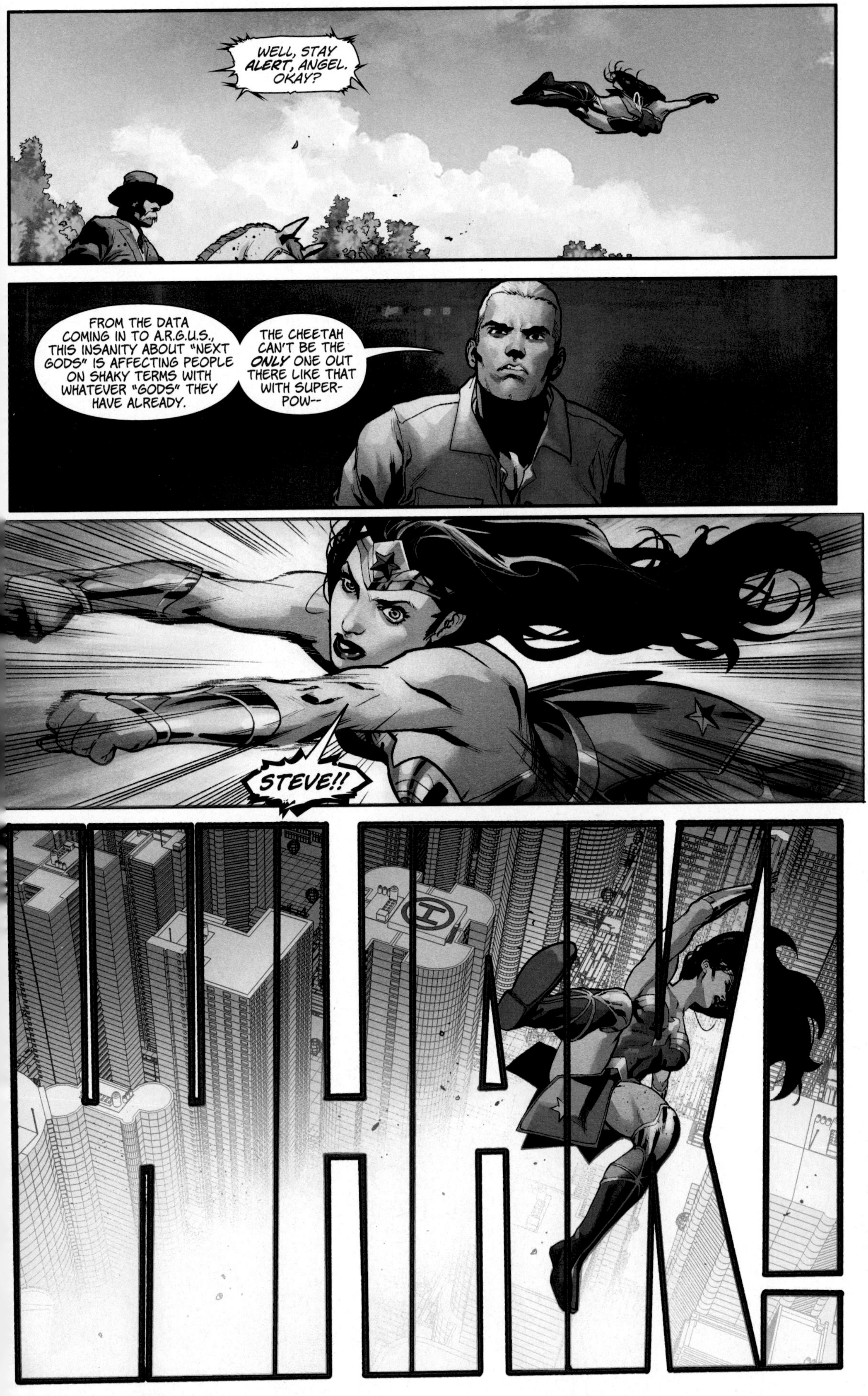
WELL, STAY ALERT, ANGEL. OKAY?
FROM THE DATA COMING IN TO A.R.G.U.S., THIS INSANITY ABOUT "NEXT GODS" IS AFFECTING PEOPLE ON SHAKY TERMS WITH WHATEVER "GODS" THEY HAVE ALREADY.
THE CHEETAH CAN'T BE THE ONLY ONE OUT THERE LIKE THAT WITH SUPER-POW--
STEVE!!
THHK!

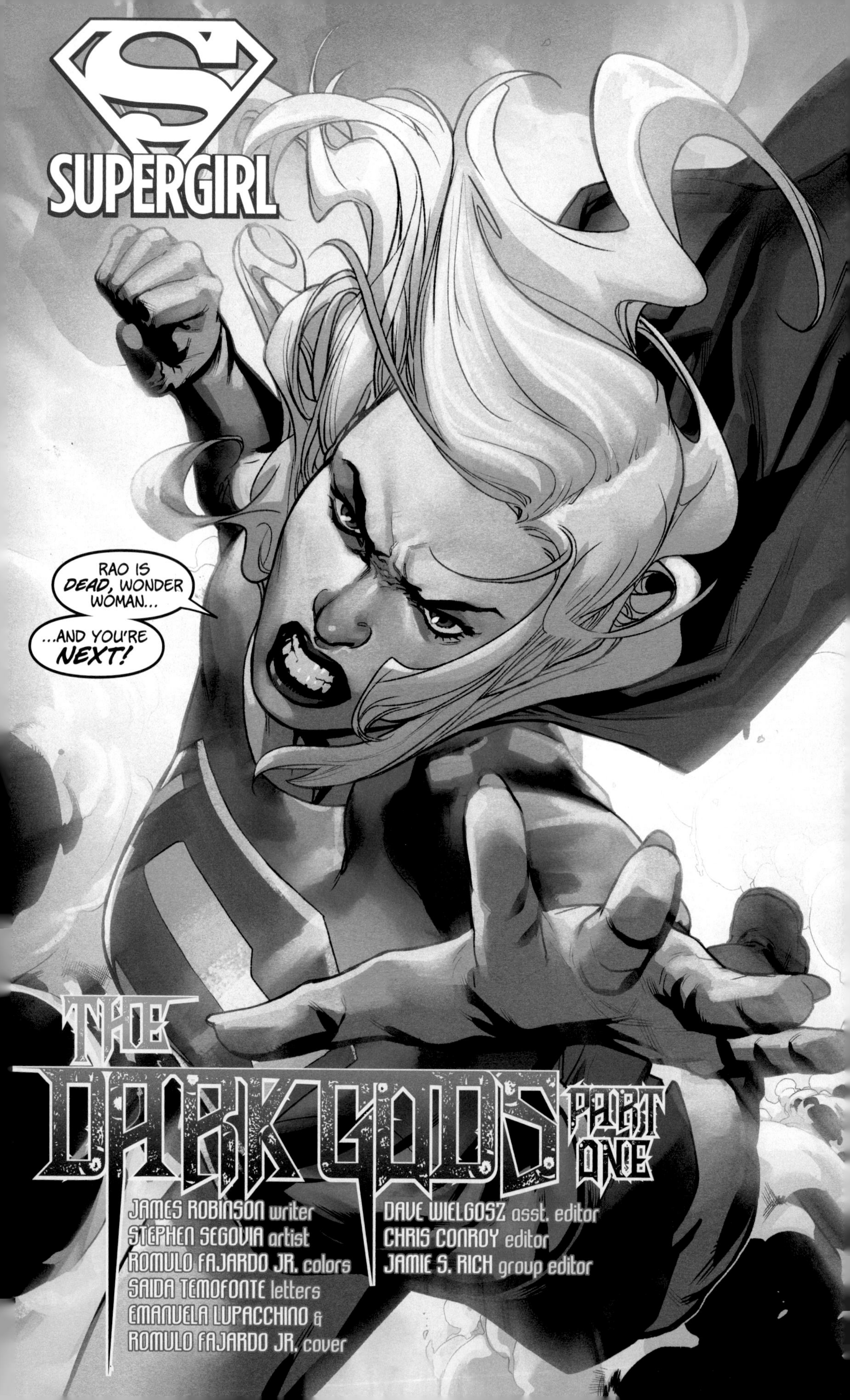
SUPERGIRL
RAO IS DEAD, WONDER WOMAN...
...AND YOU'RE NEXT!
THE DARK GODS PART ONE
JAMES ROBINSON writer
STEPHEN SEGOVIA artist
ROMULO FAJARDO JR. colors
SAIDA TEMOFONTE letters
EMANUELA LUPACCHINO & ROMULO FAJARDO JR. cover
DAVE WIELGOSZ asst. editor
CHRIS CONROY editor
JAMIE S. RICH group editor

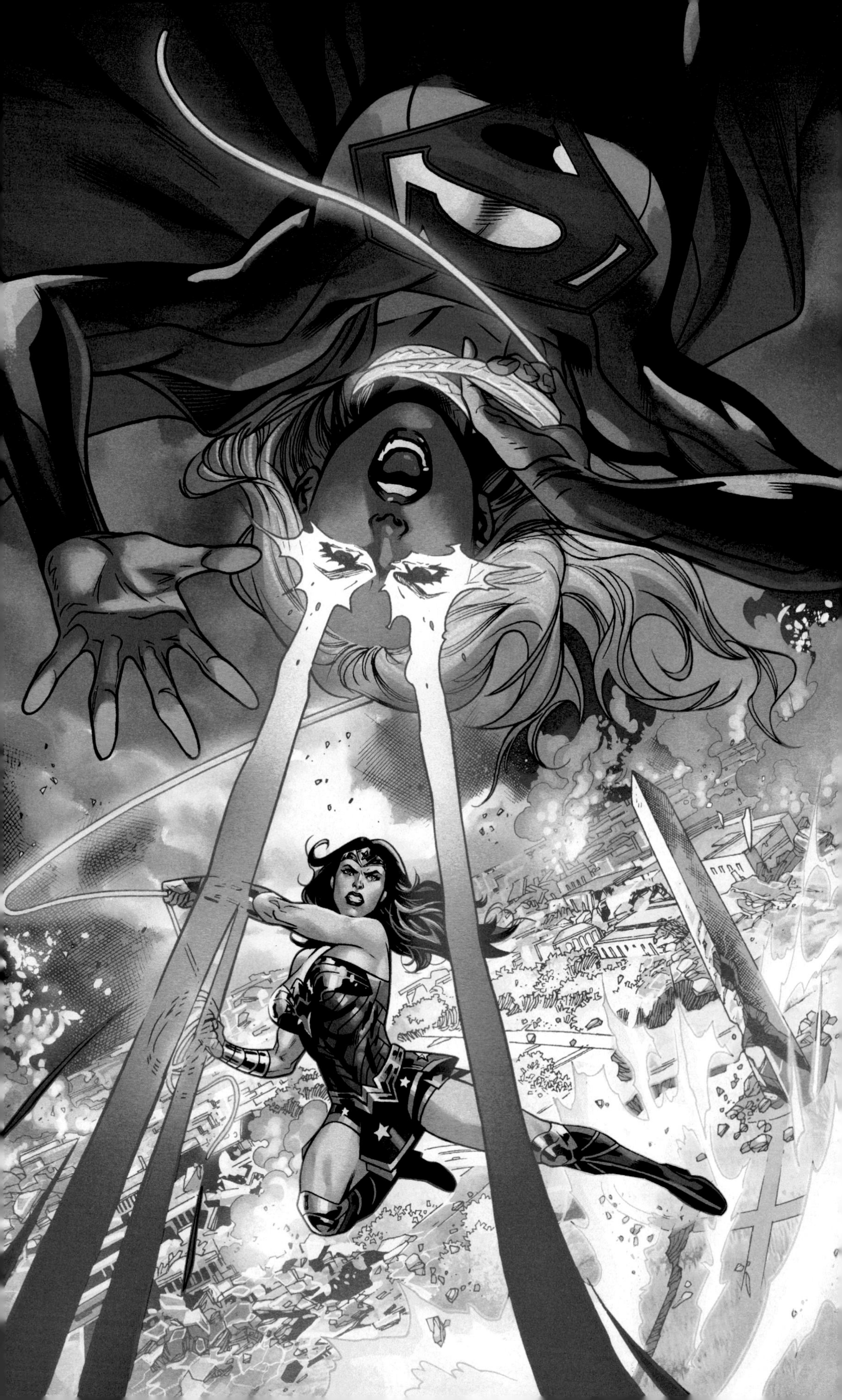

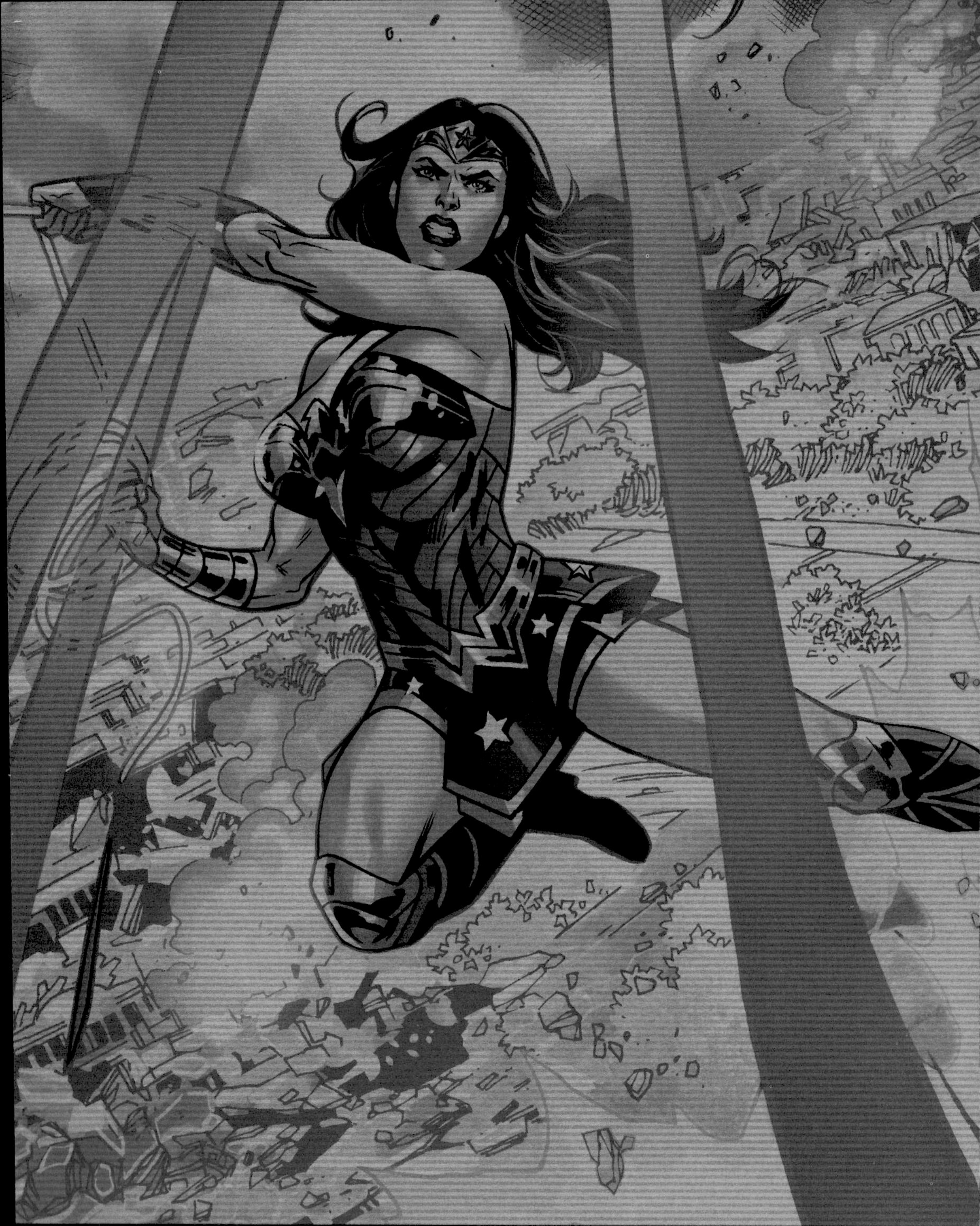

WONDER WOMAN
#47

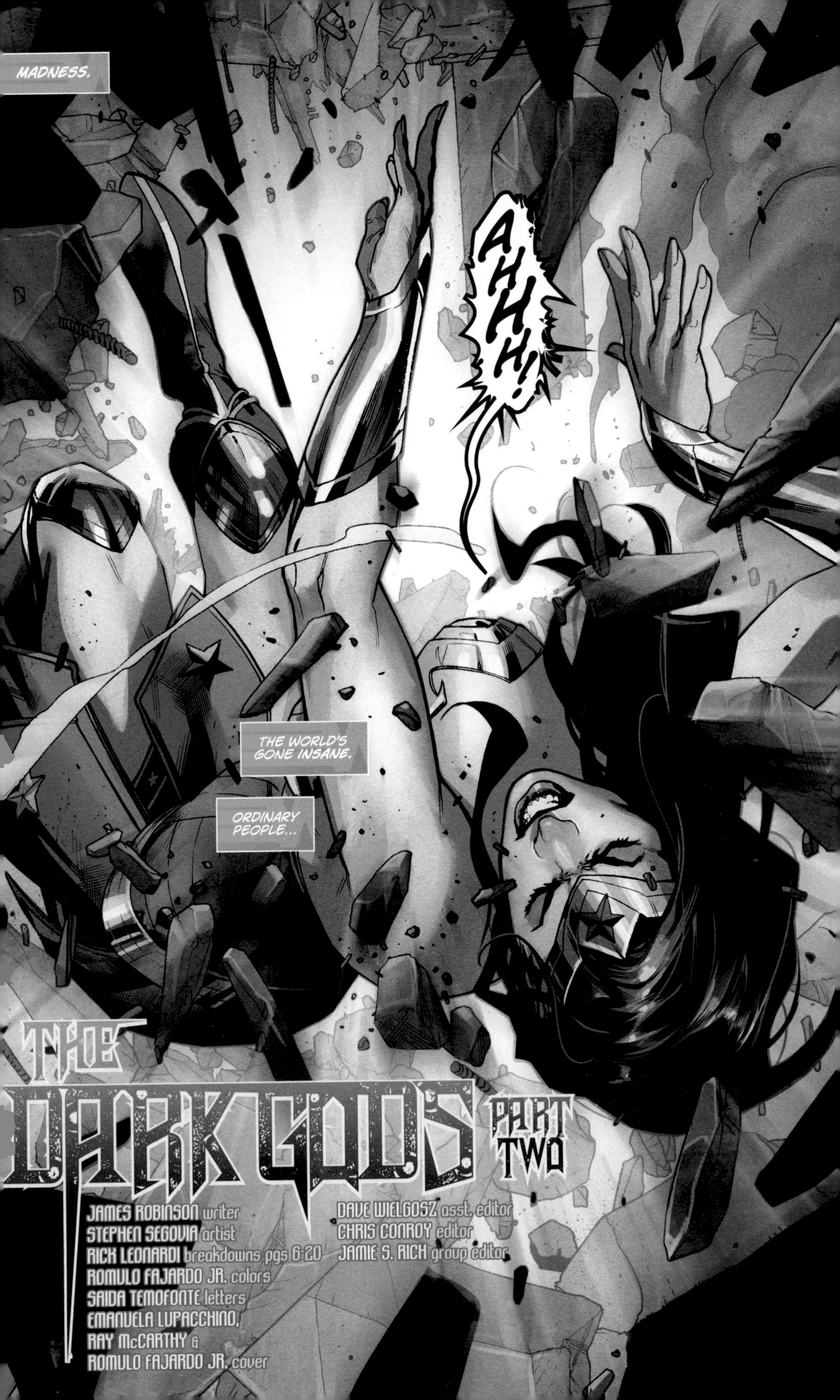

MADNESS.
AHHH!
THE WORLD'S GONE INSANE.
ORDINARY PEOPLE...
THE DARK GODS PART TWO
JAMES ROBINSON writer
STEPHEN SEGOVIA artist
RICK LEONARDI breakdowns pgs 6-20
ROMULO FAJARDO JR. colors
SAIDA TEMOFONTE letters
EMANUELA LUPACCHINO, RAY McCARTHY & ROMULO FAJARDO JR. cover
DAVE WIELGOSZ asst. editor
CHRIS CONROY editor
JAMIE S. RICH group editor

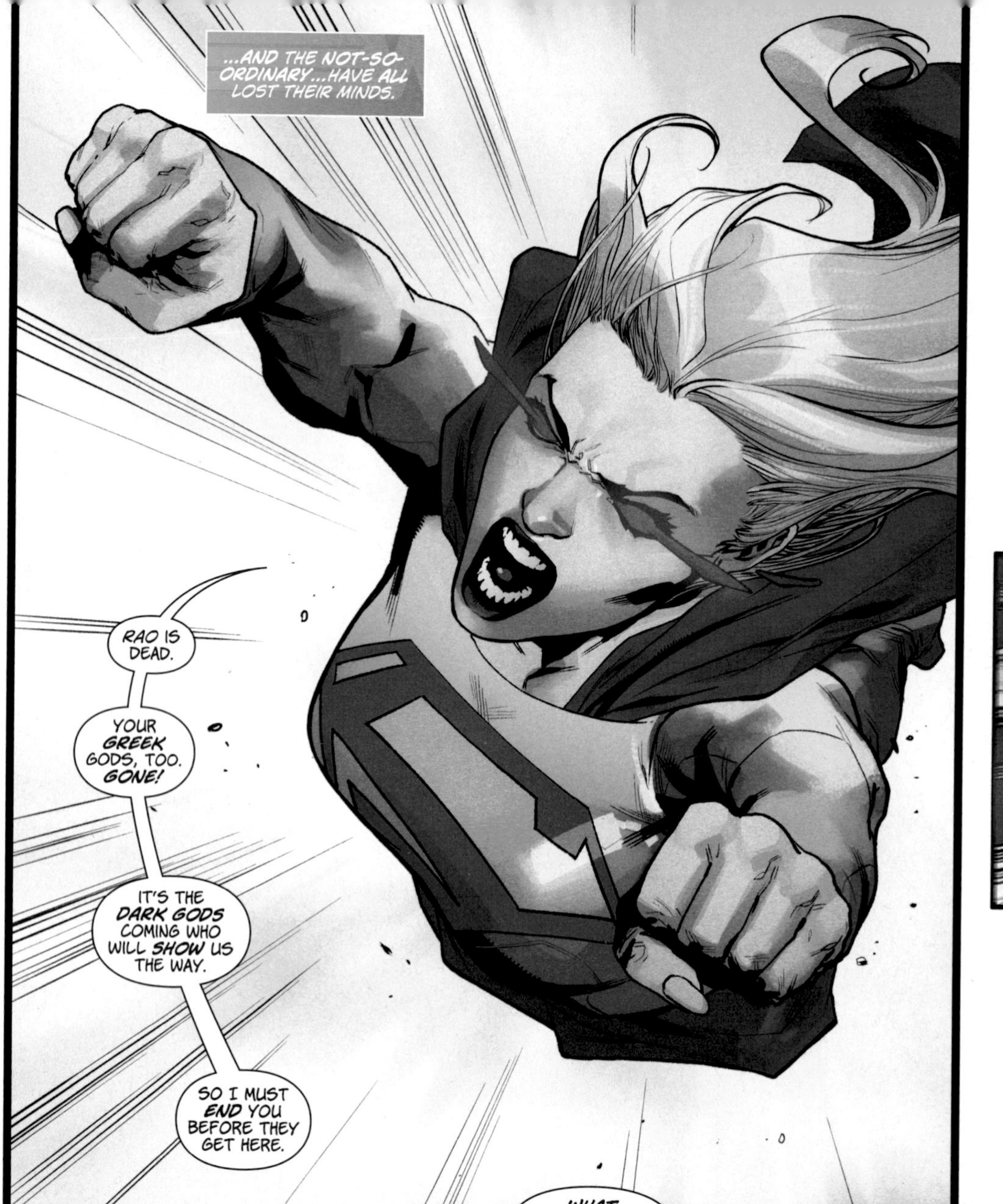
...AND THE NOT-SO-ORDINARY...HAVE ALL LOST THEIR MINDS.
RAO IS DEAD.
YOUR GREEK GODS, TOO. GONE!
IT'S THE DARK GODS COMING WHO WILL SHOW US THE WAY.
SO I MUST END YOU BEFORE THEY GET HERE.
WHAT ARE YOU TALKING ABOUT, SUPERGIRL?

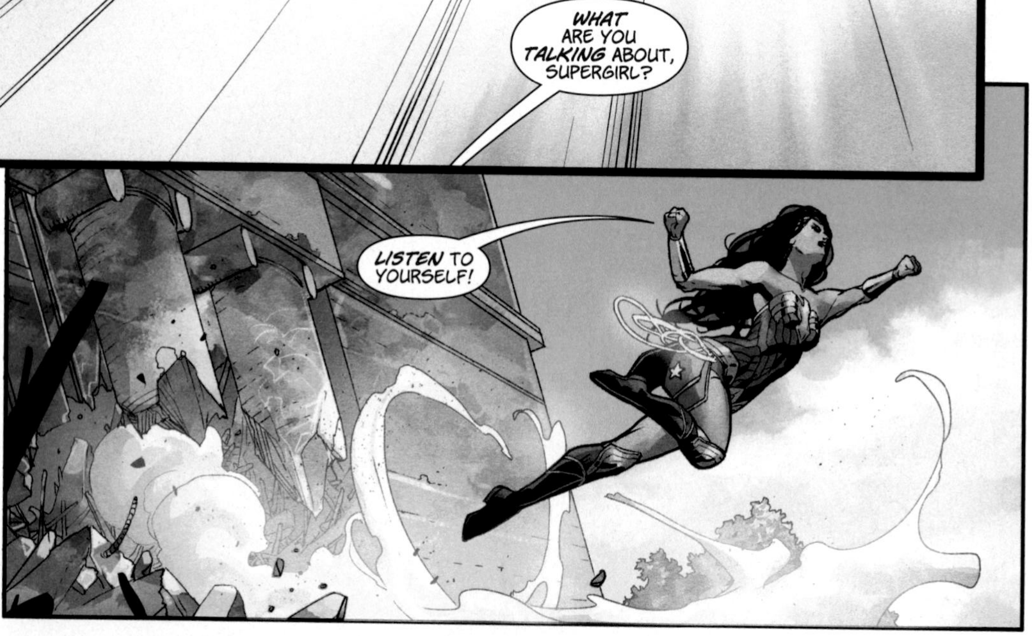
LISTEN TO YOURSELF!

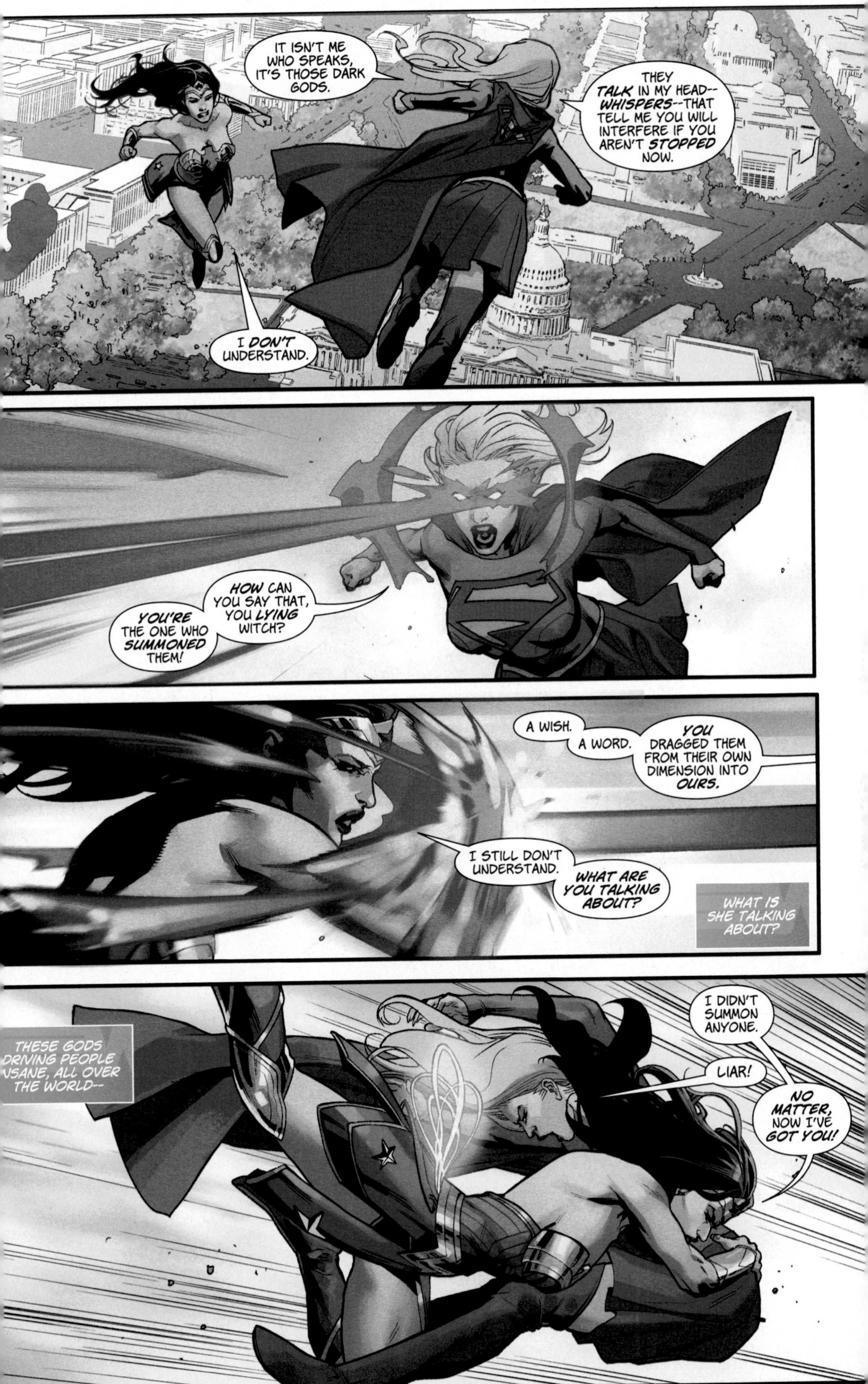
IT ISN'T ME WHO SPEAKS, IT'S THOSE DARK GODS.
THEY TALK IN MY HEAD-- WHISPERS--THAT TELL ME YOU WILL INTERFERE IF YOU AREN'T STOPPED NOW.
I DON'T UNDERSTAND.
HOW CAN YOU SAY THAT, YOU LYING WITCH?
YOU'RE THE ONE WHO SUMMONED THEM!
A WISH.
A WORD.
YOU DRAGGED THEM FROM THEIR OWN DIMENSION INTO OURS.
I STILL DON'T UNDERSTAND.
WHAT ARE YOU TALKING ABOUT?
WHAT IS SHE TALKING ABOUT?
THESE GODS DRIVING PEOPLE INSANE, ALL OVER THE WORLD--
I DIDN'T SUMMON ANYONE.
LIAR!
NO MATTER, NOW I'VE GOT YOU!

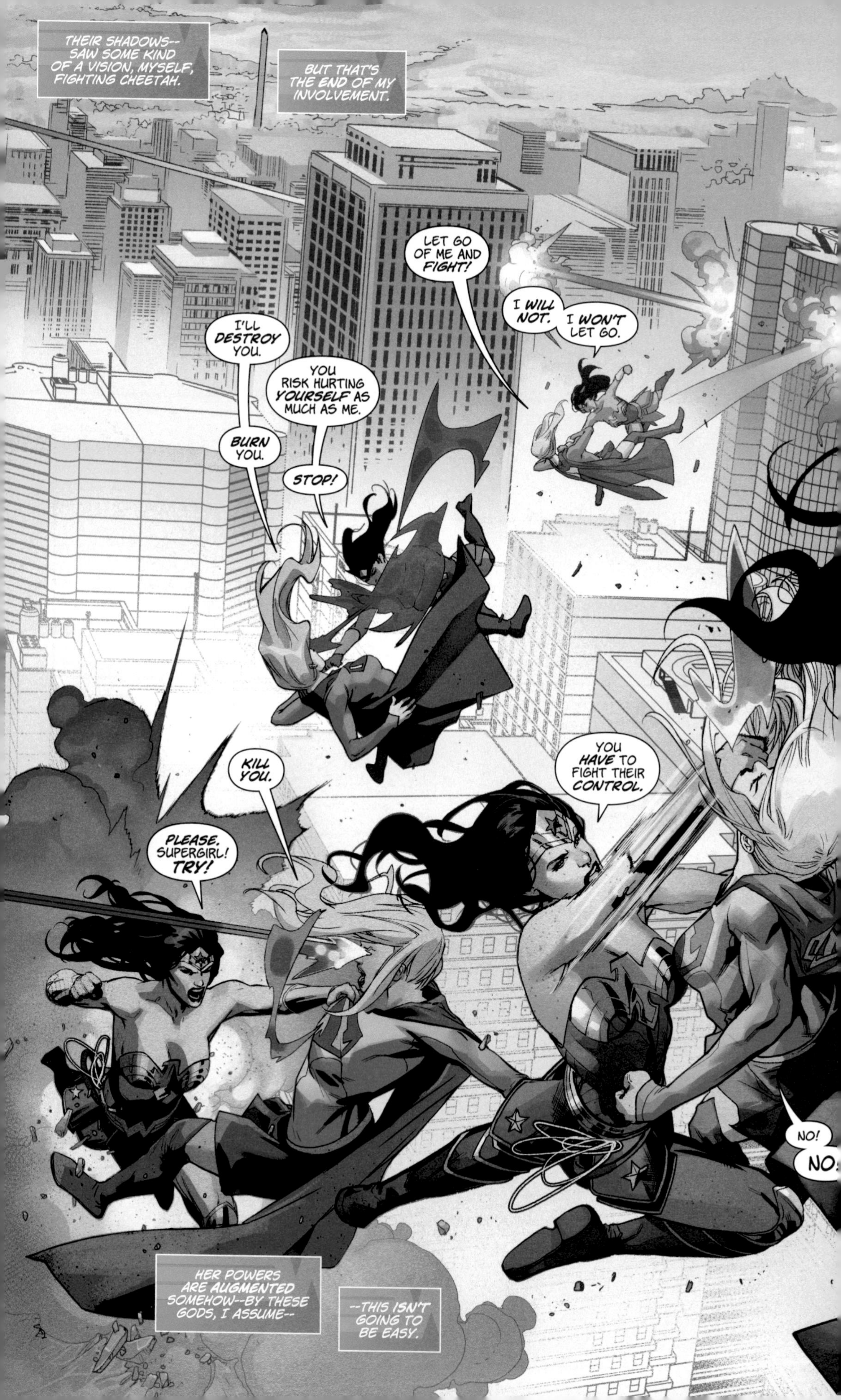
THEIR SHADOWS--SAW SOME KIND OF A VISION, MYSELF, FIGHTING CHEETAH.
BUT THAT'S THE END OF MY INVOLVEMENT.
LET GO OF ME AND FIGHT!
I WILL NOT.
I WON'T LET GO.
I'LL DESTROY YOU.
YOU RISK HURTING YOURSELF AS MUCH AS ME.
BURN YOU.
STOP!
KILL YOU.
PLEASE. SUPERGIRL! TRY!
YOU HAVE TO FIGHT THEIR CONTROL.
NO!
NO.
HER POWERS ARE AUGMENTED SOMEHOW--BY THESE GODS, I ASSUME--
--THIS ISN'T GOING TO BE EASY.

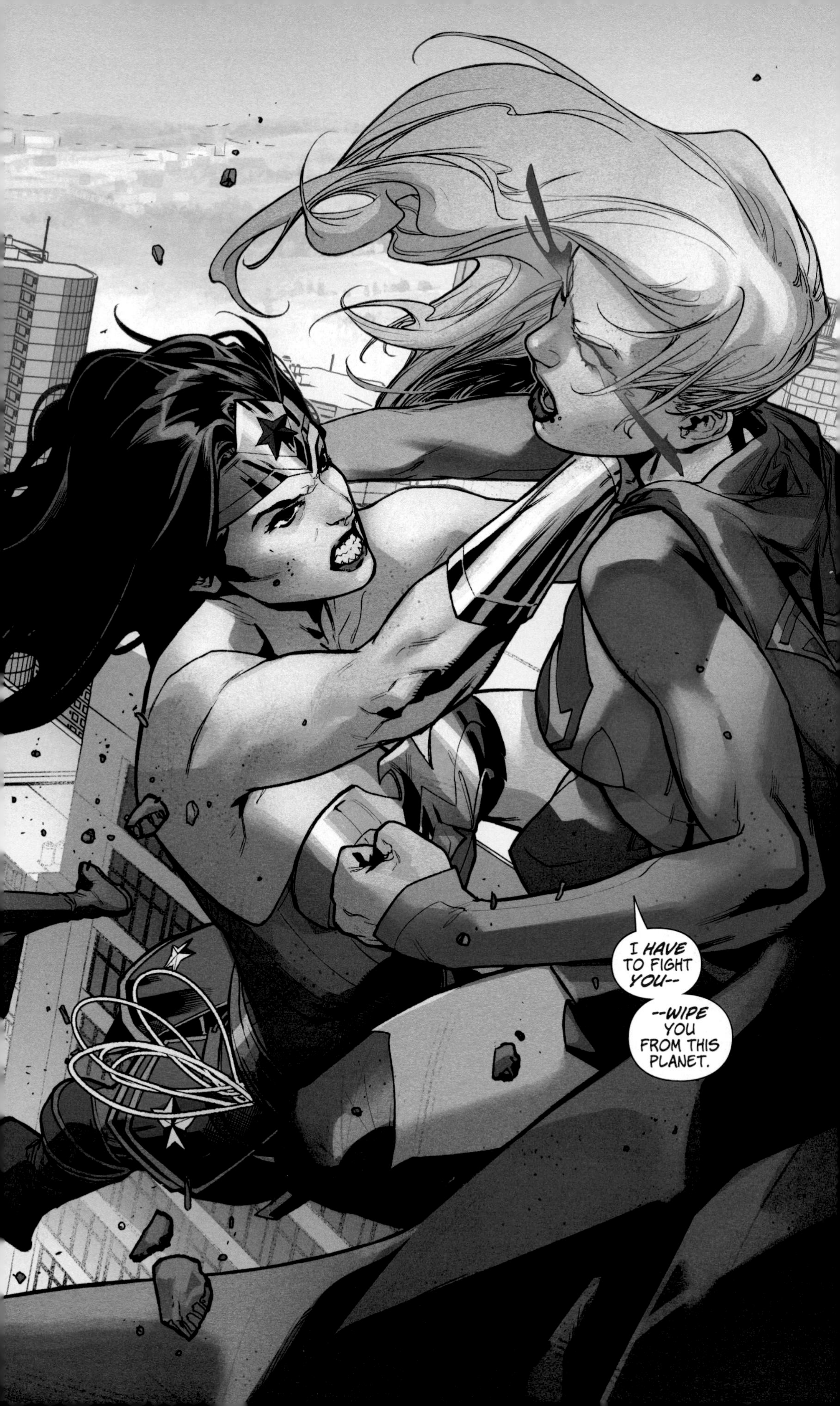
I *HAVE* TO FIGHT *YOU*--
--*WIPE* YOU FROM THIS PLANET.

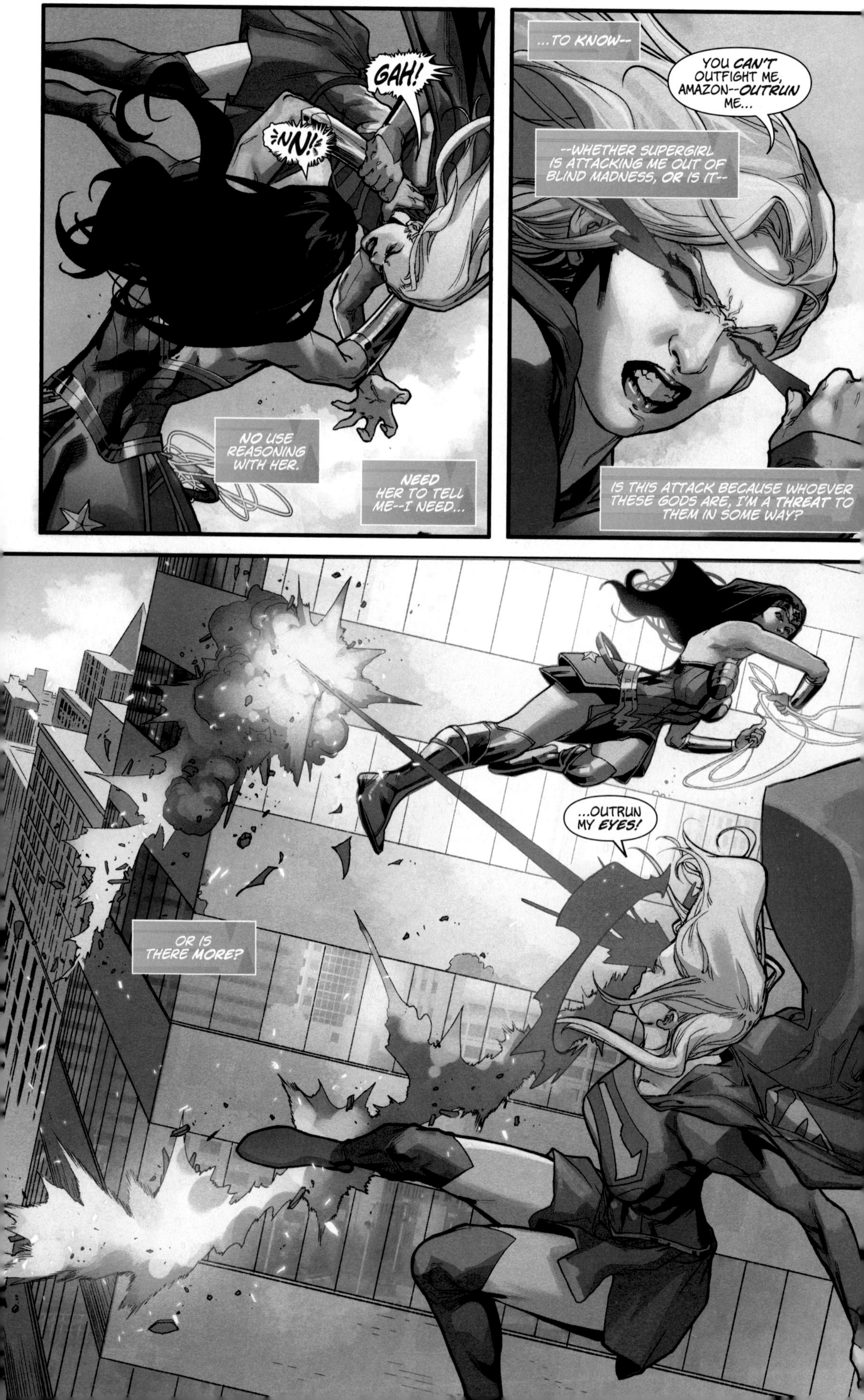
GAH!
NN!
NO USE REASONING WITH HER.
NEED HER TO TELL ME--I NEED...
...TO KNOW--
YOU CAN'T OUTFIGHT ME, AMAZON--OUTRUN ME...
--WHETHER SUPERGIRL IS ATTACKING ME OUT OF BLIND MADNESS, OR IS IT--
IS THIS ATTACK BECAUSE WHOEVER THESE GODS ARE, I'M A THREAT TO THEM IN SOME WAY?
...OUTRUN MY EYES!
OR IS THERE MORE?

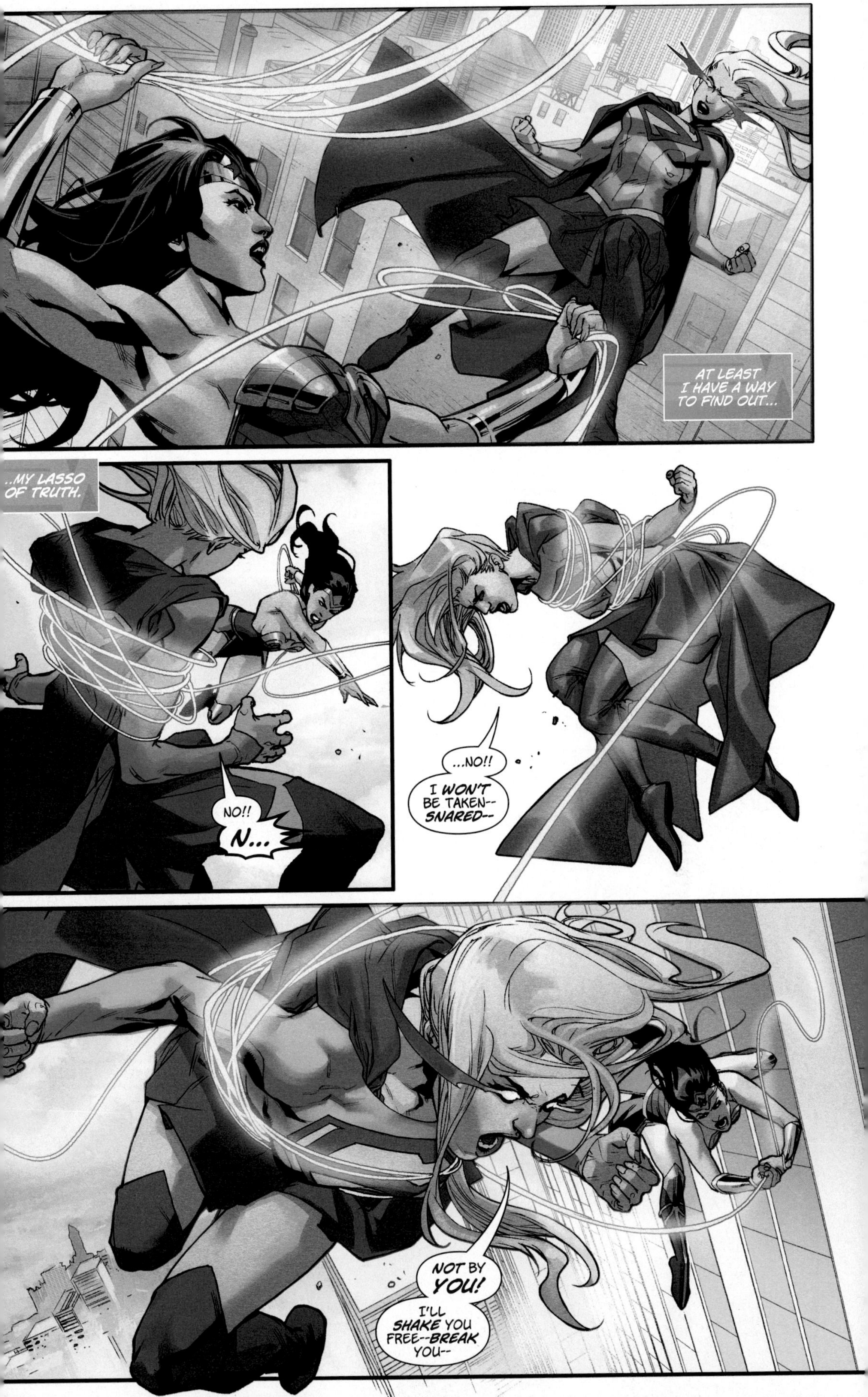
AT LEAST I HAVE A WAY TO FIND OUT...
..MY LASSO OF TRUTH.
NO!! N...
...NO!! I WON'T BE TAKEN-- SNARED--
NOT BY YOU!
I'LL SHAKE YOU FREE--BREAK YOU--

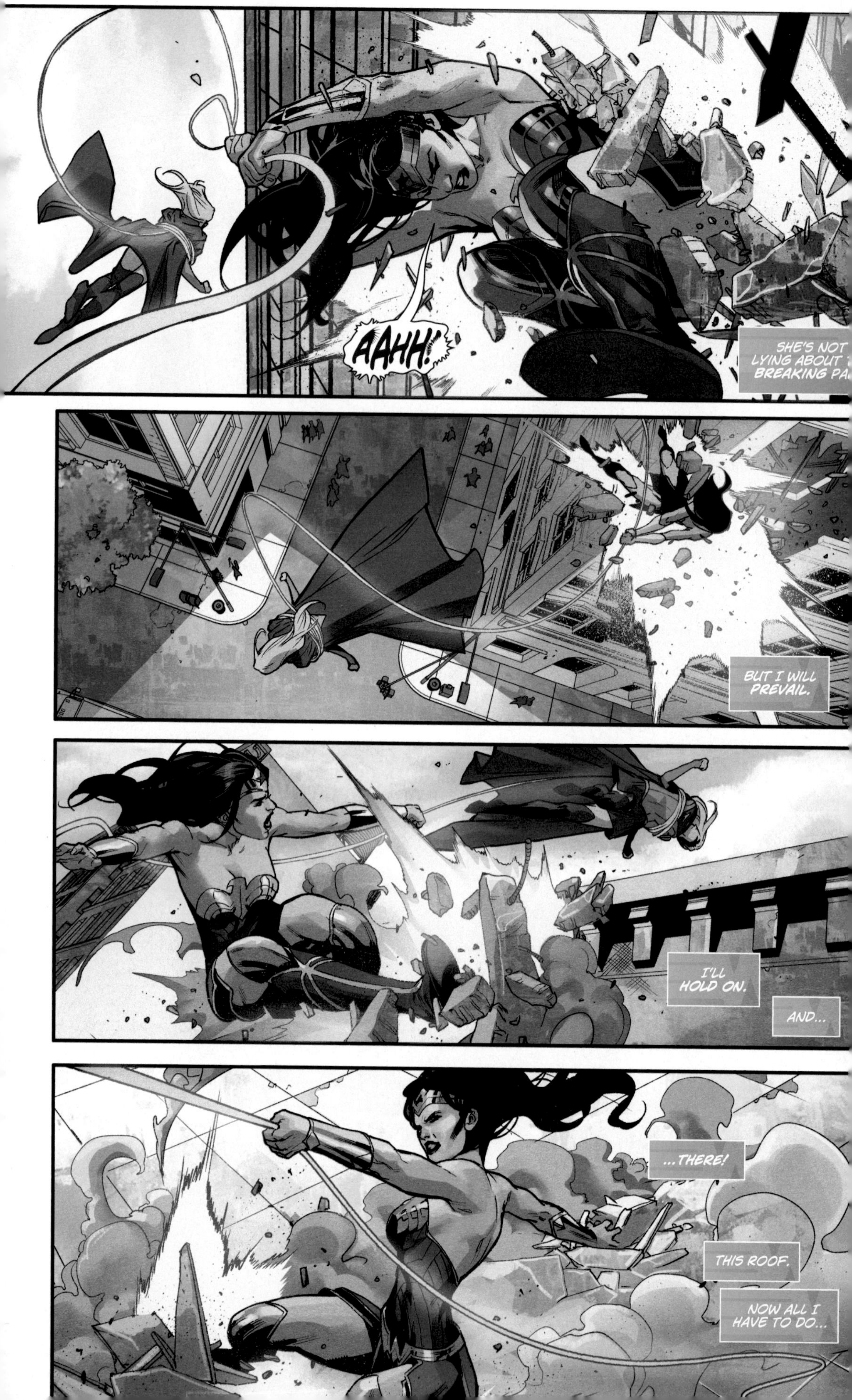
AAHH!
SHE'S NOT
LYING ABOUT
BREAKING PA
BUT I WILL PREVAIL.
I'LL HOLD ON.
AND...
...THERE!
THIS ROOF.
NOW ALL I HAVE TO DO...

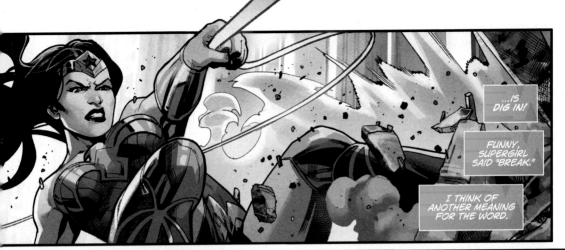

...IS DIG IN!

FUNNY, SUPERGIRL SAID "BREAK."

I THINK OF ANOTHER MEANING FOR THE WORD.

ON THEMYSCIRA--

--BEING TAUGHT TO BREAK WILD HORSES.

HOW IT TAKES GRIT AND WILL.

TALK, SUPERGIRL! I COMMAND YOU!

AND THOSE I HAVE.

TELL ME EVERYTHING YOU KNOW ABOUT THE DARK GODS!

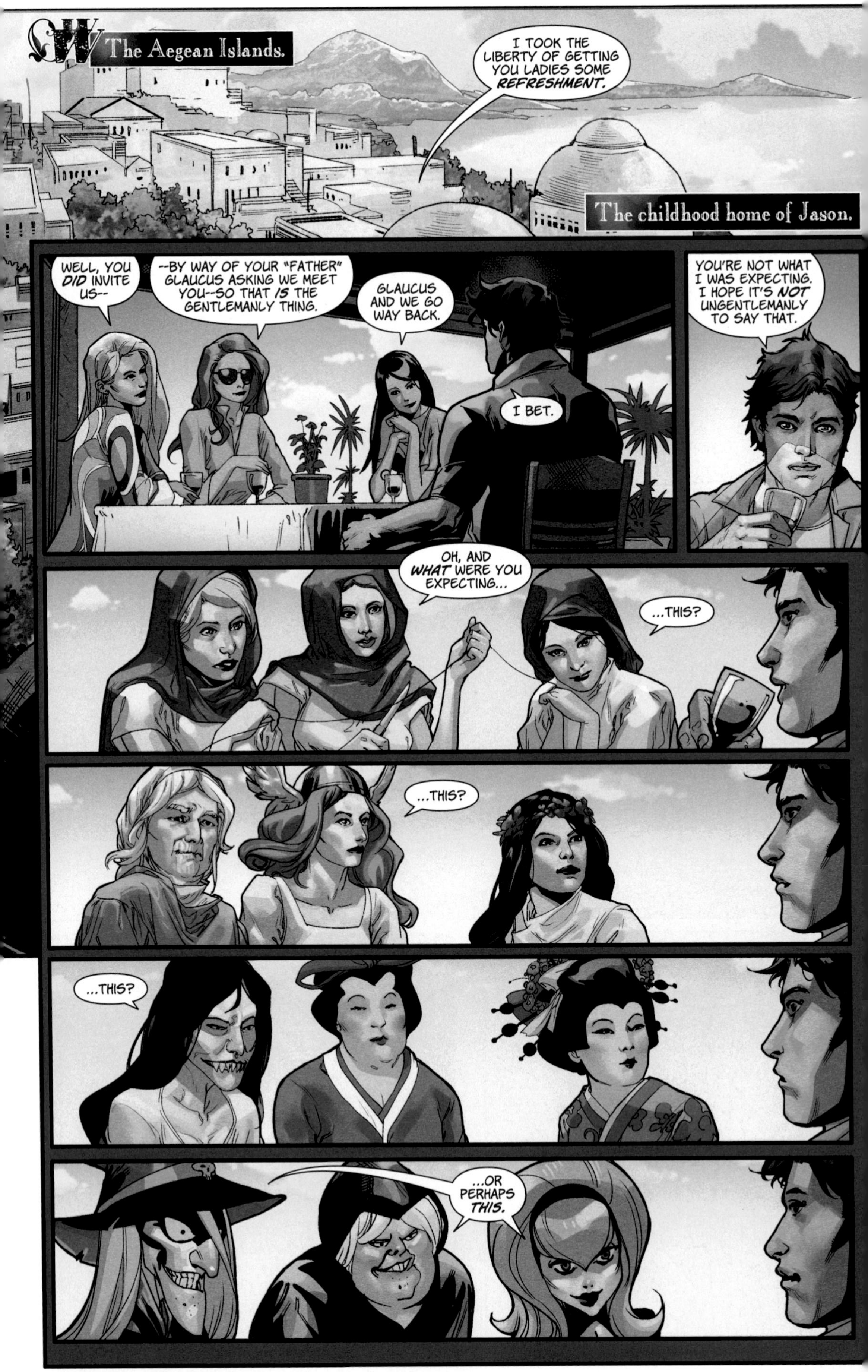

The Aegean Islands.
I TOOK THE LIBERTY OF GETTING YOU LADIES SOME REFRESHMENT.
The childhood home of Jason.
WELL, YOU DID INVITE US--
--BY WAY OF YOUR "FATHER" GLAUCUS ASKING WE MEET YOU--SO THAT IS THE GENTLEMANLY THING.
GLAUCUS AND WE GO WAY BACK.
I BET.
YOU'RE NOT WHAT I WAS EXPECTING. I HOPE IT'S NOT UNGENTLEMANLY TO SAY THAT.
OH, AND WHAT WERE YOU EXPECTING...
...THIS?
...THIS?
...THIS?
...OR PERHAPS THIS.

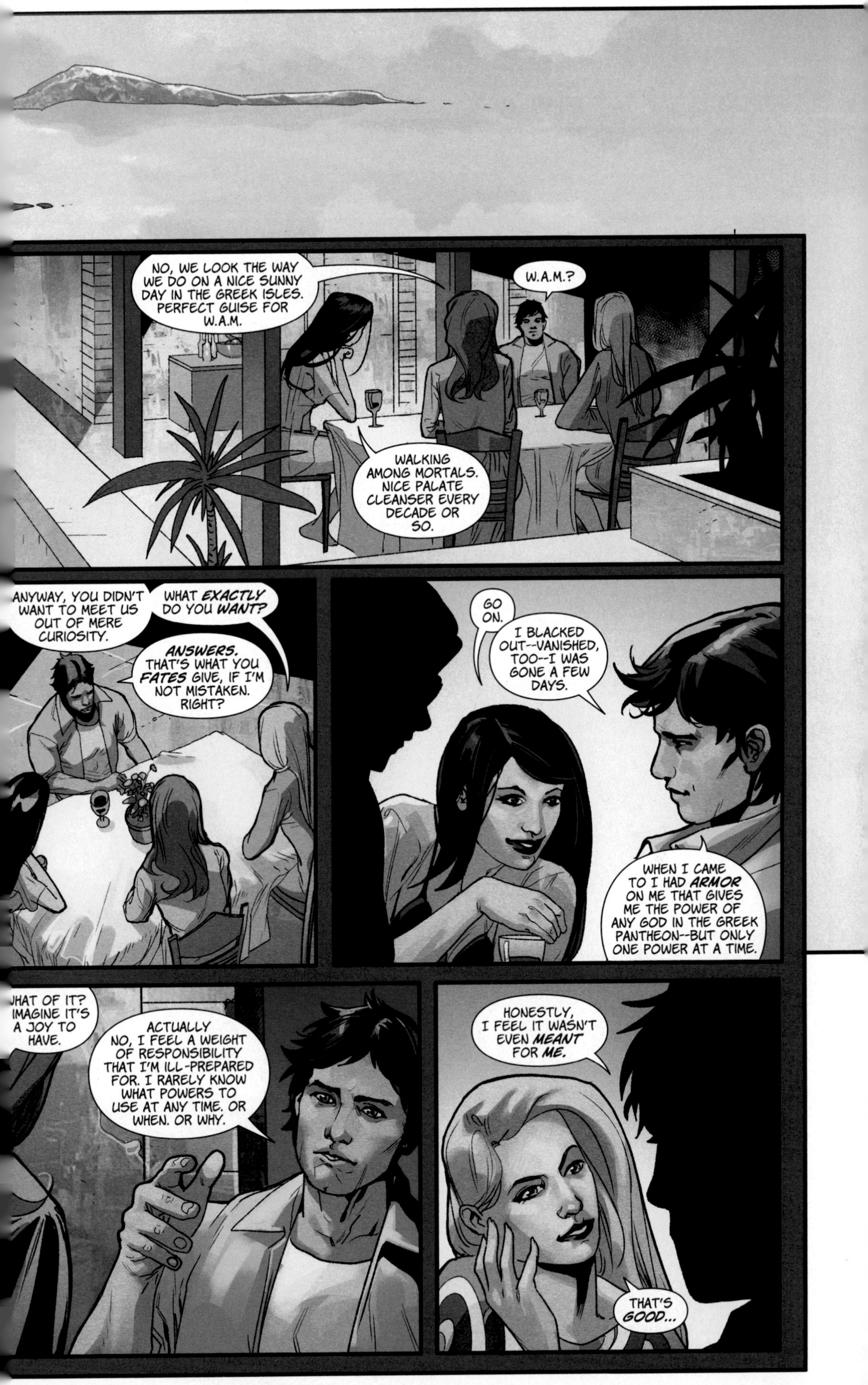

NO, WE LOOK THE WAY WE DO ON A NICE SUNNY DAY IN THE GREEK ISLES. PERFECT GUISE FOR W.A.M.
W.A.M.?
WALKING AMONG MORTALS. NICE PALATE CLEANSER EVERY DECADE OR SO.
ANYWAY, YOU DIDN'T WANT TO MEET US OUT OF MERE CURIOSITY.
WHAT *EXACTLY* DO YOU *WANT?*
ANSWERS. THAT'S WHAT YOU *FATES* GIVE, IF I'M NOT MISTAKEN. RIGHT?
GO ON.
I BLACKED OUT--VANISHED, TOO--I WAS GONE A FEW DAYS.
WHEN I CAME TO I HAD *ARMOR* ON ME THAT GIVES ME THE POWER OF ANY GOD IN THE GREEK PANTHEON--BUT ONLY ONE POWER AT A TIME.
WHAT OF IT? IMAGINE IT'S A JOY TO HAVE.
ACTUALLY NO, I FEEL A WEIGHT OF RESPONSIBILITY THAT I'M ILL-PREPARED FOR. I RARELY KNOW WHAT POWERS TO USE AT ANY TIME. OR WHEN. OR WHY.
HONESTLY, I FEEL IT WASN'T EVEN *MEANT* FOR *ME.*
THAT'S *GOOD...*

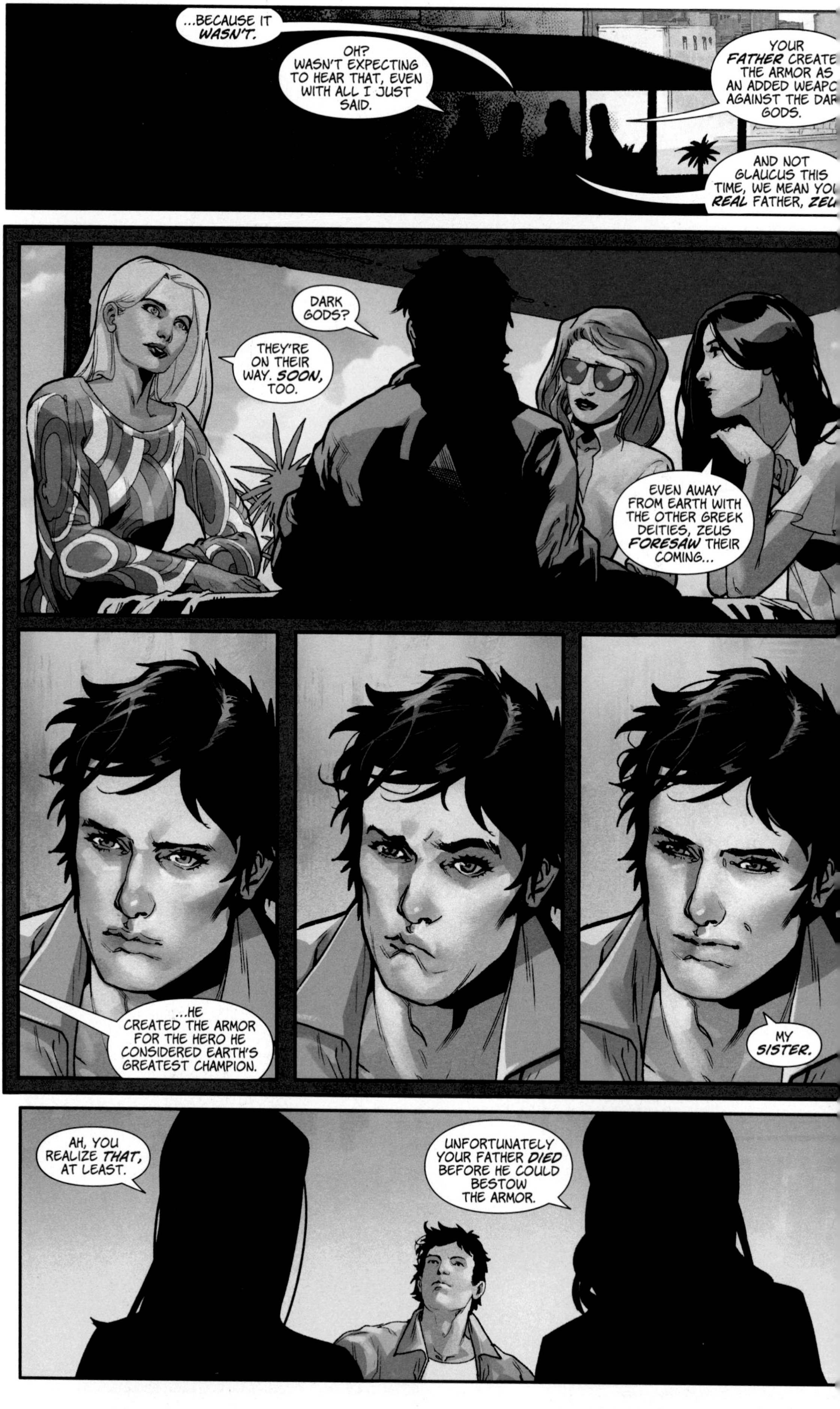
...BECAUSE IT WASN'T.
OH? WASN'T EXPECTING TO HEAR THAT, EVEN WITH ALL I JUST SAID.
YOUR FATHER CREATE THE ARMOR AS AN ADDED WEAPC AGAINST THE DAR GODS.
AND NOT GLAUCUS THIS TIME, WE MEAN YOU REAL FATHER, ZEU
DARK GODS?
THEY'RE ON THEIR WAY. SOON, TOO.
EVEN AWAY FROM EARTH WITH THE OTHER GREEK DEITIES, ZEUS FORESAW THEIR COMING...
...HE CREATED THE ARMOR FOR THE HERO HE CONSIDERED EARTH'S GREATEST CHAMPION.
MY SISTER.
AH, YOU REALIZE THAT, AT LEAST.
UNFORTUNATELY YOUR FATHER DIED BEFORE HE COULD BESTOW THE ARMOR.

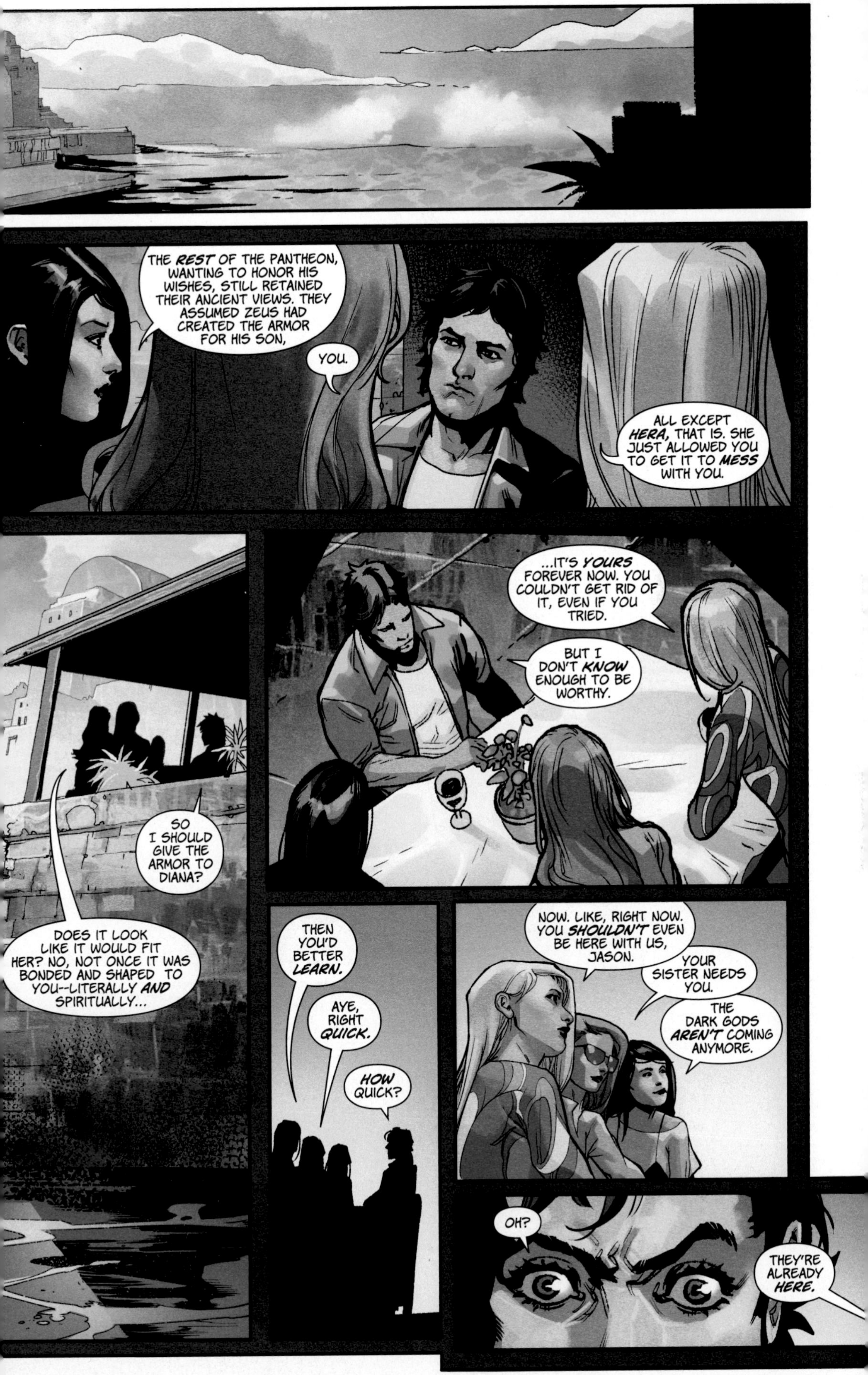

THE REST OF THE PANTHEON, WANTING TO HONOR HIS WISHES, STILL RETAINED THEIR ANCIENT VIEWS. THEY ASSUMED ZEUS HAD CREATED THE ARMOR FOR HIS SON,
YOU.
ALL EXCEPT HERA, THAT IS. SHE JUST ALLOWED YOU TO GET IT TO MESS WITH YOU.
SO I SHOULD GIVE THE ARMOR TO DIANA?
DOES IT LOOK LIKE IT WOULD FIT HER? NO, NOT ONCE IT WAS BONDED AND SHAPED TO YOU--LITERALLY AND SPIRITUALLY...
...IT'S YOURS FOREVER NOW. YOU COULDN'T GET RID OF IT, EVEN IF YOU TRIED.
BUT I DON'T KNOW ENOUGH TO BE WORTHY.
THEN YOU'D BETTER LEARN.
AYE, RIGHT QUICK.
HOW QUICK?
NOW. LIKE, RIGHT NOW. YOU SHOULDN'T EVEN BE HERE WITH US, JASON.
YOUR SISTER NEEDS YOU.
THE DARK GODS AREN'T COMING ANYMORE.
OH?
THEY'RE ALREADY HERE.

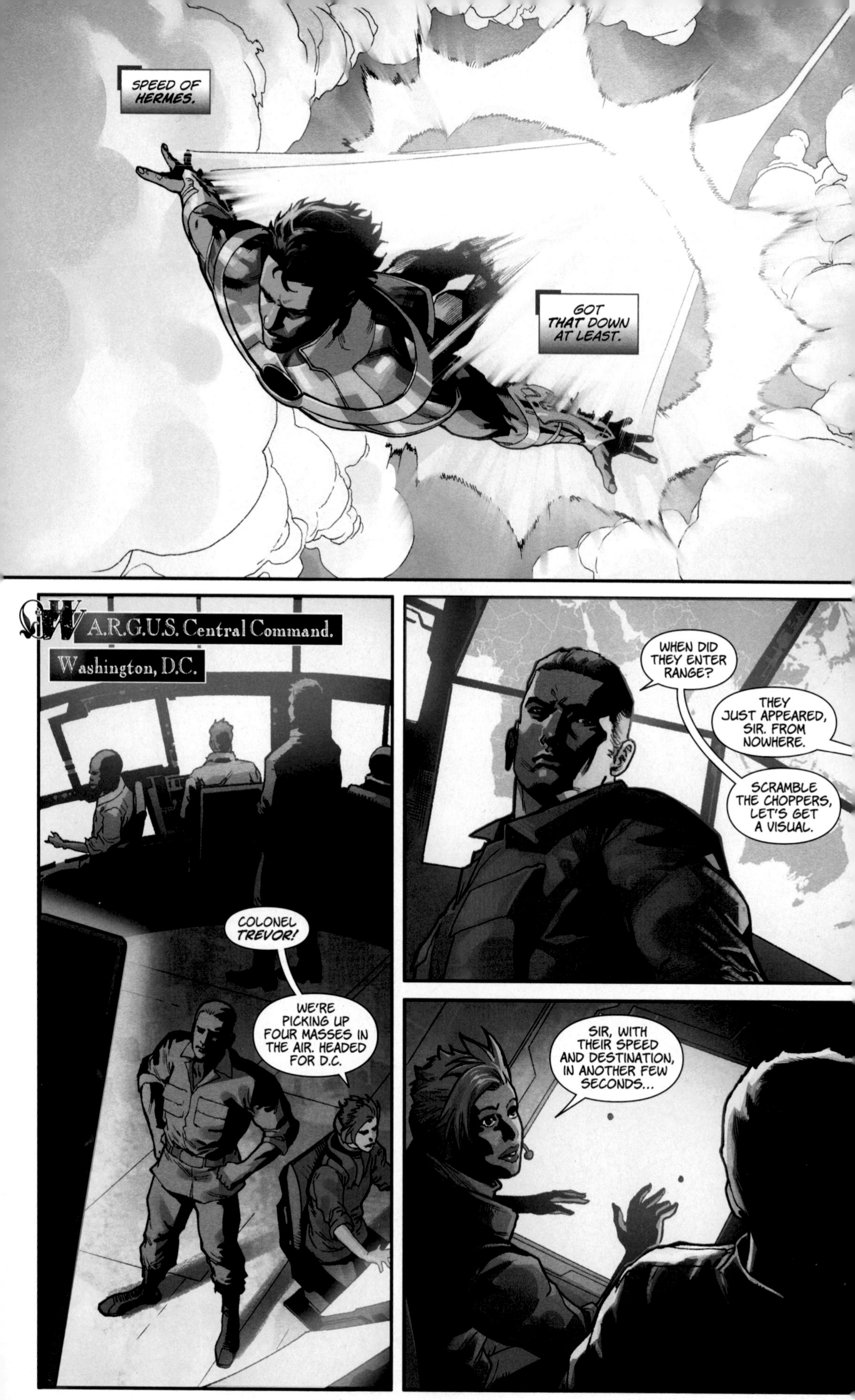
SPEED OF HERMES.
GOT THAT DOWN AT LEAST.
A.R.G.U.S. Central Command.
Washington, D.C.
COLONEL TREVOR!
WE'RE PICKING UP FOUR MASSES IN THE AIR. HEADED FOR D.C.
WHEN DID THEY ENTER RANGE?
THEY JUST APPEARED, SIR. FROM NOWHERE.
SCRAMBLE THE CHOPPERS, LET'S GET A VISUAL.
SIR, WITH THEIR SPEED AND DESTINATION, IN ANOTHER FEW SECONDS...

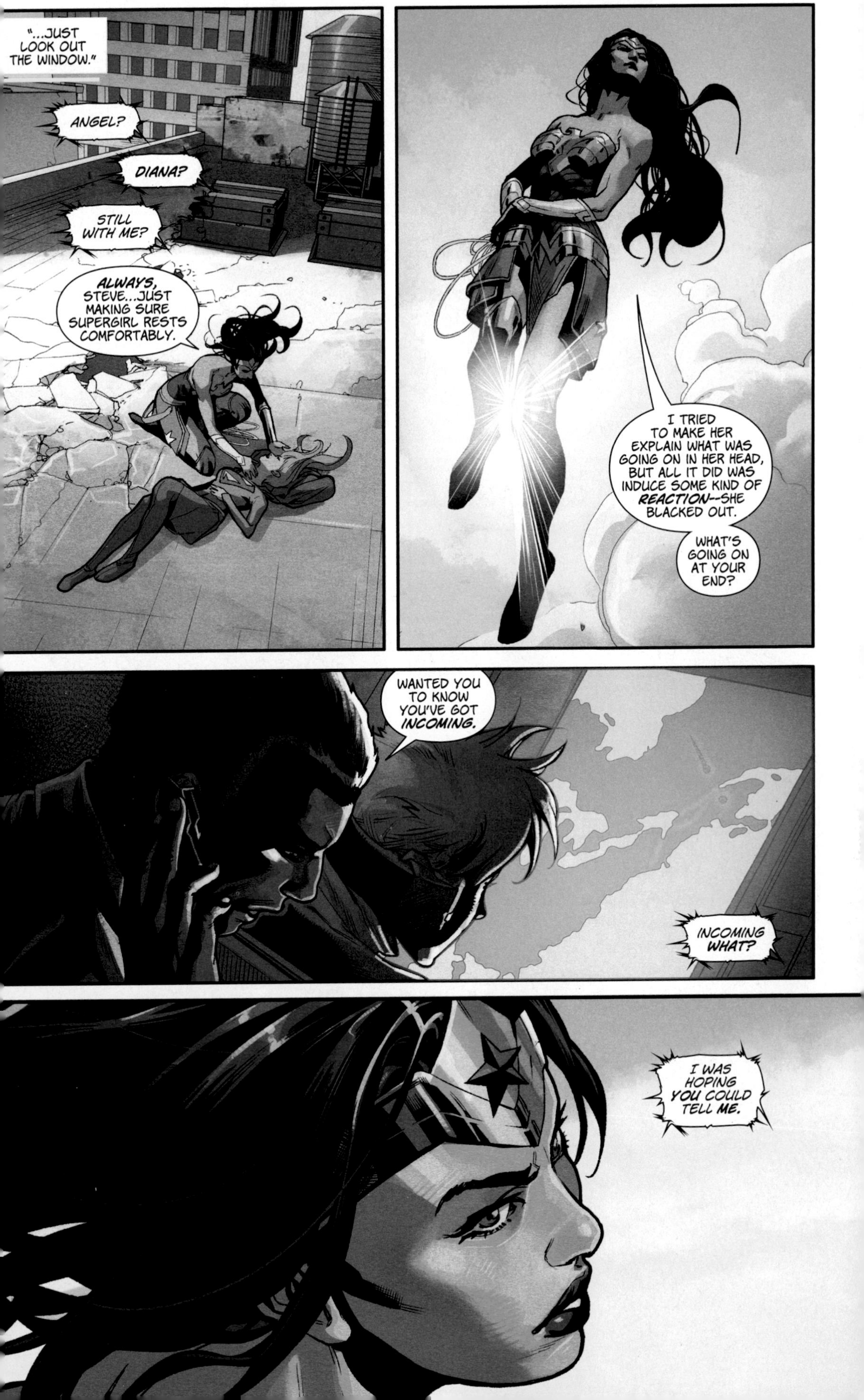
"...JUST LOOK OUT THE WINDOW."
ANGEL?
DIANA?
STILL WITH ME?
ALWAYS, STEVE...JUST MAKING SURE SUPERGIRL RESTS COMFORTABLY.
I TRIED TO MAKE HER EXPLAIN WHAT WAS GOING ON IN HER HEAD, BUT ALL IT DID WAS INDUCE SOME KIND OF REACTION--SHE BLACKED OUT.
WHAT'S GOING ON AT YOUR END?
WANTED YOU TO KNOW YOU'VE GOT INCOMING.
INCOMING WHAT?
I WAS HOPING YOU COULD TELL ME.

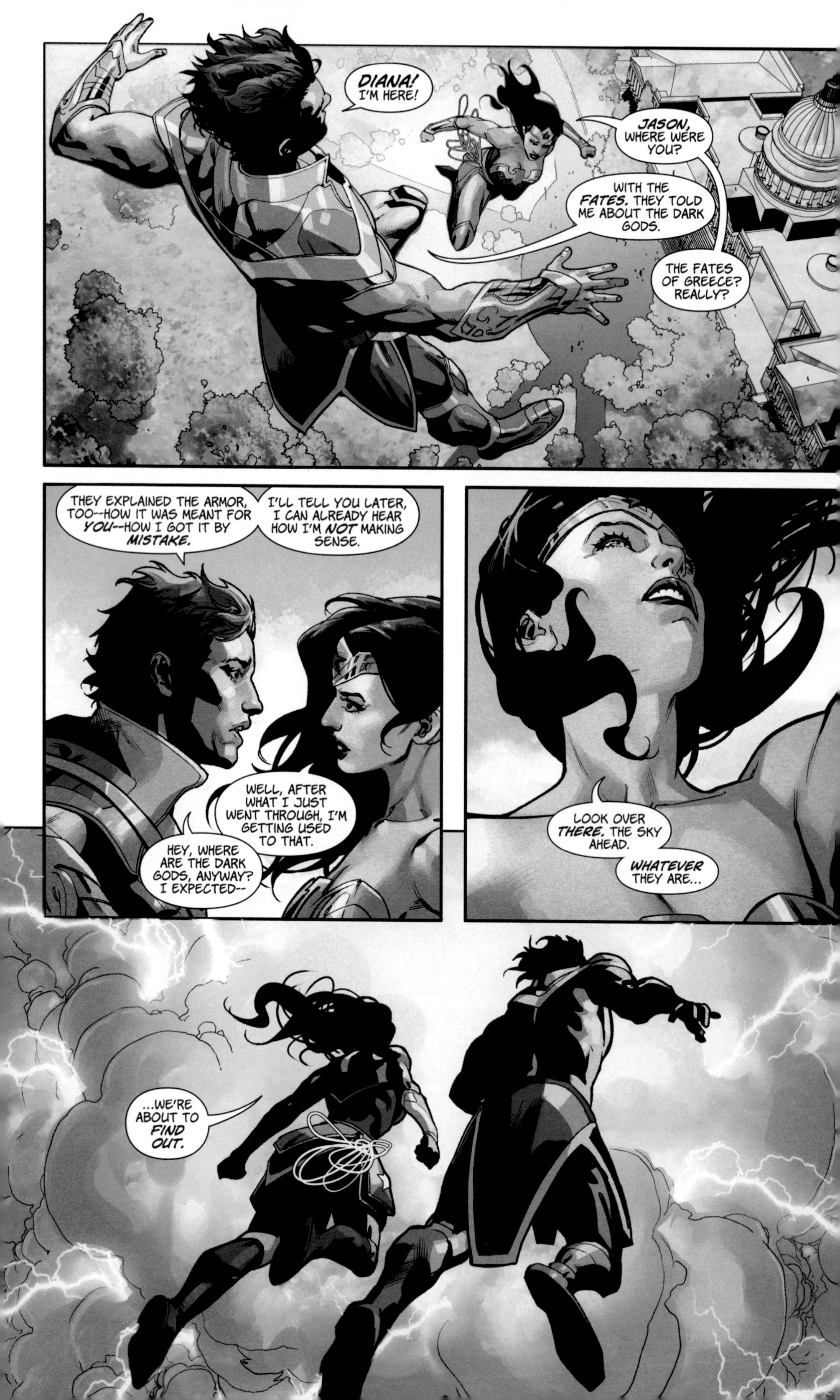
DIANA! I'M HERE!
JASON, WHERE WERE YOU?
WITH THE FATES. THEY TOLD ME ABOUT THE DARK GODS.
THE FATES OF GREECE? REALLY?
THEY EXPLAINED THE ARMOR, TOO--HOW IT WAS MEANT FOR YOU--HOW I GOT IT BY MISTAKE.
I'LL TELL YOU LATER, I CAN ALREADY HEAR HOW I'M NOT MAKING SENSE.
WELL, AFTER WHAT I JUST WENT THROUGH, I'M GETTING USED TO THAT.
HEY, WHERE ARE THE DARK GODS, ANYWAY? I EXPECTED--
LOOK OVER THERE. THE SKY AHEAD.
WHATEVER THEY ARE...
...WE'RE ABOUT TO FIND OUT.

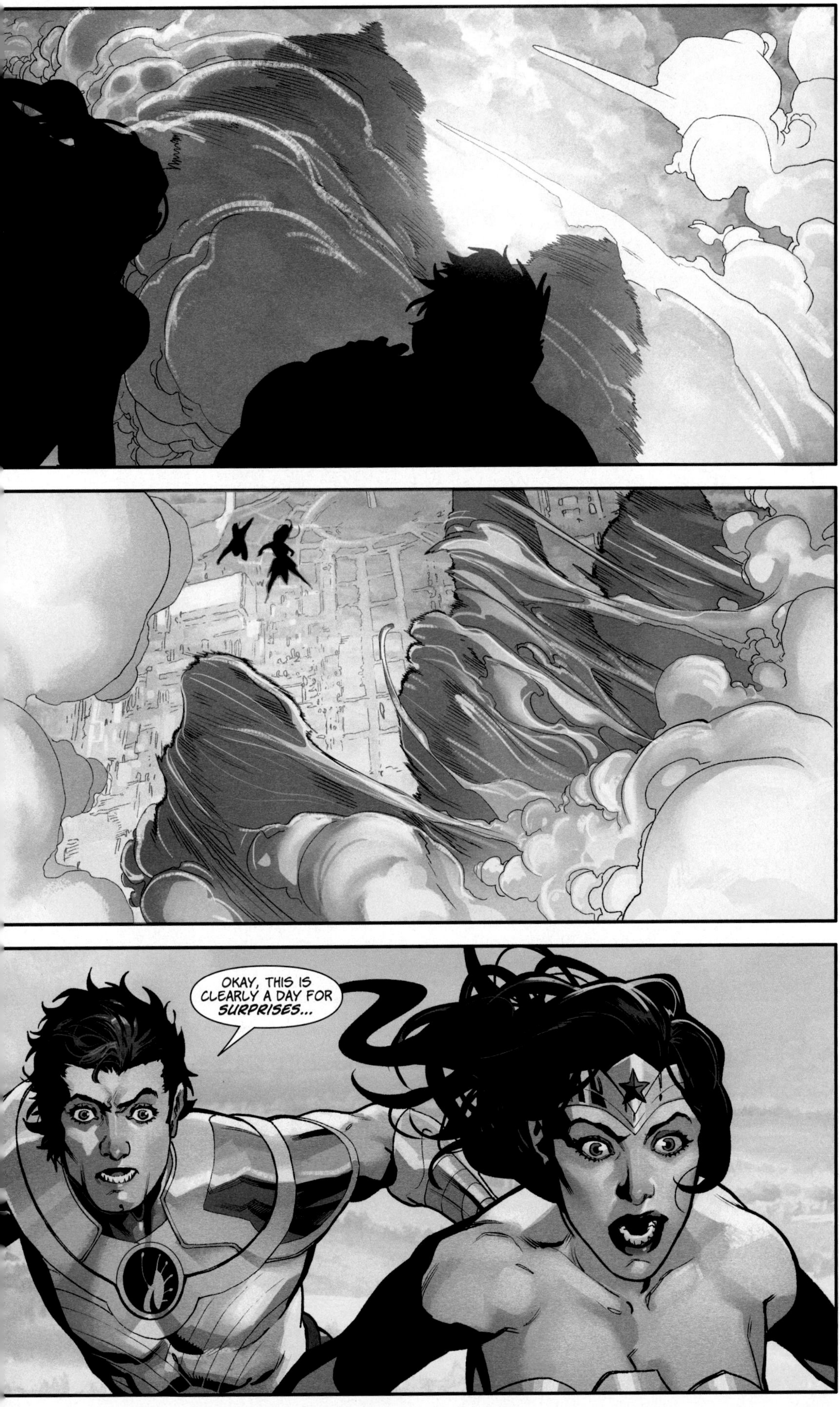
OKAY, THIS IS CLEARLY A DAY FOR *SURPRISES...*

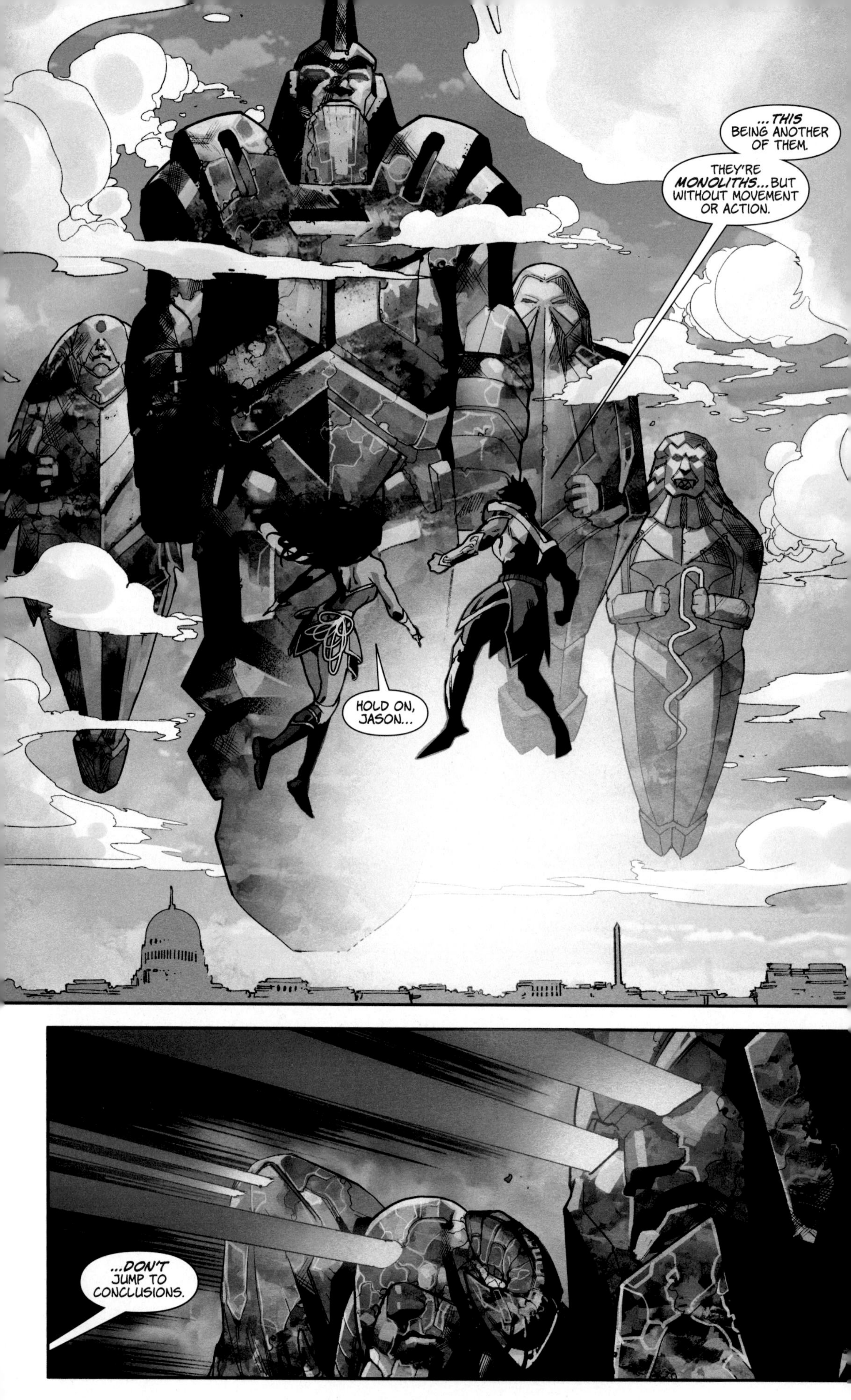
...THIS BEING ANOTHER OF THEM.
THEY'RE MONOLITHS...BUT WITHOUT MOVEMENT OR ACTION.
HOLD ON, JASON...
...DON'T JUMP TO CONCLUSIONS.

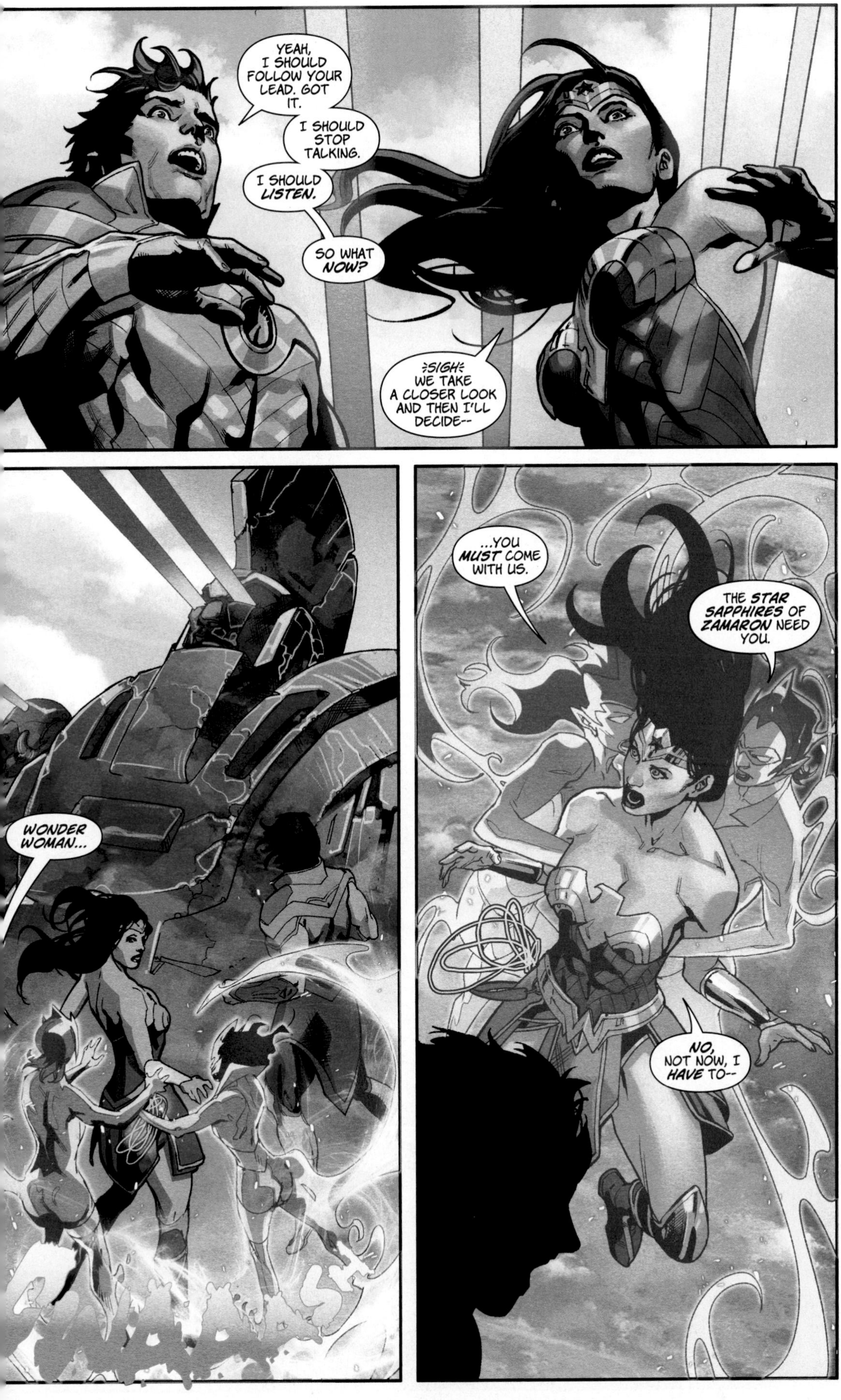
YEAH, I SHOULD FOLLOW YOUR LEAD. GOT IT.
I SHOULD STOP TALKING.
I SHOULD LISTEN.
SO WHAT NOW?
SIGH WE TAKE A CLOSER LOOK AND THEN I'LL DECIDE--
WONDER WOMAN...
...YOU MUST COME WITH US.
THE STAR SAPPHIRES OF ZAMARON NEED YOU.
NO, NOT NOW, I HAVE TO--

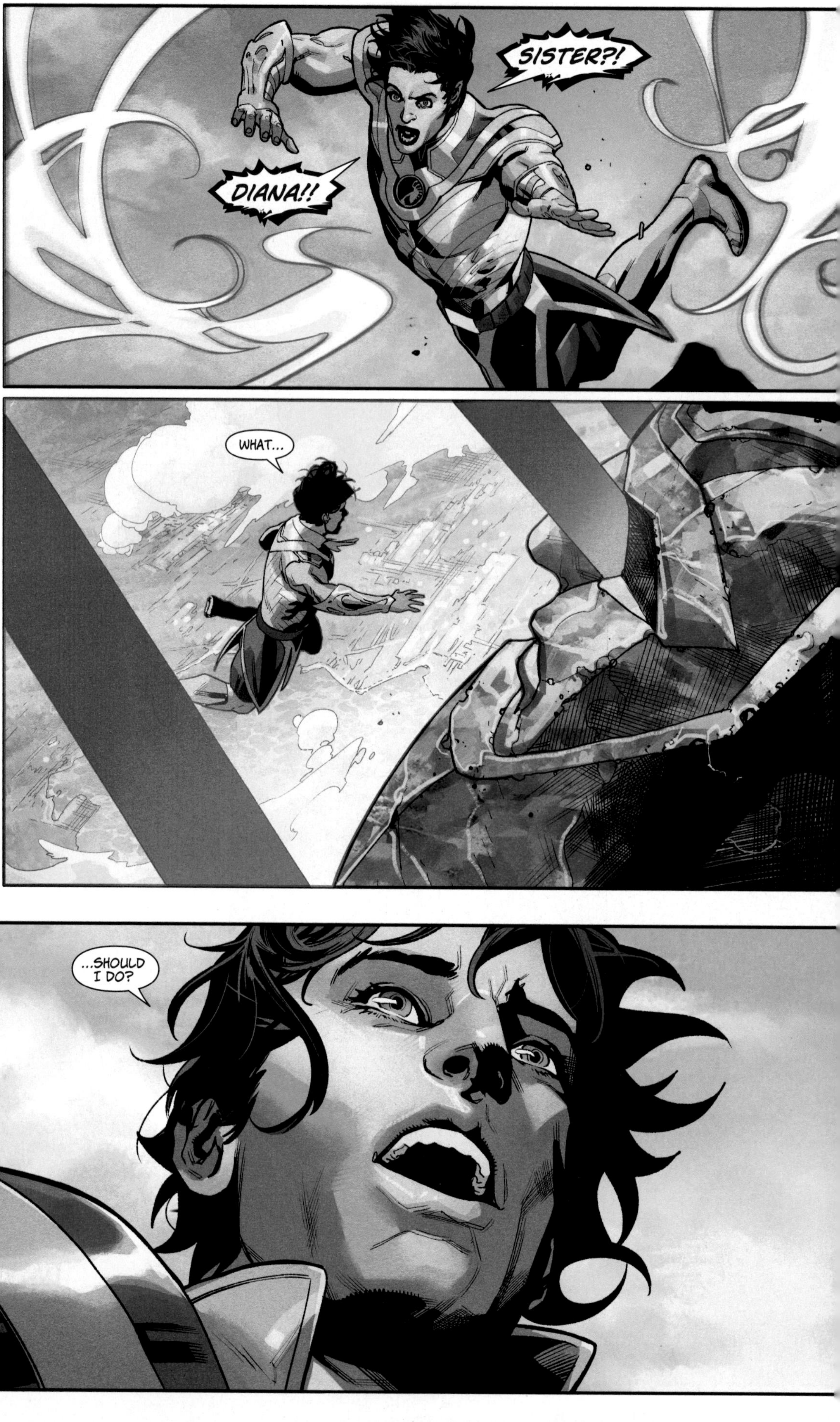
SISTER?!
DIANA!!
WHAT...
...SHOULD I DO?

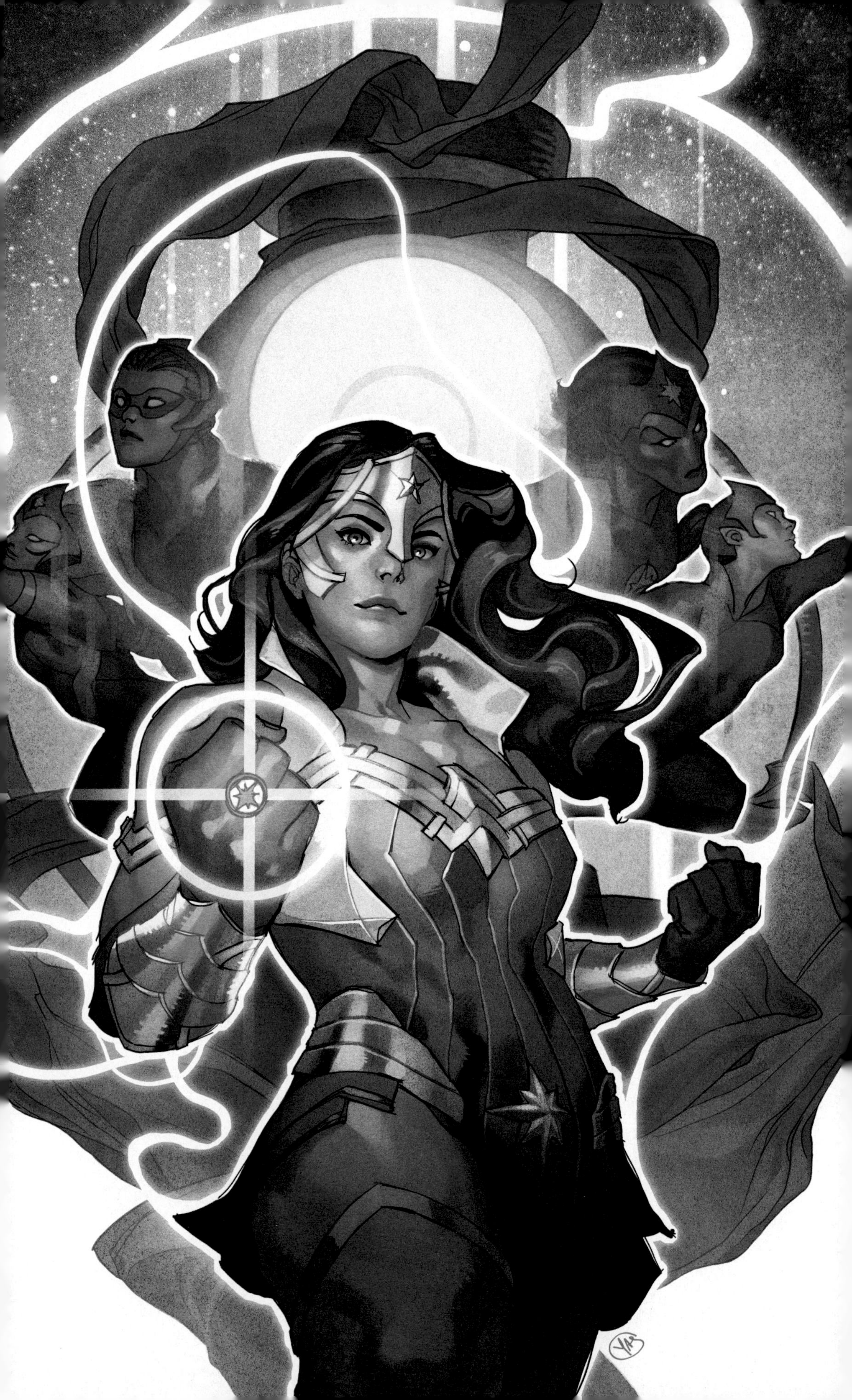

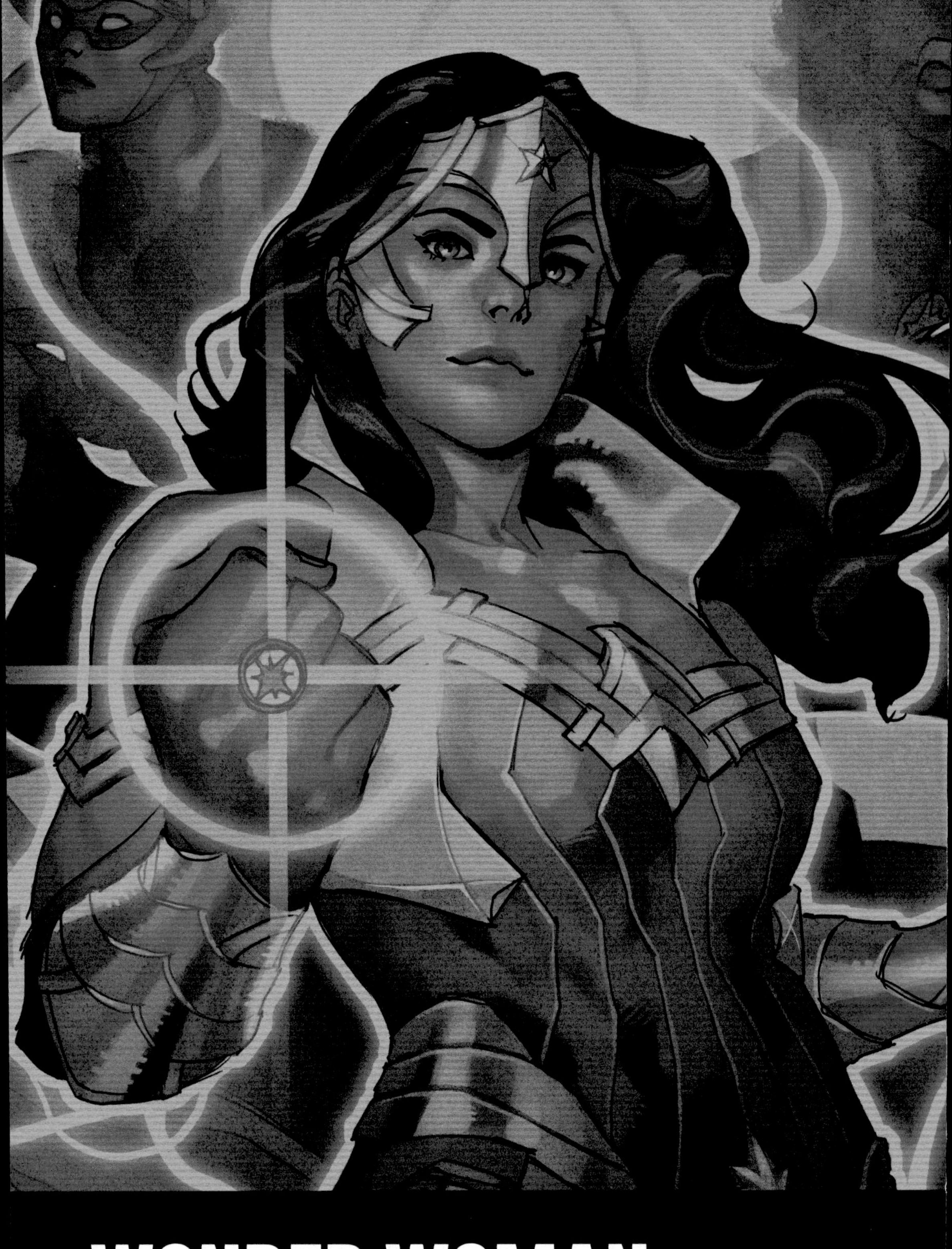

WONDER WOMAN
ANNUAL #2

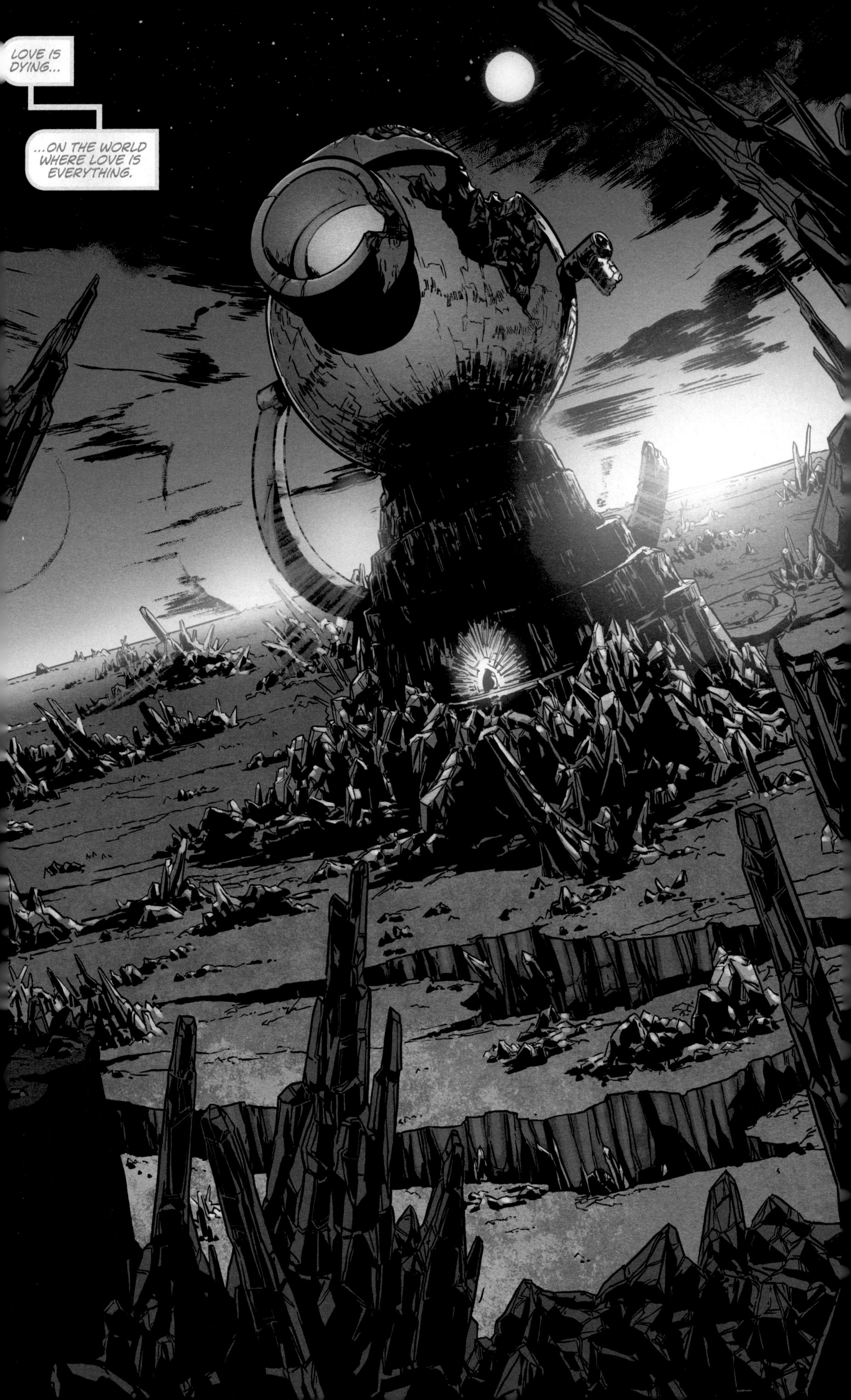
LOVE IS DYING...
...ON THE WORLD WHERE LOVE IS EVERYTHING.

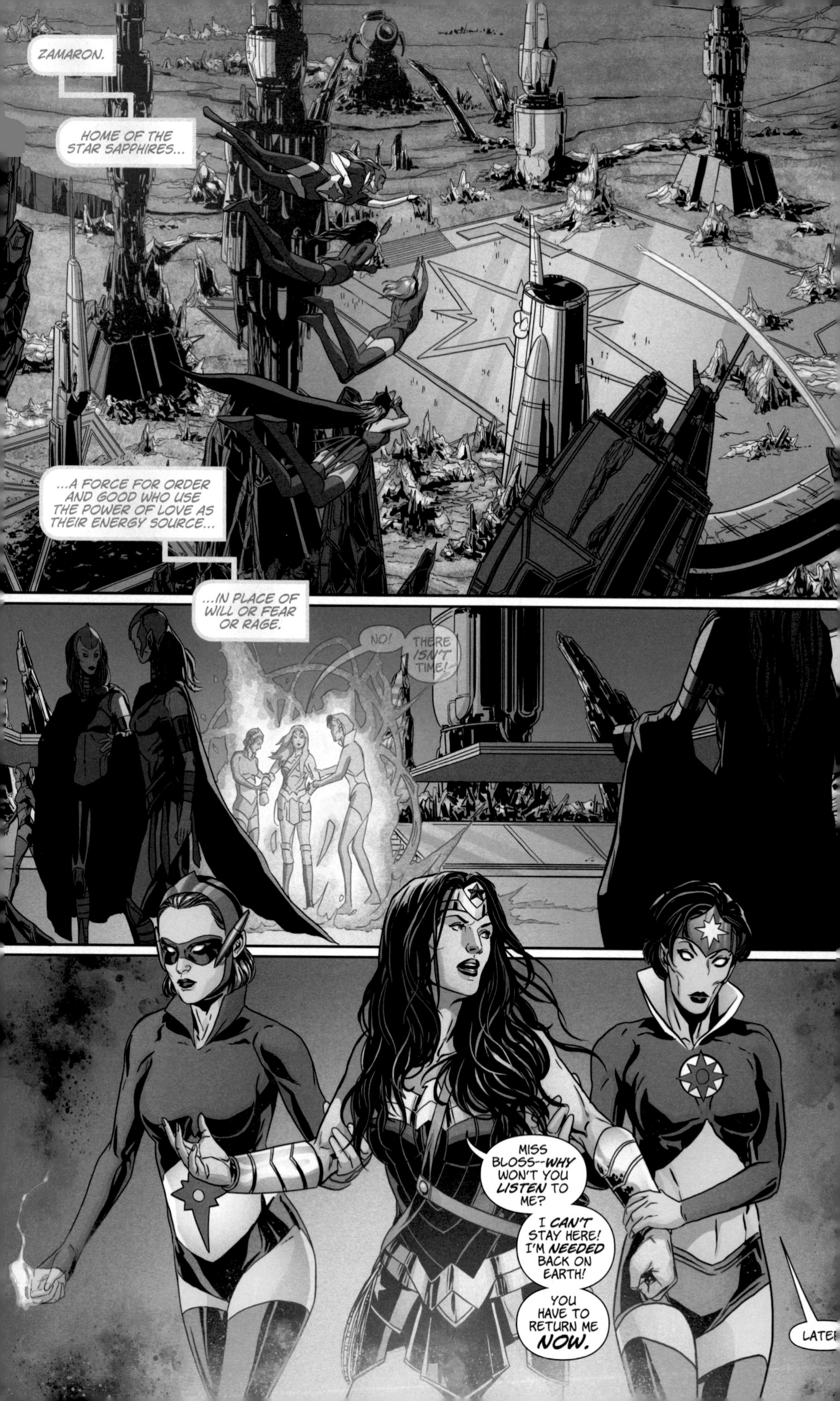
ZAMARON.
HOME OF THE STAR SAPPHIRES...
...A FORCE FOR ORDER AND GOOD WHO USE THE POWER OF LOVE AS THEIR ENERGY SOURCE...
...IN PLACE OF WILL OR FEAR OR RAGE.
NO!
THERE ISN'T TIME!
MISS BLOSS--WHY WON'T YOU LISTEN TO ME?
I CAN'T STAY HERE! I'M NEEDED BACK ON EARTH!
YOU HAVE TO RETURN ME NOW.

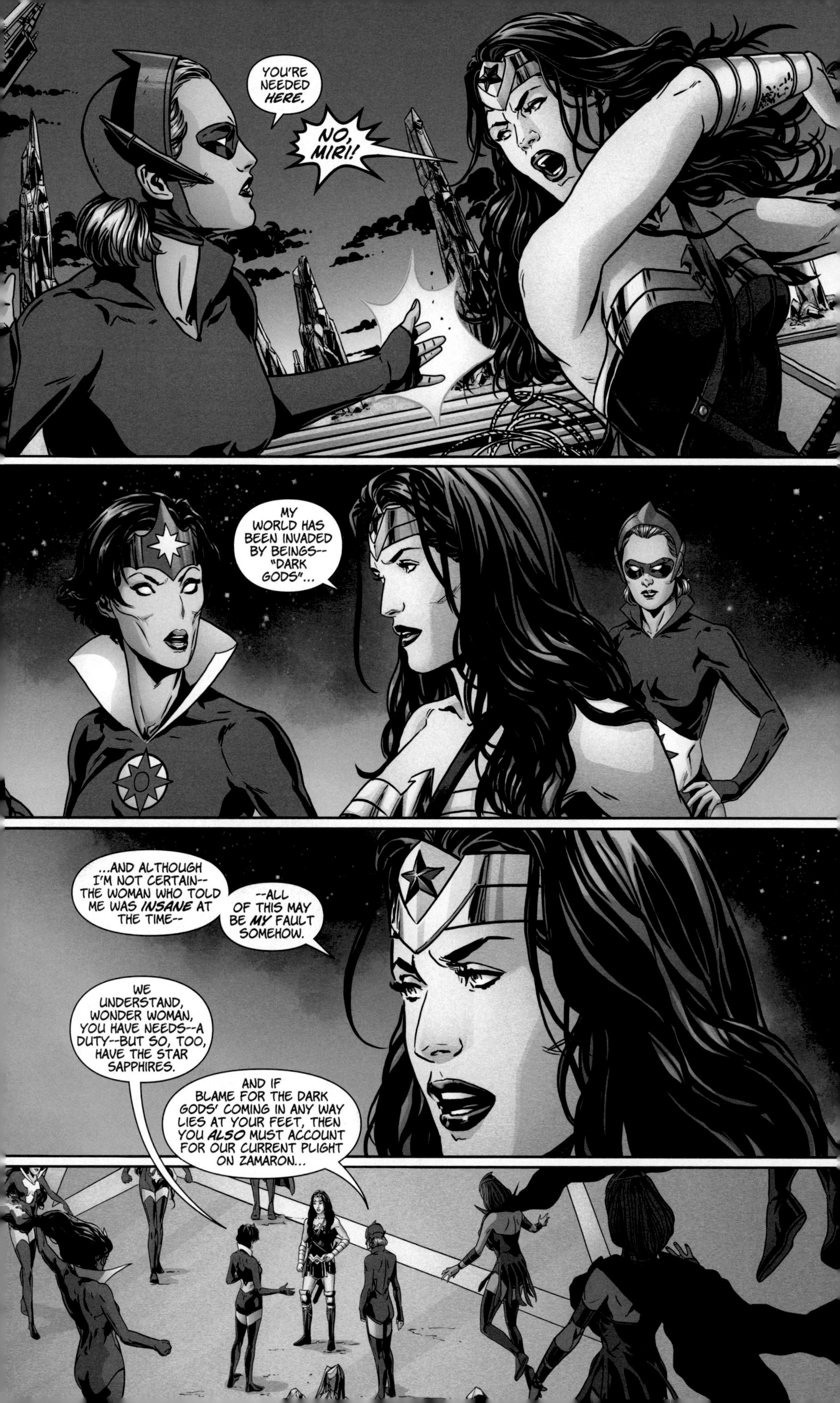

YOU'RE NEEDED HERE.
NO, MIRI!
MY WORLD HAS BEEN INVADED BY BEINGS-- "DARK GODS"...
...AND ALTHOUGH I'M NOT CERTAIN-- THE WOMAN WHO TOLD ME WAS INSANE AT THE TIME--
--ALL OF THIS MAY BE MY FAULT SOMEHOW.
WE UNDERSTAND, WONDER WOMAN, YOU HAVE NEEDS--A DUTY--BUT SO, TOO, HAVE THE STAR SAPPHIRES.
AND IF BLAME FOR THE DARK GODS' COMING IN ANY WAY LIES AT YOUR FEET, THEN YOU ALSO MUST ACCOUNT FOR OUR CURRENT PLIGHT ON ZAMARON...

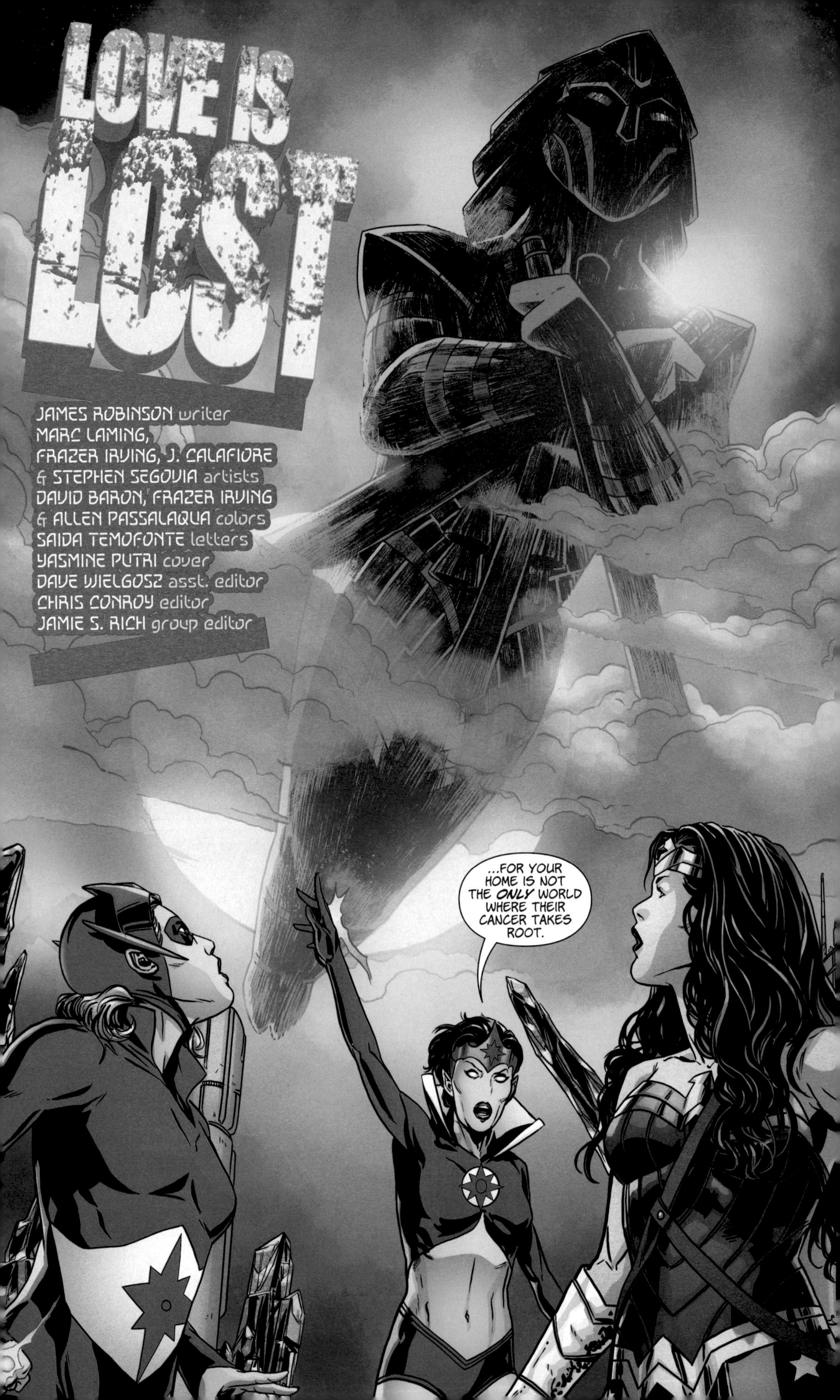
LOVE IS LOST
JAMES ROBINSON writer
MARC LAMING,
FRAZER IRVING, J. CALAFIORE
& STEPHEN SEGOVIA artists
DAVID BARON, FRAZER IRVING
& ALLEN PASSALAQUA colors
SAIDA TEMOFONTE letters
YASMINE PUTRI cover
DAVE WIELGOSZ asst. editor
CHRIS CONROY editor
JAMIE S. RICH group editor
...FOR YOUR HOME IS NOT THE *ONLY* WORLD WHERE THEIR CANCER TAKES ROOT.

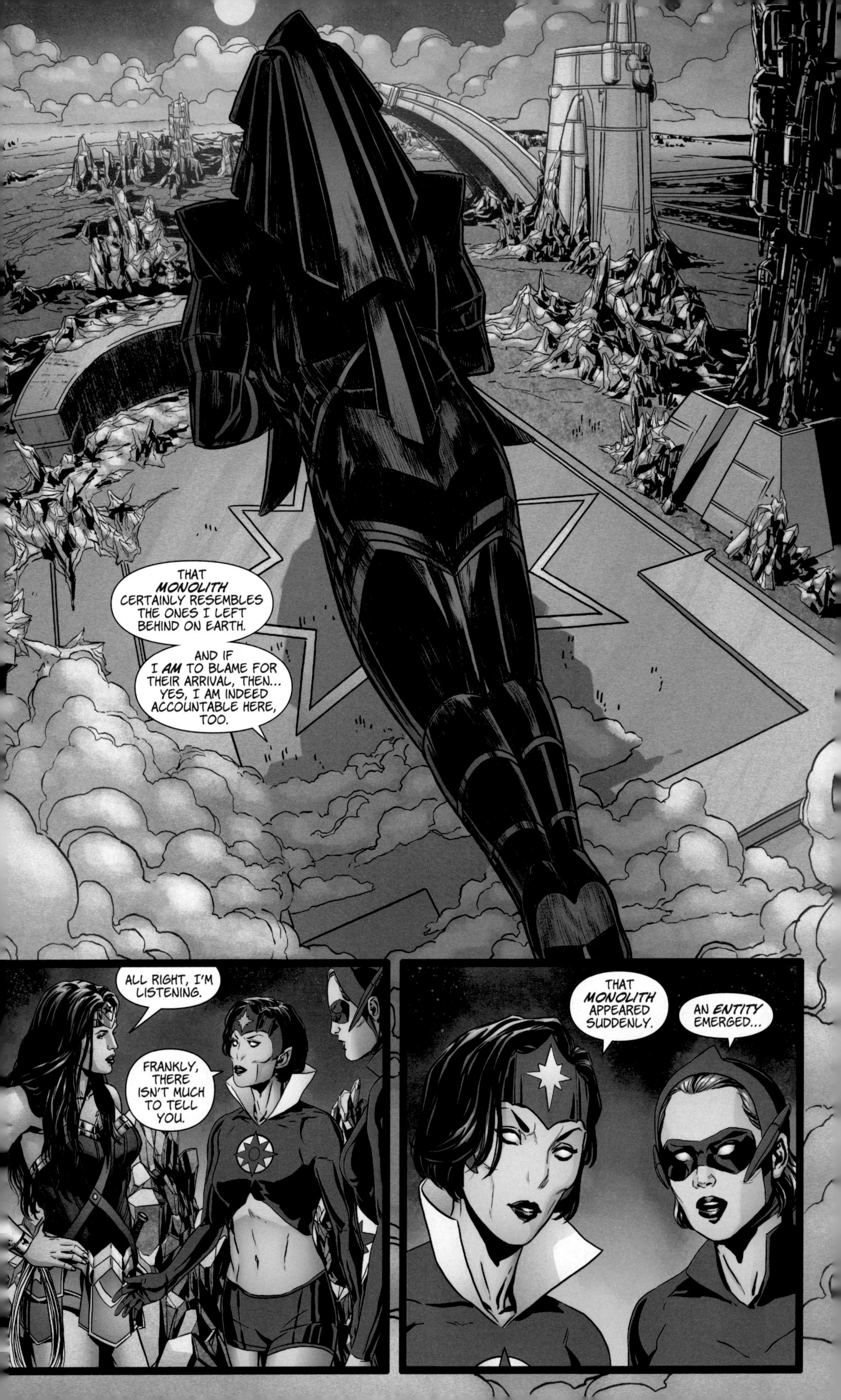

THAT *MONOLITH* CERTAINLY RESEMBLES THE ONES I LEFT BEHIND ON EARTH.
AND IF I *AM* TO BLAME FOR THEIR ARRIVAL, THEN... YES, I AM INDEED ACCOUNTABLE HERE, TOO.
ALL RIGHT, I'M LISTENING.
FRANKLY, THERE ISN'T MUCH TO TELL YOU.
THAT *MONOLITH* APPEARED SUDDENLY.
AN *ENTITY* EMERGED...

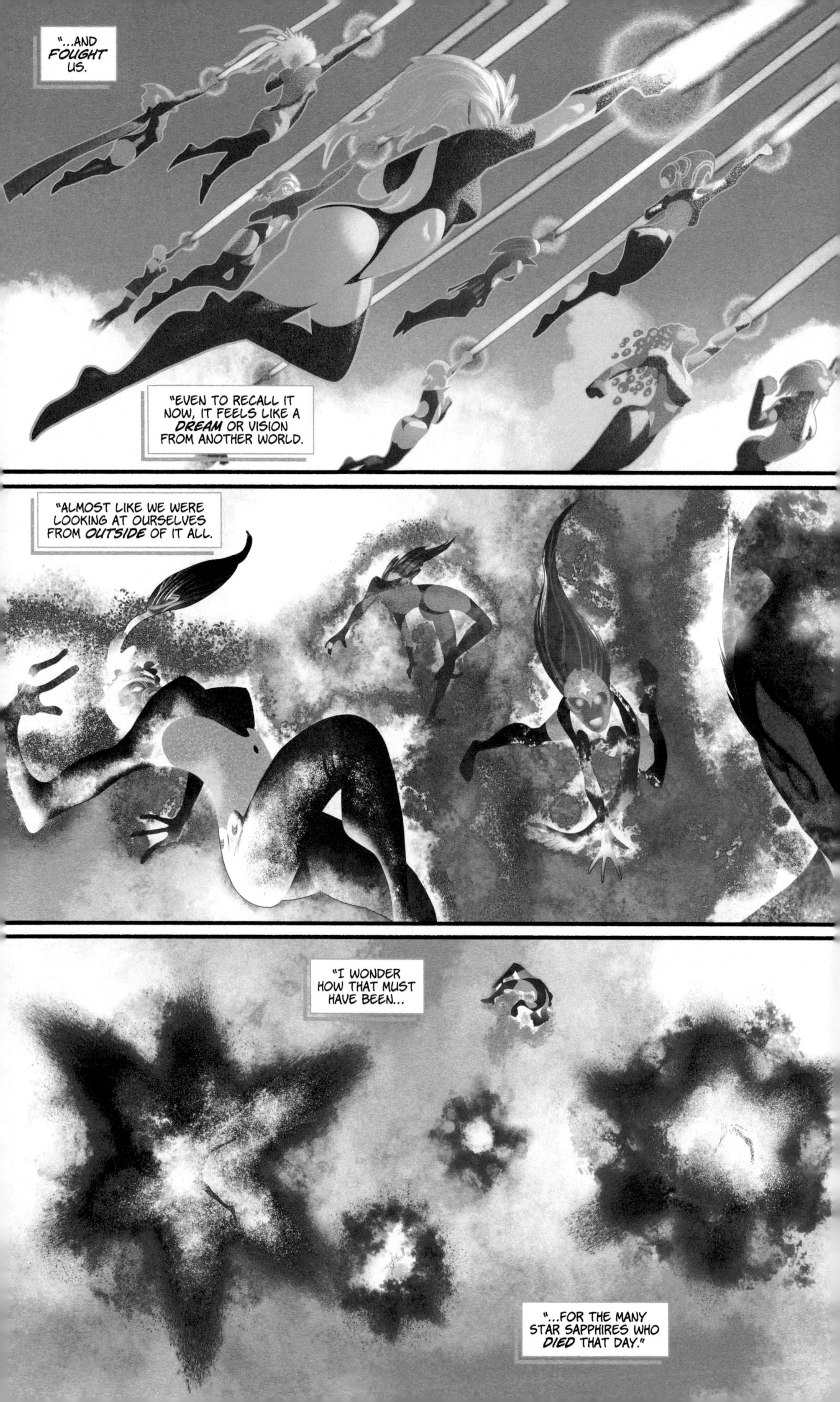
"...AND *FOUGHT* US.
"EVEN TO RECALL IT NOW, IT FEELS LIKE A *DREAM* OR VISION FROM ANOTHER WORLD.
"ALMOST LIKE WE WERE LOOKING AT OURSELVES FROM *OUTSIDE* OF IT ALL.
"I WONDER HOW THAT MUST HAVE BEEN...
"...FOR THE MANY STAR SAPPHIRES WHO *DIED* THAT DAY."

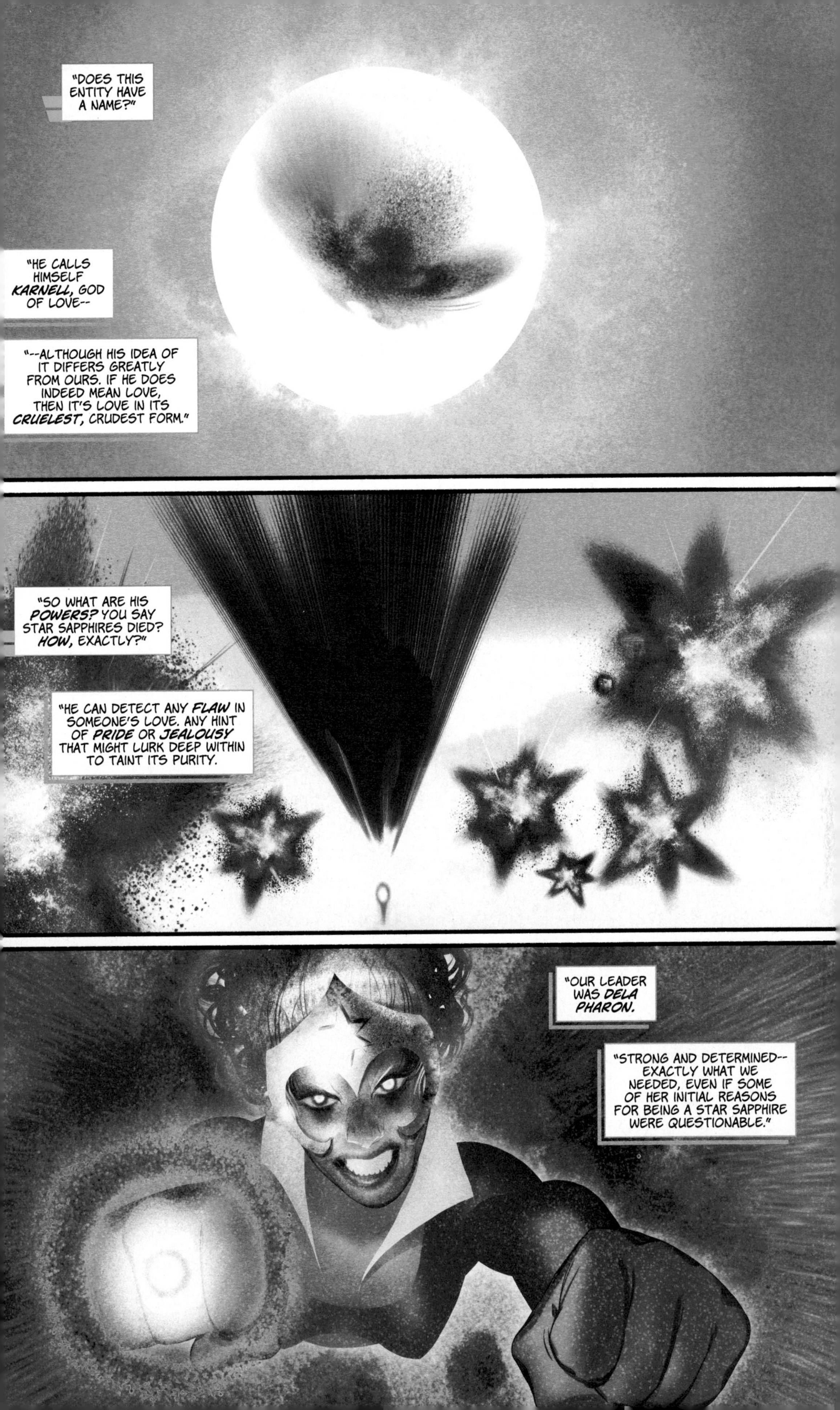
"DOES THIS ENTITY HAVE A NAME?"
"HE CALLS HIMSELF KARNELL, GOD OF LOVE--
"--ALTHOUGH HIS IDEA OF IT DIFFERS GREATLY FROM OURS. IF HE DOES INDEED MEAN LOVE, THEN IT'S LOVE IN ITS CRUELEST, CRUDEST FORM."
"SO WHAT ARE HIS POWERS? YOU SAY STAR SAPPHIRES DIED? HOW, EXACTLY?"
"HE CAN DETECT ANY FLAW IN SOMEONE'S LOVE. ANY HINT OF PRIDE OR JEALOUSY THAT MIGHT LURK DEEP WITHIN TO TAINT ITS PURITY.
"OUR LEADER WAS DELA PHARON.
"STRONG AND DETERMINED-- EXACTLY WHAT WE NEEDED, EVEN IF SOME OF HER INITIAL REASONS FOR BEING A STAR SAPPHIRE WERE QUESTIONABLE."

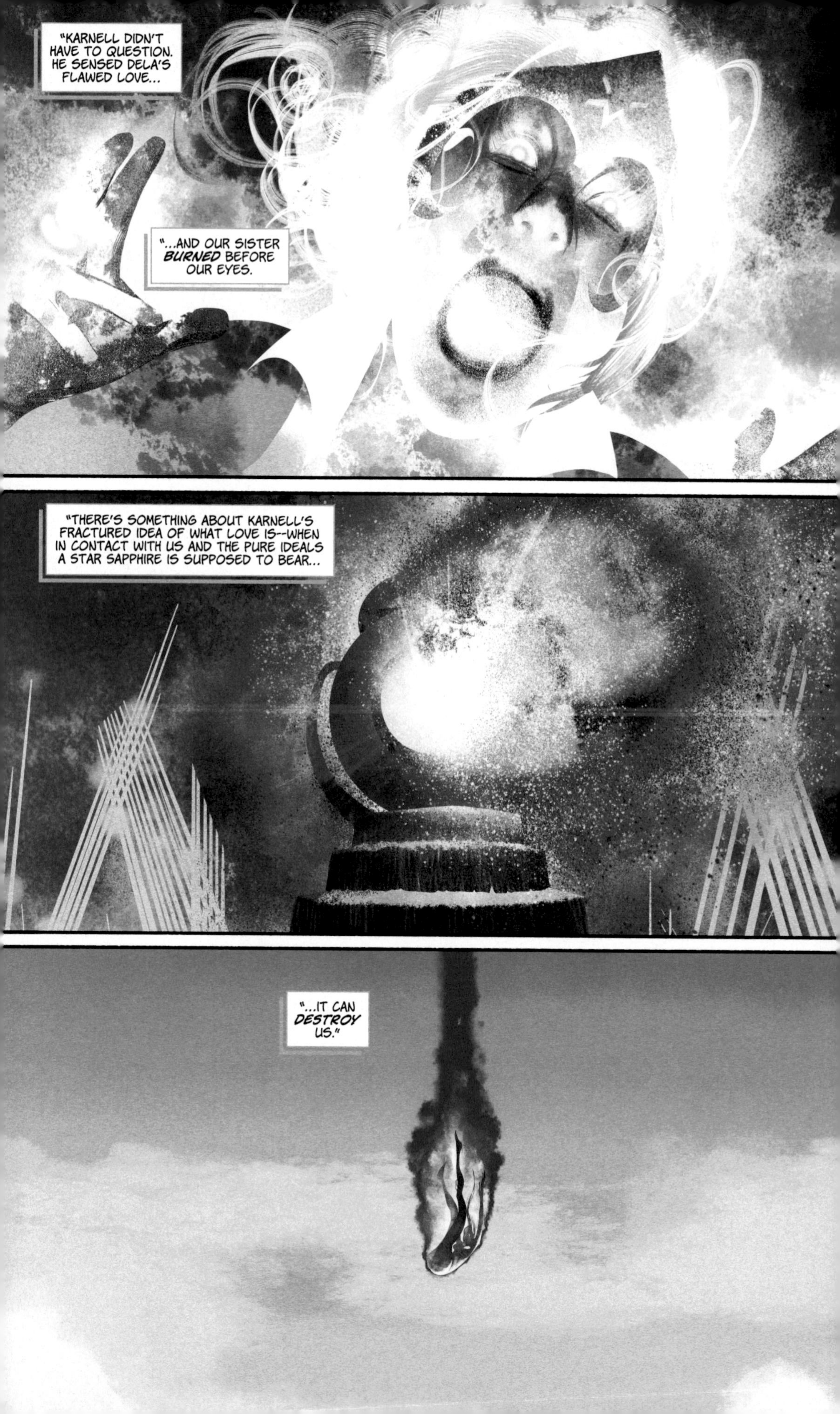
"KARNELL DIDN'T HAVE TO QUESTION. HE SENSED DELA'S FLAWED LOVE...
"...AND OUR SISTER BURNED BEFORE OUR EYES.
"THERE'S SOMETHING ABOUT KARNELL'S FRACTURED IDEA OF WHAT LOVE IS--WHEN IN CONTACT WITH US AND THE PURE IDEALS A STAR SAPPHIRE IS SUPPOSED TO BEAR...
"...IT CAN DESTROY US."

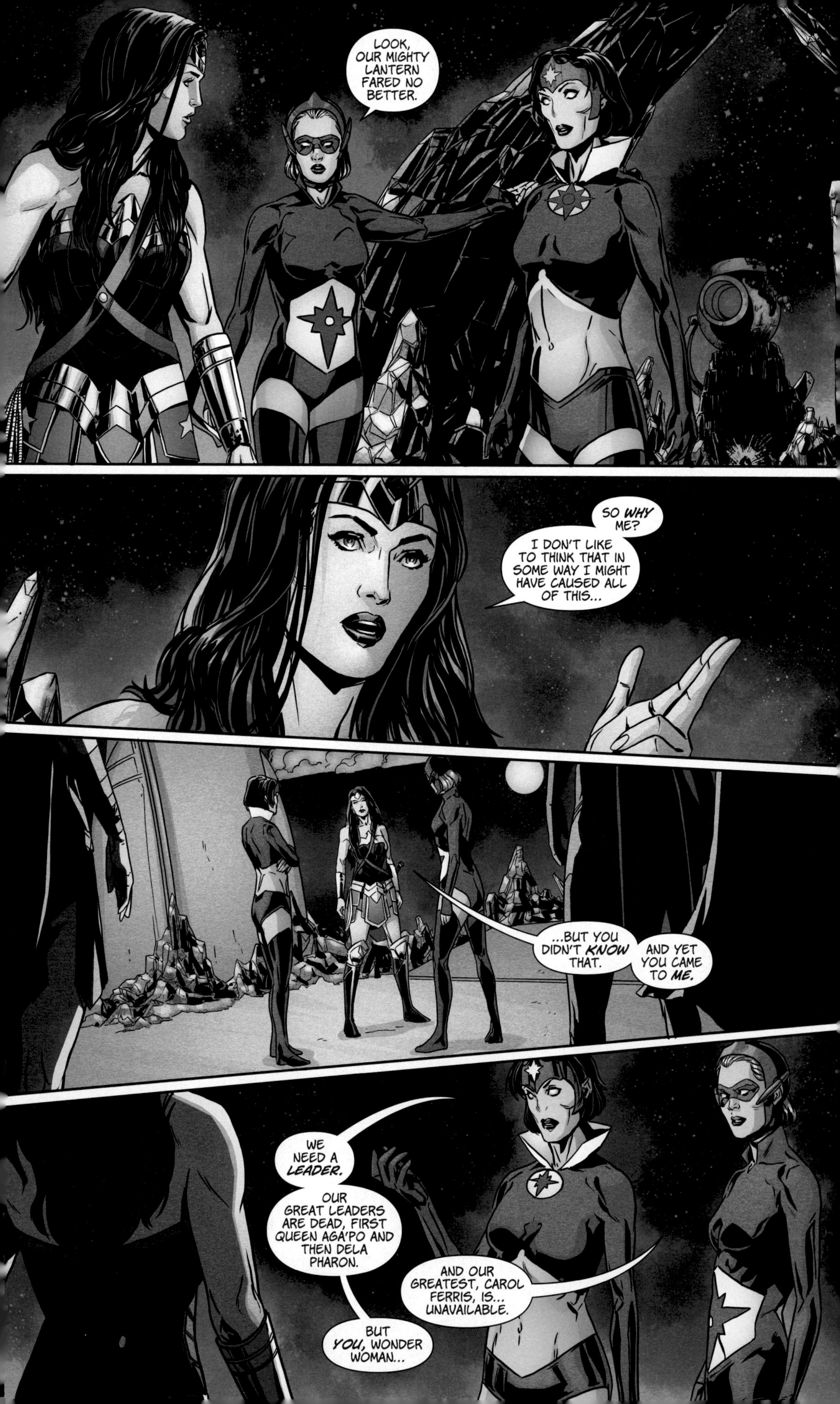

LOOK, OUR MIGHTY LANTERN FARED NO BETTER.
SO WHY ME?
I DON'T LIKE TO THINK THAT IN SOME WAY I MIGHT HAVE CAUSED ALL OF THIS...
...BUT YOU DIDN'T KNOW THAT.
AND YET YOU CAME TO ME.
WE NEED A LEADER.
OUR GREAT LEADERS ARE DEAD, FIRST QUEEN AGA'PO AND THEN DELA PHARON.
AND OUR GREATEST, CAROL FERRIS, IS... UNAVAILABLE.
BUT YOU, WONDER WOMAN...

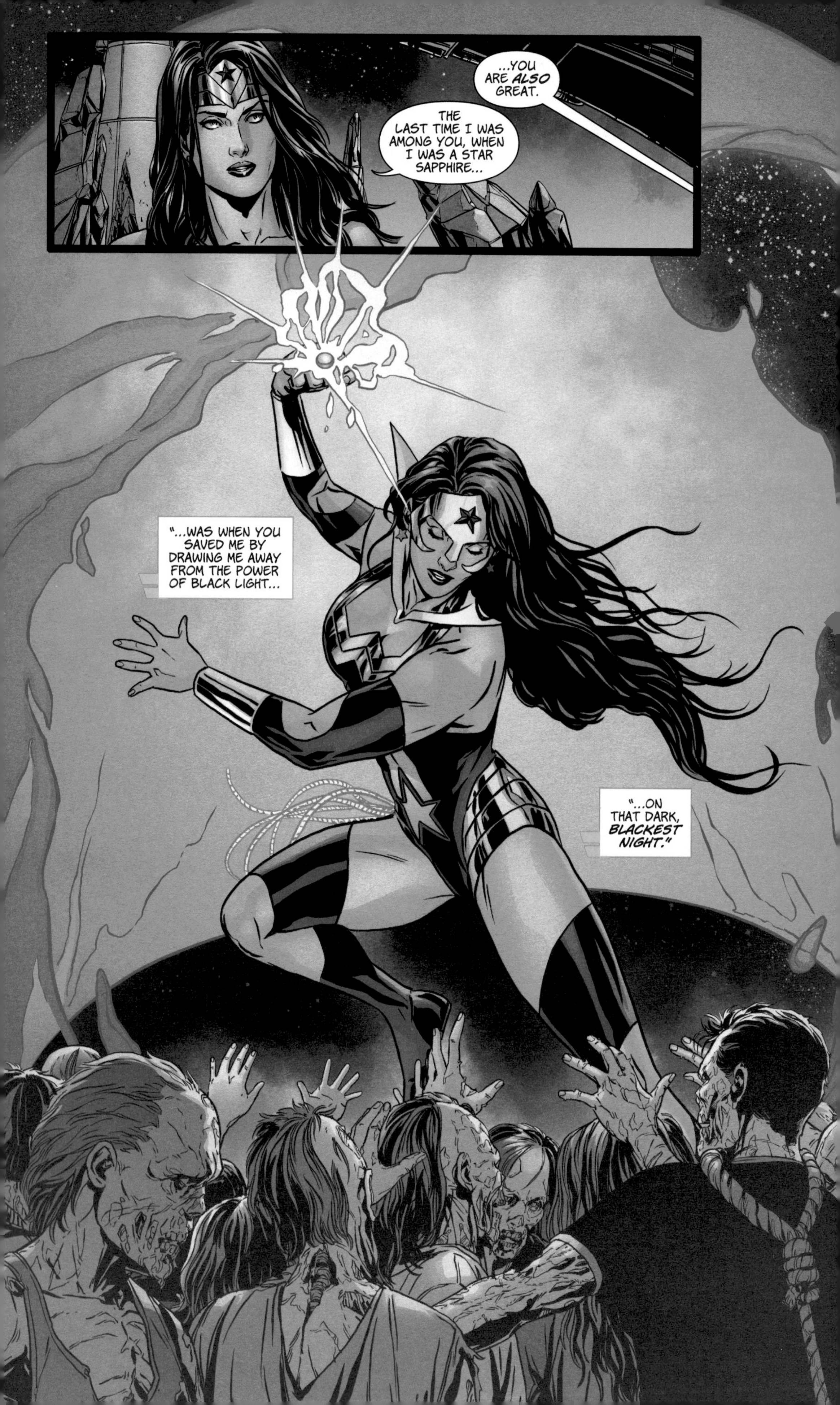
...YOU ARE ALSO GREAT.
THE LAST TIME I WAS AMONG YOU, WHEN I WAS A STAR SAPPHIRE...
"...WAS WHEN YOU SAVED ME BY DRAWING ME AWAY FROM THE POWER OF BLACK LIGHT...
"...ON THAT DARK, BLACKEST NIGHT."

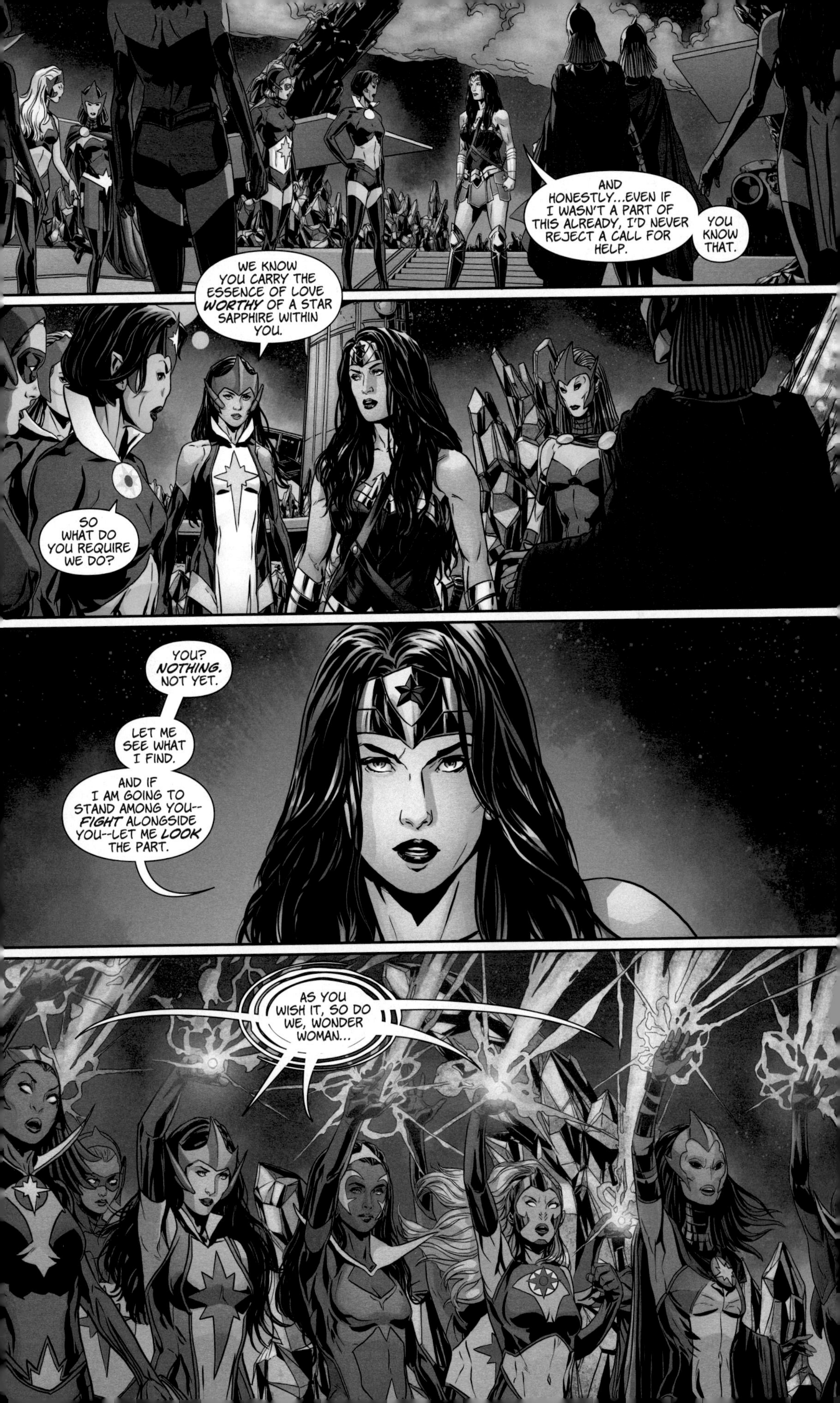

AND HONESTLY...EVEN IF I WASN'T A PART OF THIS ALREADY, I'D NEVER REJECT A CALL FOR HELP.
YOU KNOW THAT.
WE KNOW YOU CARRY THE ESSENCE OF LOVE WORTHY OF A STAR SAPPHIRE WITHIN YOU.
SO WHAT DO YOU REQUIRE WE DO?
YOU? NOTHING. NOT YET.
LET ME SEE WHAT I FIND.
AND IF I AM GOING TO STAND AMONG YOU--FIGHT ALONGSIDE YOU--LET ME LOOK THE PART.
AS YOU WISH IT, SO DO WE, WONDER WOMAN...

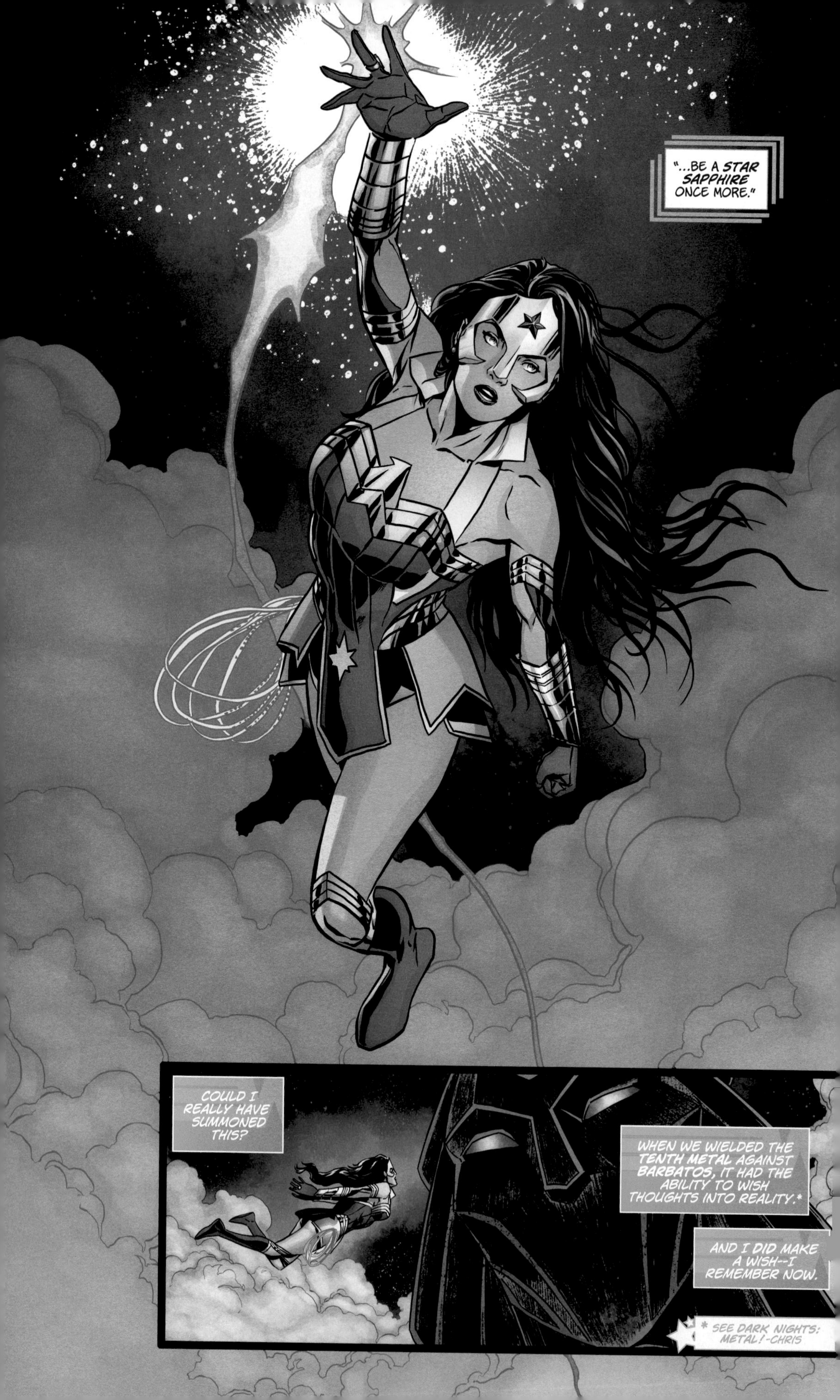
"...BE A STAR SAPPHIRE ONCE MORE."
COULD I REALLY HAVE SUMMONED THIS?
WHEN WE WIELDED THE TENTH METAL AGAINST BARBATOS, IT HAD THE ABILITY TO WISH THOUGHTS INTO REALITY.*
AND I DID MAKE A WISH--I REMEMBER NOW.
* SEE DARK NIGHTS: METAL! -CHRIS

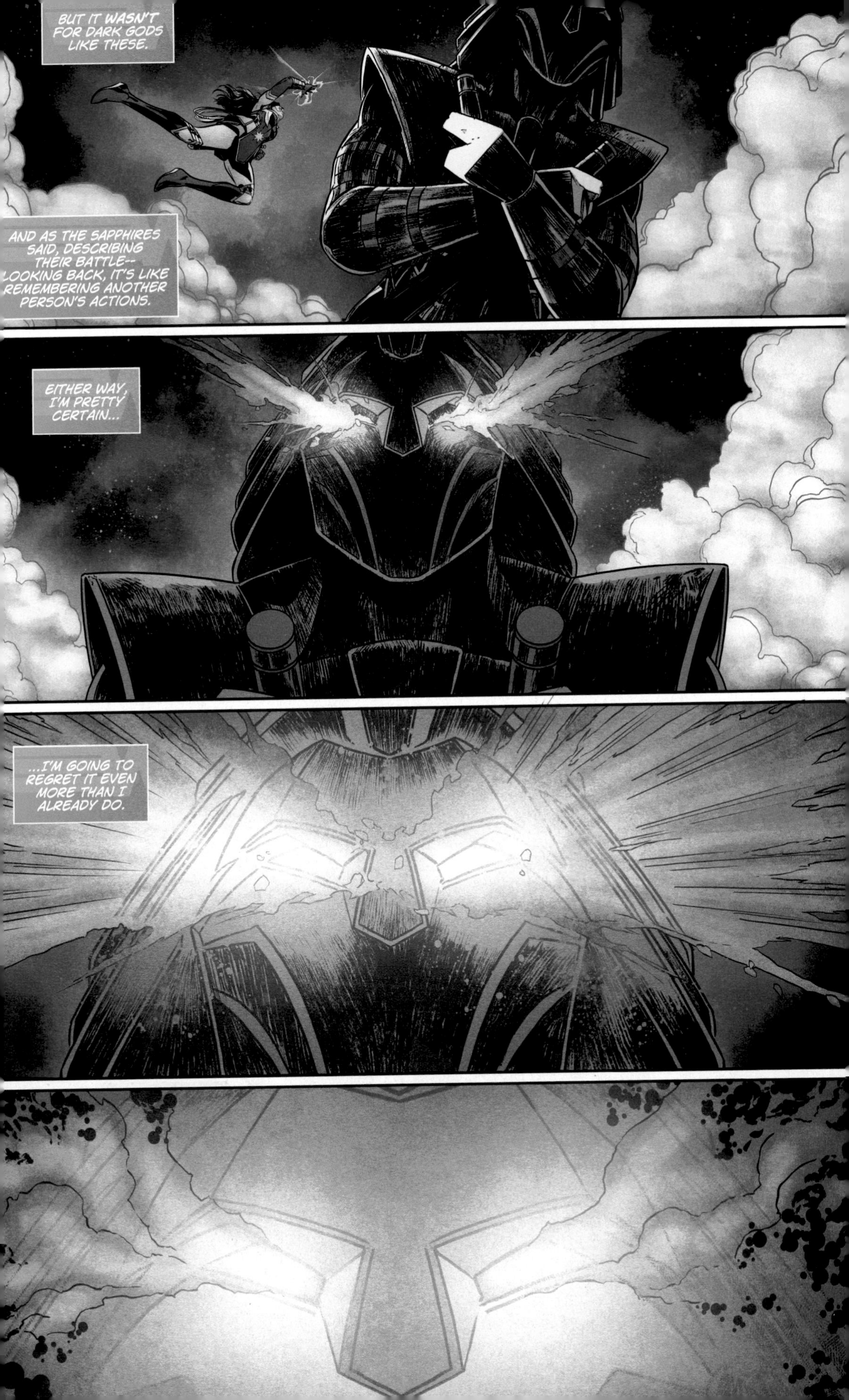
BUT IT WASN'T FOR DARK GODS LIKE THESE.
AND AS THE SAPPHIRES SAID, DESCRIBING THEIR BATTLE-- LOOKING BACK, IT'S LIKE REMEMBERING ANOTHER PERSON'S ACTIONS.
EITHER WAY, I'M PRETTY CERTAIN...
...I'M GOING TO REGRET IT EVEN MORE THAN I ALREADY DO.

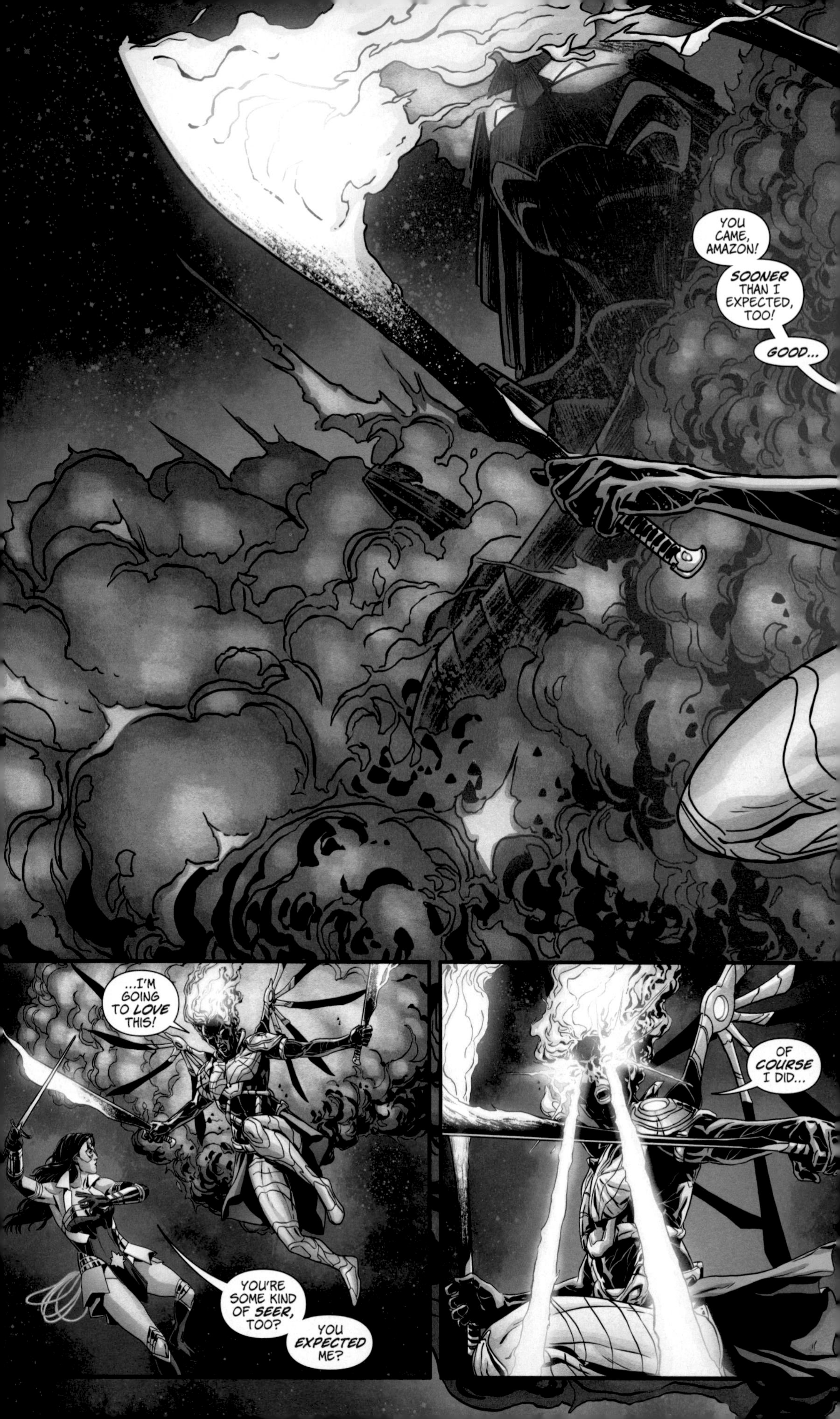
YOU CAME, AMAZON!
SOONER THAN I EXPECTED, TOO!
GOOD...
...I'M GOING TO LOVE THIS!
YOU'RE SOME KIND OF SEER, TOO?
YOU EXPECTED ME?
OF COURSE I DID...

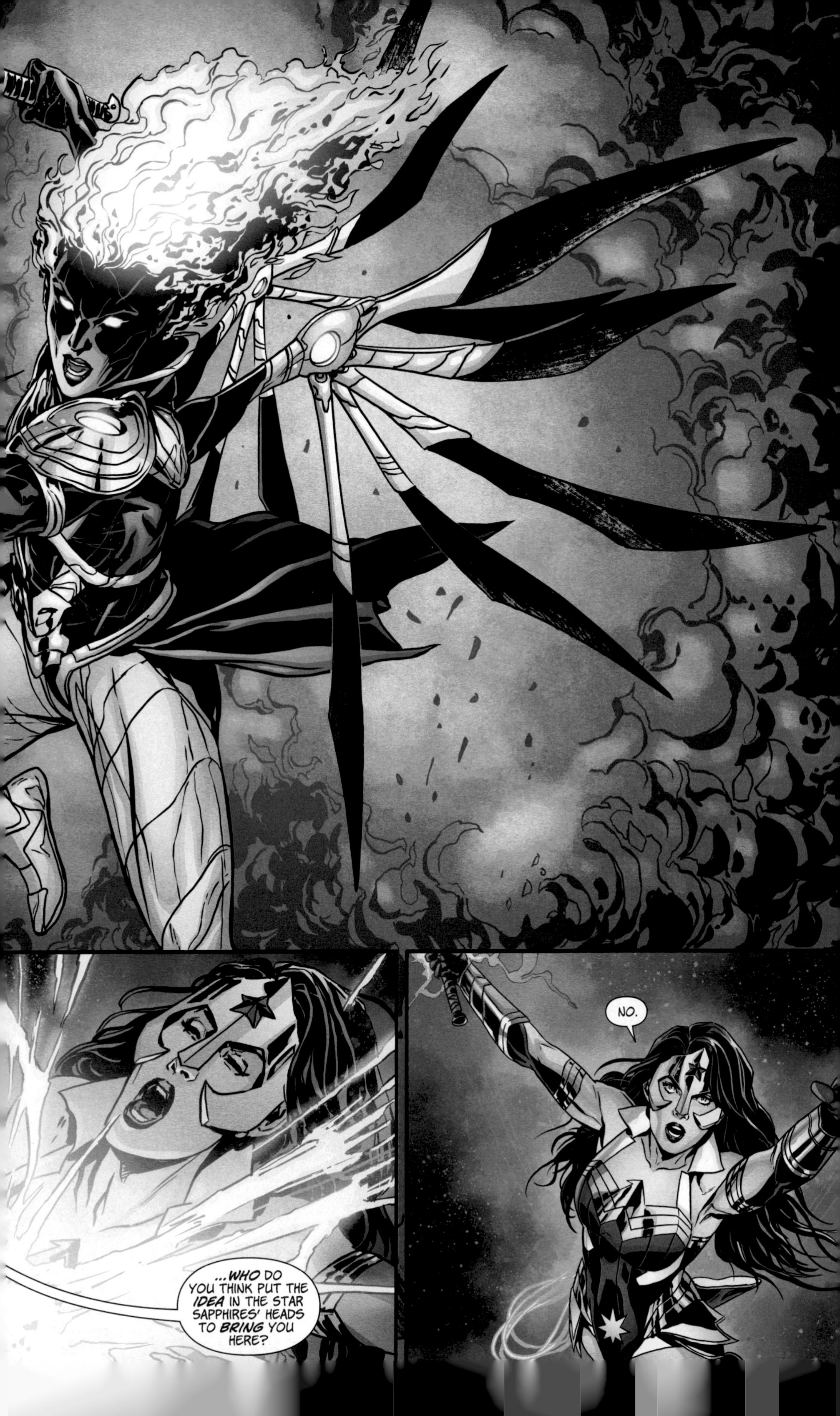
...WHO DO YOU THINK PUT THE IDEA IN THE STAR SAPPHIRES' HEADS TO BRING YOU HERE?
NO.

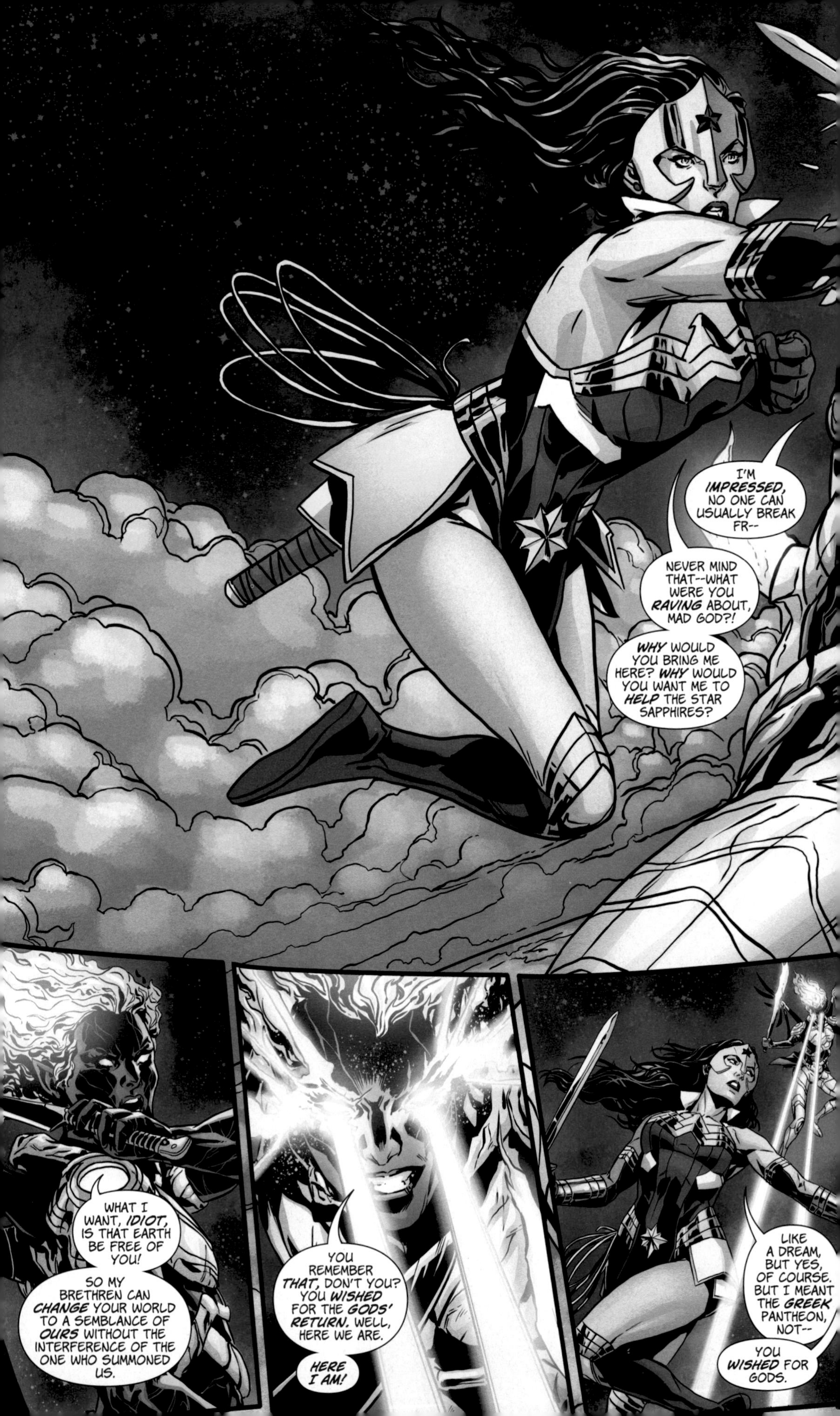

I'M IMPRESSED, NO ONE CAN USUALLY BREAK FR--
NEVER MIND THAT--WHAT WERE YOU RAVING ABOUT, MAD GOD?!
WHY WOULD YOU BRING ME HERE? WHY WOULD YOU WANT ME TO HELP THE STAR SAPPHIRES?
WHAT I WANT, IDIOT, IS THAT EARTH BE FREE OF YOU!
SO MY BRETHREN CAN CHANGE YOUR WORLD TO A SEMBLANCE OF OURS WITHOUT THE INTERFERENCE OF THE ONE WHO SUMMONED US.
YOU REMEMBER THAT, DON'T YOU? YOU WISHED FOR THE GODS' RETURN. WELL, HERE WE ARE.
HERE I AM!
LIKE A DREAM, BUT YES, OF COURSE. BUT I MEANT THE GREEK PANTHEON, NOT--
YOU WISHED FOR GODS.

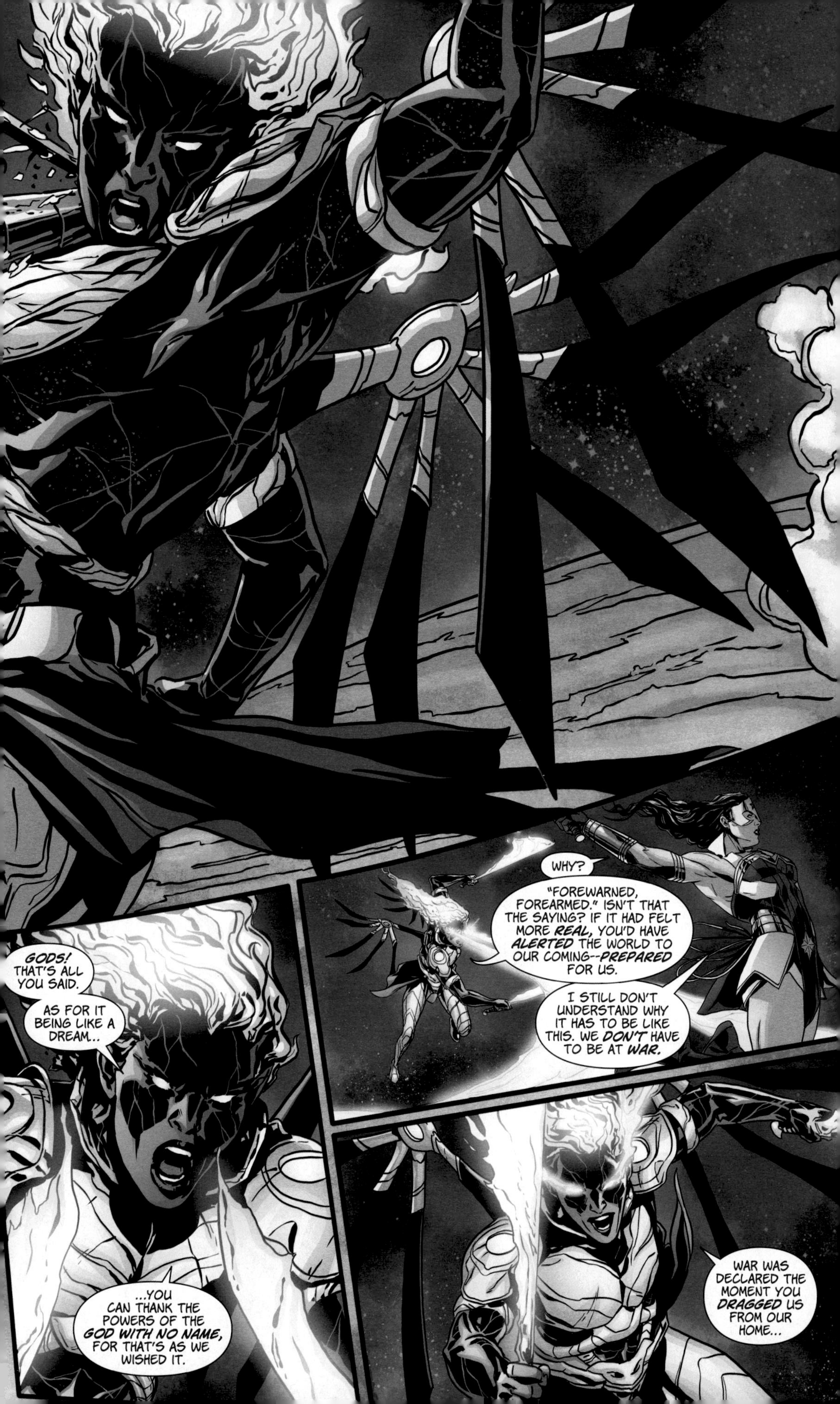
WHY?
"FOREWARNED, FOREARMED." ISN'T THAT THE SAYING? IF IT HAD FELT MORE REAL, YOU'D HAVE ALERTED THE WORLD TO OUR COMING--PREPARED FOR US.
I STILL DON'T UNDERSTAND WHY IT HAS TO BE LIKE THIS. WE DON'T HAVE TO BE AT WAR.
GODS! THAT'S ALL YOU SAID.
AS FOR IT BEING LIKE A DREAM...
...YOU CAN THANK THE POWERS OF THE GOD WITH NO NAME, FOR THAT'S AS WE WISHED IT.
WAR WAS DECLARED THE MOMENT YOU DRAGGED US FROM OUR HOME...

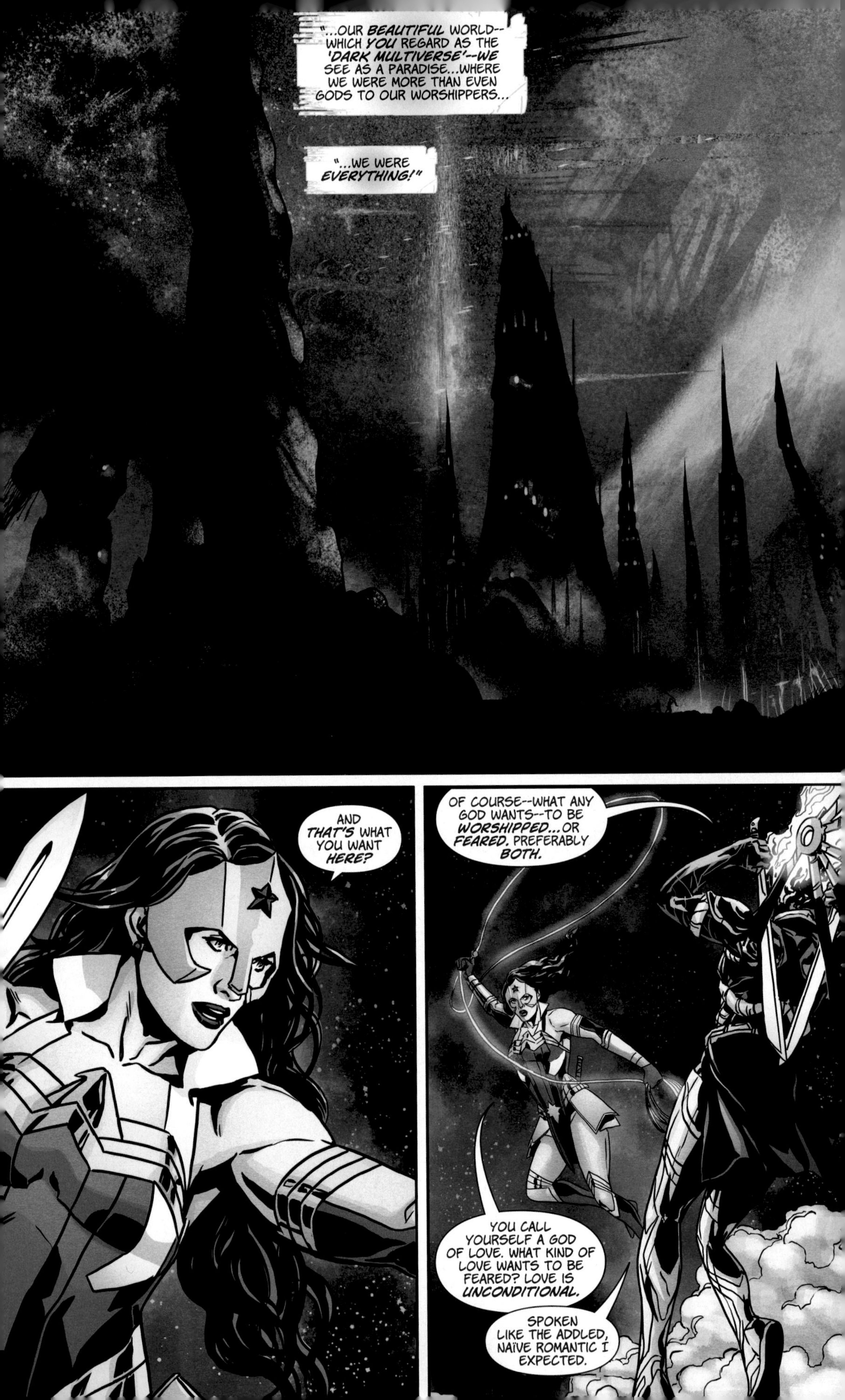
"...OUR BEAUTIFUL WORLD--WHICH YOU REGARD AS THE 'DARK MULTIVERSE'--WE SEE AS A PARADISE...WHERE WE WERE MORE THAN EVEN GODS TO OUR WORSHIPPERS...
"...WE WERE EVERYTHING!"
AND THAT'S WHAT YOU WANT HERE?
OF COURSE--WHAT ANY GOD WANTS--TO BE WORSHIPPED...OR FEARED. PREFERABLY BOTH.
YOU CALL YOURSELF A GOD OF LOVE. WHAT KIND OF LOVE WANTS TO BE FEARED? LOVE IS UNCONDITIONAL.
SPOKEN LIKE THE ADDLED, NAÏVE ROMANTIC I EXPECTED.

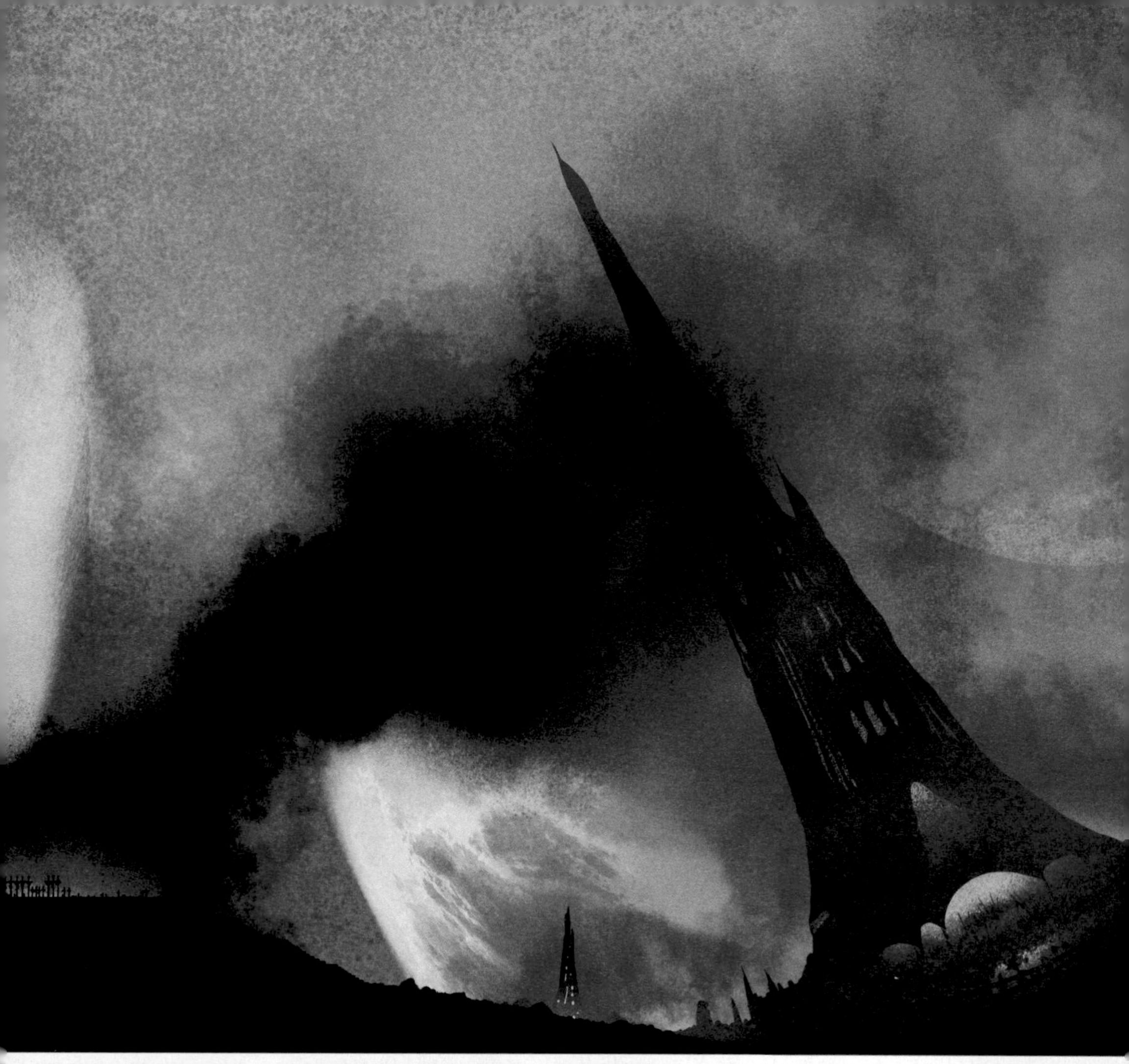

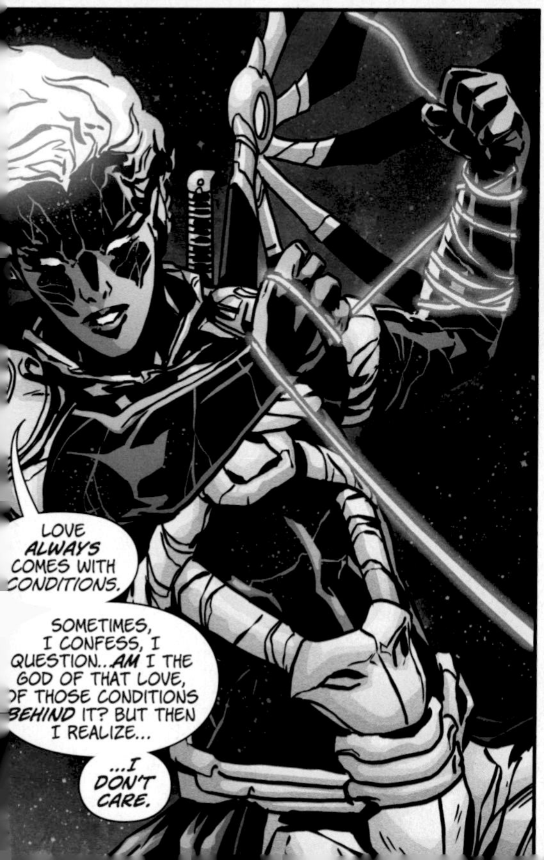
LOVE ALWAYS COMES WITH CONDITIONS.
SOMETIMES, I CONFESS, I QUESTION...AM I THE GOD OF THAT LOVE, OF THOSE CONDITIONS BEHIND IT? BUT THEN I REALIZE...
...I DON'T CARE.

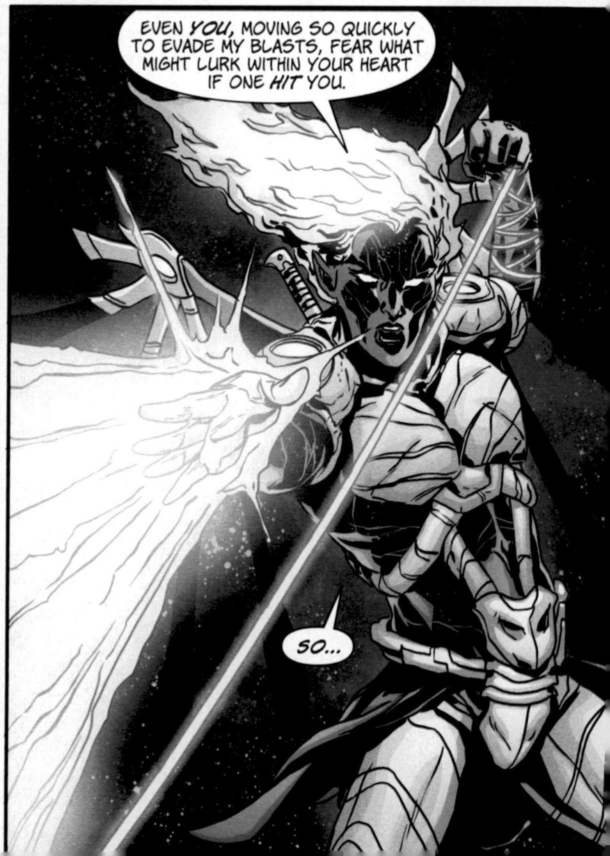
EVEN YOU, MOVING SO QUICKLY TO EVADE MY BLASTS, FEAR WHAT MIGHT LURK WITHIN YOUR HEART IF ONE HIT YOU.
SO...

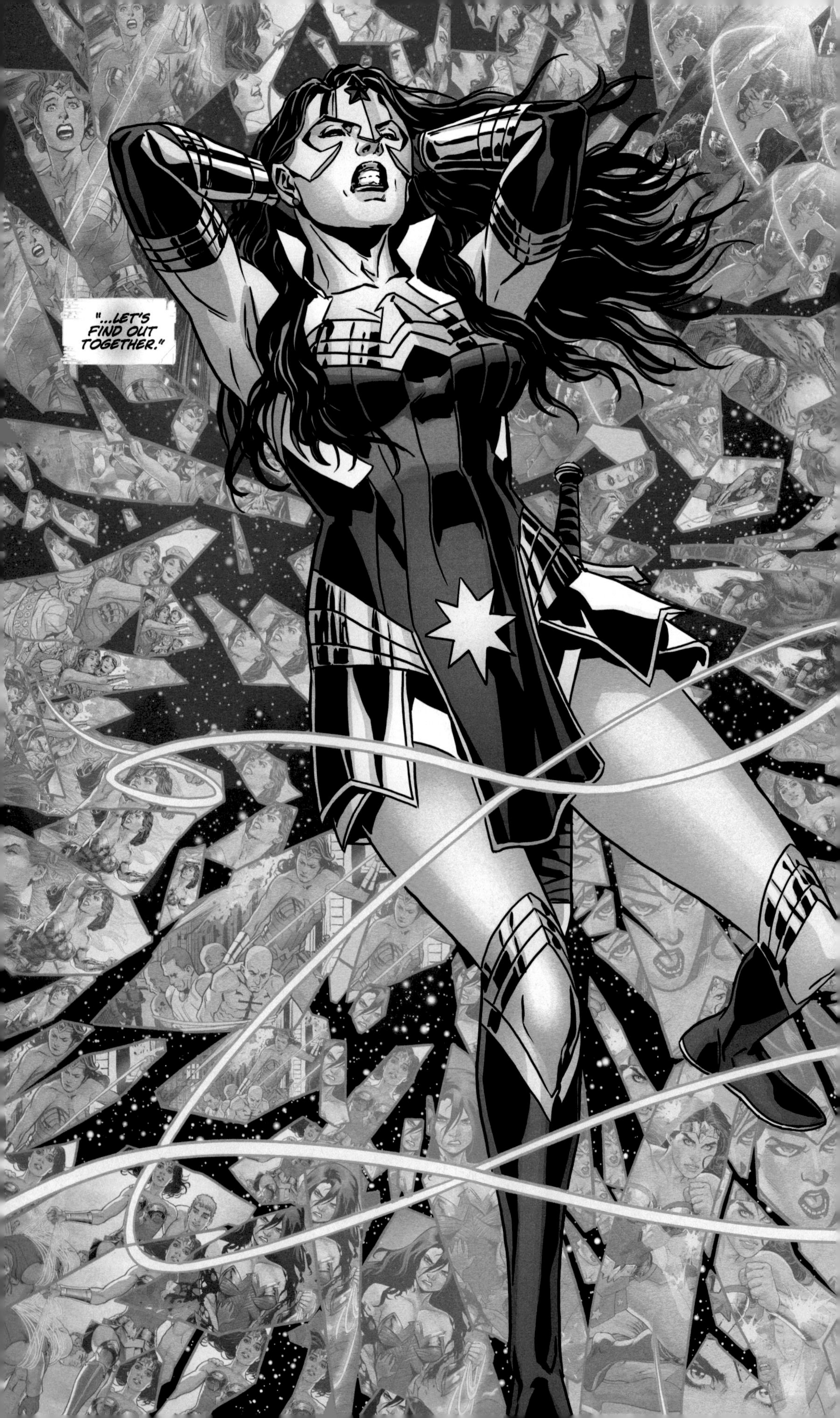
"...LET'S FIND OUT TOGETHER."

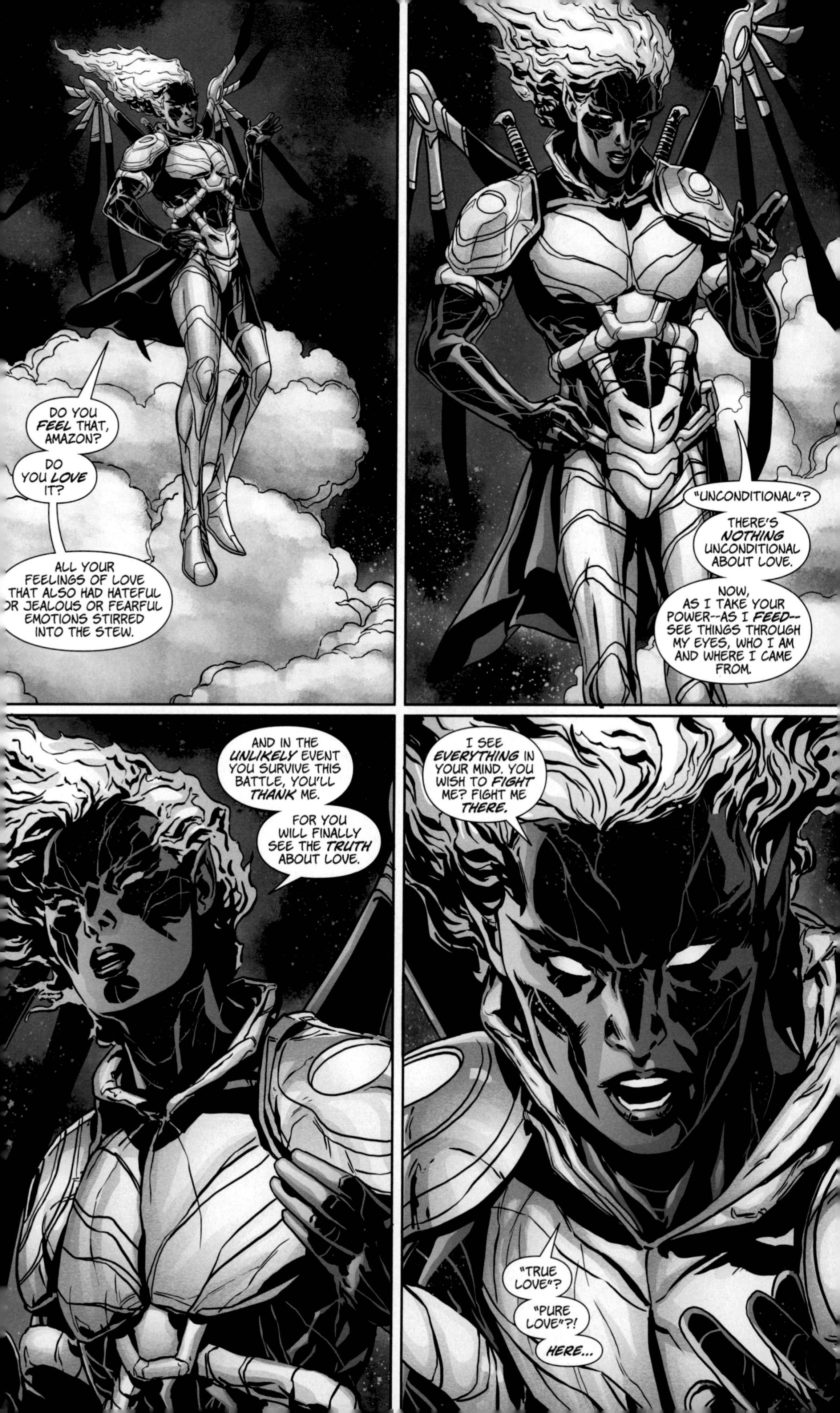
DO YOU FEEL THAT, AMAZON?
DO YOU LOVE IT?
ALL YOUR FEELINGS OF LOVE THAT ALSO HAD HATEFUL OR JEALOUS OR FEARFUL EMOTIONS STIRRED INTO THE STEW.
"UNCONDITIONAL"?
THERE'S NOTHING UNCONDITIONAL ABOUT LOVE.
NOW, AS I TAKE YOUR POWER--AS I FEED--SEE THINGS THROUGH MY EYES, WHO I AM AND WHERE I CAME FROM.
AND IN THE UNLIKELY EVENT YOU SURVIVE THIS BATTLE, YOU'LL THANK ME.
FOR YOU WILL FINALLY SEE THE TRUTH ABOUT LOVE.
I SEE EVERYTHING IN YOUR MIND. YOU WISH TO FIGHT ME? FIGHT ME THERE.
"TRUE LOVE"?
"PURE LOVE"?!
HERE...

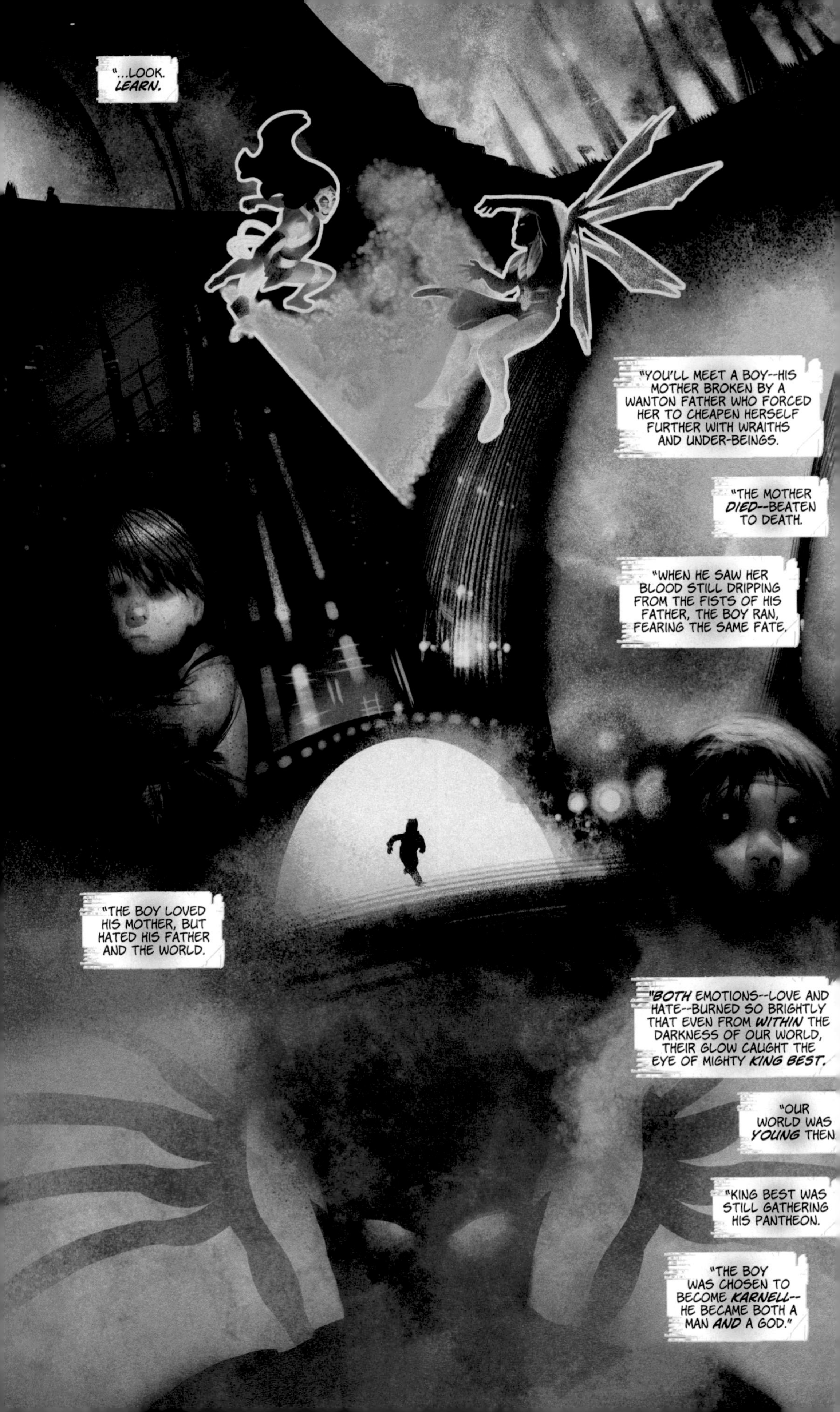
"...LOOK. LEARN.
"YOU'LL MEET A BOY--HIS MOTHER BROKEN BY A WANTON FATHER WHO FORCED HER TO CHEAPEN HERSELF FURTHER WITH WRAITHS AND UNDER-BEINGS.
"THE MOTHER DIED--BEATEN TO DEATH.
"WHEN HE SAW HER BLOOD STILL DRIPPING FROM THE FISTS OF HIS FATHER, THE BOY RAN, FEARING THE SAME FATE.
"THE BOY LOVED HIS MOTHER, BUT HATED HIS FATHER AND THE WORLD.
"BOTH EMOTIONS--LOVE AND HATE--BURNED SO BRIGHTLY THAT EVEN FROM WITHIN THE DARKNESS OF OUR WORLD, THEIR GLOW CAUGHT THE EYE OF MIGHTY KING BEST.
"OUR WORLD WAS YOUNG THEN.
"KING BEST WAS STILL GATHERING HIS PANTHEON.
"THE BOY WAS CHOSEN TO BECOME KARNELL--HE BECAME BOTH A MAN AND A GOD."

"KING BEST? WHO?
"AND YOUR WORLD... WHEN WAS THIS-- 'YOUNG WORLD,' YOU SAID?
"I CAN'T TALK-- BRAIN LIKE TAR. TELL ME W--"
"MY WORLD--THE WORLD OF KING BEST AND MY FELLOW GODS..."
"...WAS FORGED BY THE TITANS, MUCH LIKE THE REALITY OF YOUR OWN GREEK PANTHEON, AMAZON.
"ALTHOUGH OUR TITANS DESTROYED FIVE OTHER REALITIES--SMASHED THEM INTO NOTHING--TO CREATE THE ENERGY THAT FORGED OUR PLANE OF EXISTENCE."

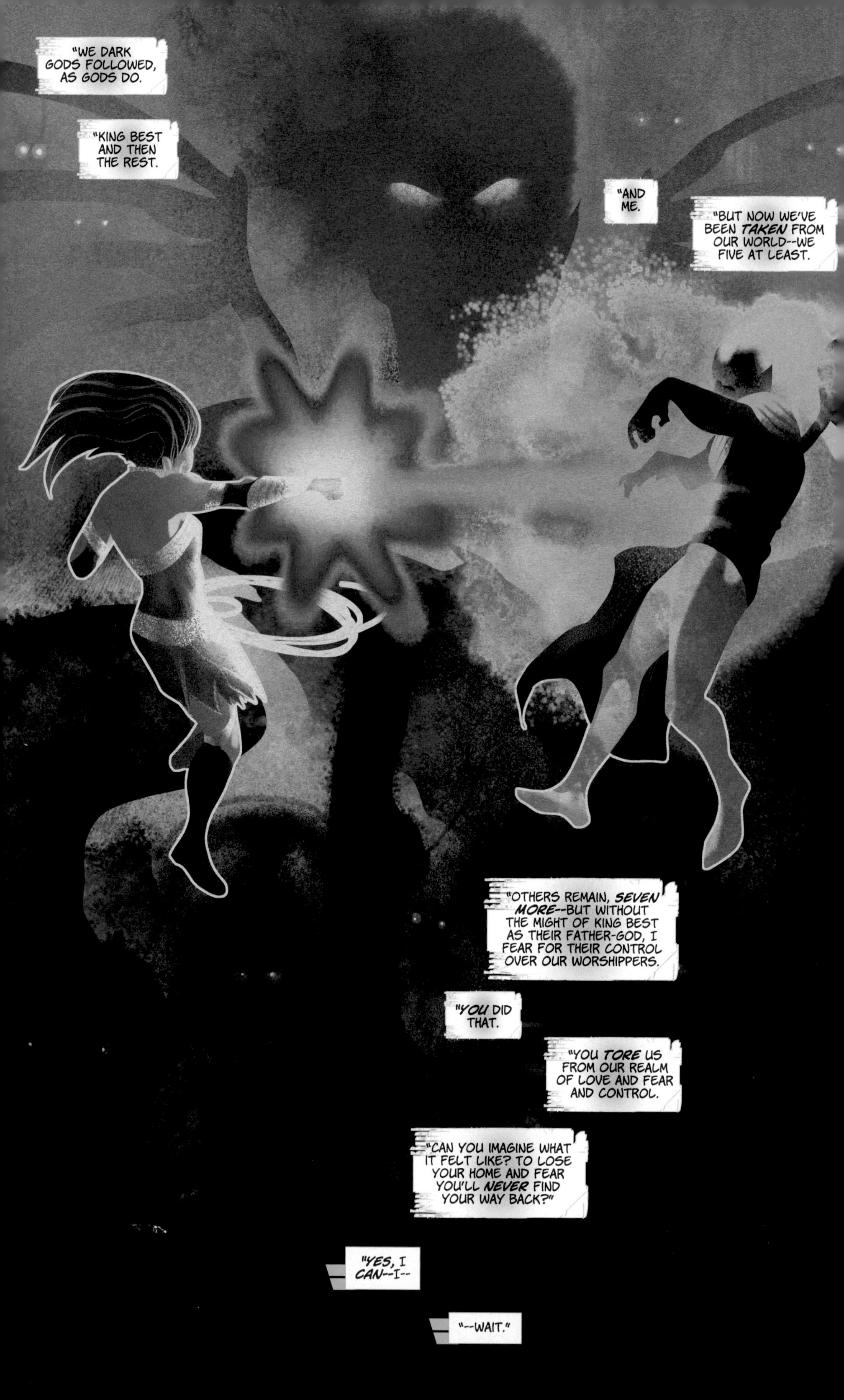
"WE DARK GODS FOLLOWED, AS GODS DO.
"KING BEST AND THEN THE REST.
"AND ME.
"BUT NOW WE'VE BEEN TAKEN FROM OUR WORLD--WE FIVE AT LEAST.
"OTHERS REMAIN, SEVEN MORE--BUT WITHOUT THE MIGHT OF KING BEST AS THEIR FATHER-GOD, I FEAR FOR THEIR CONTROL OVER OUR WORSHIPPERS.
"YOU DID THAT.
"YOU TORE US FROM OUR REALM OF LOVE AND FEAR AND CONTROL.
"CAN YOU IMAGINE WHAT IT FELT LIKE? TO LOSE YOUR HOME AND FEAR YOU'LL NEVER FIND YOUR WAY BACK?"
"YES, I CAN--I--
"--WAIT."

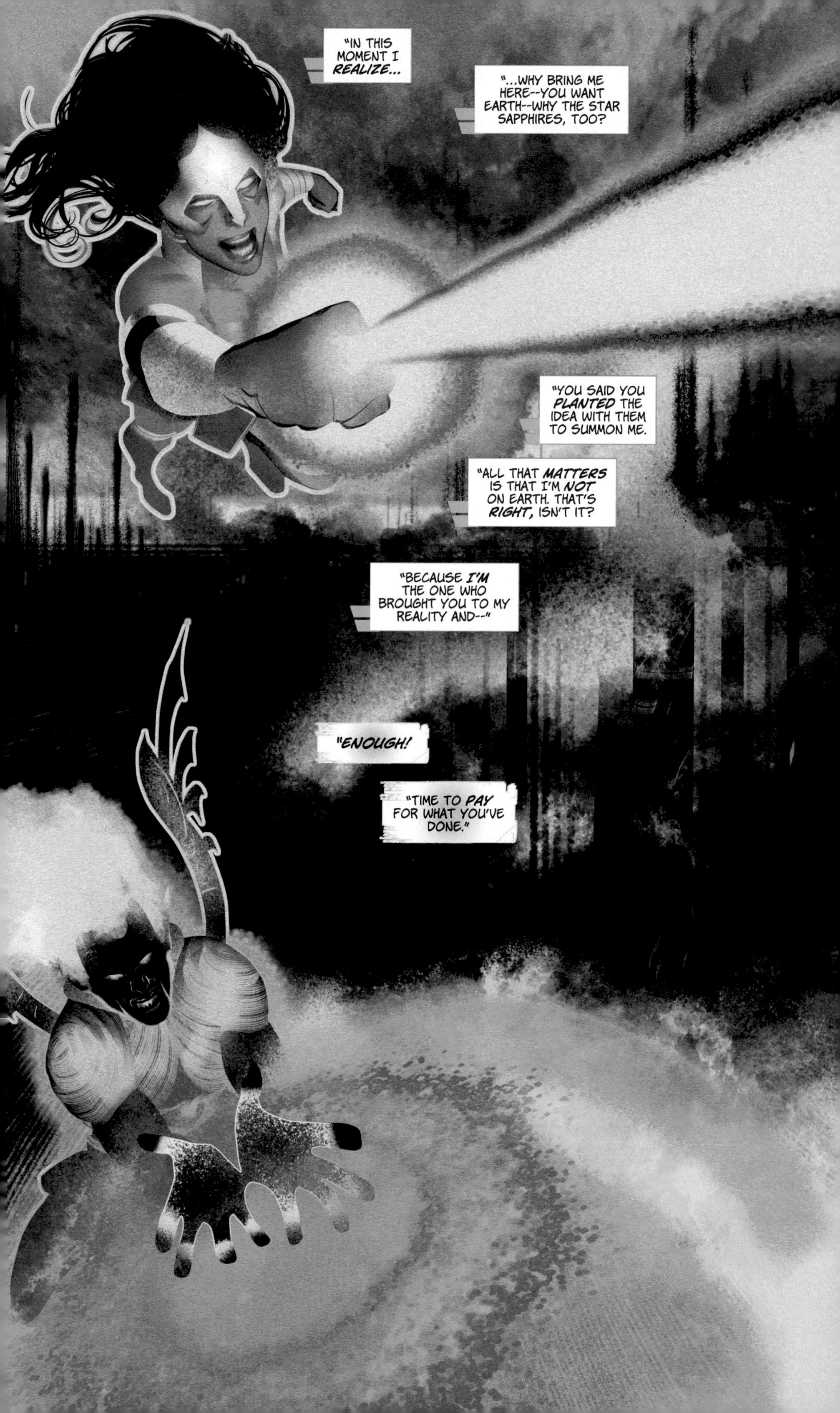
"IN THIS MOMENT I REALIZE...
"...WHY BRING ME HERE--YOU WANT EARTH--WHY THE STAR SAPPHIRES, TOO?
"YOU SAID YOU PLANTED THE IDEA WITH THEM TO SUMMON ME.
"ALL THAT MATTERS IS THAT I'M NOT ON EARTH. THAT'S RIGHT, ISN'T IT?
"BECAUSE I'M THE ONE WHO BROUGHT YOU TO MY REALITY AND--"
"ENOUGH!
"TIME TO PAY FOR WHAT YOU'VE DONE."

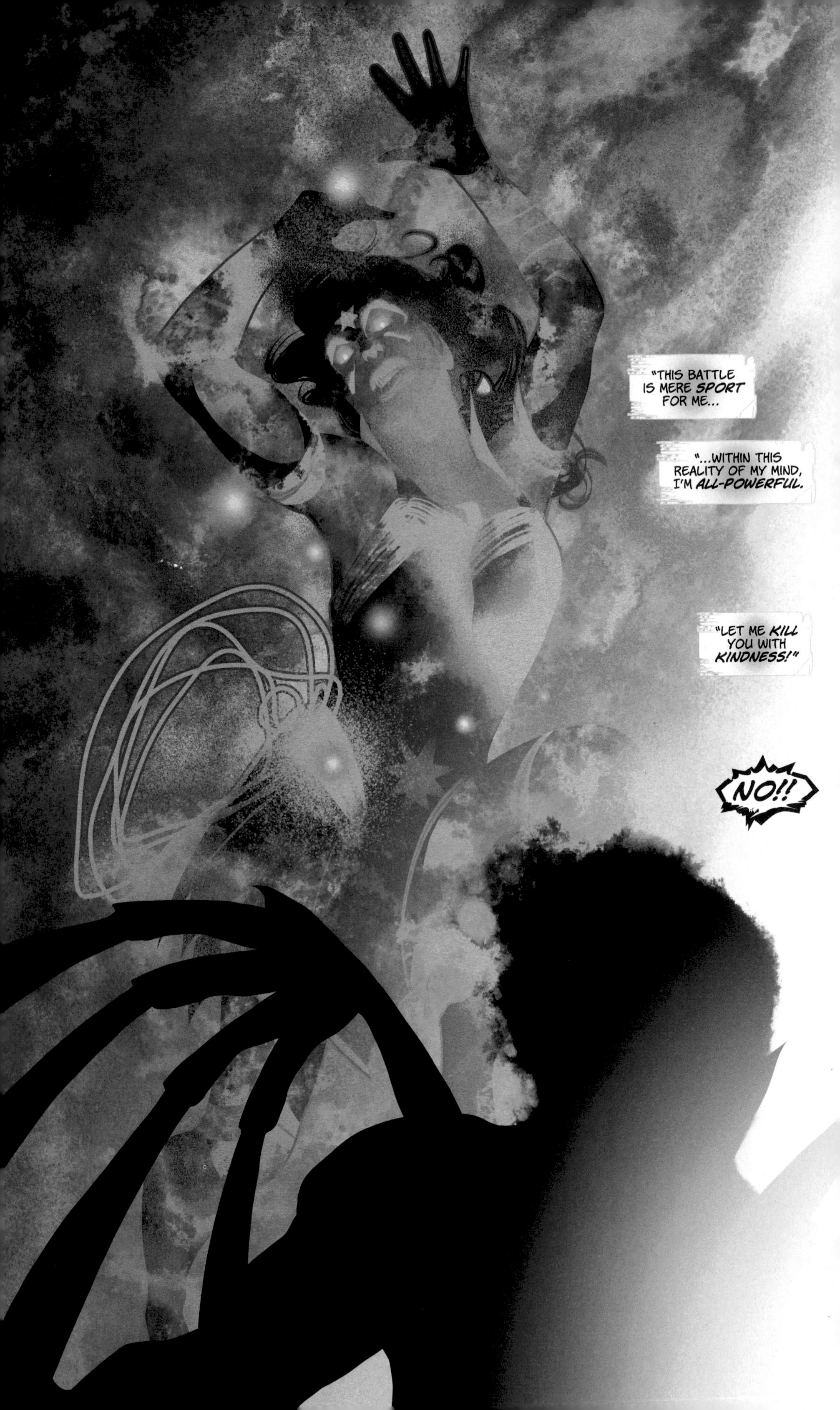

"THIS BATTLE IS MERE SPORT FOR ME...
"...WITHIN THIS REALITY OF MY MIND, I'M ALL-POWERFUL.
"LET ME KILL YOU WITH KINDNESS!"
NO!!

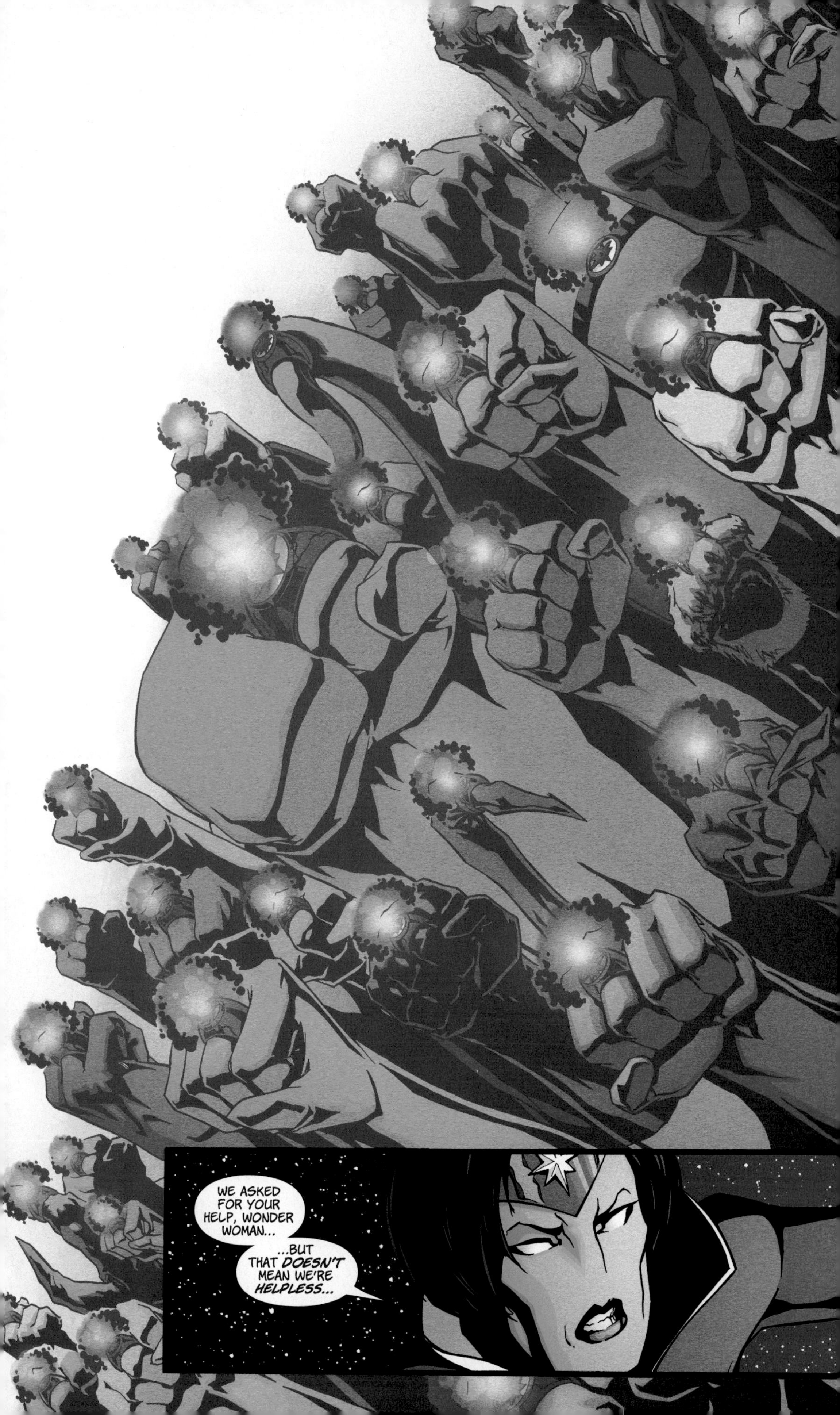
WE ASKED FOR YOUR HELP, WONDER WOMAN...
...BUT THAT *DOESN'T* MEAN WE'RE *HELPLESS...*

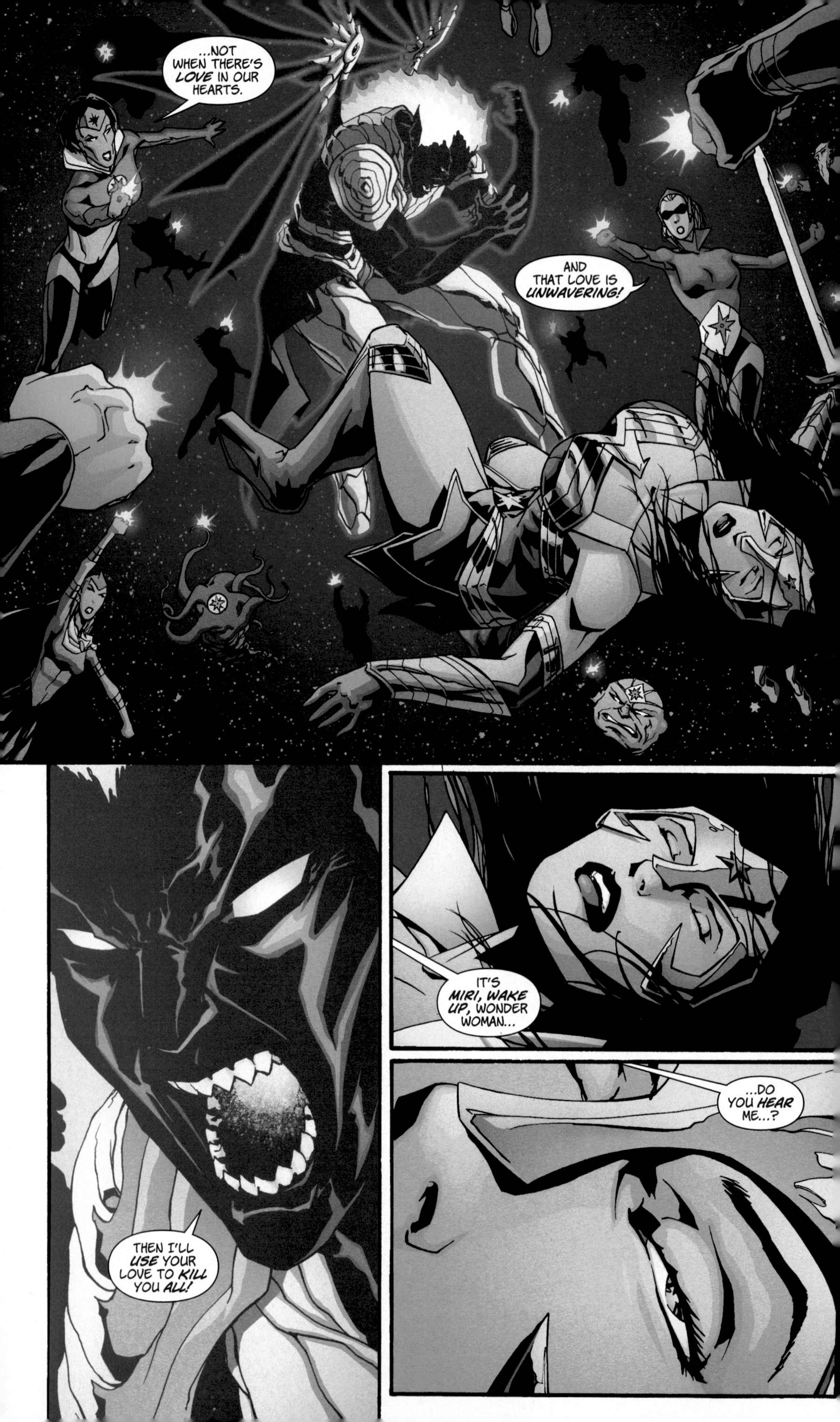
...NOT WHEN THERE'S LOVE IN OUR HEARTS.
AND THAT LOVE IS UNWAVERING!
THEN I'LL USE YOUR LOVE TO KILL YOU ALL!
IT'S MIRI, WAKE UP, WONDER WOMAN...
...DO YOU HEAR ME...?

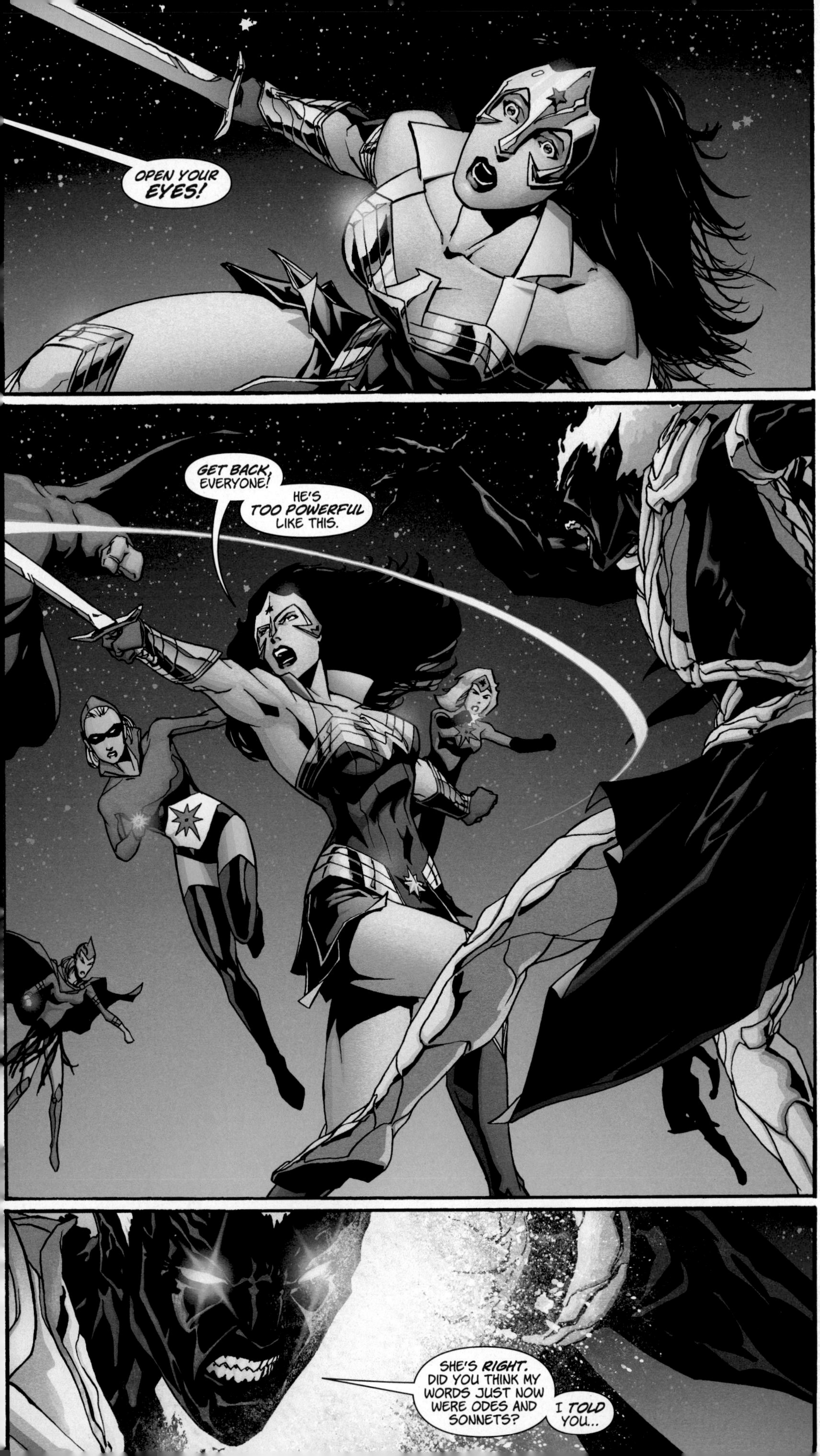
OPEN YOUR EYES!
GET BACK, EVERYONE!
HE'S TOO POWERFUL LIKE THIS.
SHE'S RIGHT. DID YOU THINK MY WORDS JUST NOW WERE ODES AND SONNETS?
I TOLD YOU...

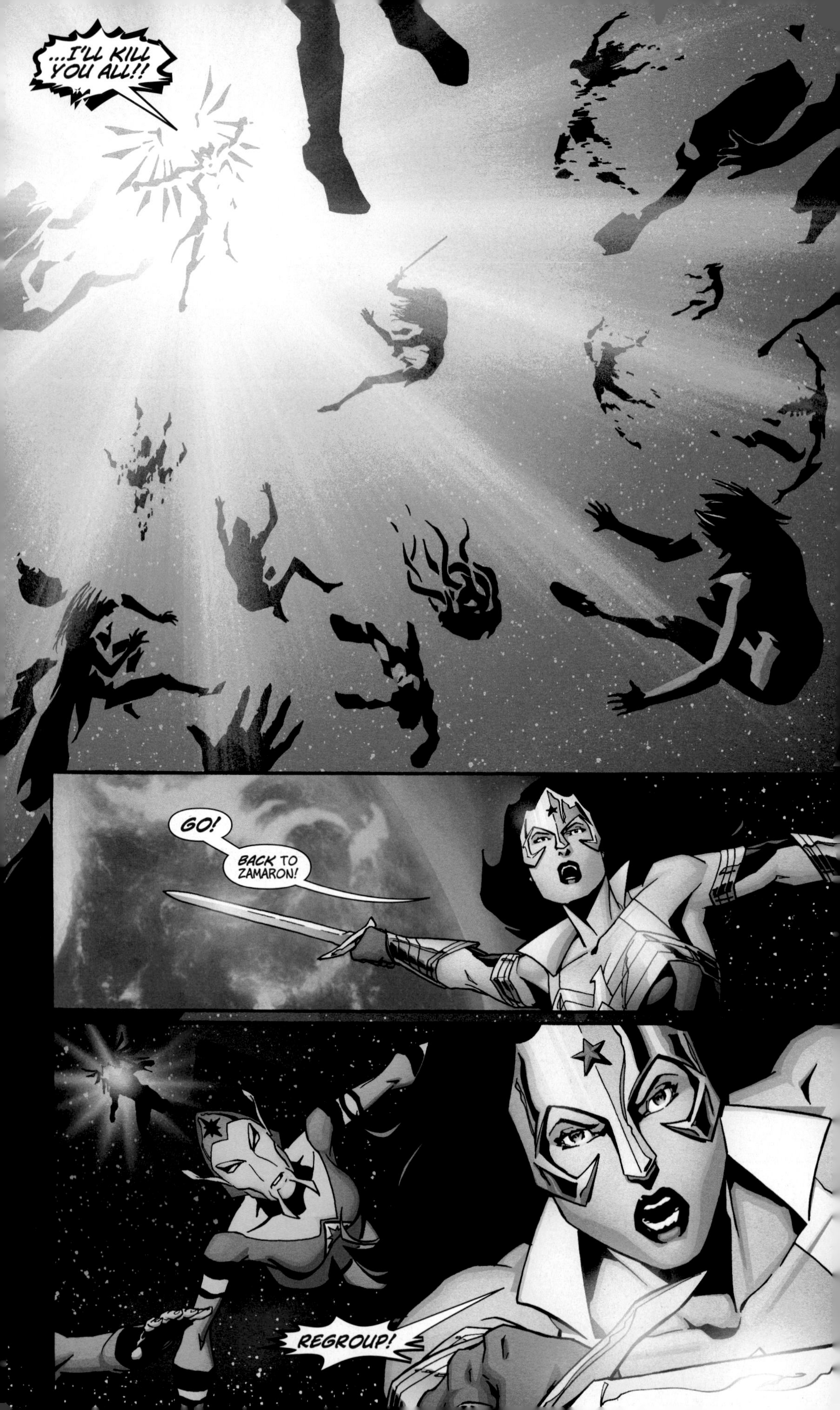
...I'LL KILL YOU ALL!!
GO!
BACK TO ZAMARON!
REGROUP!

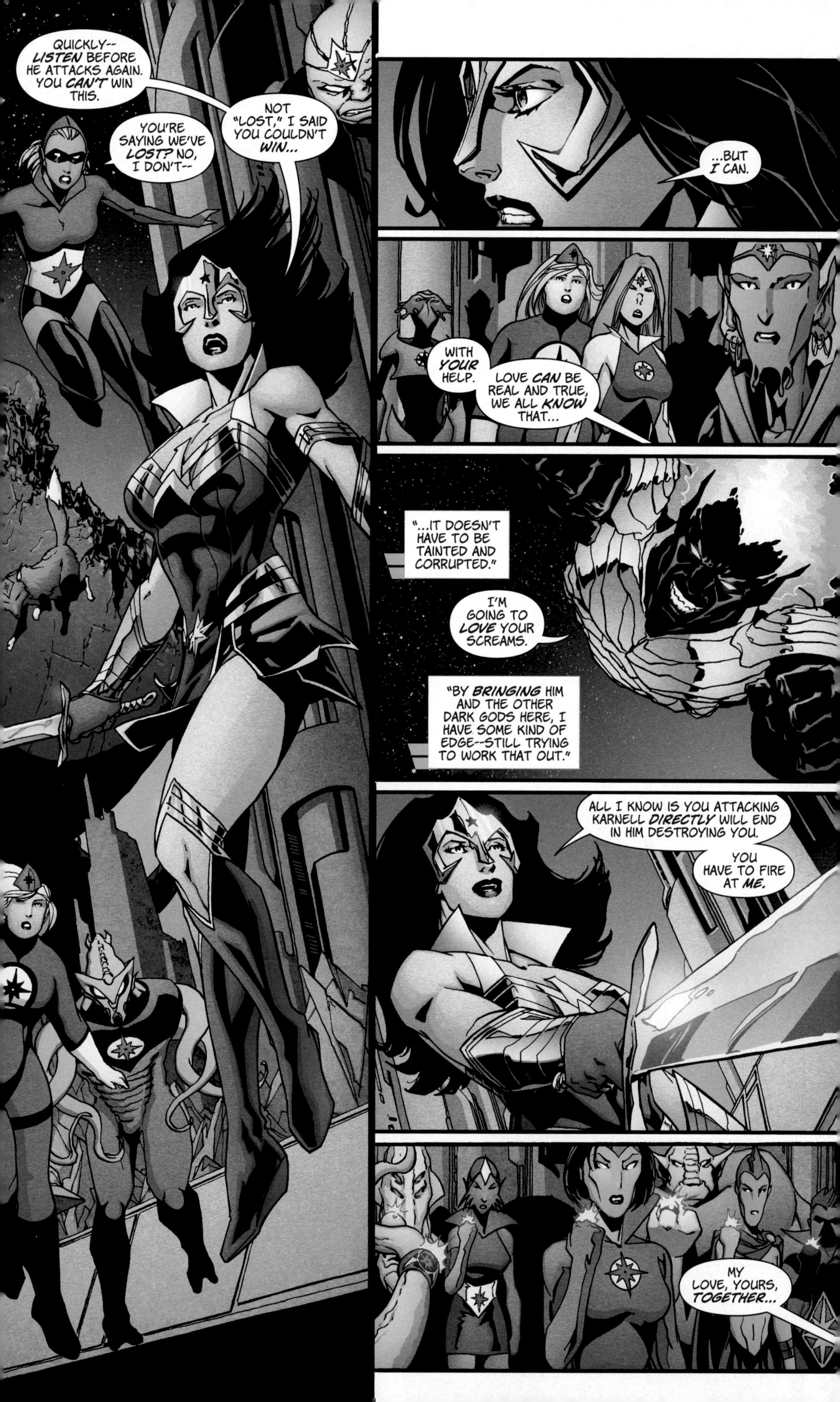
QUICKLY-- LISTEN BEFORE HE ATTACKS AGAIN. YOU CAN'T WIN THIS.
YOU'RE SAYING WE'VE LOST? NO, I DON'T--
NOT "LOST," I SAID YOU COULDN'T WIN...
...BUT I CAN.
WITH YOUR HELP.
LOVE CAN BE REAL AND TRUE, WE ALL KNOW THAT...
"...IT DOESN'T HAVE TO BE TAINTED AND CORRUPTED."
I'M GOING TO LOVE YOUR SCREAMS.
"BY BRINGING HIM AND THE OTHER DARK GODS HERE, I HAVE SOME KIND OF EDGE--STILL TRYING TO WORK THAT OUT."
ALL I KNOW IS YOU ATTACKING KARNELL DIRECTLY WILL END IN HIM DESTROYING YOU.
YOU HAVE TO FIRE AT ME.
MY LOVE, YOURS, TOGETHER...

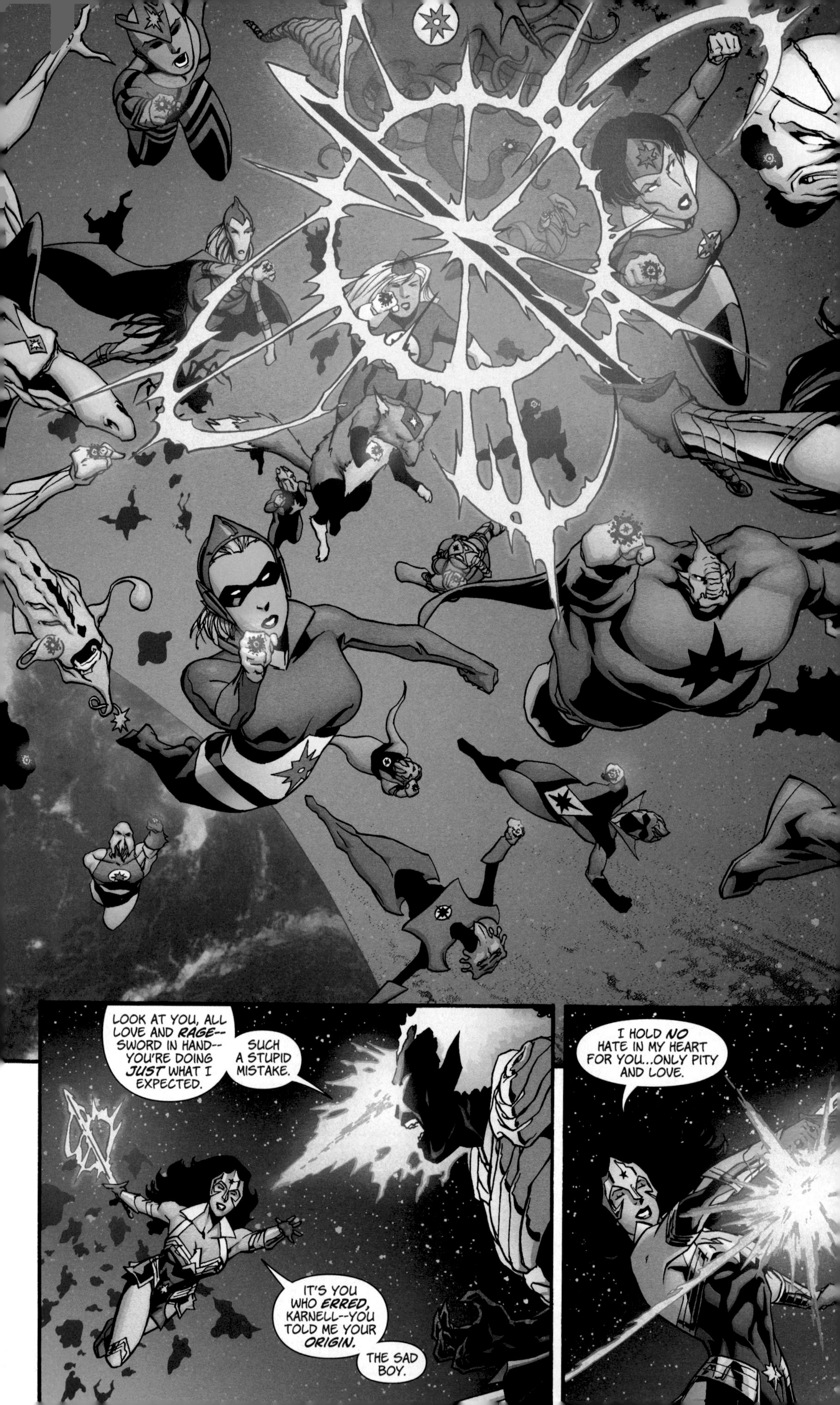
LOOK AT YOU, ALL LOVE AND *RAGE*-- SWORD IN HAND-- YOU'RE DOING *JUST* WHAT I EXPECTED.
SUCH A STUPID MISTAKE.
IT'S YOU WHO *ERRED*, KARNELL--YOU TOLD ME YOUR *ORIGIN*.
THE SAD BOY.
I HOLD *NO* HATE IN MY HEART FOR YOU...ONLY PITY AND LOVE.

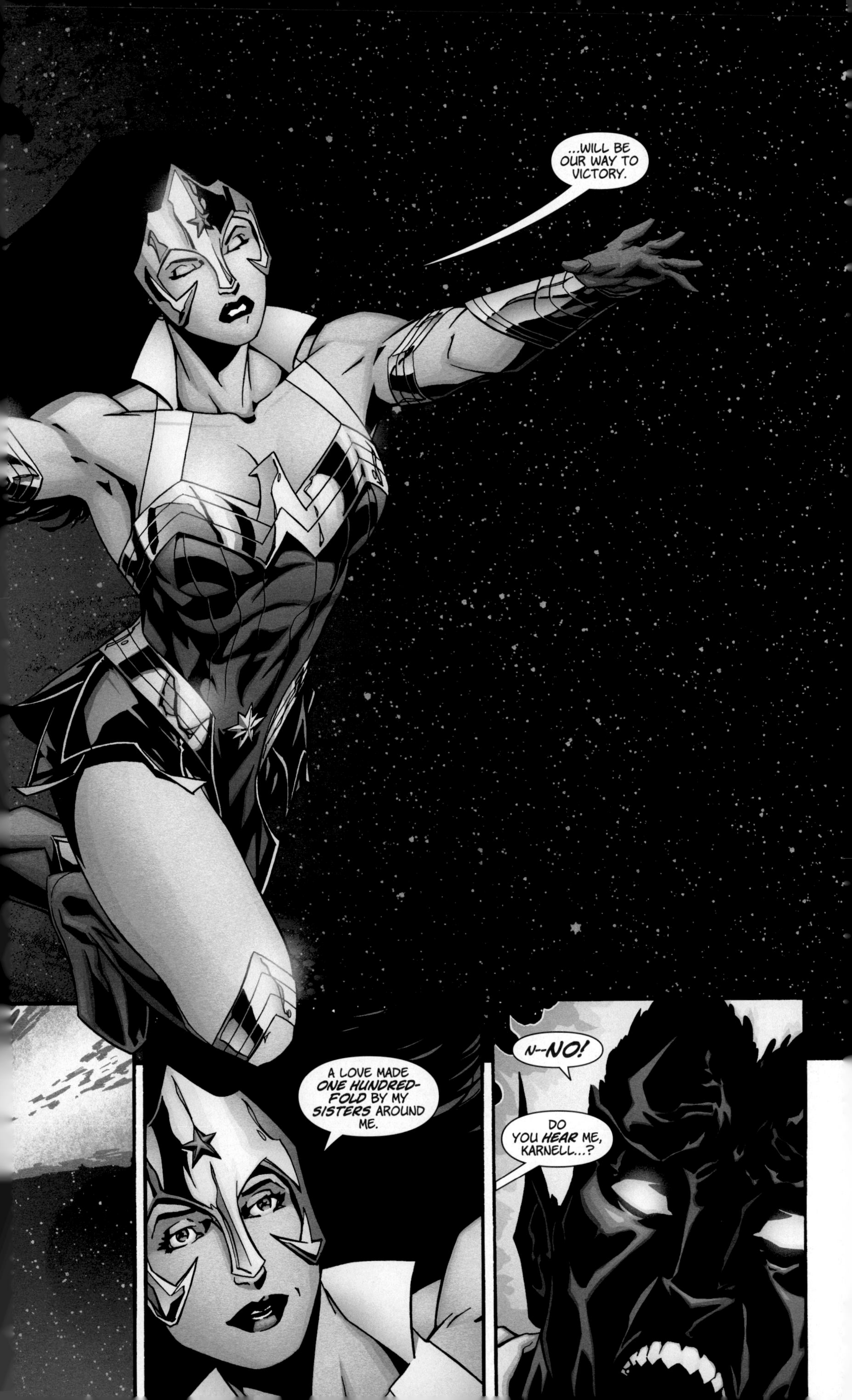
...WILL BE OUR WAY TO VICTORY.
A LOVE MADE ONE HUNDRED-FOLD BY MY SISTERS AROUND ME.
N--NO!
DO YOU HEAR ME, KARNELL...?

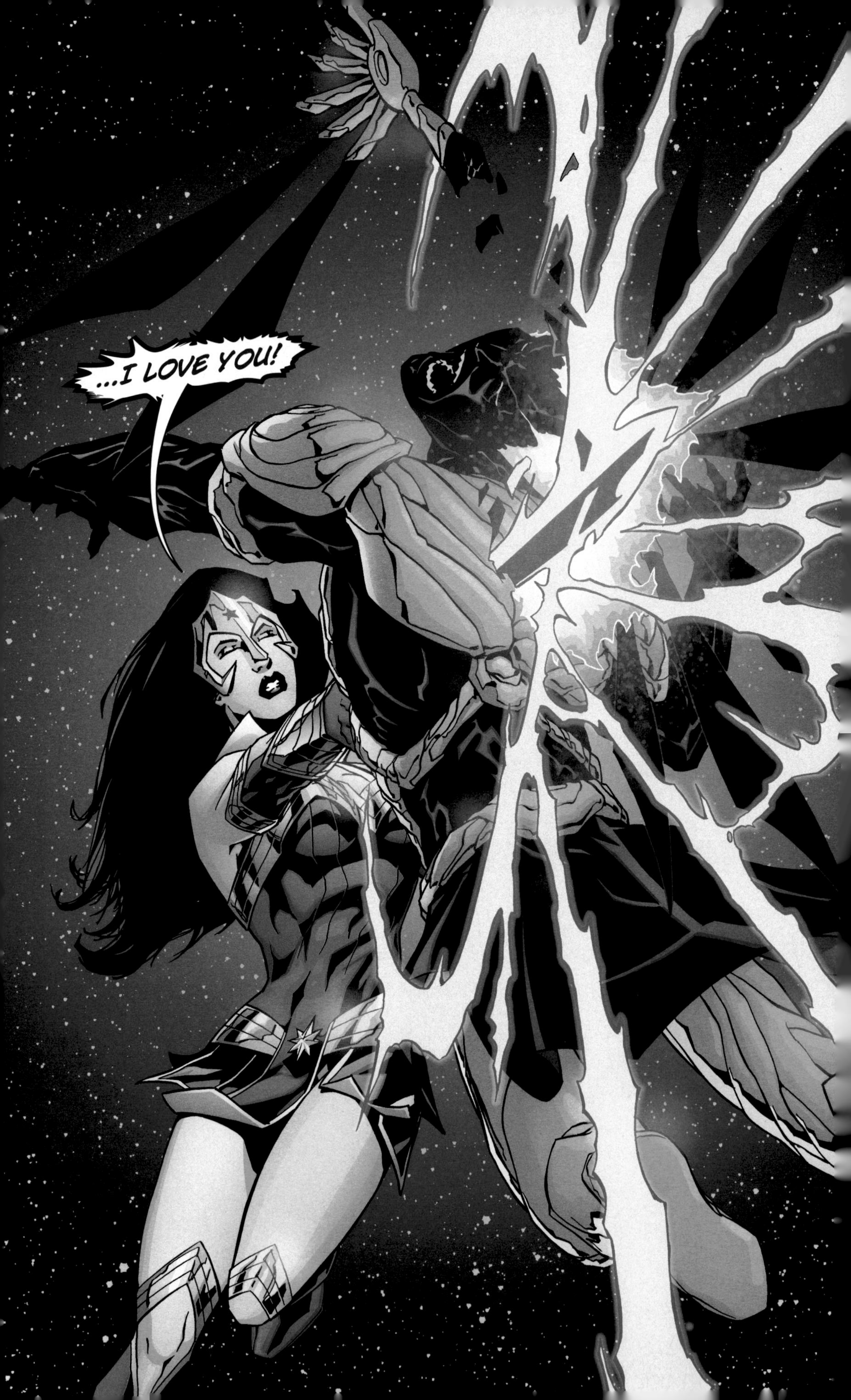
...I LOVE YOU!

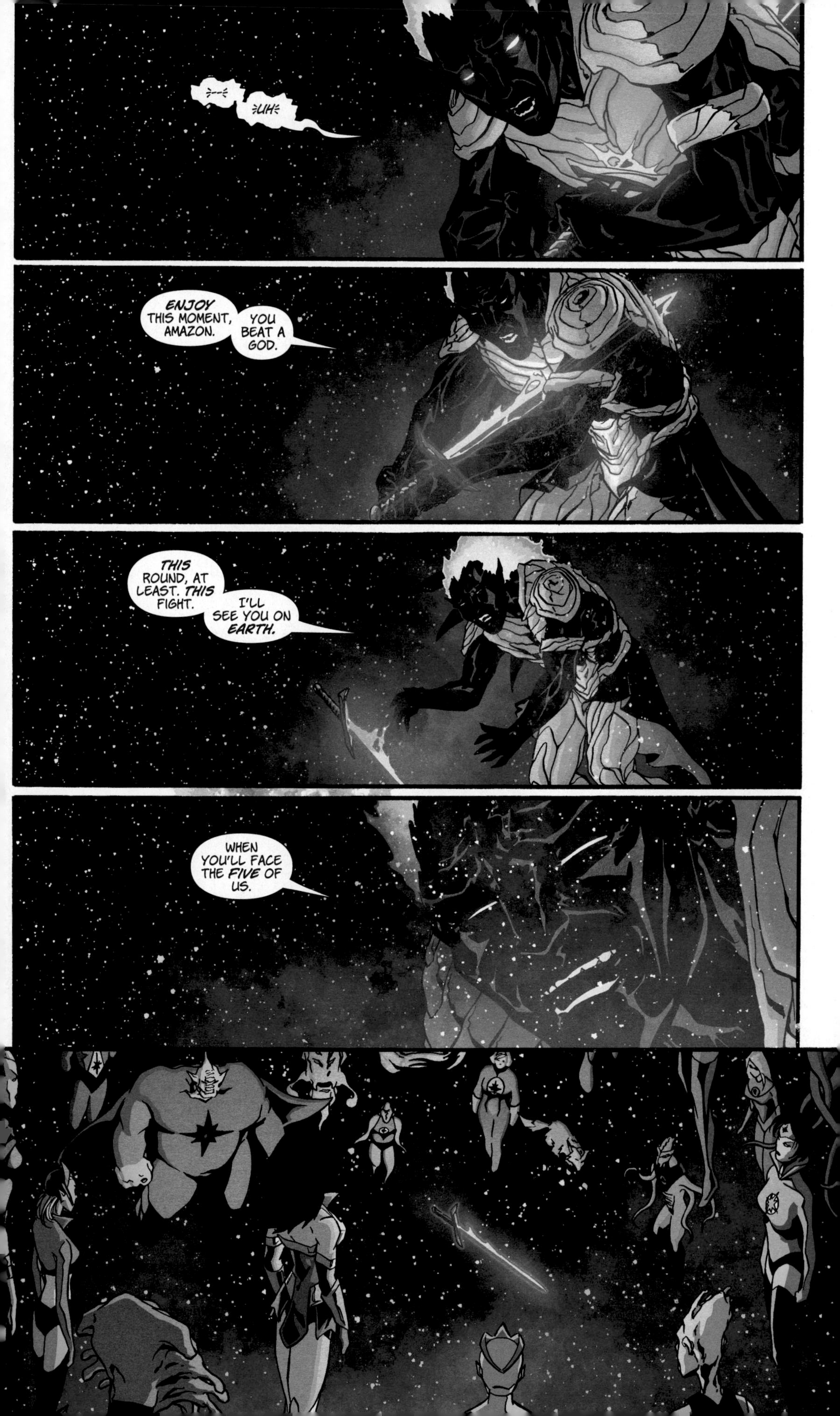
--
UH
ENJOY THIS MOMENT, AMAZON.
YOU BEAT A GOD.
THIS ROUND, AT LEAST. THIS FIGHT.
I'LL SEE YOU ON EARTH.
WHEN YOU'LL FACE THE FIVE OF US.

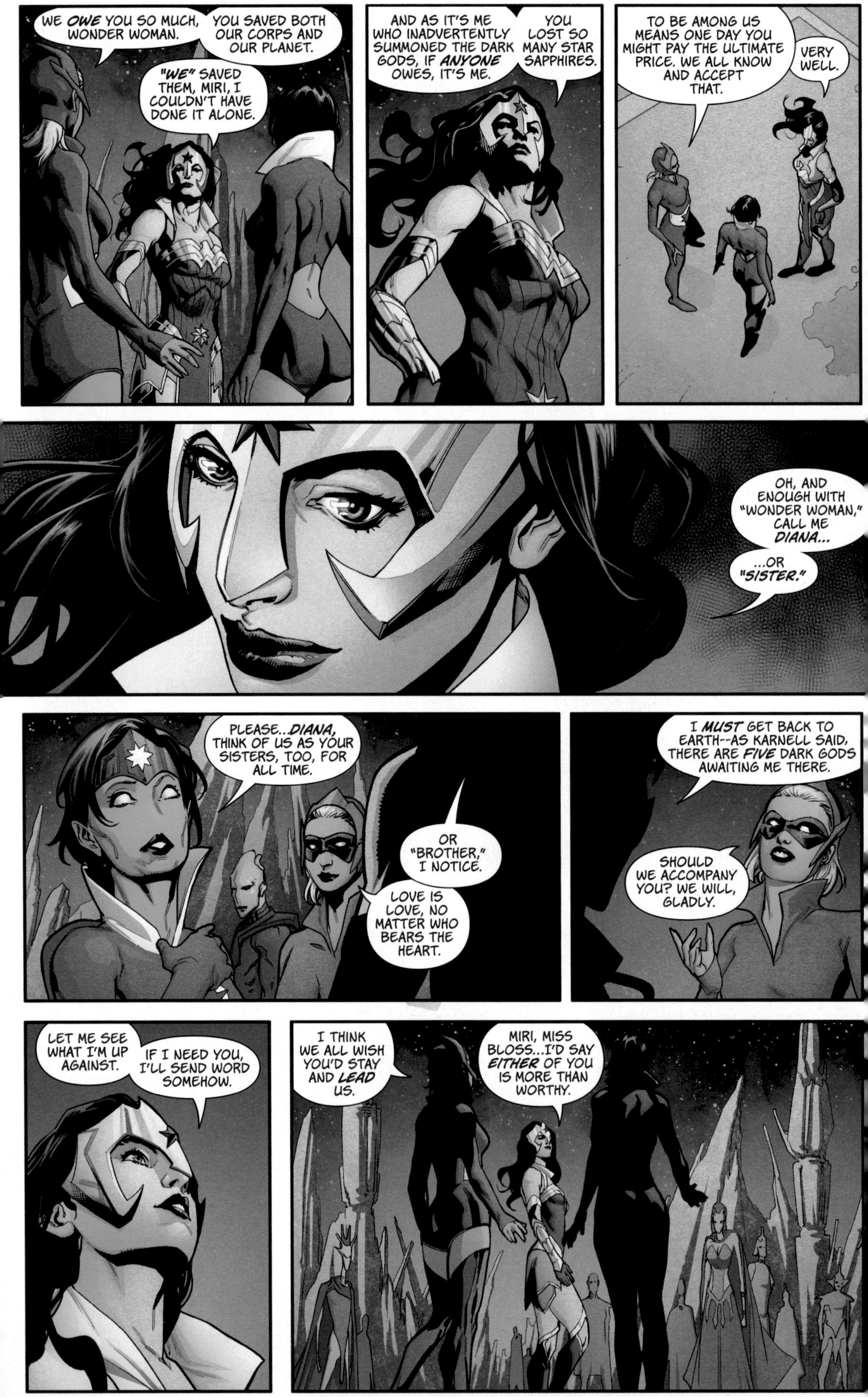

WE OWE YOU SO MUCH, WONDER WOMAN.
YOU SAVED BOTH OUR CORPS AND OUR PLANET.
"WE" SAVED THEM, MIRI, I COULDN'T HAVE DONE IT ALONE.
AND AS IT'S ME WHO INADVERTENTLY SUMMONED THE DARK GODS, IF ANYONE OWES, IT'S ME.
YOU LOST SO MANY STAR SAPPHIRES.
TO BE AMONG US MEANS ONE DAY YOU MIGHT PAY THE ULTIMATE PRICE. WE ALL KNOW AND ACCEPT THAT.
VERY WELL.
OH, AND ENOUGH WITH "WONDER WOMAN," CALL ME DIANA...
...OR "SISTER."
PLEASE...DIANA, THINK OF US AS YOUR SISTERS, TOO, FOR ALL TIME.
OR "BROTHER," I NOTICE.
LOVE IS LOVE, NO MATTER WHO BEARS THE HEART.
I MUST GET BACK TO EARTH--AS KARNELL SAID, THERE ARE FIVE DARK GODS AWAITING ME THERE.
SHOULD WE ACCOMPANY YOU? WE WILL, GLADLY.
LET ME SEE WHAT I'M UP AGAINST.
IF I NEED YOU, I'LL SEND WORD SOMEHOW.
I THINK WE ALL WISH YOU'D STAY AND LEAD US.
MIRI, MISS BLOSS...I'D SAY EITHER OF YOU IS MORE THAN WORTHY.

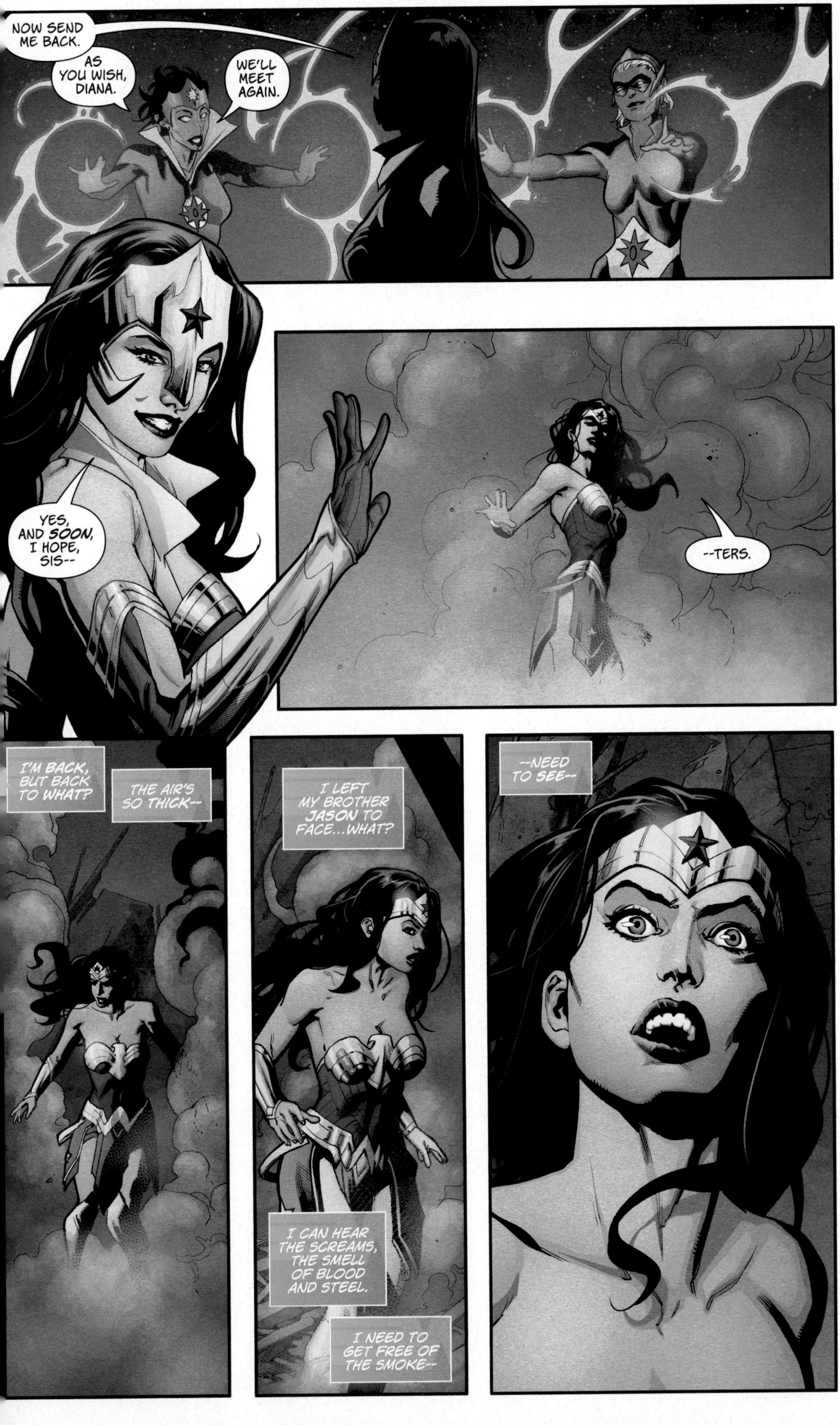
NOW SEND ME BACK.
AS YOU WISH, DIANA.
WE'LL MEET AGAIN.
YES, AND SOON, I HOPE, SIS--
--TERS.
I'M BACK, BUT BACK TO WHAT?
THE AIR'S SO THICK--
I LEFT MY BROTHER JASON TO FACE...WHAT?
I CAN HEAR THE SCREAMS, THE SMELL OF BLOOD AND STEEL.
I NEED TO GET FREE OF THE SMOKE--
--NEED TO SEE--

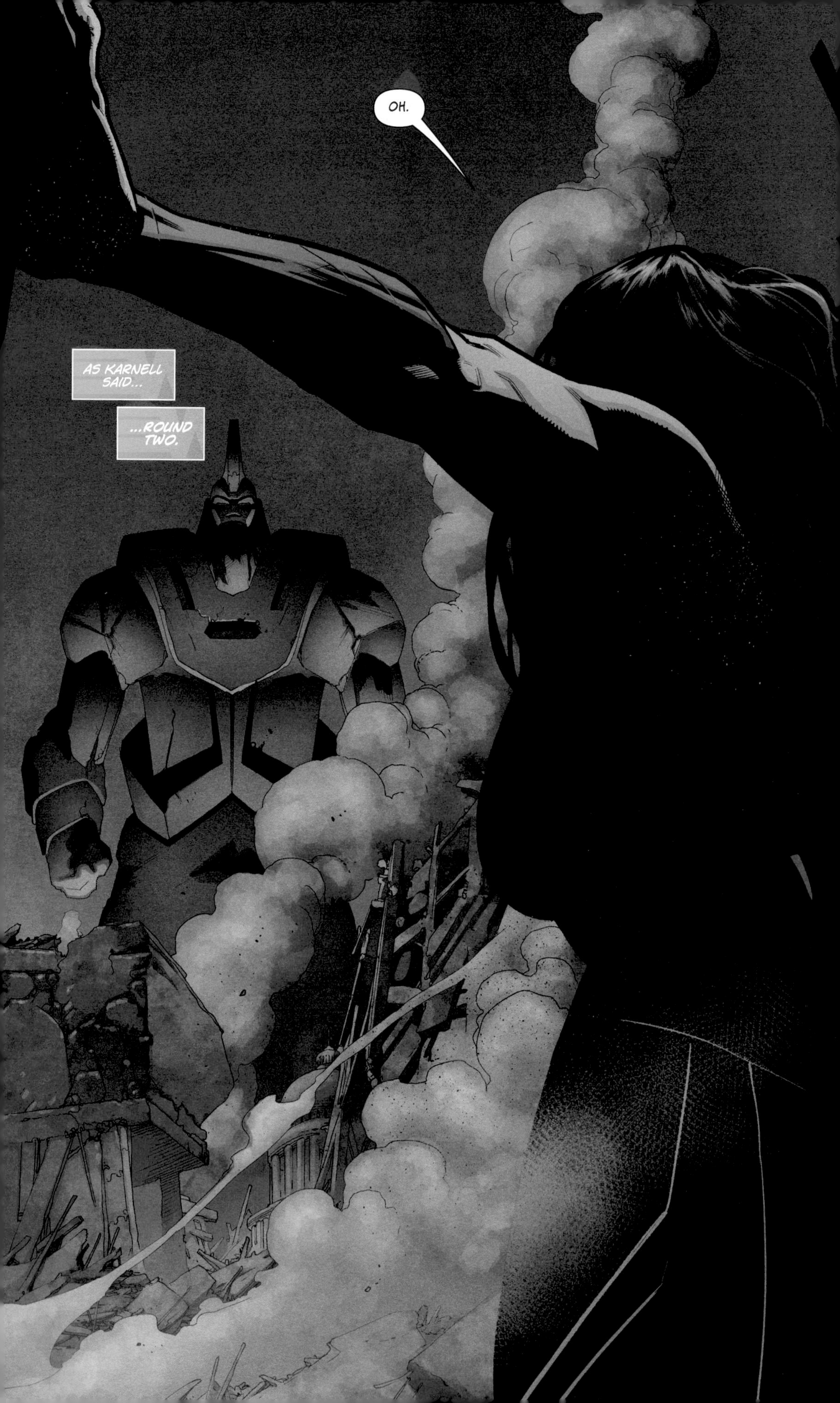
OH.
AS KARNELL SAID...
...ROUND TWO.

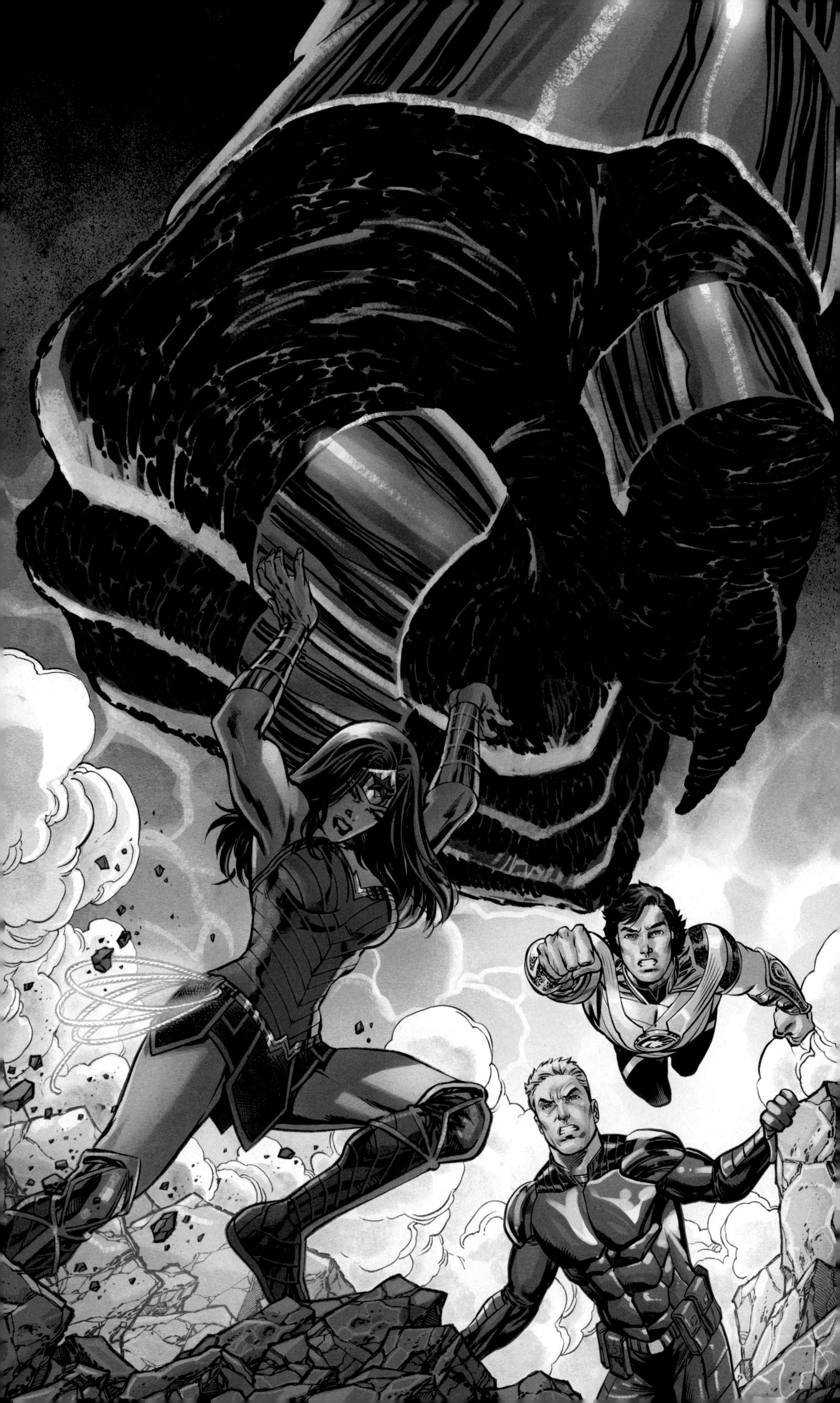

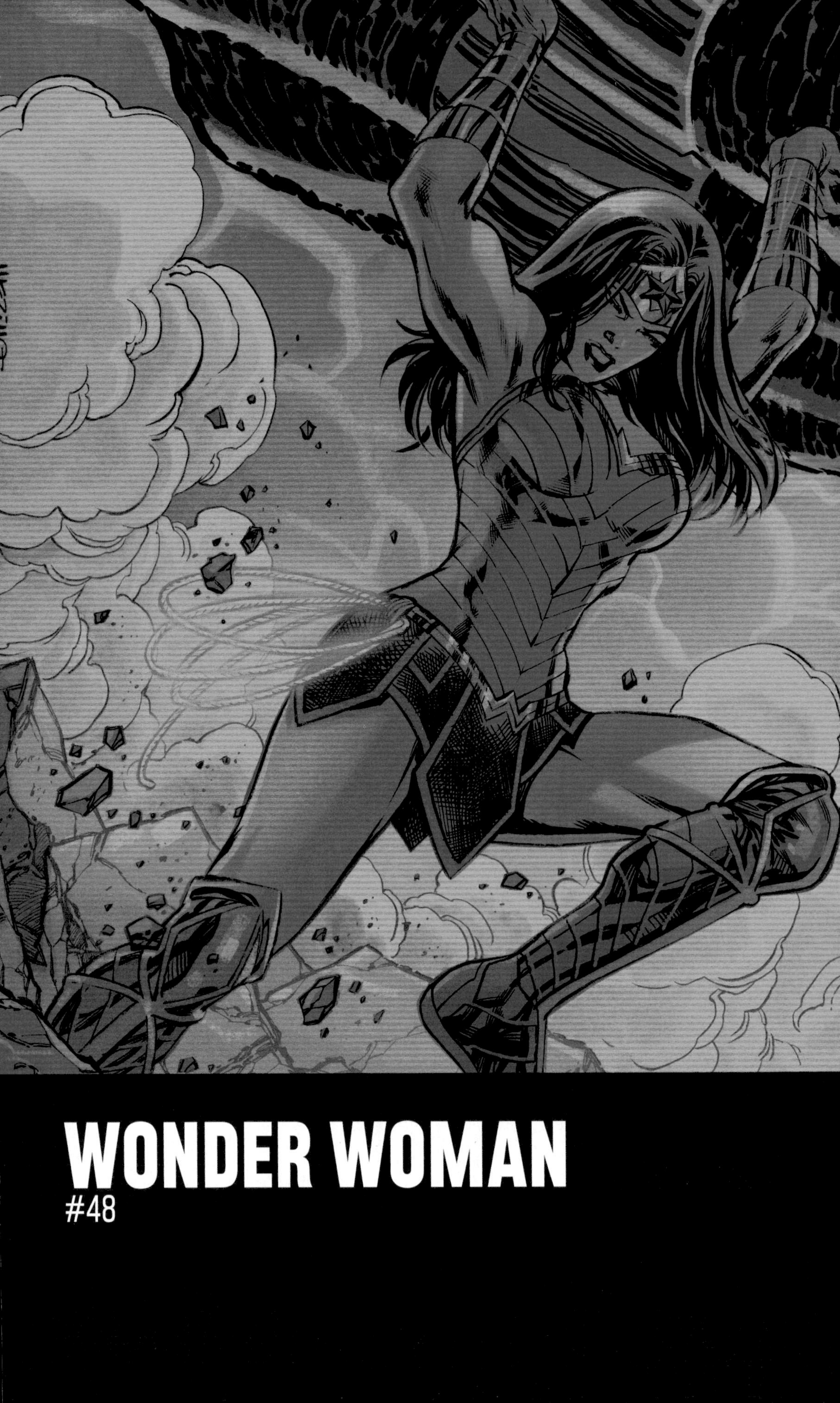

WONDER WOMAN
#48

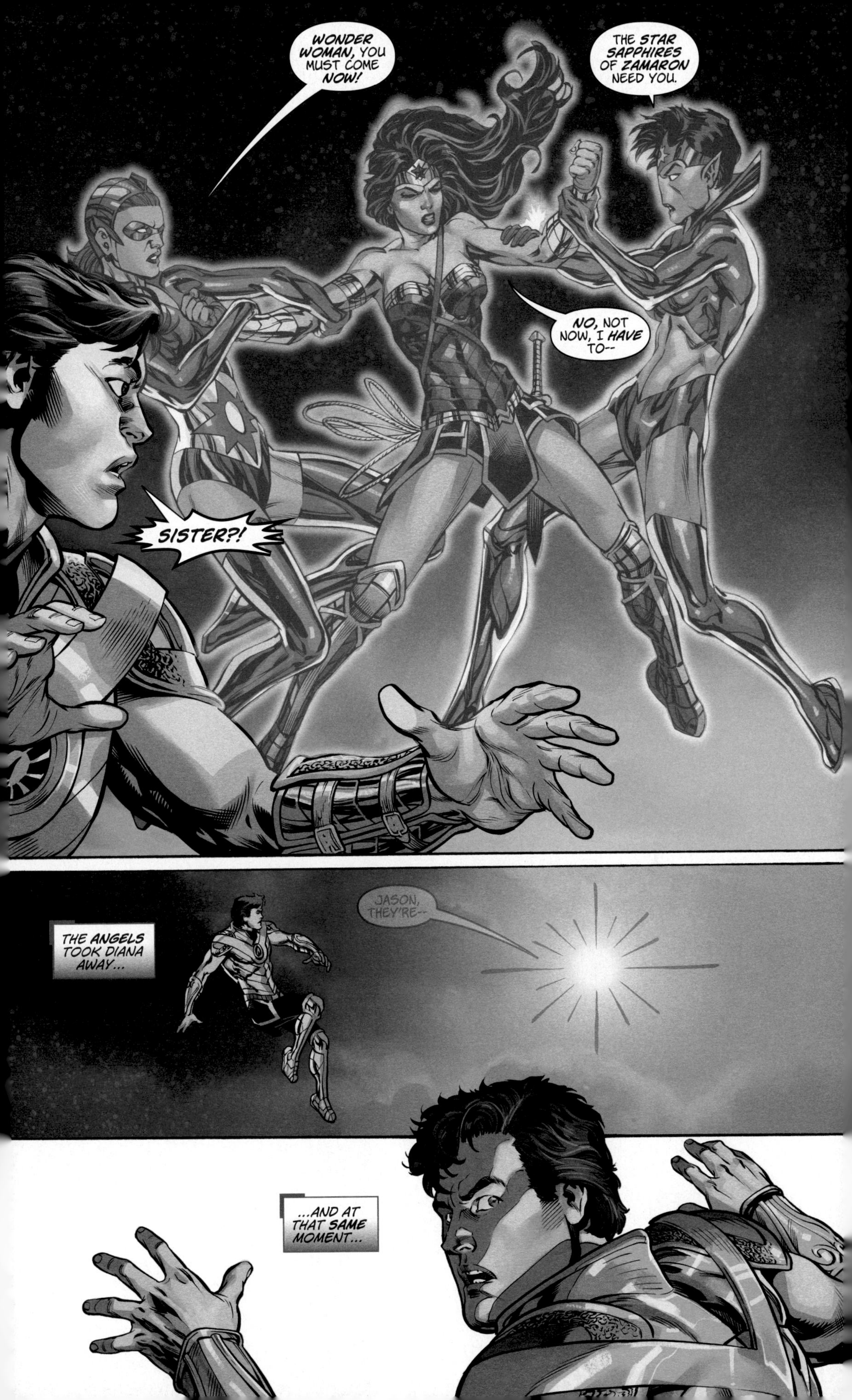
WONDER WOMAN, YOU MUST COME NOW!
THE STAR SAPPHIRES OF ZAMARON NEED YOU.
NO, NOT NOW, I HAVE TO--
SISTER?!
THE ANGELS TOOK DIANA AWAY...
JASON, THEY'RE--
...AND AT THAT SAME MOMENT...

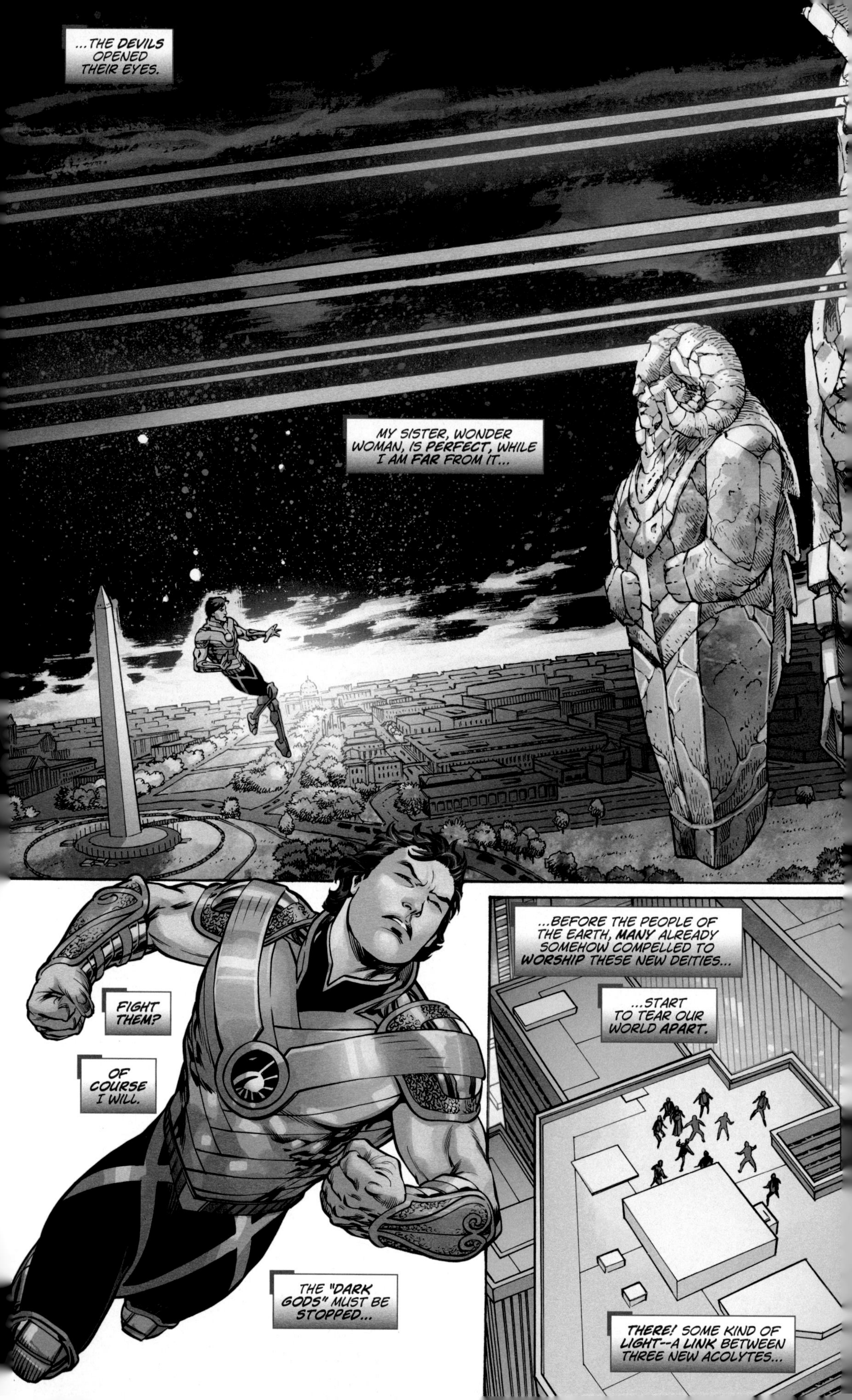
...THE DEVILS OPENED THEIR EYES.
MY SISTER, WONDER WOMAN, IS PERFECT, WHILE I AM FAR FROM IT...
...BEFORE THE PEOPLE OF THE EARTH, MANY ALREADY SOMEHOW COMPELLED TO WORSHIP THESE NEW DEITIES...
...START TO TEAR OUR WORLD APART.
FIGHT THEM?
OF COURSE I WILL.
THE "DARK GODS" MUST BE STOPPED...
THERE! SOME KIND OF LIGHT--A LINK BETWEEN THREE NEW ACOLYTES...

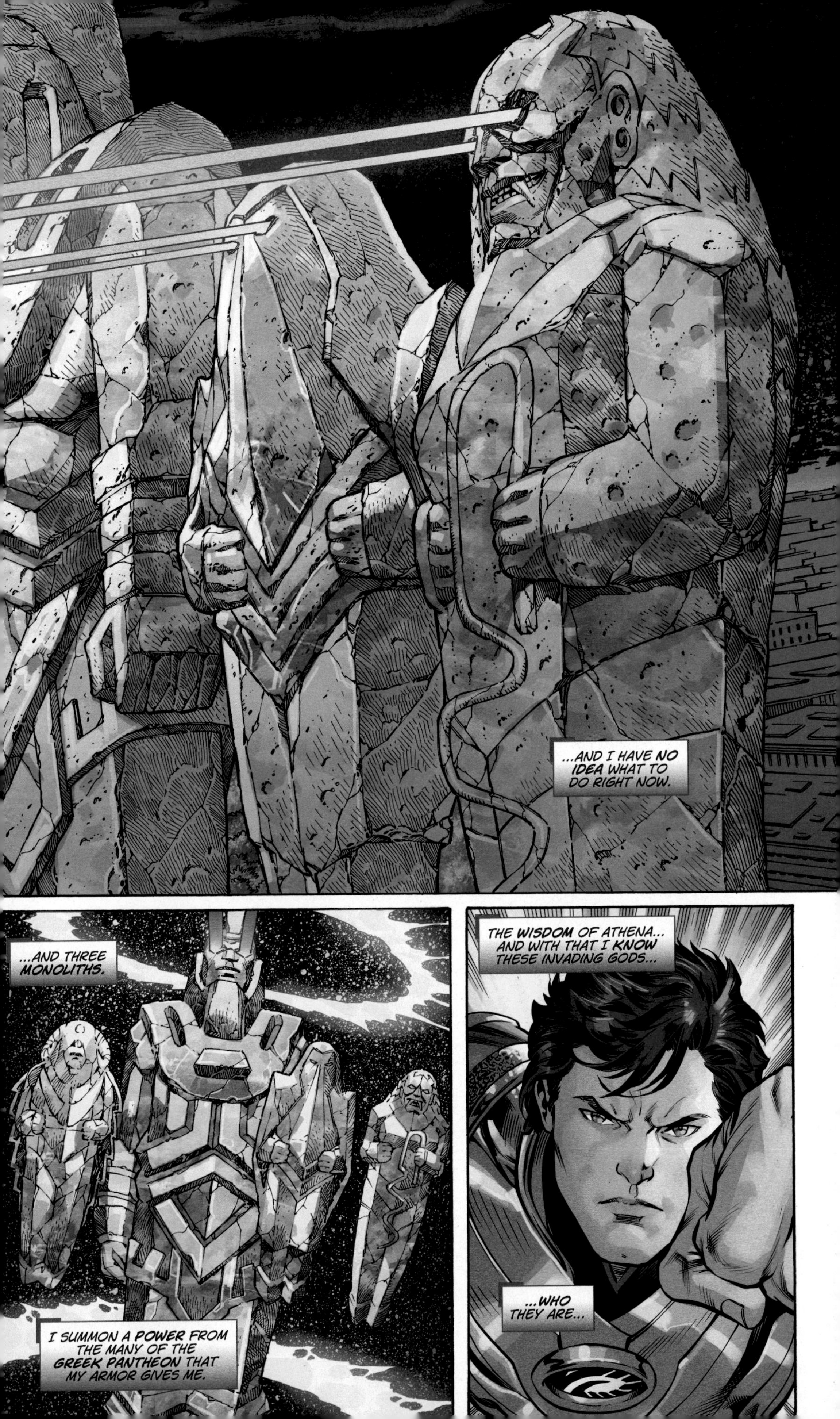
...AND I HAVE NO IDEA WHAT TO DO RIGHT NOW.
...AND THREE MONOLITHS.
I SUMMON A POWER FROM THE MANY OF THE GREEK PANTHEON THAT MY ARMOR GIVES ME.
THE WISDOM OF ATHENA... AND WITH THAT I KNOW THESE INVADING GODS...
...WHO THEY ARE...

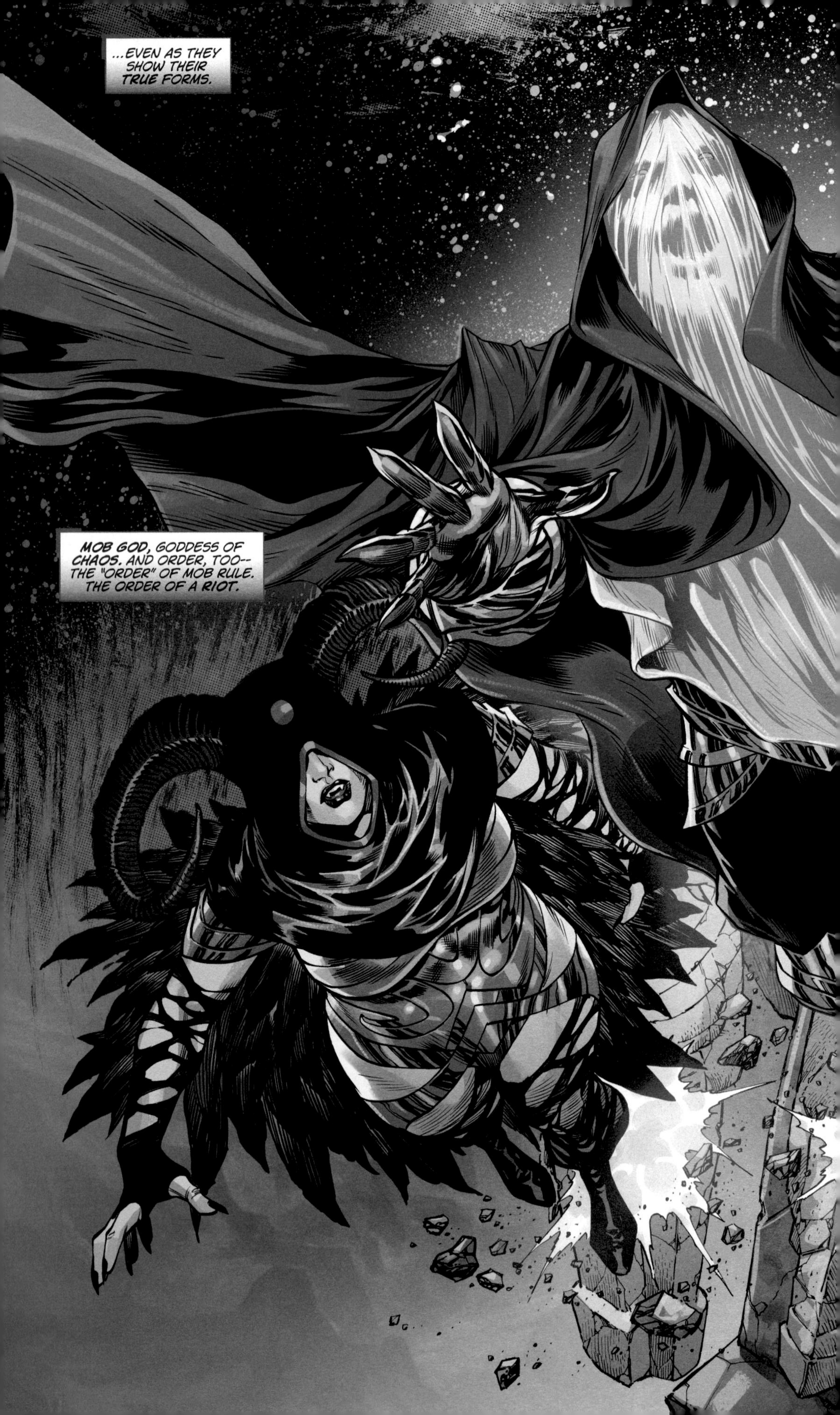
...EVEN AS THEY SHOW THEIR TRUE FORMS.
MOB GOD, GODDESS OF CHAOS. AND ORDER, TOO-- THE "ORDER" OF MOB RULE. THE ORDER OF A RIOT.

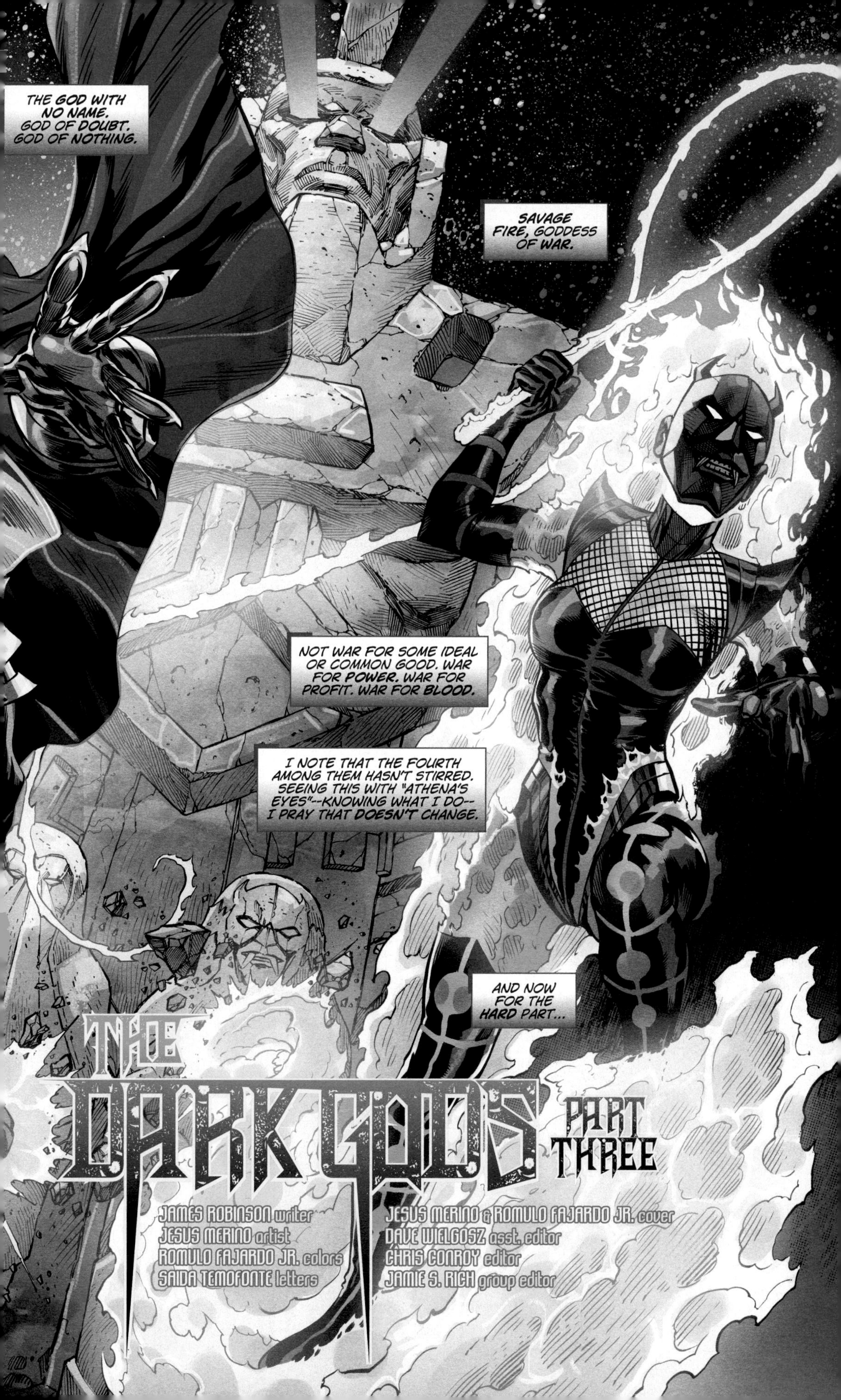

THE GOD WITH NO NAME. GOD OF DOUBT. GOD OF NOTHING.
SAVAGE FIRE, GODDESS OF WAR.
NOT WAR FOR SOME IDEAL OR COMMON GOOD. WAR FOR POWER. WAR FOR PROFIT. WAR FOR BLOOD.
I NOTE THAT THE FOURTH AMONG THEM HASN'T STIRRED. SEEING THIS WITH "ATHENA'S EYES"--KNOWING WHAT I DO--I PRAY THAT DOESN'T CHANGE.
AND NOW FOR THE HARD PART...
THE DARK GODS PART THREE
JAMES ROBINSON writer
JESUS MERINO artist
ROMULO FAJARDO JR. colors
SAIDA TEMOFONTE letters
JESUS MERINO & ROMULO FAJARDO JR. cover
DAVE WIELGOSZ asst. editor
CHRIS CONROY editor
JAMIE S. RICH group editor

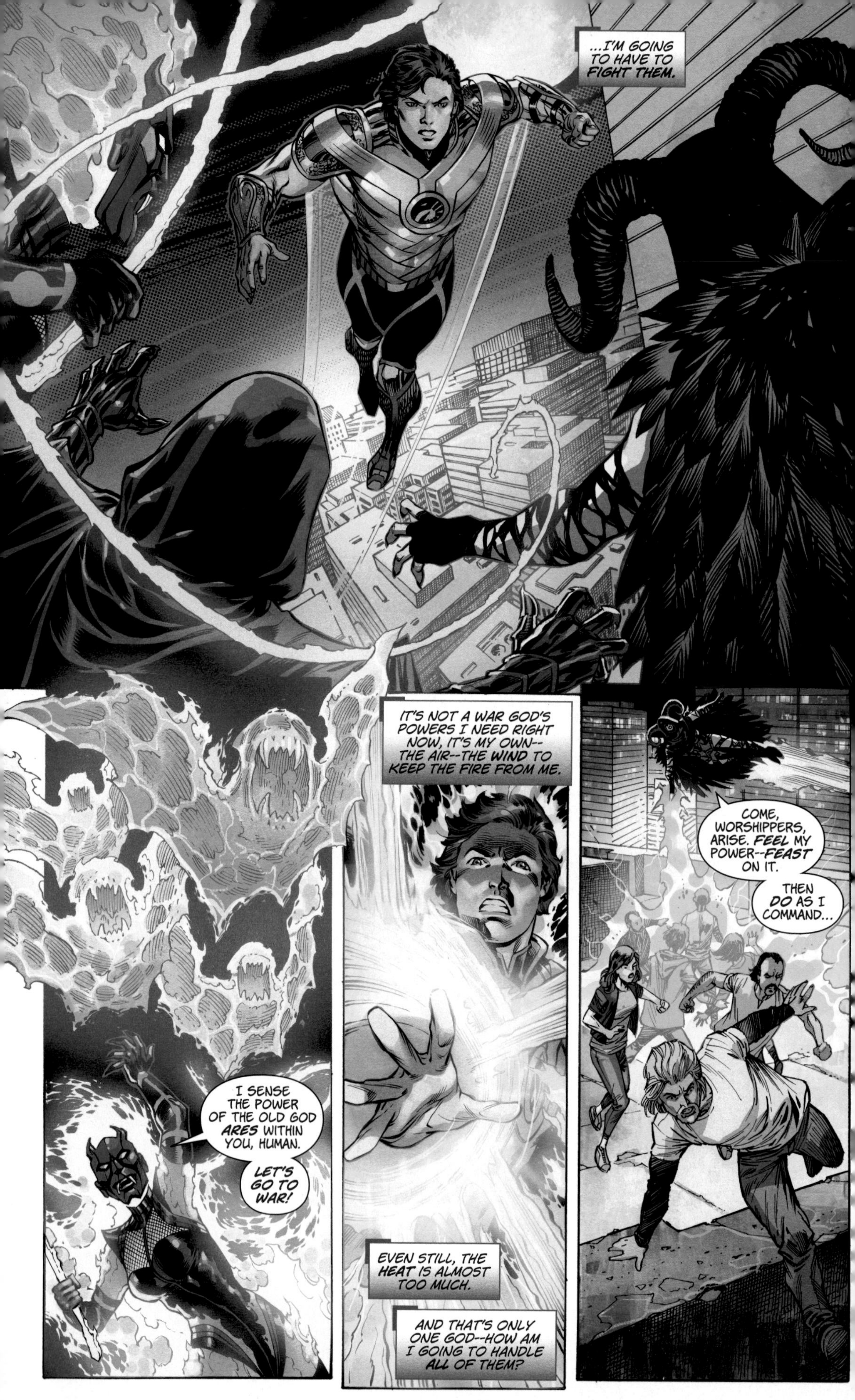

...I'M GOING TO HAVE TO FIGHT THEM.
I SENSE THE POWER OF THE OLD GOD ARES WITHIN YOU, HUMAN.
LET'S GO TO WAR!
IT'S NOT A WAR GOD'S POWERS I NEED RIGHT NOW, IT'S MY OWN-- THE AIR--THE WIND TO KEEP THE FIRE FROM ME.
EVEN STILL, THE HEAT IS ALMOST TOO MUCH.
AND THAT'S ONLY ONE GOD--HOW AM I GOING TO HANDLE ALL OF THEM?
COME, WORSHIPPERS, ARISE. FEEL MY POWER--FEAST ON IT.
THEN DO AS I COMMAND...

"...AND LEAP!"

NEED THE SPEED OF HERMES TO CATCH EVERYONE.

MY ARMOR, TOO, JUST TO KEEP THEM FROM RIPPING ME APART WHILE I DO IT.

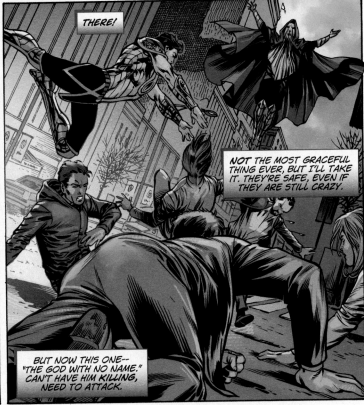

THERE!

NOT THE MOST GRACEFUL THING EVER, BUT I'LL TAKE IT. THEY'RE SAFE, EVEN IF THEY ARE STILL CRAZY.

BUT NOW THIS ONE-- "THE GOD WITH NO NAME." CAN'T HAVE HIM KILLING, NEED TO ATTACK.

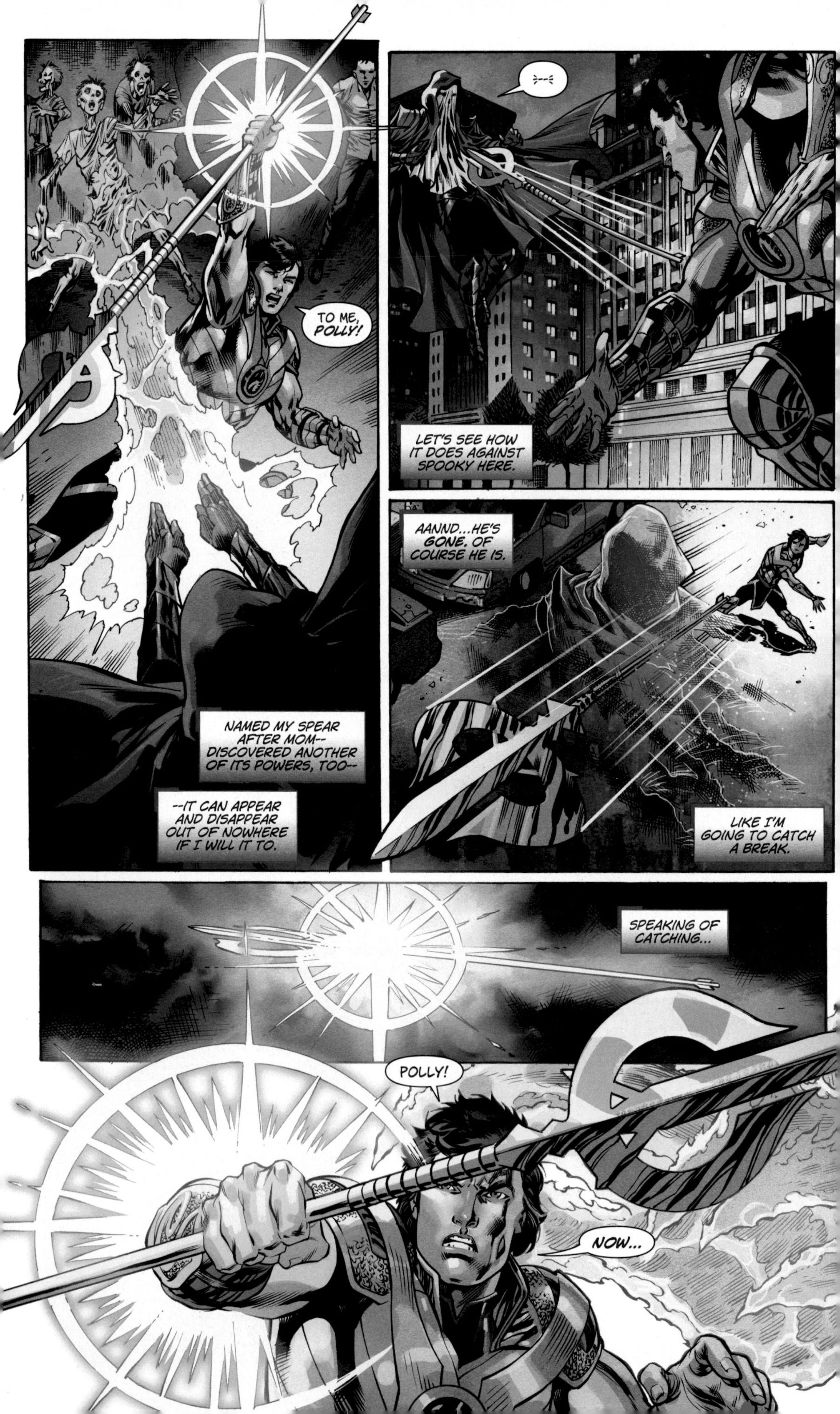
TO ME, POLLY!
NAMED MY SPEAR AFTER MOM--DISCOVERED ANOTHER OF ITS POWERS, TOO--
--IT CAN APPEAR AND DISAPPEAR OUT OF NOWHERE IF I WILL IT TO.
LET'S SEE HOW IT DOES AGAINST SPOOKY HERE.
AANND...HE'S GONE. OF COURSE HE IS.
LIKE I'M GOING TO CATCH A BREAK.
SPEAKING OF CATCHING...
POLLY!
NOW...

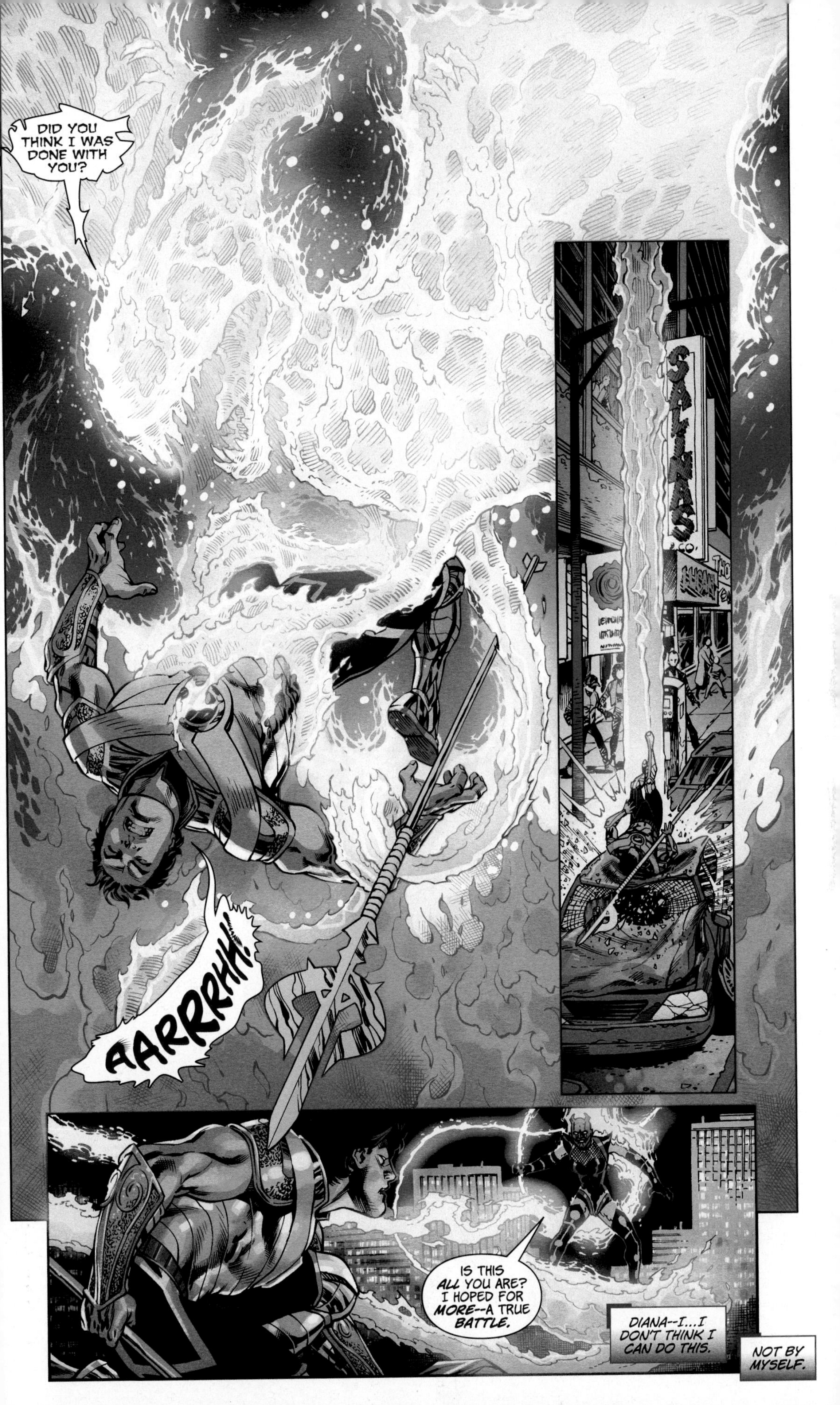
DID YOU THINK I WAS DONE WITH YOU?
AARRRHH!
IS THIS *ALL* YOU ARE? I HOPED FOR *MORE*--A TRUE *BATTLE.*
DIANA--I...I DON'T THINK I CAN DO THIS.
NOT BY MYSELF.

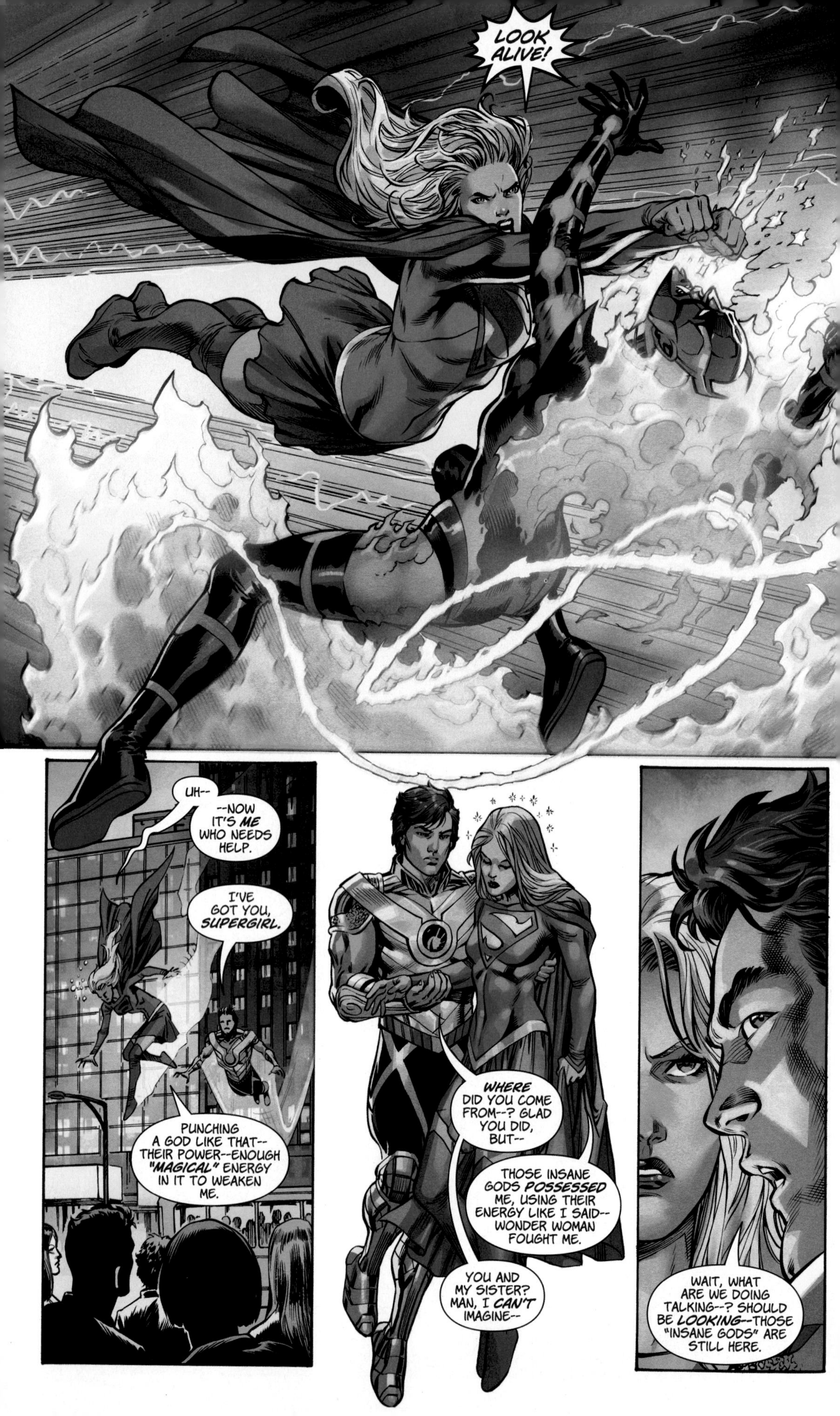
LOOK ALIVE!
UH--
--NOW IT'S ME WHO NEEDS HELP.
I'VE GOT YOU, SUPERGIRL.
PUNCHING A GOD LIKE THAT--THEIR POWER--ENOUGH "MAGICAL" ENERGY IN IT TO WEAKEN ME.
WHERE DID YOU COME FROM--? GLAD YOU DID, BUT--
THOSE INSANE GODS POSSESSED ME, USING THEIR ENERGY LIKE I SAID--WONDER WOMAN FOUGHT ME.
YOU AND MY SISTER? MAN, I CAN'T IMAGINE--
WAIT, WHAT ARE WE DOING TALKING--? SHOULD BE LOOKING--THOSE "INSANE GODS" ARE STILL HERE.

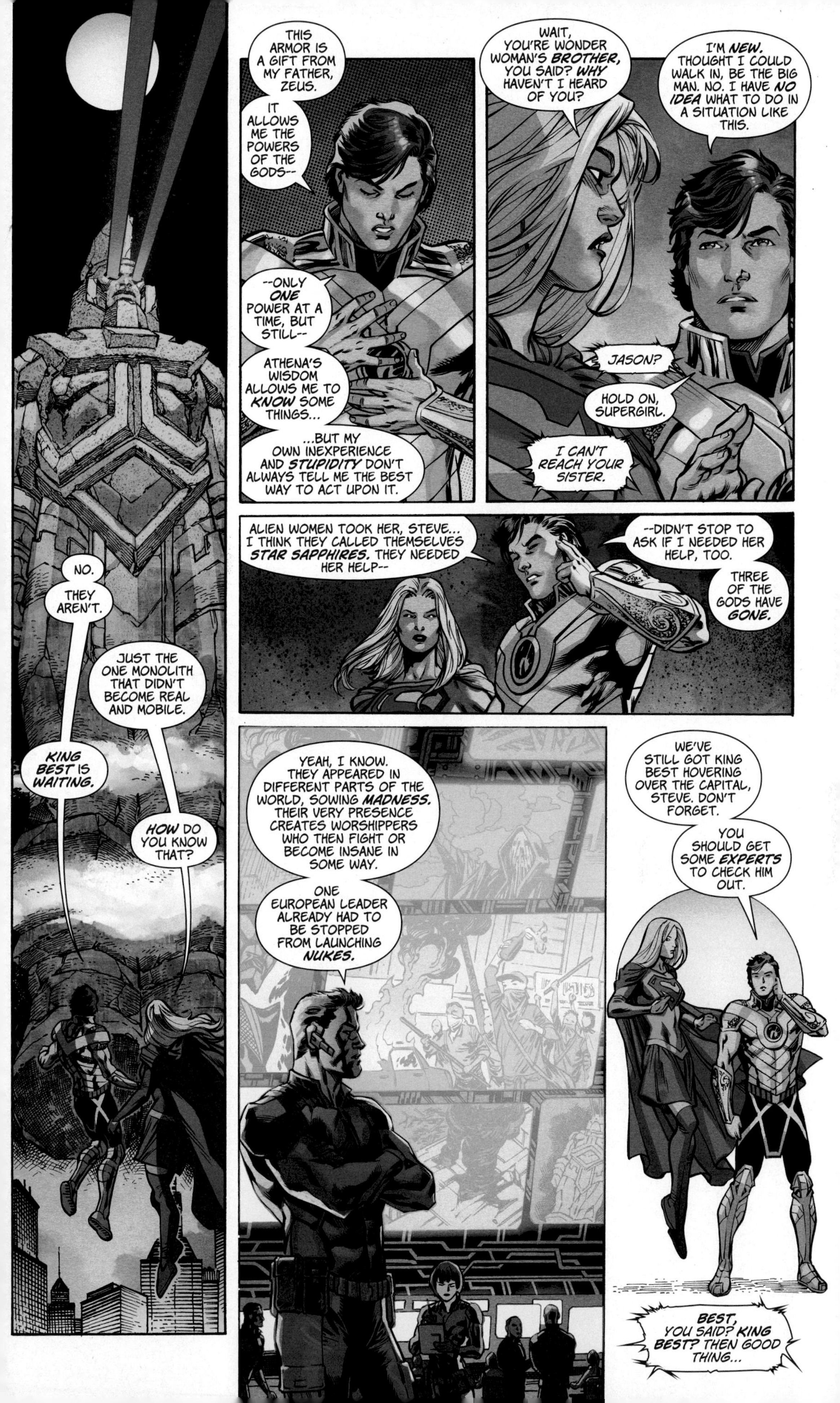

THIS ARMOR IS A GIFT FROM MY FATHER, ZEUS.
IT ALLOWS ME THE POWERS OF THE GODS--
--ONLY ONE POWER AT A TIME, BUT STILL--
ATHENA'S WISDOM ALLOWS ME TO KNOW SOME THINGS...
...BUT MY OWN INEXPERIENCE AND STUPIDITY DON'T ALWAYS TELL ME THE BEST WAY TO ACT UPON IT.
WAIT, YOU'RE WONDER WOMAN'S BROTHER, YOU SAID? WHY HAVEN'T I HEARD OF YOU?
I'M NEW. THOUGHT I COULD WALK IN, BE THE BIG MAN. NO. I HAVE NO IDEA WHAT TO DO IN A SITUATION LIKE THIS.
JASON?
HOLD ON, SUPERGIRL.
I CAN'T REACH YOUR SISTER.
ALIEN WOMEN TOOK HER, STEVE... I THINK THEY CALLED THEMSELVES STAR SAPPHIRES. THEY NEEDED HER HELP--
--DIDN'T STOP TO ASK IF I NEEDED HER HELP, TOO.
THREE OF THE GODS HAVE GONE.
NO.
THEY AREN'T.
JUST THE ONE MONOLITH THAT DIDN'T BECOME REAL AND MOBILE.
KING BEST IS WAITING.
HOW DO YOU KNOW THAT?
YEAH, I KNOW. THEY APPEARED IN DIFFERENT PARTS OF THE WORLD, SOWING MADNESS. THEIR VERY PRESENCE CREATES WORSHIPPERS WHO THEN FIGHT OR BECOME INSANE IN SOME WAY.
ONE EUROPEAN LEADER ALREADY HAD TO BE STOPPED FROM LAUNCHING NUKES.
WE'VE STILL GOT KING BEST HOVERING OVER THE CAPITAL, STEVE. DON'T FORGET.
YOU SHOULD GET SOME EXPERTS TO CHECK HIM OUT.
BEST, YOU SAID? KING BEST? THEN GOOD THING...

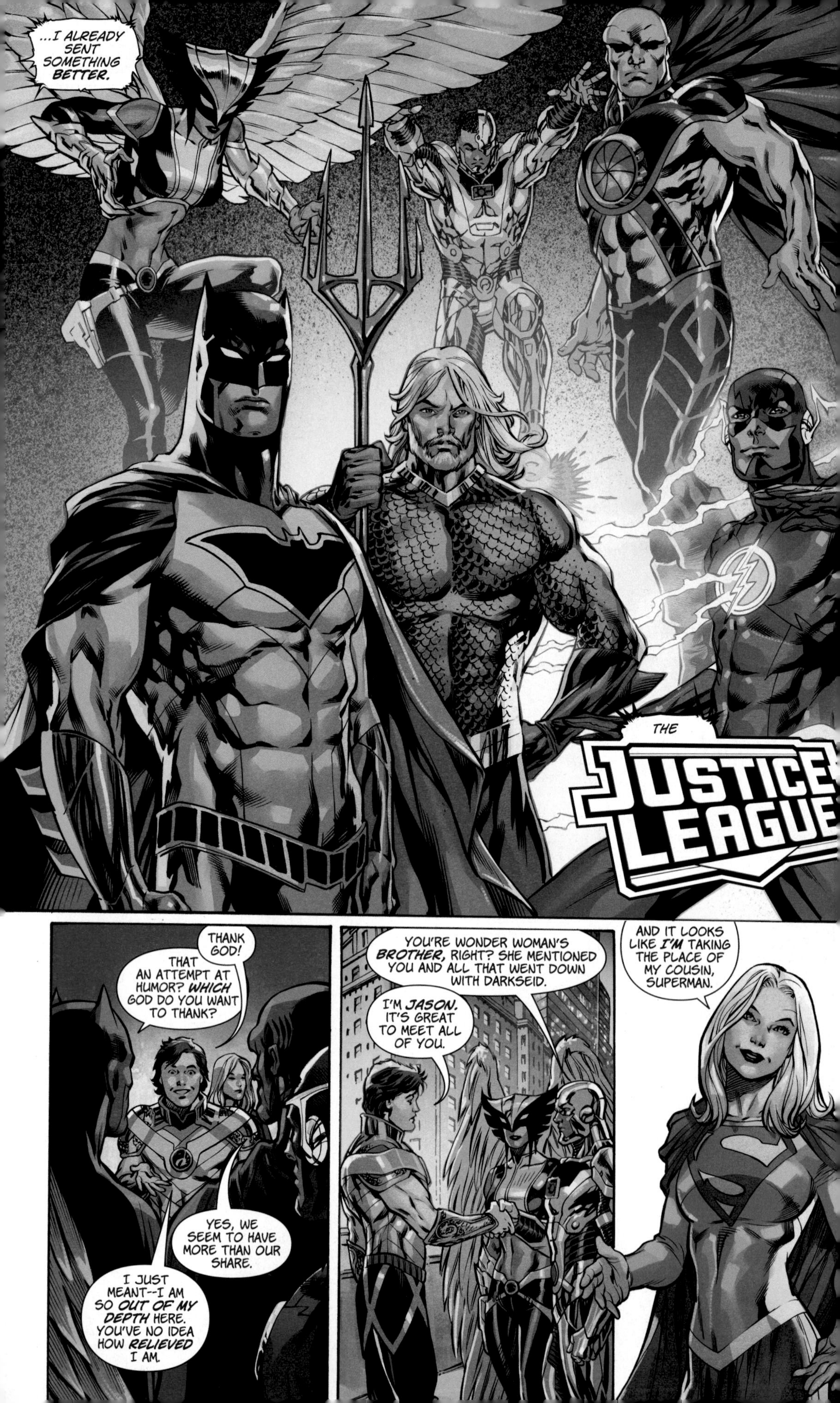
...I ALREADY SENT SOMETHING BETTER.
THE JUSTICE LEAGUE
THANK GOD!
THAT AN ATTEMPT AT HUMOR? WHICH GOD DO YOU WANT TO THANK?
YES, WE SEEM TO HAVE MORE THAN OUR SHARE.
I JUST MEANT--I AM SO OUT OF MY DEPTH HERE. YOU'VE NO IDEA HOW RELIEVED I AM.
YOU'RE WONDER WOMAN'S BROTHER, RIGHT? SHE MENTIONED YOU AND ALL THAT WENT DOWN WITH DARKSEID.
I'M JASON. IT'S GREAT TO MEET ALL OF YOU.
AND IT LOOKS LIKE I'M TAKING THE PLACE OF MY COUSIN, SUPERMAN.

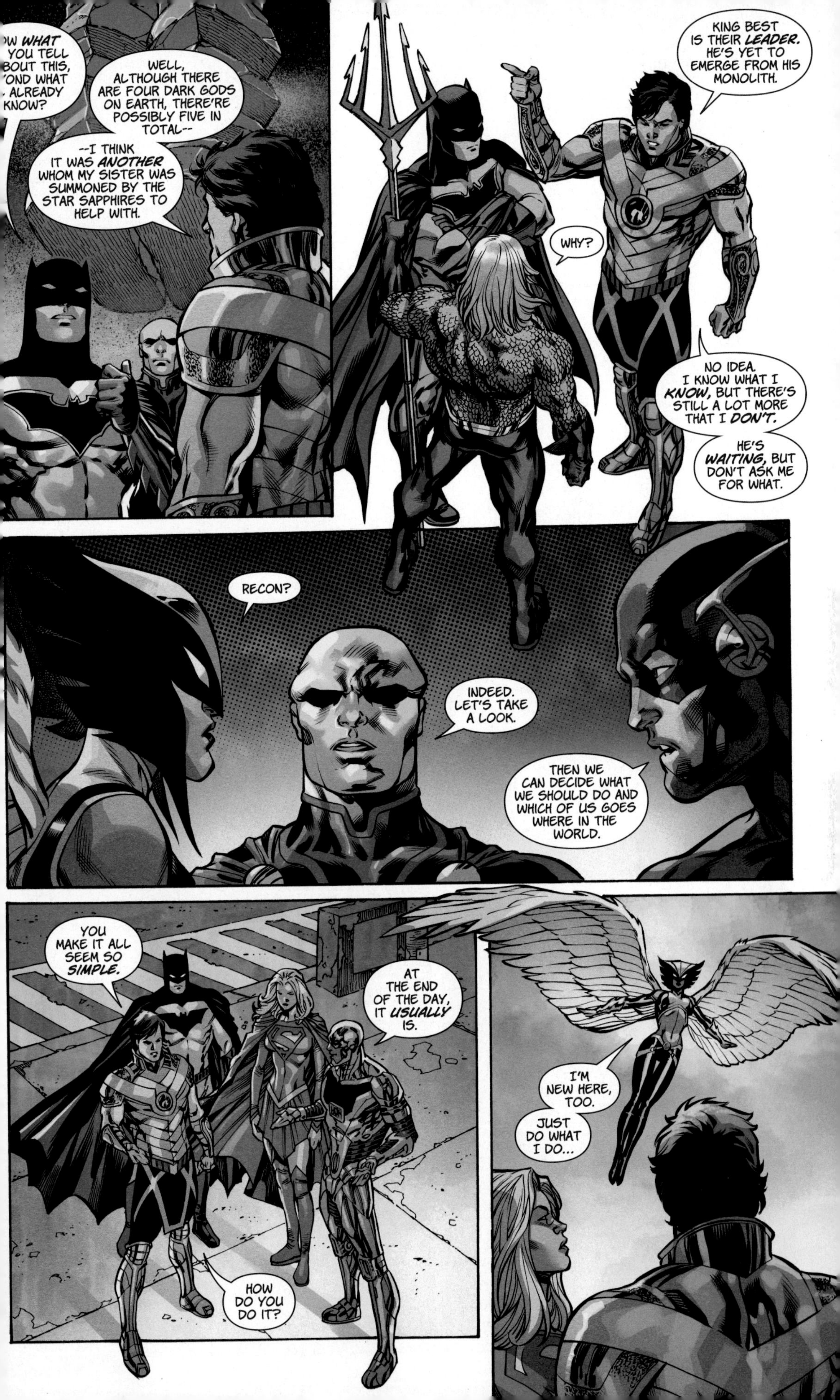

...OW WHAT YOU TELL ...BOUT THIS, ...YOND WHAT ... ALREADY KNOW?
WELL, ALTHOUGH THERE ARE FOUR DARK GODS ON EARTH, THERE'RE POSSIBLY FIVE IN TOTAL--
--I THINK IT WAS ANOTHER WHOM MY SISTER WAS SUMMONED BY THE STAR SAPPHIRES TO HELP WITH.
KING BEST IS THEIR LEADER. HE'S YET TO EMERGE FROM HIS MONOLITH.
WHY?
NO IDEA. I KNOW WHAT I KNOW, BUT THERE'S STILL A LOT MORE THAT I DON'T.
HE'S WAITING, BUT DON'T ASK ME FOR WHAT.
RECON?
INDEED. LET'S TAKE A LOOK.
THEN WE CAN DECIDE WHAT WE SHOULD DO AND WHICH OF US GOES WHERE IN THE WORLD.
YOU MAKE IT ALL SEEM SO SIMPLE.
AT THE END OF THE DAY, IT USUALLY IS.
HOW DO YOU DO IT?
I'M NEW HERE, TOO.
JUST DO WHAT I DO...

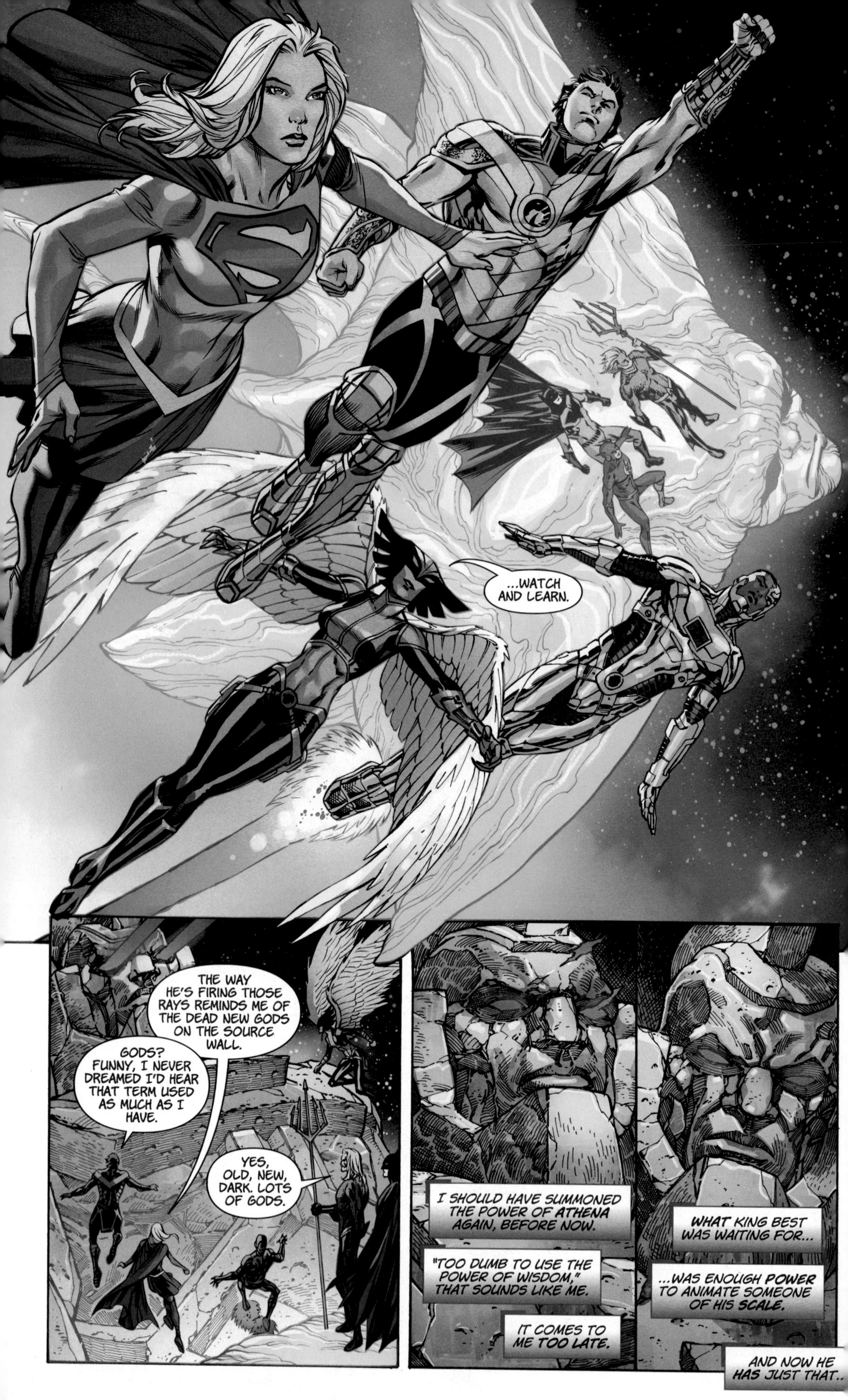
...WATCH AND LEARN.
THE WAY HE'S FIRING THOSE RAYS REMINDS ME OF THE DEAD NEW GODS ON THE SOURCE WALL.
GODS? FUNNY, I NEVER DREAMED I'D HEAR THAT TERM USED AS MUCH AS I HAVE.
YES, OLD, NEW, DARK. LOTS OF GODS.
I SHOULD HAVE SUMMONED THE POWER OF ATHENA AGAIN, BEFORE NOW.
"TOO DUMB TO USE THE POWER OF WISDOM," THAT SOUNDS LIKE ME.
IT COMES TO ME TOO LATE.
WHAT KING BEST WAS WAITING FOR...
...WAS ENOUGH POWER TO ANIMATE SOMEONE OF HIS SCALE.
AND NOW HE HAS JUST THAT.

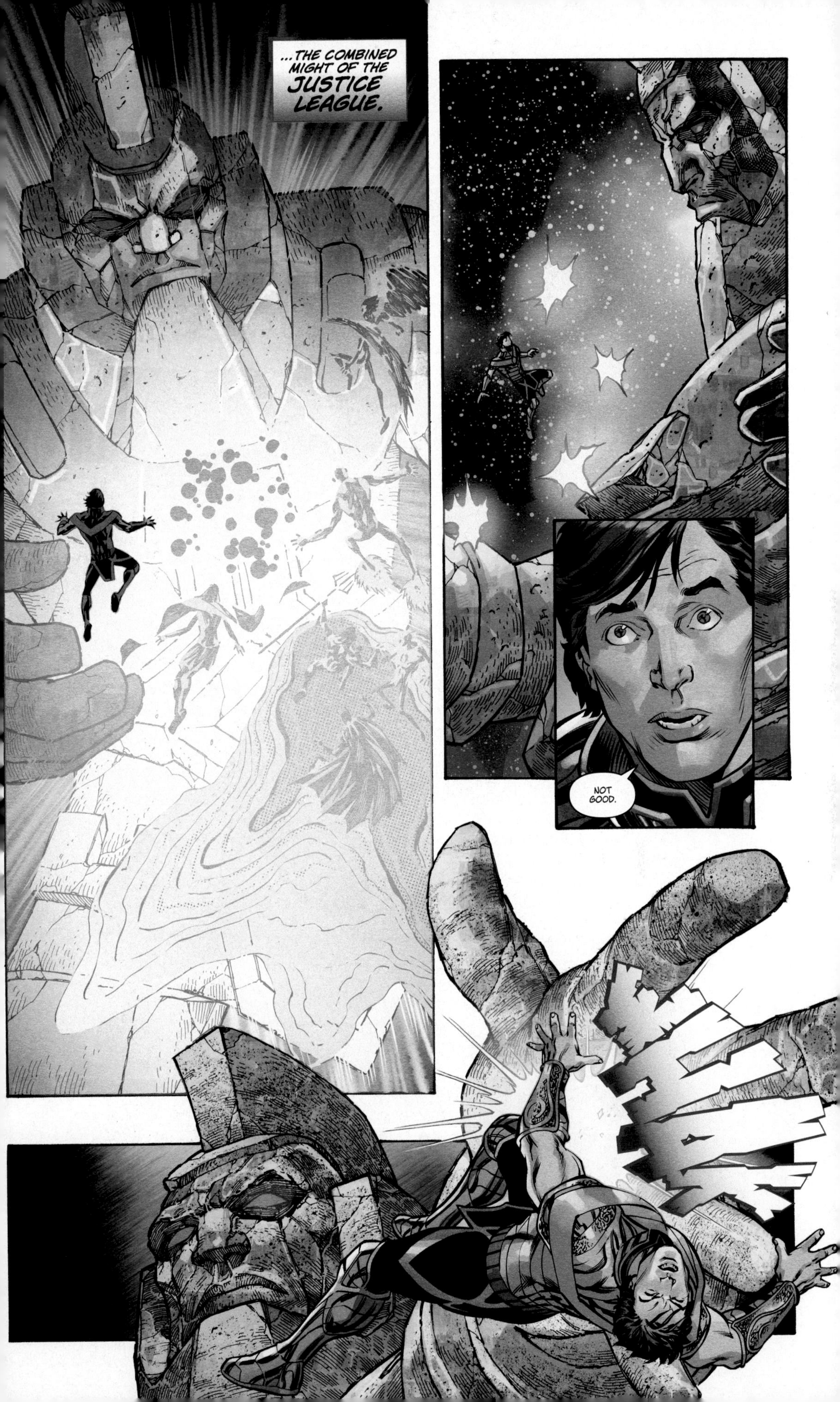
...THE COMBINED MIGHT OF THE JUSTICE LEAGUE.
NOT GOOD.

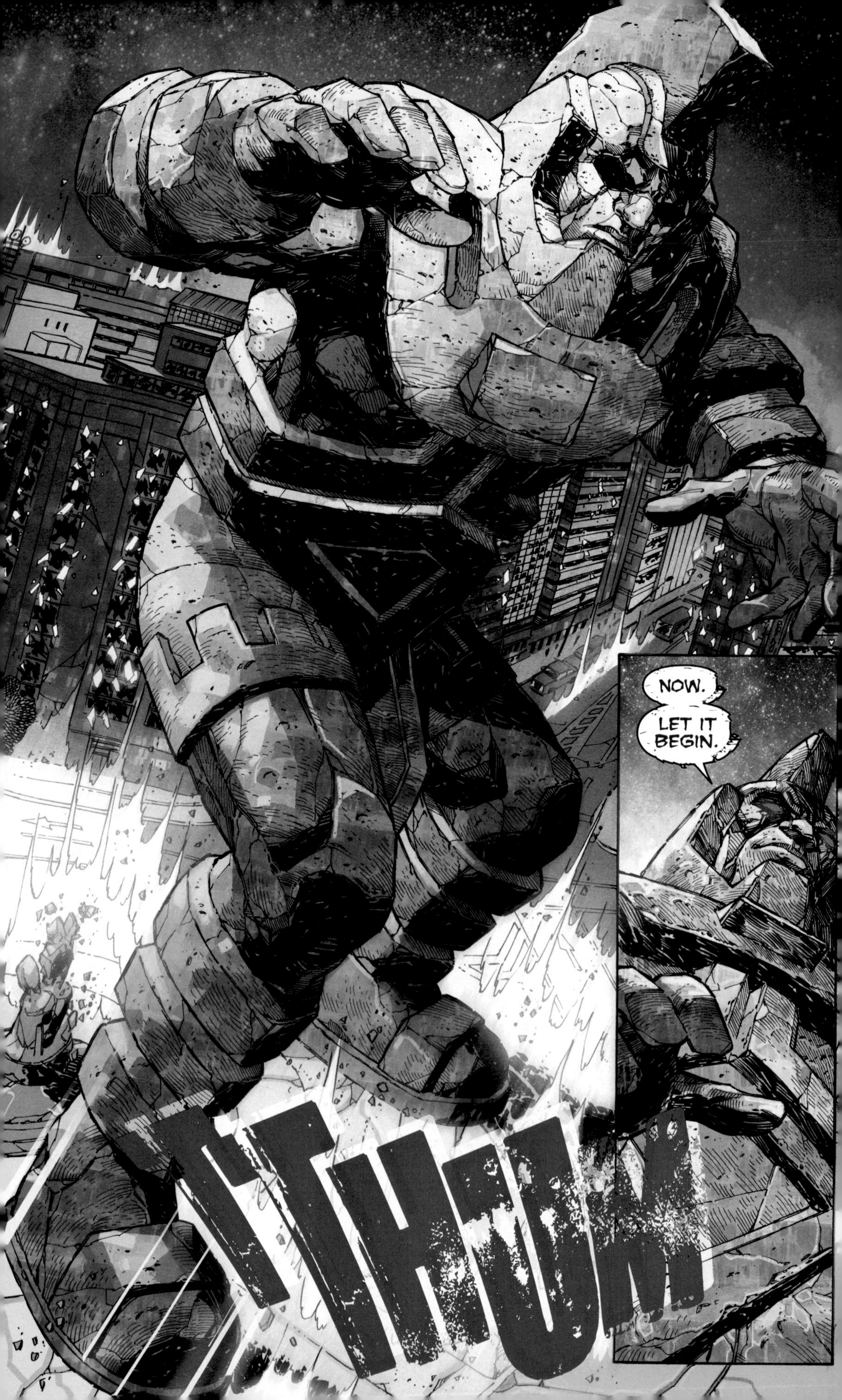
NOW.
LET IT BEGIN.
THUM

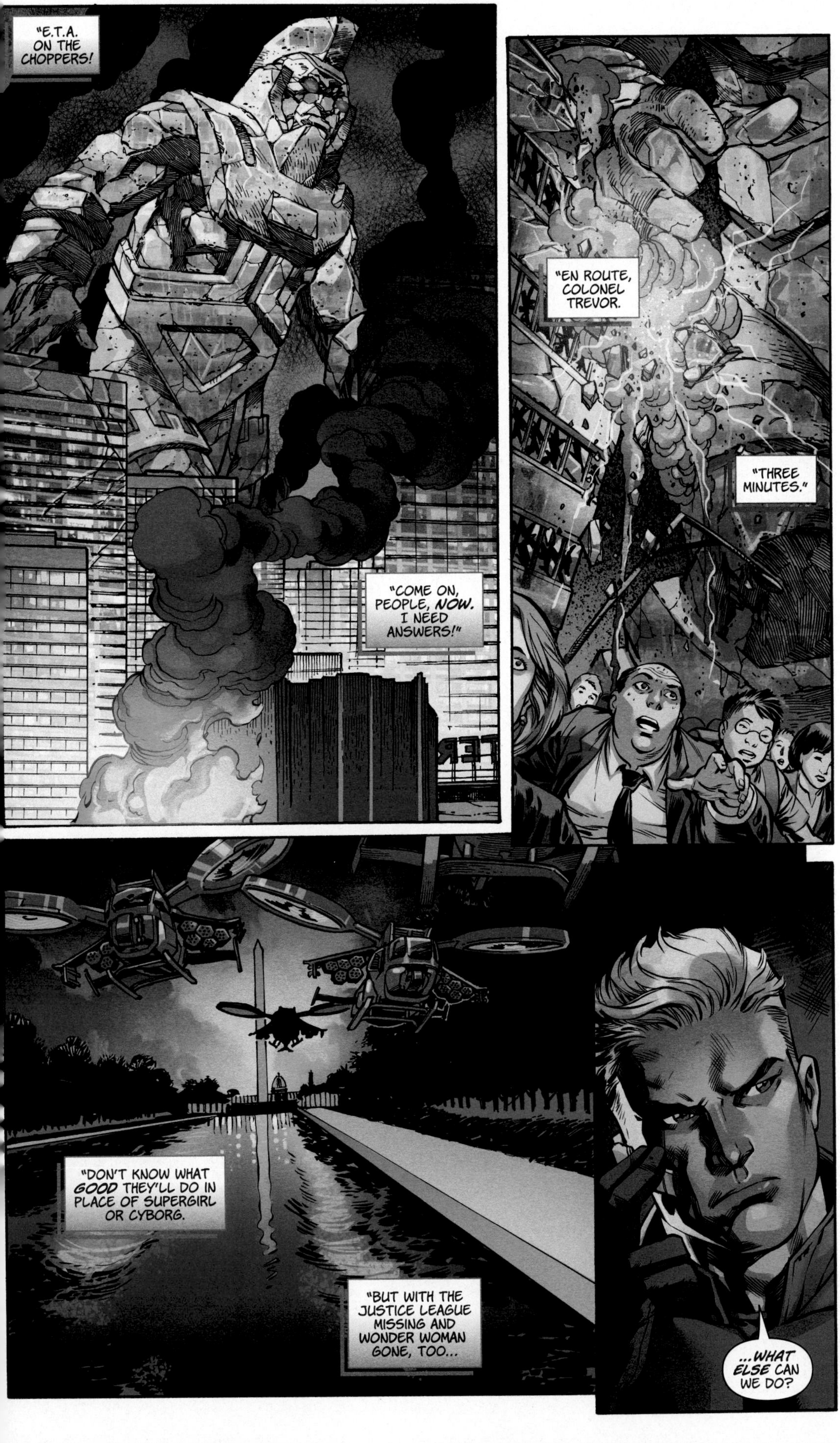
"E.T.A. ON THE CHOPPERS!
"COME ON, PEOPLE, NOW. I NEED ANSWERS!"
"EN ROUTE, COLONEL TREVOR.
"THREE MINUTES."
"DON'T KNOW WHAT GOOD THEY'LL DO IN PLACE OF SUPERGIRL OR CYBORG.
"BUT WITH THE JUSTICE LEAGUE MISSING AND WONDER WOMAN GONE, TOO...
...WHAT ELSE CAN WE DO?

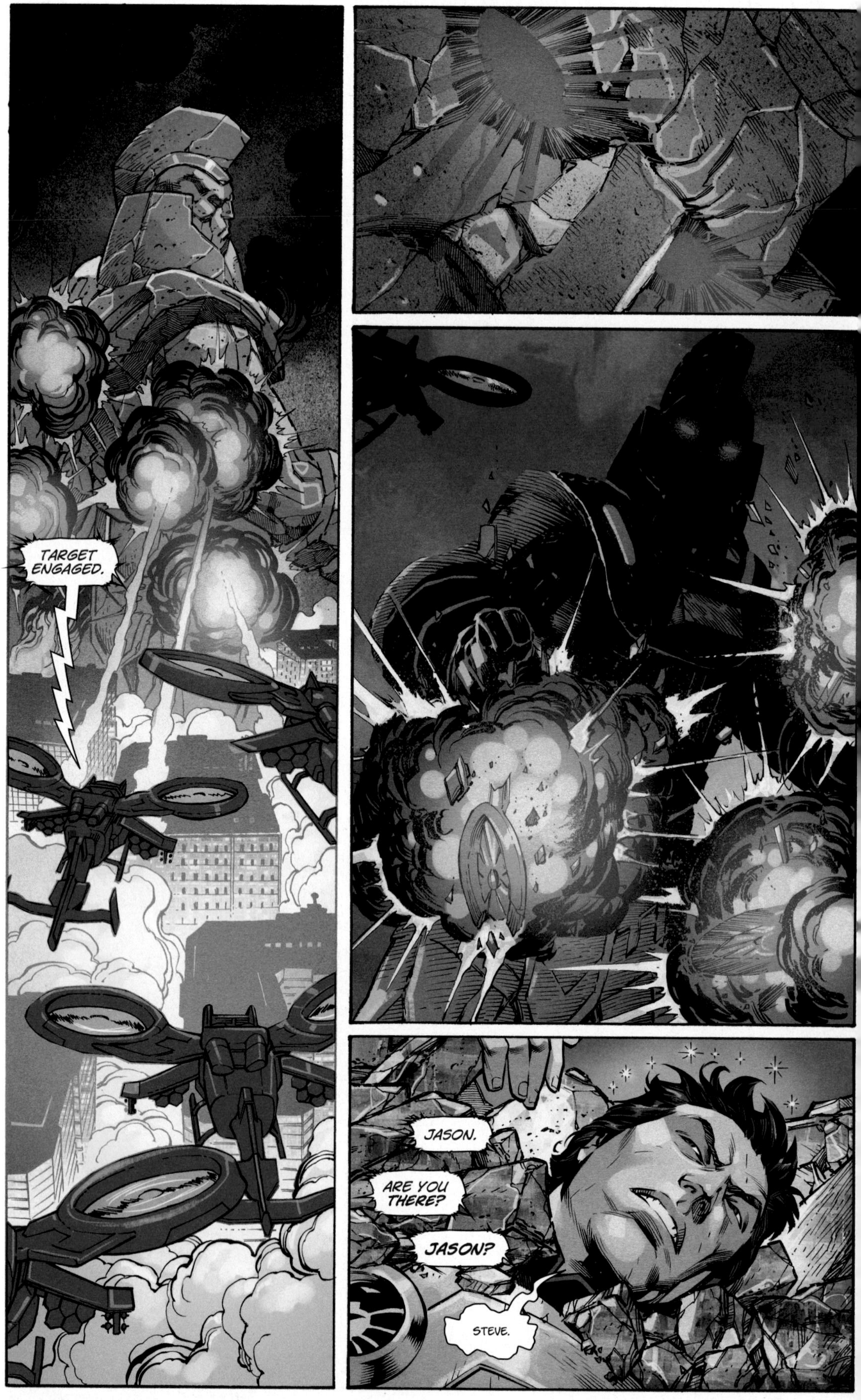
TARGET ENGAGED.
JASON.
ARE YOU THERE?
JASON?
STEVE.

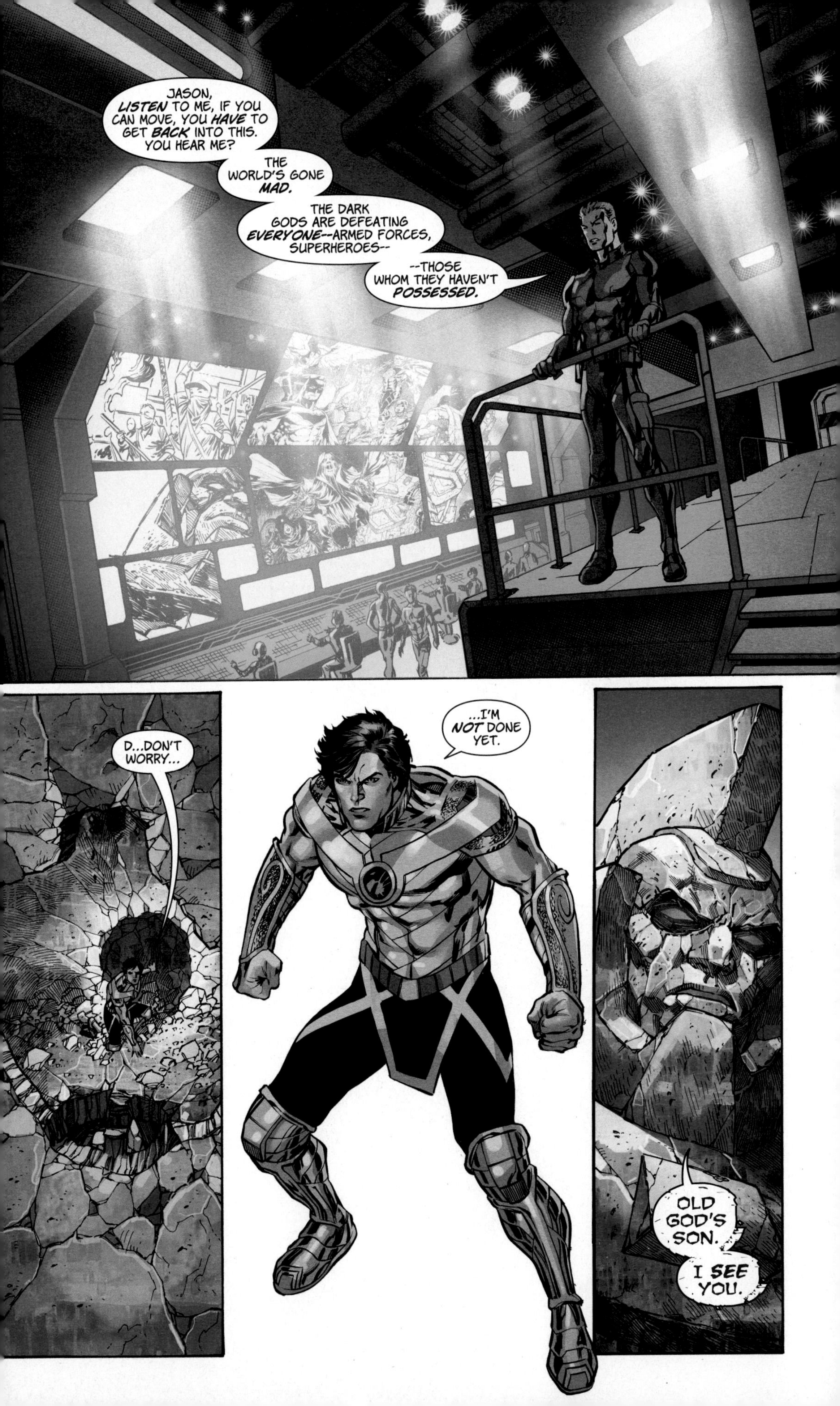
JASON, LISTEN TO ME, IF YOU CAN MOVE, YOU HAVE TO GET BACK INTO THIS. YOU HEAR ME?
THE WORLD'S GONE MAD.
THE DARK GODS ARE DEFEATING EVERYONE--ARMED FORCES, SUPERHEROES--
--THOSE WHOM THEY HAVEN'T POSSESSED.
D...DON'T WORRY...
...I'M NOT DONE YET.
OLD GOD'S SON.
I SEE YOU.

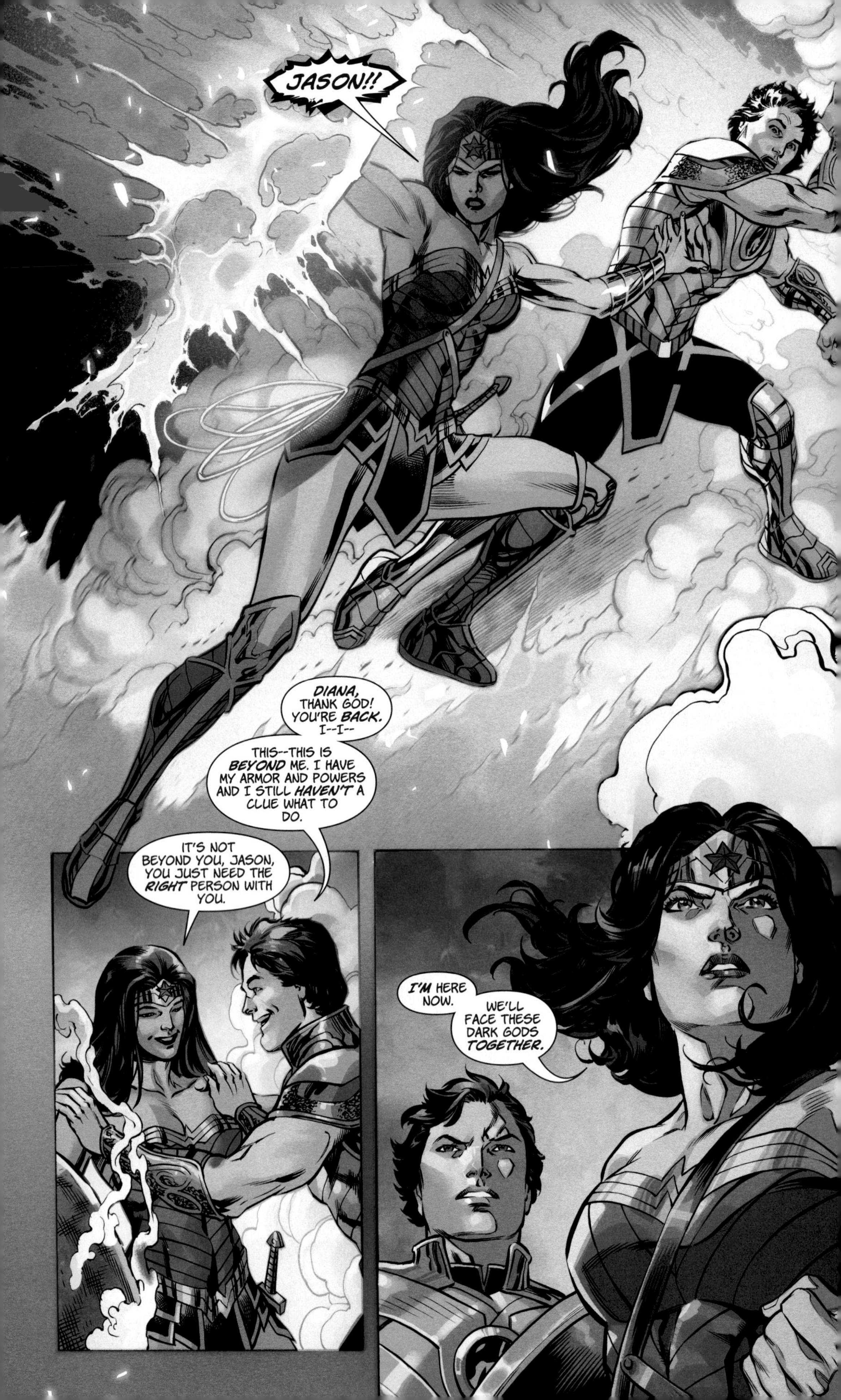
JASON!!
DIANA, THANK GOD! YOU'RE BACK. I--I--
THIS--THIS IS BEYOND ME. I HAVE MY ARMOR AND POWERS AND I STILL HAVEN'T A CLUE WHAT TO DO.
IT'S NOT BEYOND YOU, JASON, YOU JUST NEED THE RIGHT PERSON WITH YOU.
I'M HERE NOW.
WE'LL FACE THESE DARK GODS TOGETHER.

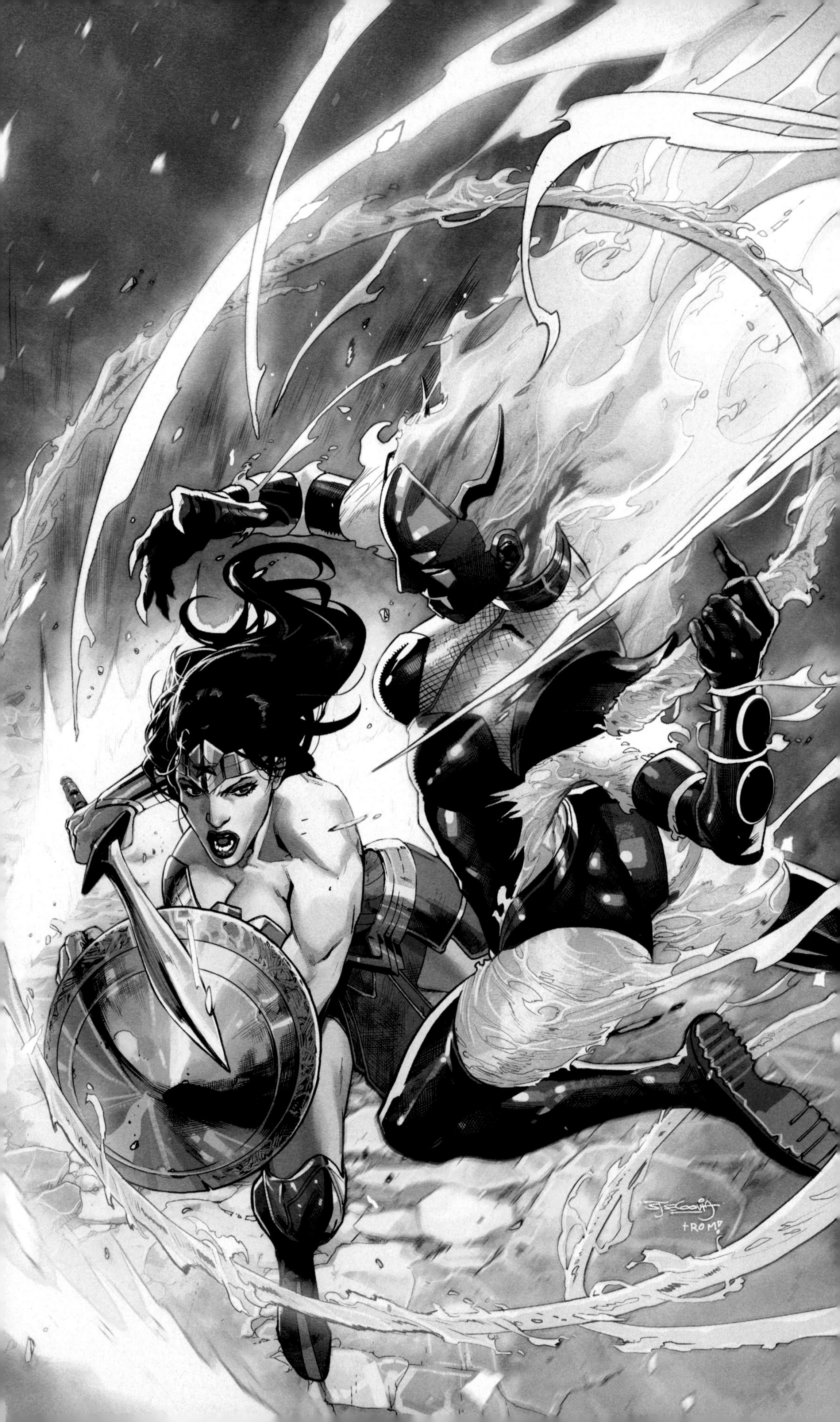

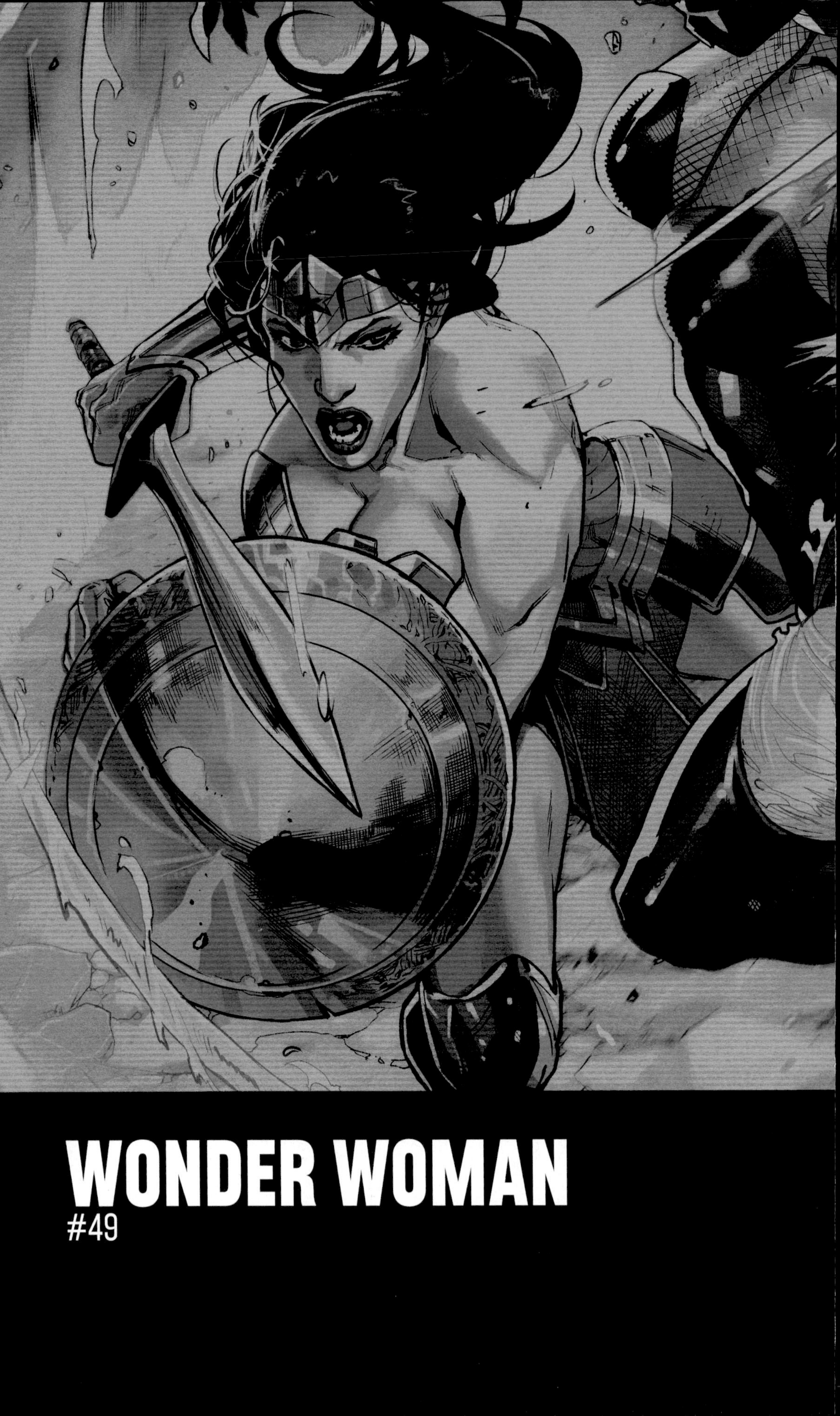

WONDER WOMAN
#49

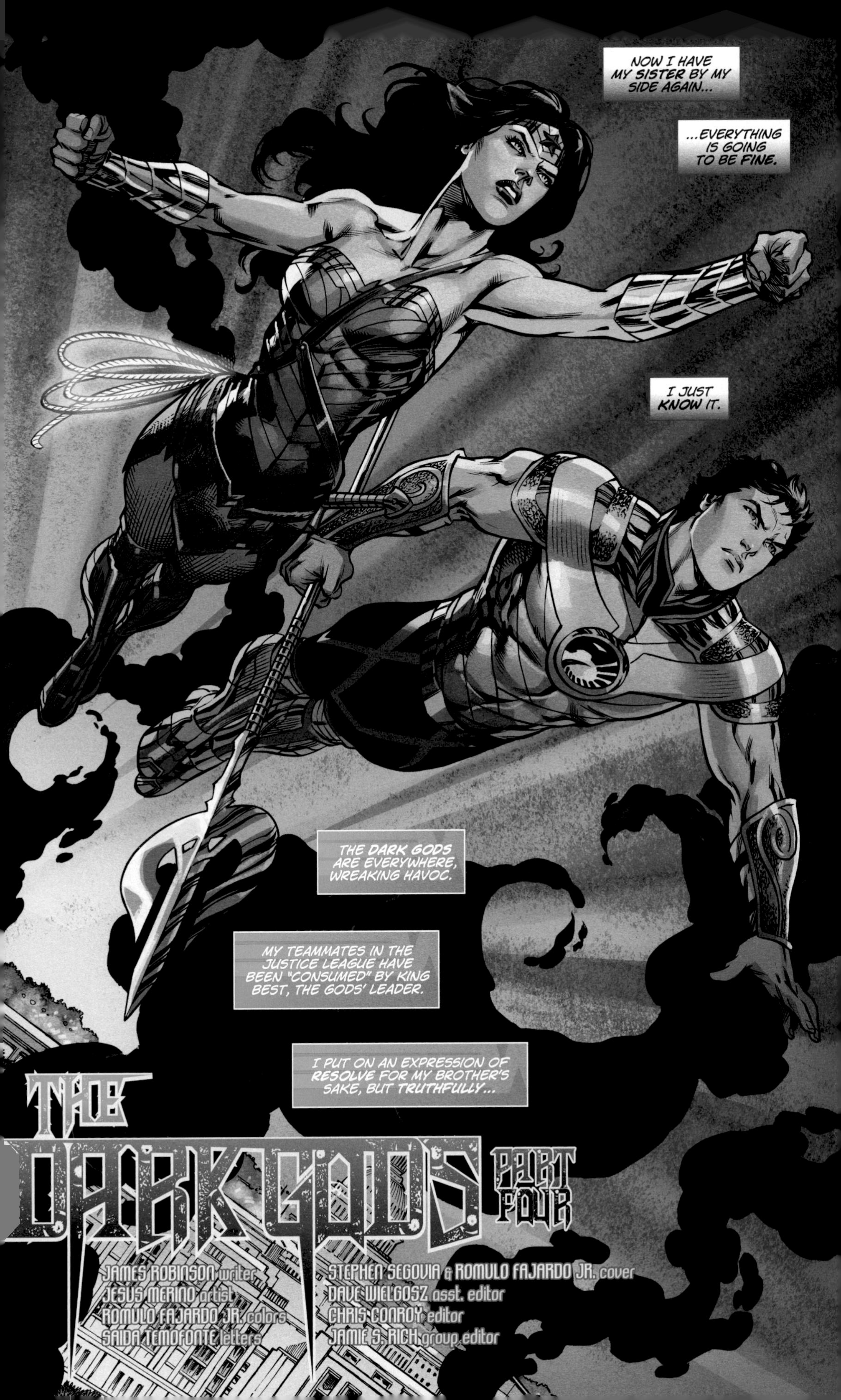

NOW I HAVE MY SISTER BY MY SIDE AGAIN...
...EVERYTHING IS GOING TO BE FINE.
I JUST KNOW IT.
THE DARK GODS ARE EVERYWHERE, WREAKING HAVOC.
MY TEAMMATES IN THE JUSTICE LEAGUE HAVE BEEN "CONSUMED" BY KING BEST, THE GODS' LEADER.
I PUT ON AN EXPRESSION OF RESOLVE FOR MY BROTHER'S SAKE, BUT TRUTHFULLY...
THE DARK GODS PART FOUR
JAMES ROBINSON writer
JESUS MERINO artist
ROMULO FAJARDO JR. colors
SAIDA TEMOFONTE letters
STEPHEN SEGOVIA & ROMULO FAJARDO JR. cover
DAVE WIELGOSZ asst. editor
CHRIS CONROY editor
JAMIE S. RICH group editor

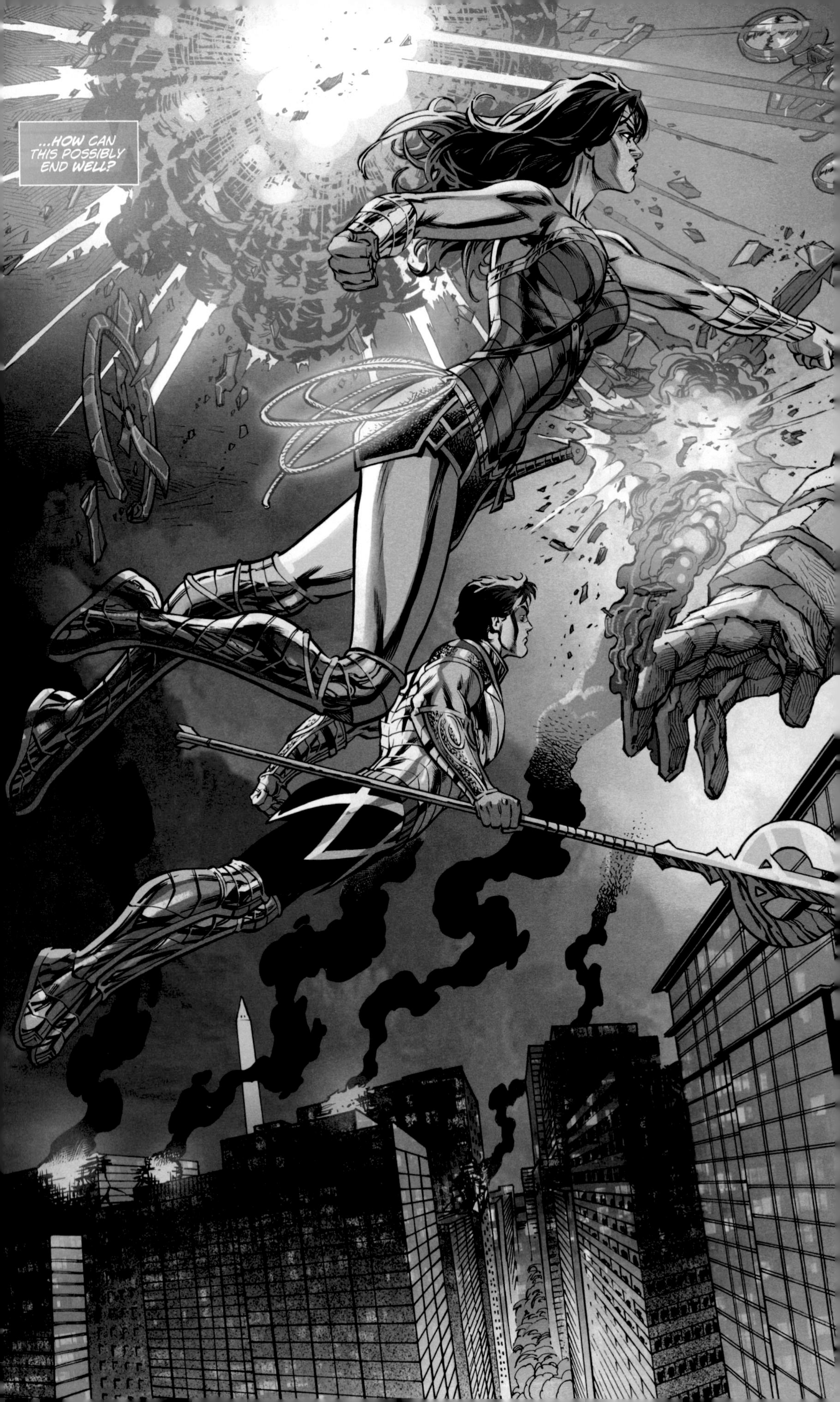
...HOW CAN THIS POSSIBLY END WELL?

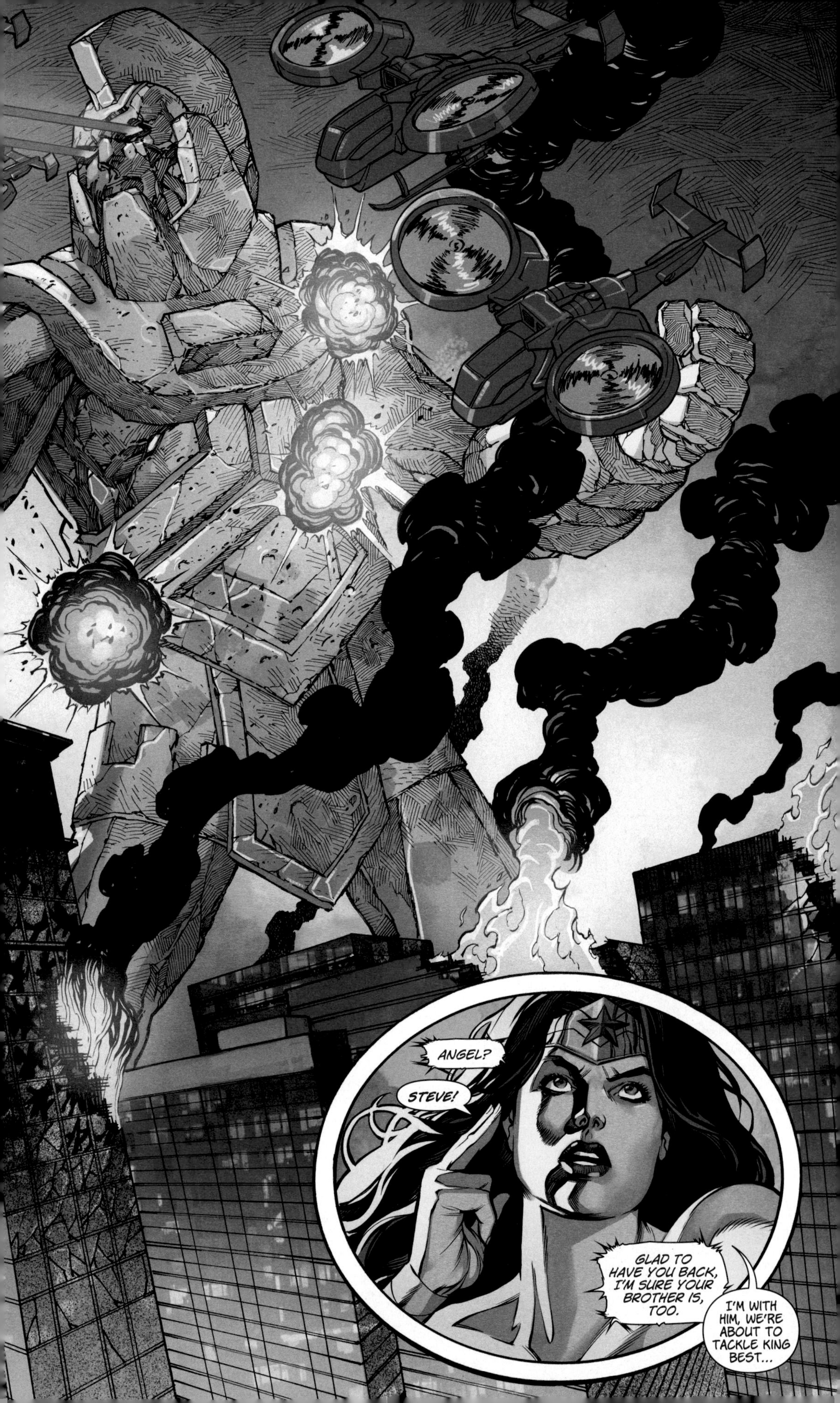
ANGEL?
STEVE!
GLAD TO HAVE YOU BACK, I'M SURE YOUR BROTHER IS, TOO.
I'M WITH HIM, WE'RE ABOUT TO TACKLE KING BEST...

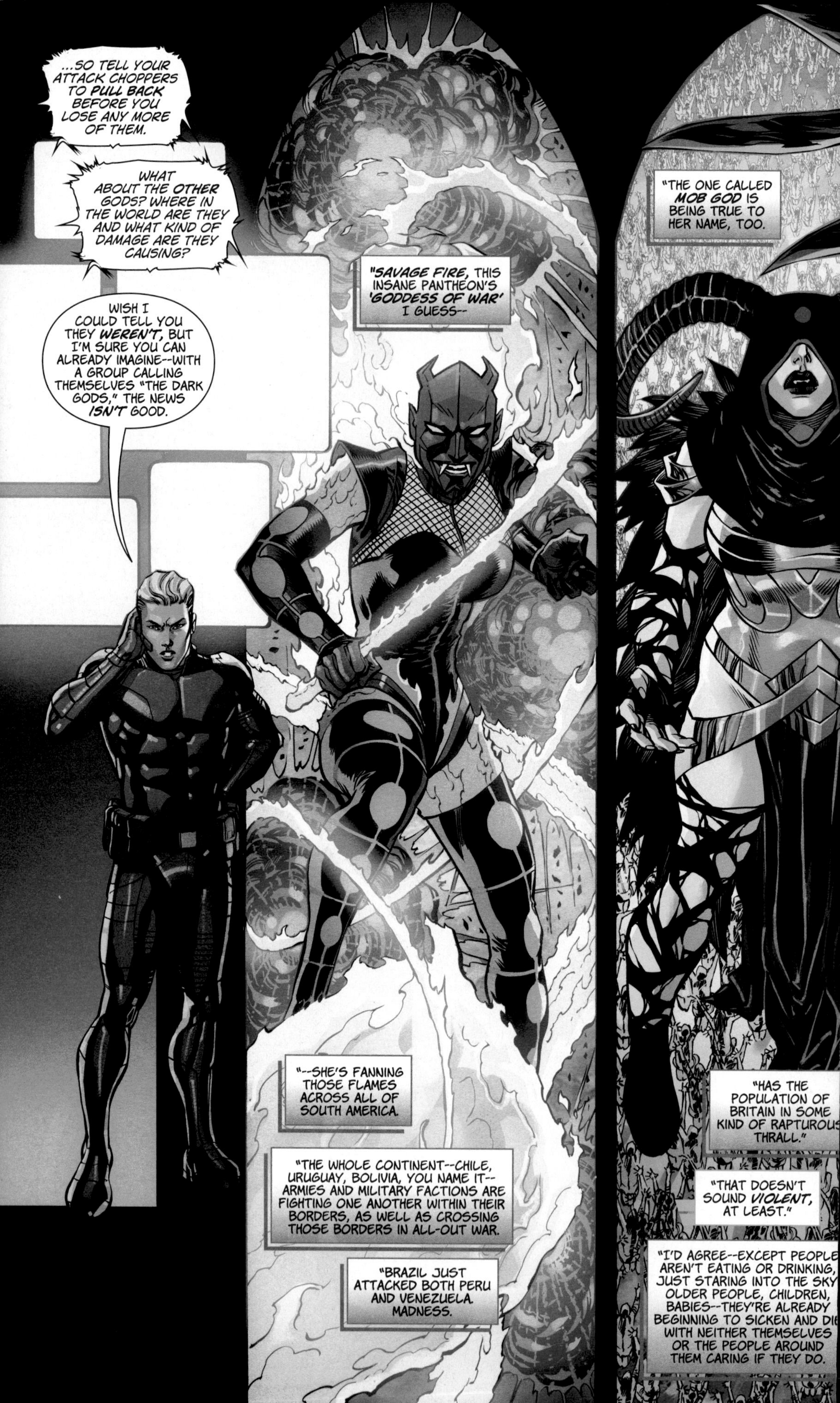
...SO TELL YOUR ATTACK CHOPPERS TO PULL BACK BEFORE YOU LOSE ANY MORE OF THEM.
WHAT ABOUT THE OTHER GODS? WHERE IN THE WORLD ARE THEY AND WHAT KIND OF DAMAGE ARE THEY CAUSING?
WISH I COULD TELL YOU THEY WEREN'T, BUT I'M SURE YOU CAN ALREADY IMAGINE--WITH A GROUP CALLING THEMSELVES "THE DARK GODS," THE NEWS ISN'T GOOD.
"SAVAGE FIRE, THIS INSANE PANTHEON'S 'GODDESS OF WAR' I GUESS--
"--SHE'S FANNING THOSE FLAMES ACROSS ALL OF SOUTH AMERICA.
"THE WHOLE CONTINENT--CHILE, URUGUAY, BOLIVIA, YOU NAME IT--ARMIES AND MILITARY FACTIONS ARE FIGHTING ONE ANOTHER WITHIN THEIR BORDERS, AS WELL AS CROSSING THOSE BORDERS IN ALL-OUT WAR.
"BRAZIL JUST ATTACKED BOTH PERU AND VENEZUELA. MADNESS.
"THE ONE CALLED MOB GOD IS BEING TRUE TO HER NAME, TOO.
"HAS THE POPULATION OF BRITAIN IN SOME KIND OF RAPTUROUS THRALL."
"THAT DOESN'T SOUND VIOLENT, AT LEAST."
"I'D AGREE--EXCEPT PEOPLE AREN'T EATING OR DRINKING, JUST STARING INTO THE SKY. OLDER PEOPLE, CHILDREN, BABIES--THEY'RE ALREADY BEGINNING TO SICKEN AND DIE WITH NEITHER THEMSELVES OR THE PEOPLE AROUND THEM CARING IF THEY DO.

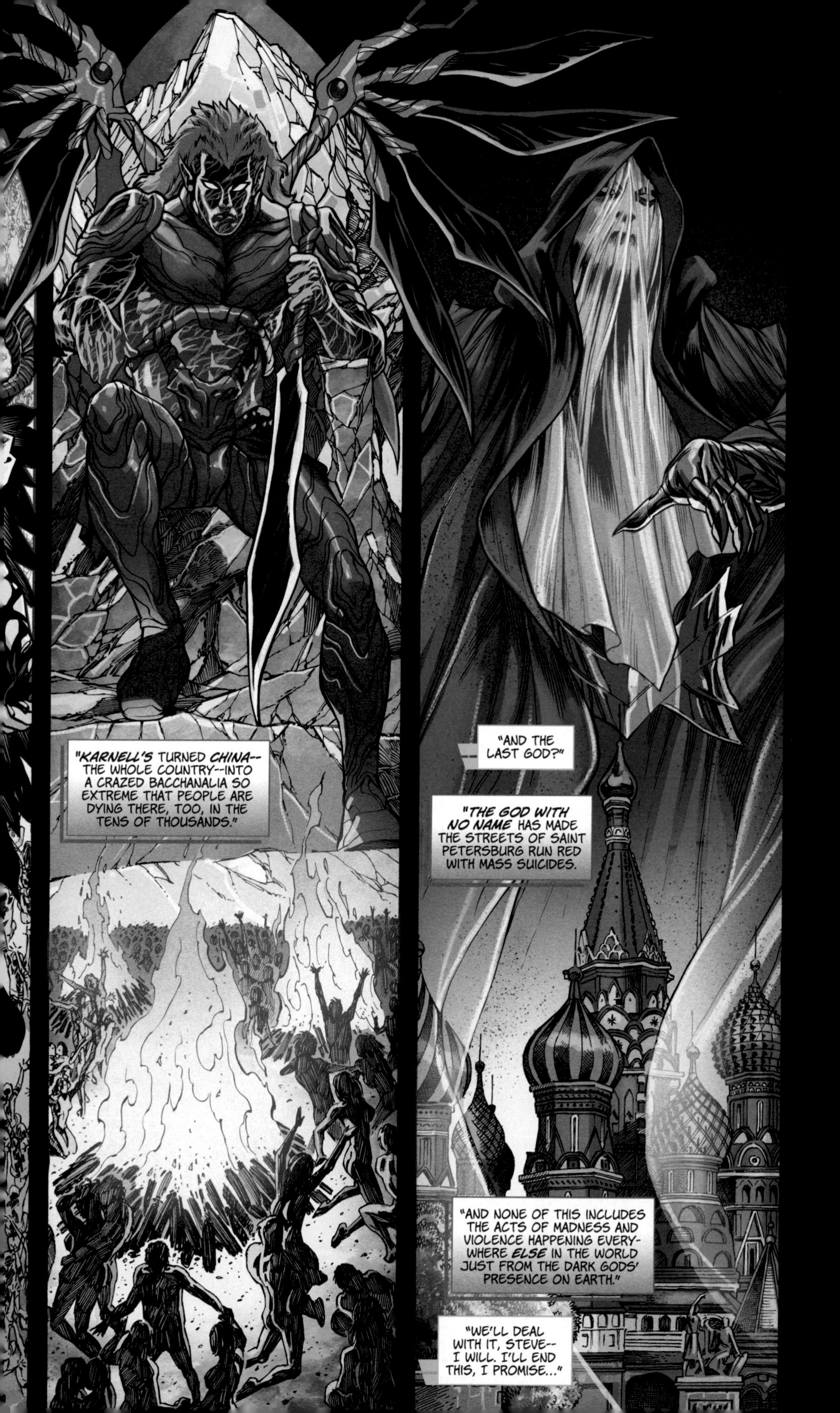
"KARNELL'S TURNED CHINA--THE WHOLE COUNTRY--INTO A CRAZED BACCHANALIA SO EXTREME THAT PEOPLE ARE DYING THERE, TOO, IN THE TENS OF THOUSANDS."
"AND THE LAST GOD?"
"THE GOD WITH NO NAME HAS MADE THE STREETS OF SAINT PETERSBURG RUN RED WITH MASS SUICIDES.
"AND NONE OF THIS INCLUDES THE ACTS OF MADNESS AND VIOLENCE HAPPENING EVERY-WHERE ELSE IN THE WORLD JUST FROM THE DARK GODS' PRESENCE ON EARTH."
"WE'LL DEAL WITH IT, STEVE--I WILL. I'LL END THIS, I PROMISE..."

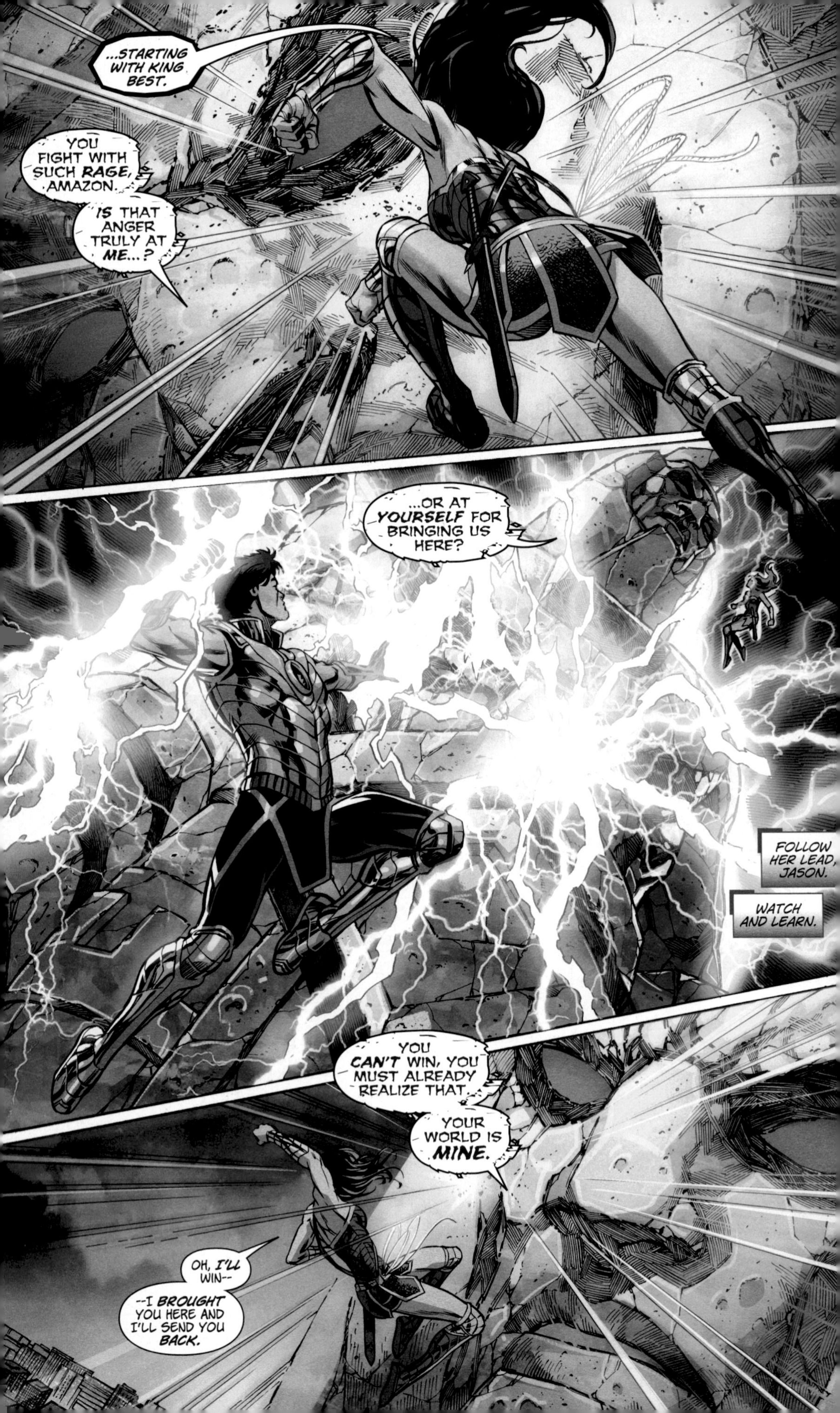
...STARTING WITH KING BEST.
YOU FIGHT WITH SUCH RAGE, AMAZON.
IS THAT ANGER TRULY AT ME...?
...OR AT YOURSELF FOR BRINGING US HERE?
FOLLOW HER LEAD, JASON.
WATCH AND LEARN.
YOU CAN'T WIN, YOU MUST ALREADY REALIZE THAT.
YOUR WORLD IS MINE.
OH, I'LL WIN--
--I BROUGHT YOU HERE AND I'LL SEND YOU BACK.

Buenos Aires, Argentina.

THE DAYS OF THE MAD JUNTAS ARE LONG OVER. CONSIGNED TO THE HISTORY BOOKS...

...LIKE THE ONE ISABELLA PUTS DOWN ON THE CHAIR.

← Way Out   ← Southern platform 3   ← Southern platform 4

London, England.

DANNY IS LATE FOR WORK, NOT THAT HE CARES IF THEY FIRE HIM.

TWENTY YEARS HE'S GIVEN THEM, AND FOR WHAT?

Wuhan, China.

AI AWAKENS TO THE SOUND OF HER HUSBAND CLEARING HIS THROAT.

A TYPICAL MORNING.

AI LOOKS AT THE CLOCK AND DECIDES HER BED SHOULD NOT REMAIN A LURE--THE DAY AWAITS.

Saint Petersburg, Russia.

"PEOPLE STILL INVOKE THE TERROR THAT WAS STALIN. HA!"

"LIKE ANY OF THEM REMEMBER," VITALY THINKS.

VITALY DOES REMEMBER. HE WAS A BOY, OF COURSE, BUT HE STILL RECALLS THE FEAR IN HIS PARENTS' EYES.

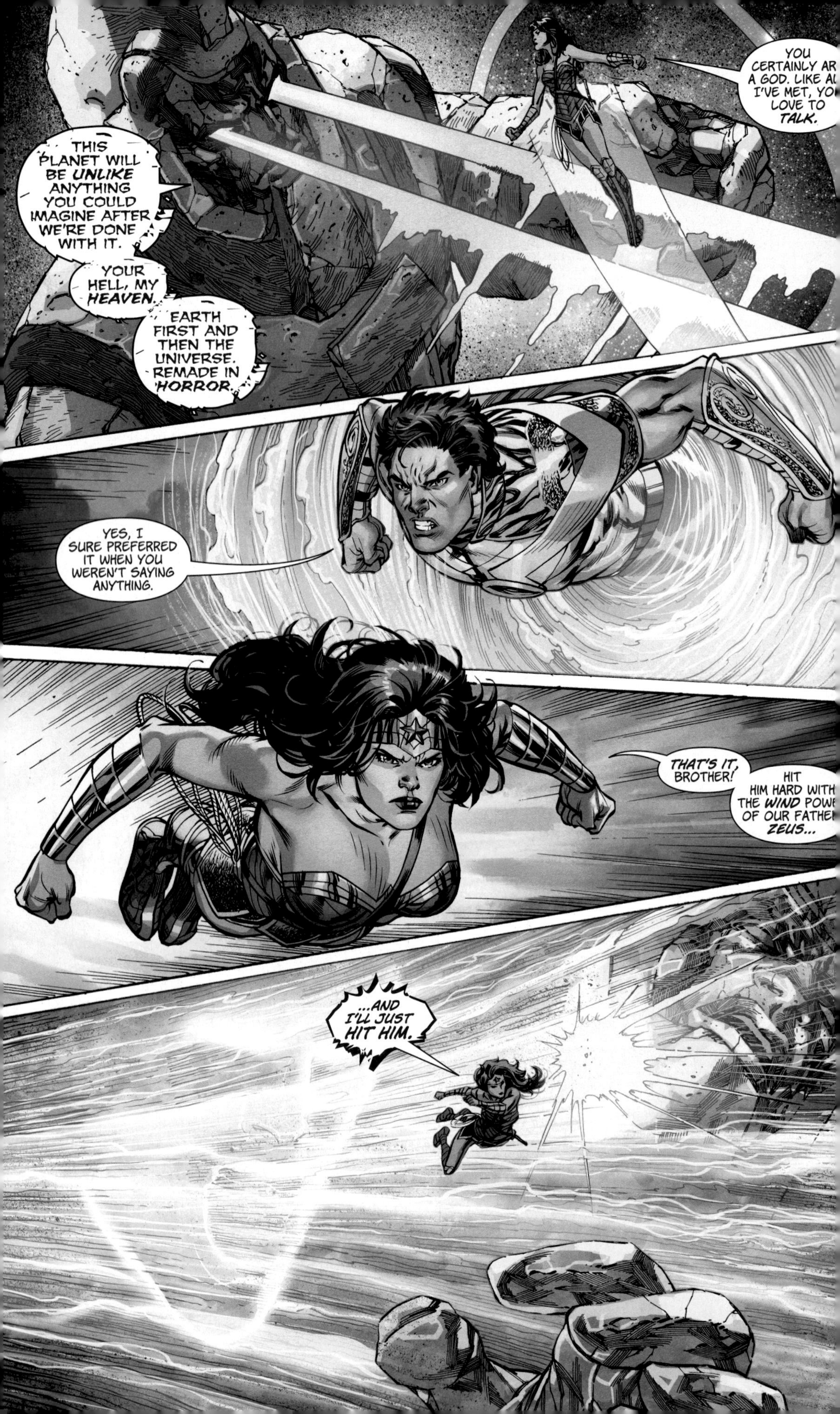
YOU CERTAINLY AR A GOD. LIKE AL I'VE MET, YO LOVE TO TALK.
THIS PLANET WILL BE UNLIKE ANYTHING YOU COULD IMAGINE AFTER WE'RE DONE WITH IT.
YOUR HELL, MY HEAVEN.
EARTH FIRST AND THEN THE UNIVERSE. REMADE IN HORROR.
YES, I SURE PREFERRED IT WHEN YOU WEREN'T SAYING ANYTHING.
THAT'S IT, BROTHER!
HIT HIM HARD WITH THE WIND POWE OF OUR FATHE ZEUS...
...AND I'LL JUST HIT HIM.

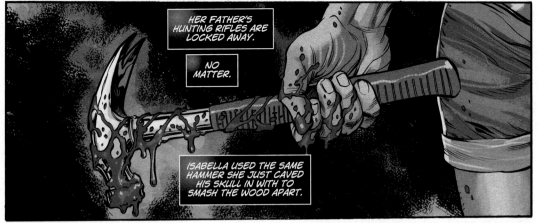

HER FATHER'S HUNTING RIFLES ARE LOCKED AWAY.

NO MATTER.

ISABELLA USED THE SAME HAMMER SHE JUST CAVED HIS SKULL IN WITH TO SMASH THE WOOD APART.

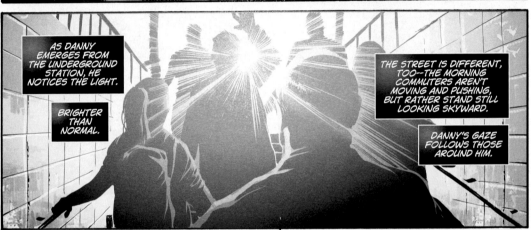

AS DANNY EMERGES FROM THE UNDERGROUND STATION, HE NOTICES THE LIGHT.

BRIGHTER THAN NORMAL.

THE STREET IS DIFFERENT, TOO--THE MORNING COMMUTERS AREN'T MOVING AND PUSHING, BUT RATHER STAND STILL LOOKING SKYWARD.

DANNY'S GAZE FOLLOWS THOSE AROUND HIM.

TAI CHI IN THE SQUARE, SUCH A PLEASANT WAY TO BEGIN--TO BEND AND STRETCH.

BUT STEPPING OUTSIDE, AI IS LOST WITHIN MOMENTS--HER MEMORIES AND MIND.

TODAY, HOWEVER, VITALY SEES THAT SAME FEAR EVERYWHERE--IN EVERYONE AROUND HIM.

SEES THAT FEAR AND FEELS IT.

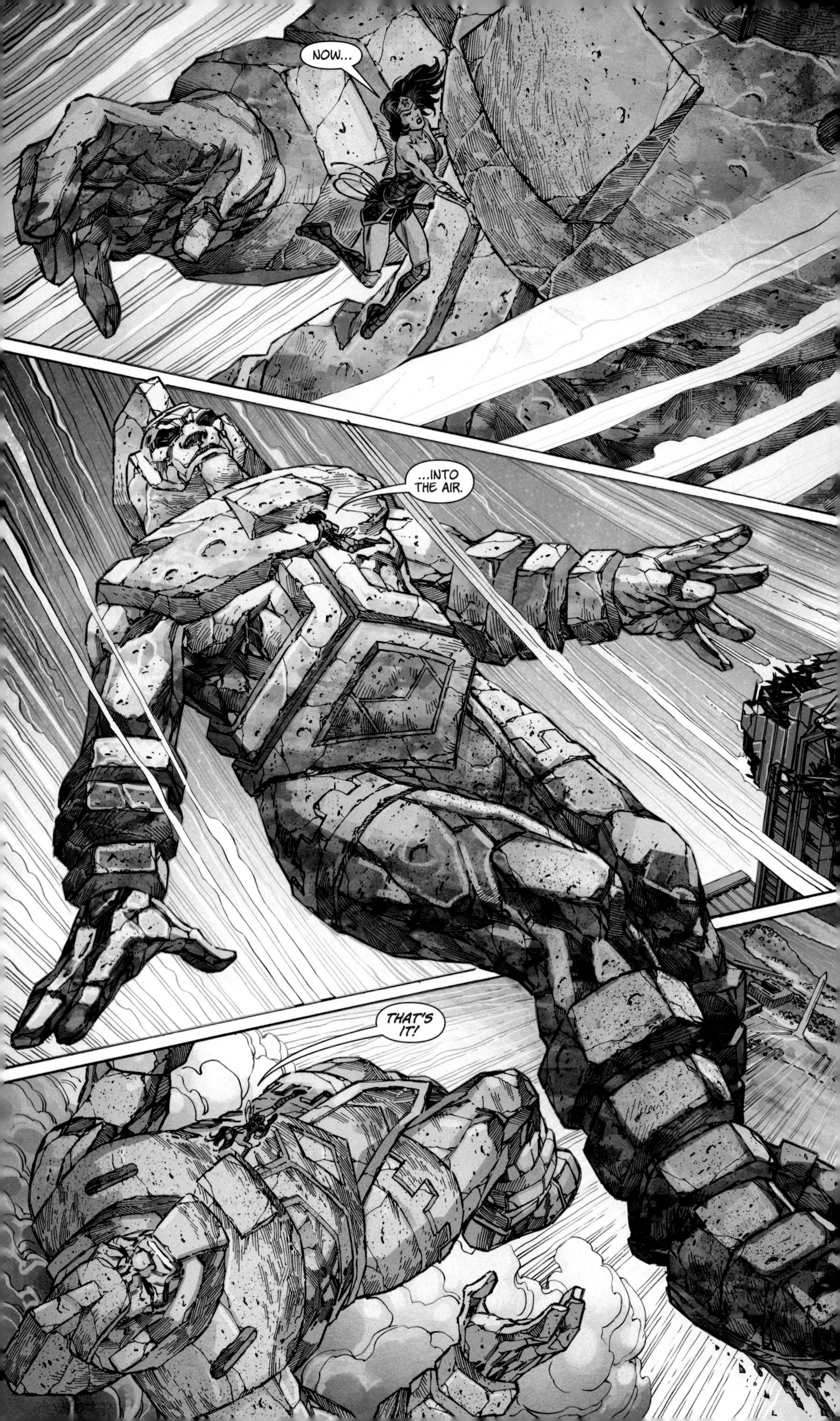
NOW...
...INTO THE AIR.
THAT'S IT!

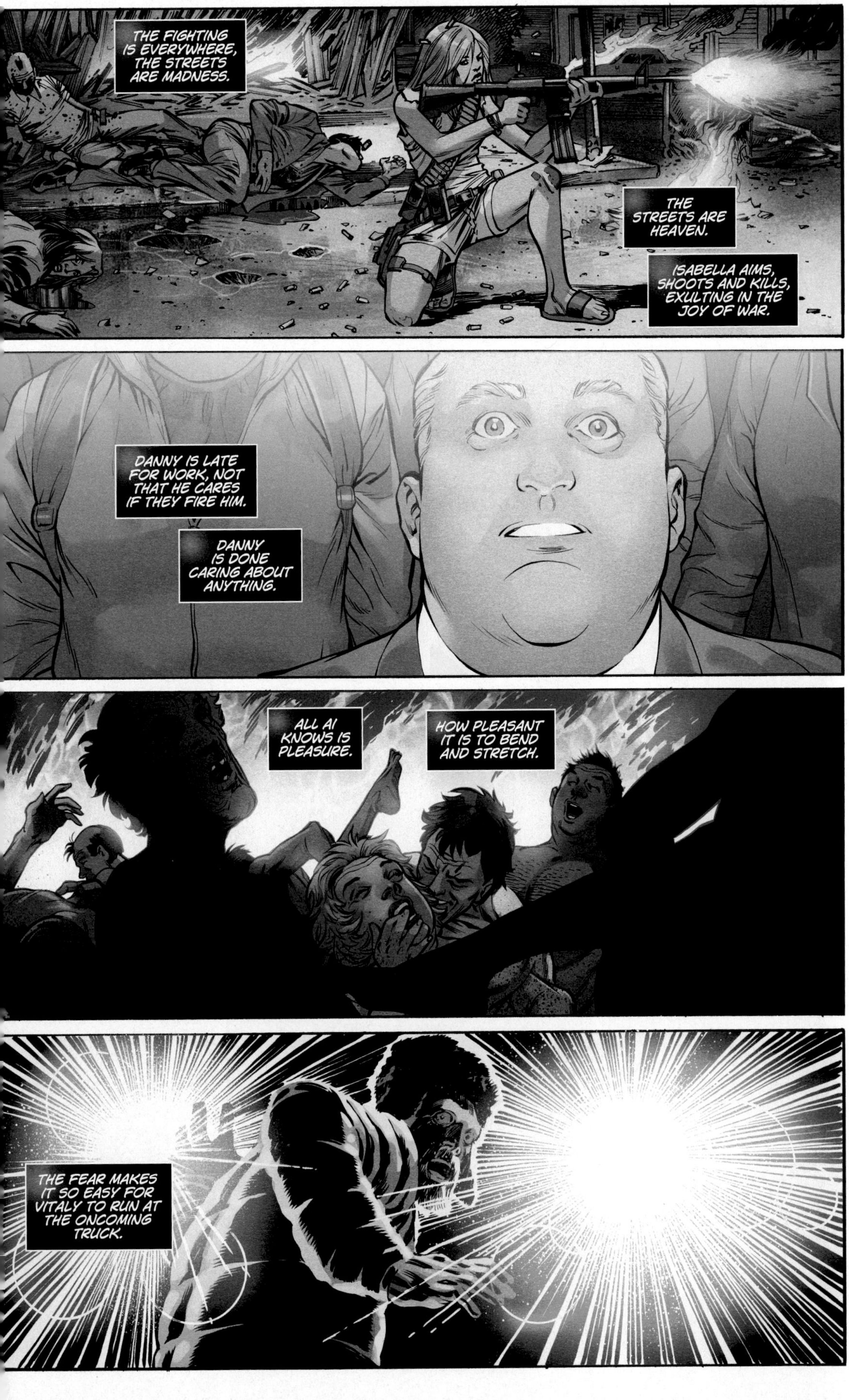
THE FIGHTING IS EVERYWHERE, THE STREETS ARE MADNESS.
THE STREETS ARE HEAVEN.
ISABELLA AIMS, SHOOTS AND KILLS, EXULTING IN THE JOY OF WAR.
DANNY IS LATE FOR WORK, NOT THAT HE CARES IF THEY FIRE HIM.
DANNY IS DONE CARING ABOUT ANYTHING.
ALL AI KNOWS IS PLEASURE.
HOW PLEASANT IT IS TO BEND AND STRETCH.
THE FEAR MAKES IT SO EASY FOR VITALY TO RUN AT THE ONCOMING TRUCK.

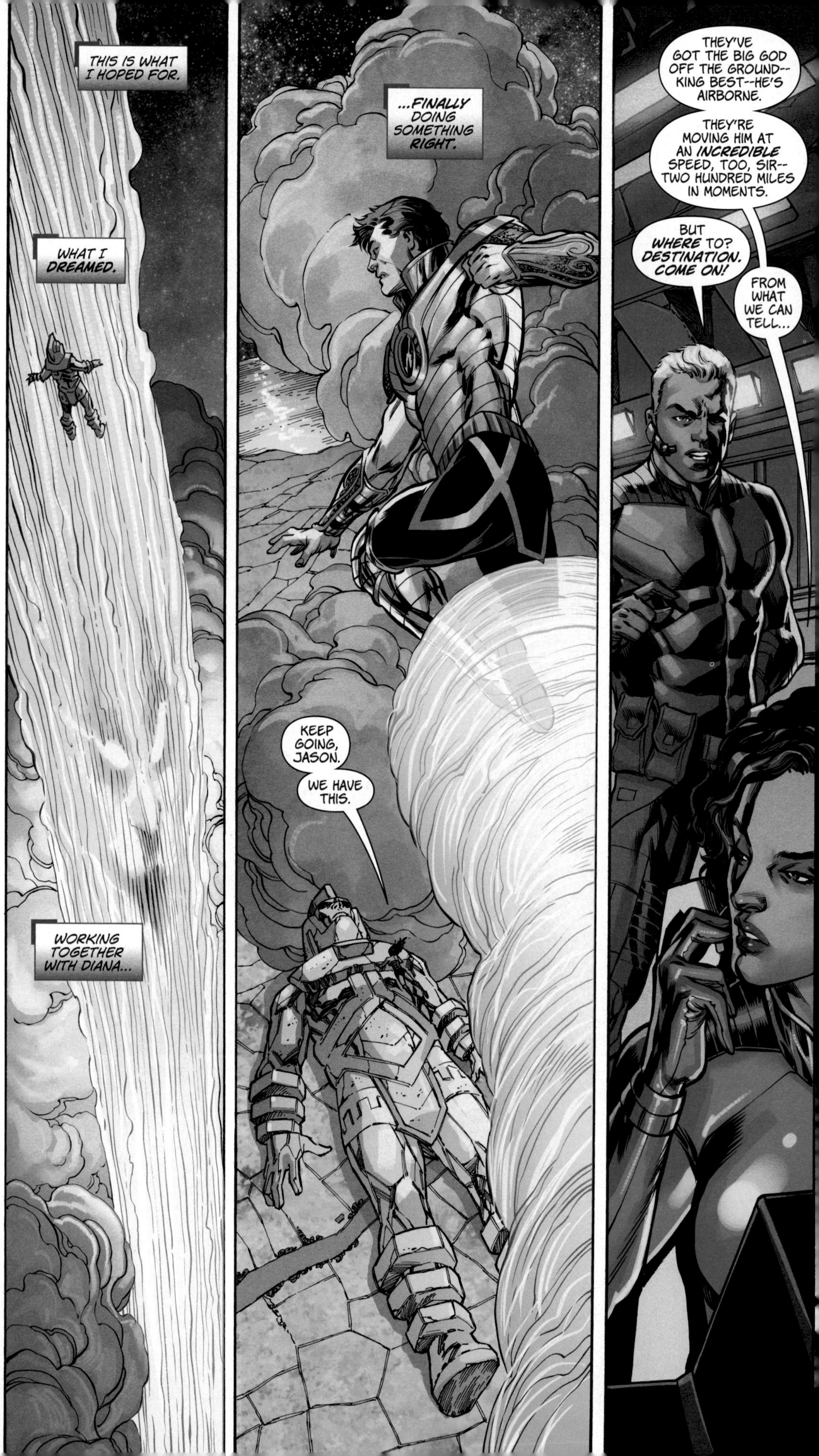
THIS IS WHAT I HOPED FOR.
WHAT I DREAMED.
WORKING TOGETHER WITH DIANA...
...FINALLY DOING SOMETHING RIGHT.
KEEP GOING, JASON.
WE HAVE THIS.
THEY'VE GOT THE BIG GOD OFF THE GROUND--KING BEST--HE'S AIRBORNE.
THEY'RE MOVING HIM AT AN INCREDIBLE SPEED, TOO, SIR--TWO HUNDRED MILES IN MOMENTS.
BUT WHERE TO? DESTINATION. COME ON!
FROM WHAT WE CAN TELL...

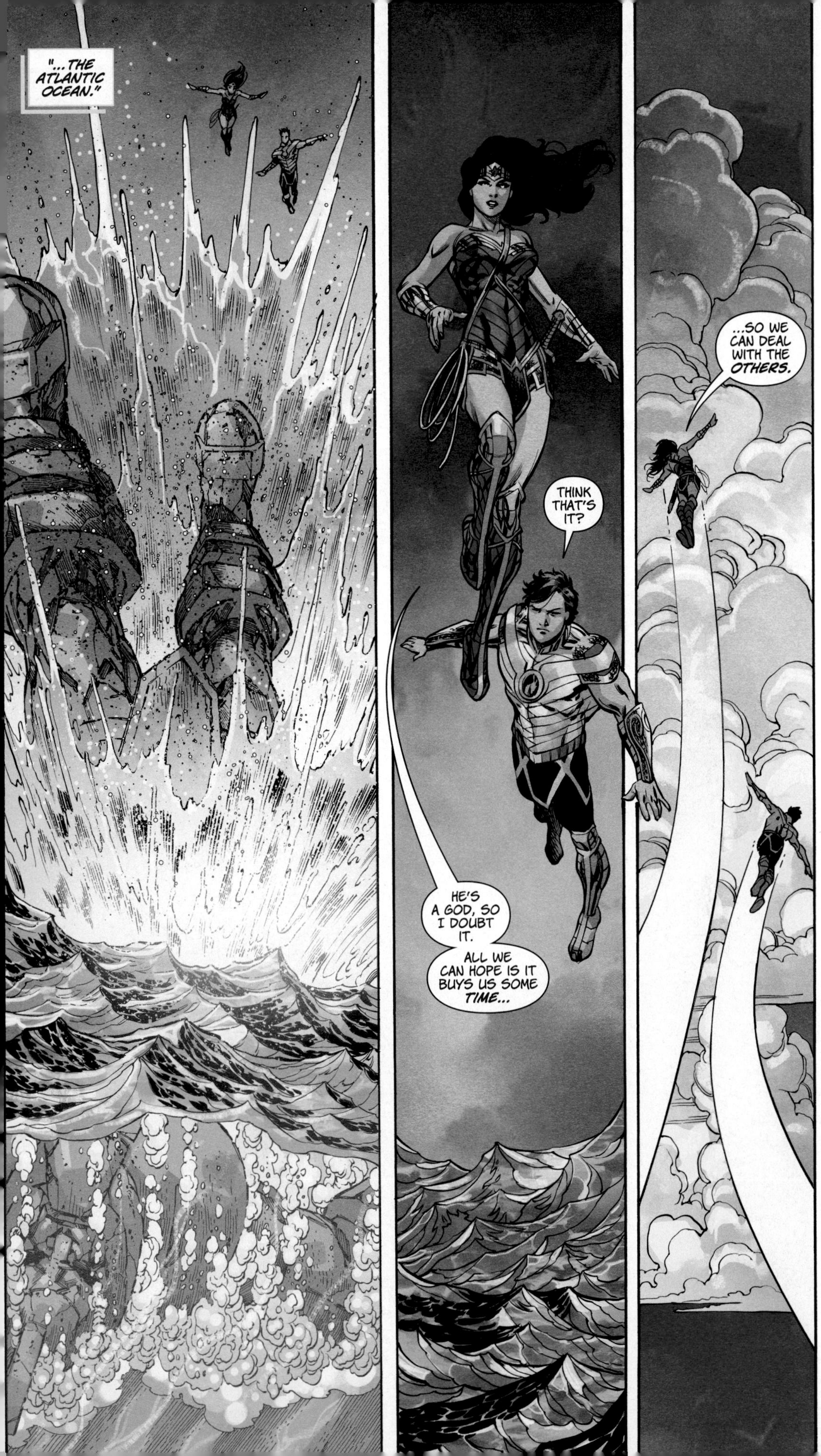
"...THE ATLANTIC OCEAN."
THINK THAT'S IT?
HE'S A GOD, SO I DOUBT IT.
ALL WE CAN HOPE IS IT BUYS US SOME *TIME*...
...SO WE CAN DEAL WITH THE *OTHERS*.

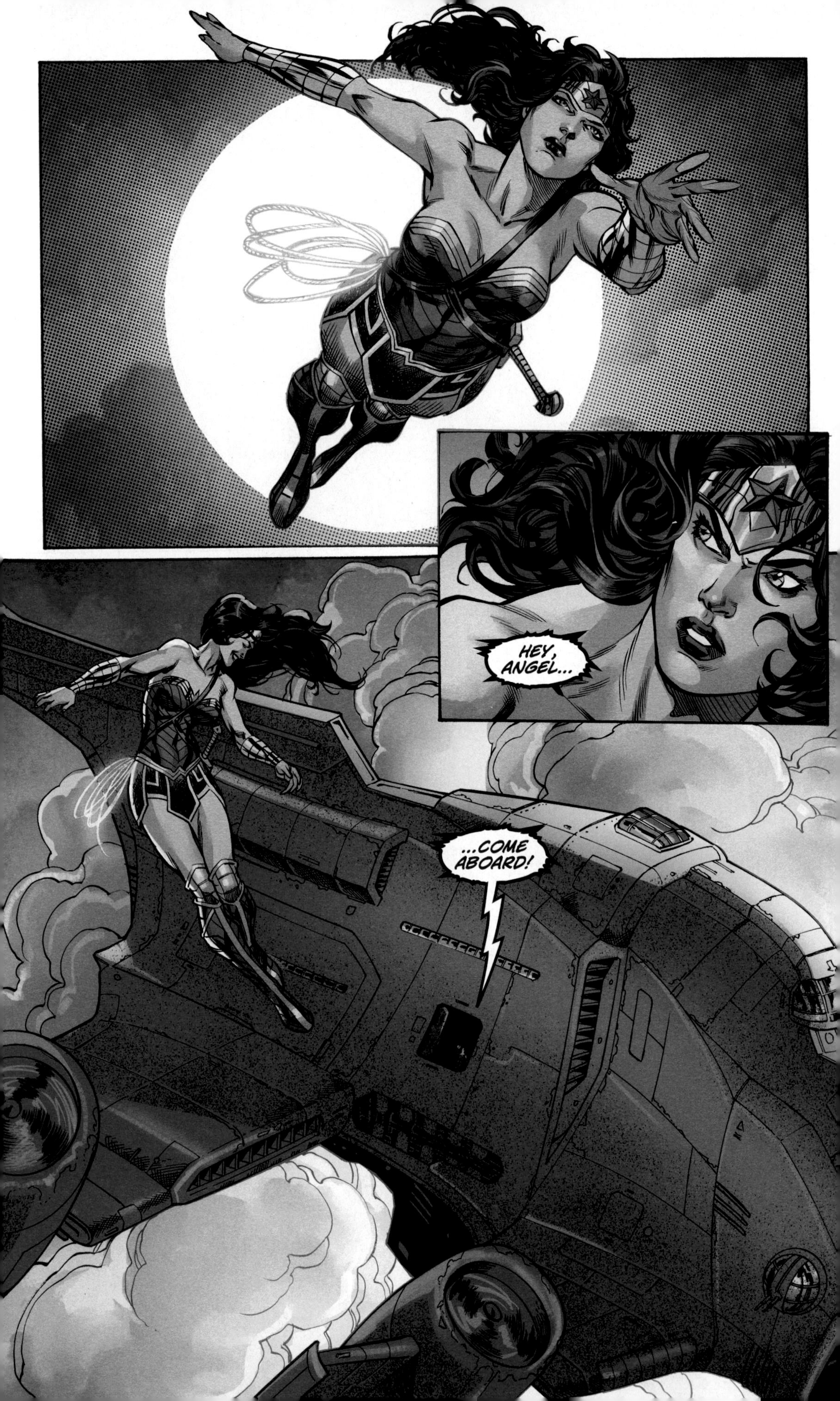
HEY, ANGEL...
...COME ABOARD!

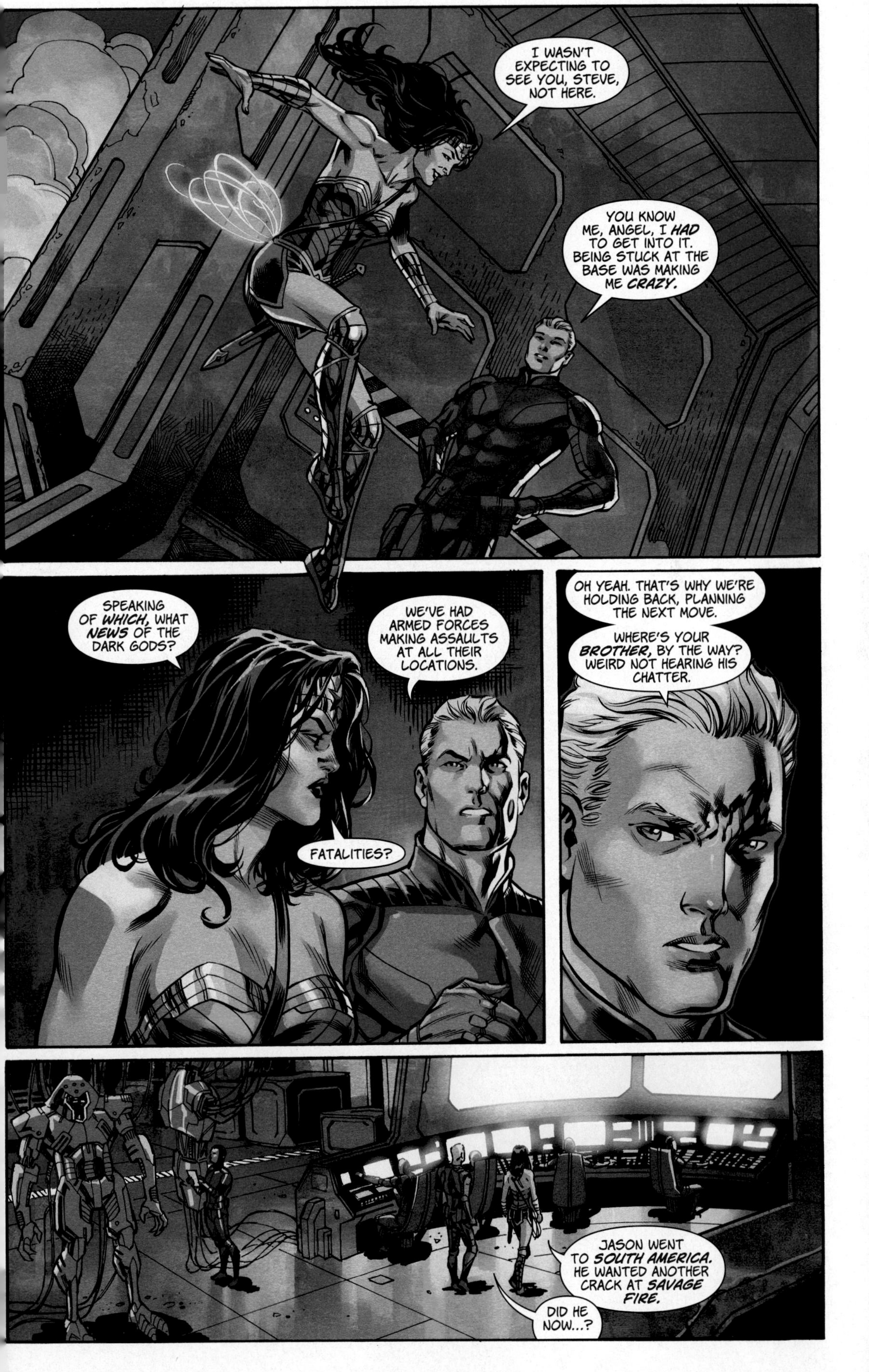
I WASN'T EXPECTING TO SEE YOU, STEVE, NOT HERE.
YOU KNOW ME, ANGEL, I HAD TO GET INTO IT. BEING STUCK AT THE BASE WAS MAKING ME CRAZY.
SPEAKING OF WHICH, WHAT NEWS OF THE DARK GODS?
WE'VE HAD ARMED FORCES MAKING ASSAULTS AT ALL THEIR LOCATIONS.
FATALITIES?
OH YEAH. THAT'S WHY WE'RE HOLDING BACK, PLANNING THE NEXT MOVE.
WHERE'S YOUR BROTHER, BY THE WAY? WEIRD NOT HEARING HIS CHATTER.
JASON WENT TO SOUTH AMERICA. HE WANTED ANOTHER CRACK AT SAVAGE FIRE.
DID HE NOW...?

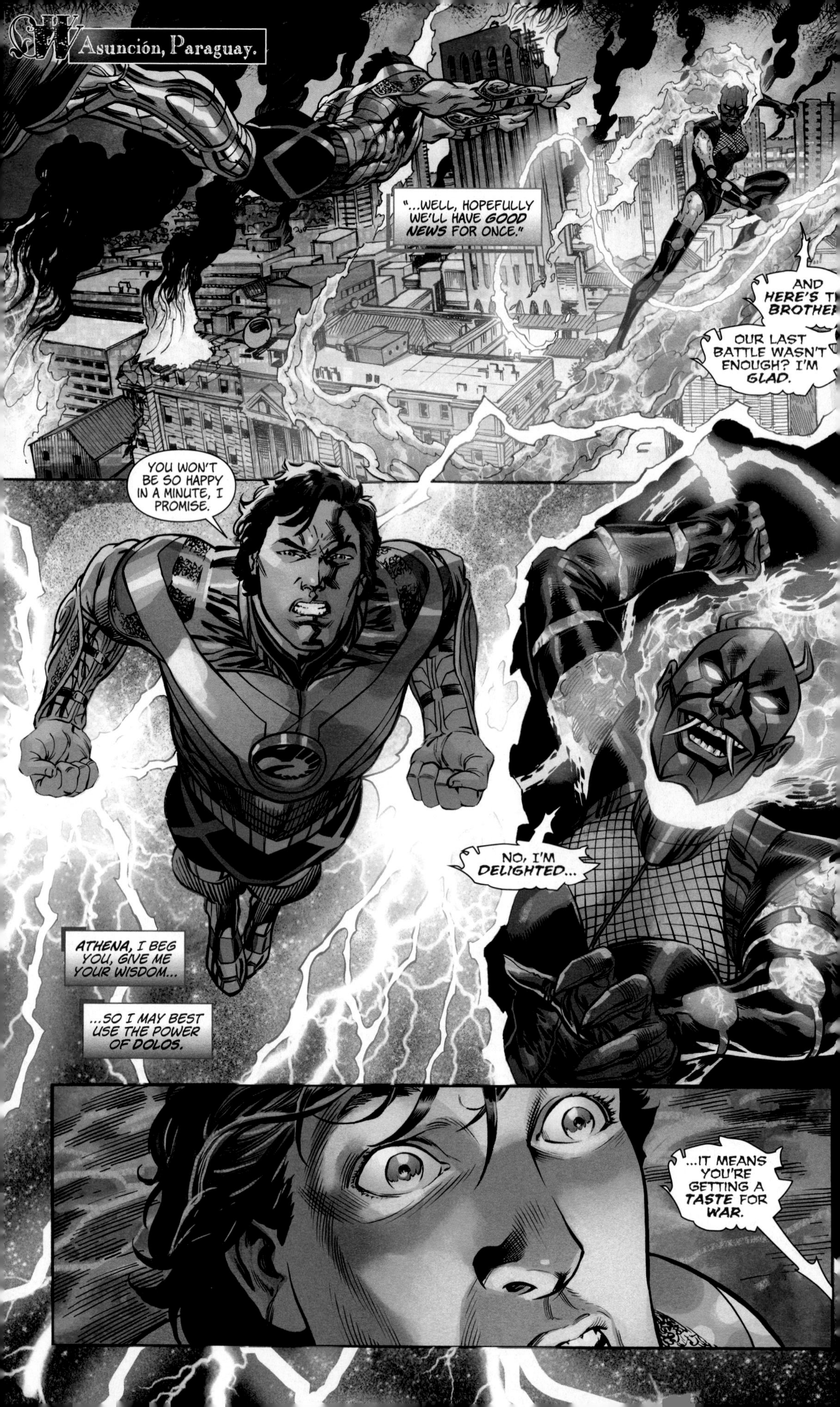
Asunción, Paraguay.
"...WELL, HOPEFULLY WE'LL HAVE GOOD NEWS FOR ONCE."
AND HERE'S TH BROTHER
OUR LAST BATTLE WASN'T ENOUGH? I'M GLAD.
YOU WON'T BE SO HAPPY IN A MINUTE, I PROMISE.
NO, I'M DELIGHTED...
ATHENA, I BEG YOU, GIVE ME YOUR WISDOM...
...SO I MAY BEST USE THE POWER OF DOLOS.
...IT MEANS YOU'RE GETTING A TASTE FOR WAR.

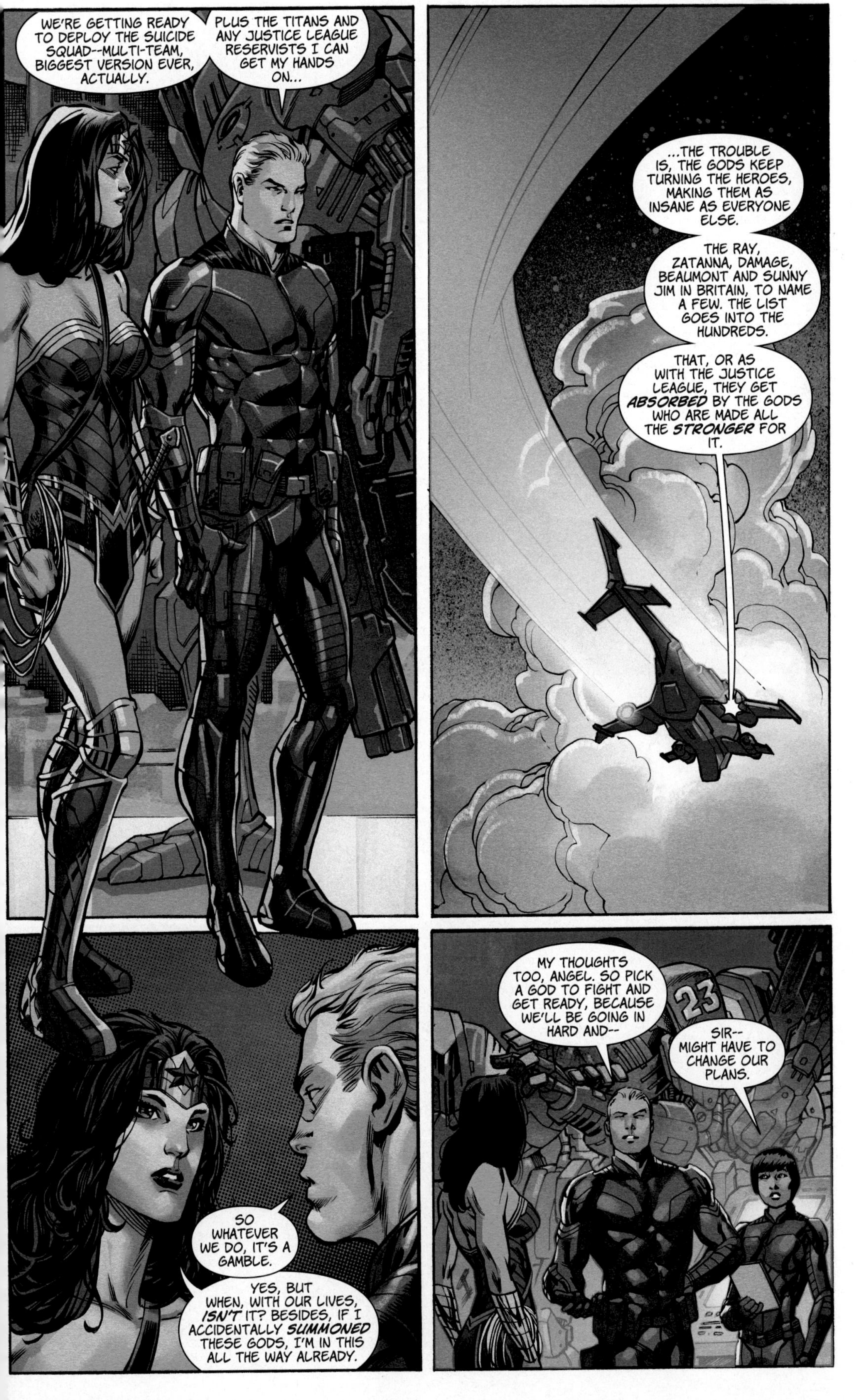
WE'RE GETTING READY TO DEPLOY THE SUICIDE SQUAD--MULTI-TEAM, BIGGEST VERSION EVER, ACTUALLY.
PLUS THE TITANS AND ANY JUSTICE LEAGUE RESERVISTS I CAN GET MY HANDS ON...
...THE TROUBLE IS, THE GODS KEEP TURNING THE HEROES, MAKING THEM AS INSANE AS EVERYONE ELSE.
THE RAY, ZATANNA, DAMAGE, BEAUMONT AND SUNNY JIM IN BRITAIN, TO NAME A FEW. THE LIST GOES INTO THE HUNDREDS.
THAT, OR AS WITH THE JUSTICE LEAGUE, THEY GET ABSORBED BY THE GODS WHO ARE MADE ALL THE STRONGER FOR IT.
SO WHATEVER WE DO, IT'S A GAMBLE.
YES, BUT WHEN, WITH OUR LIVES, ISN'T IT? BESIDES, IF I ACCIDENTALLY SUMMONED THESE GODS, I'M IN THIS ALL THE WAY ALREADY.
MY THOUGHTS TOO, ANGEL. SO PICK A GOD TO FIGHT AND GET READY, BECAUSE WE'LL BE GOING IN HARD AND--
23
SIR-- MIGHT HAVE TO CHANGE OUR PLANS.

THE DARK GOD JUST *VANISHED.*

WHAT?

ALL OF THEM, LIKE GHOSTS. *GONE.* NO LONGER AT ANY OF THEIR PRIOR LOCATIONS.

NO, *WAIT.* NEW SIGHTINGS, SIR. *CONFIRMED.*

THEY'RE ALL TOGETHER IN *ONE PLACE--* INCLUDING KING BEST-- THE SKIES OVER *PARAGUAY.*

JASON.

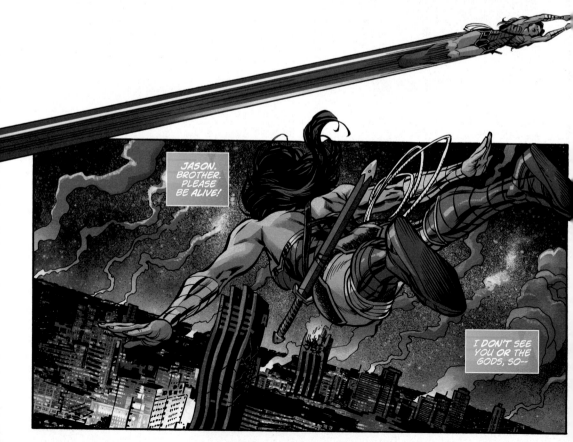

JASON. BROTHER. PLEASE BE ALIVE!

I DON'T SEE YOU OR THE GODS, SO--

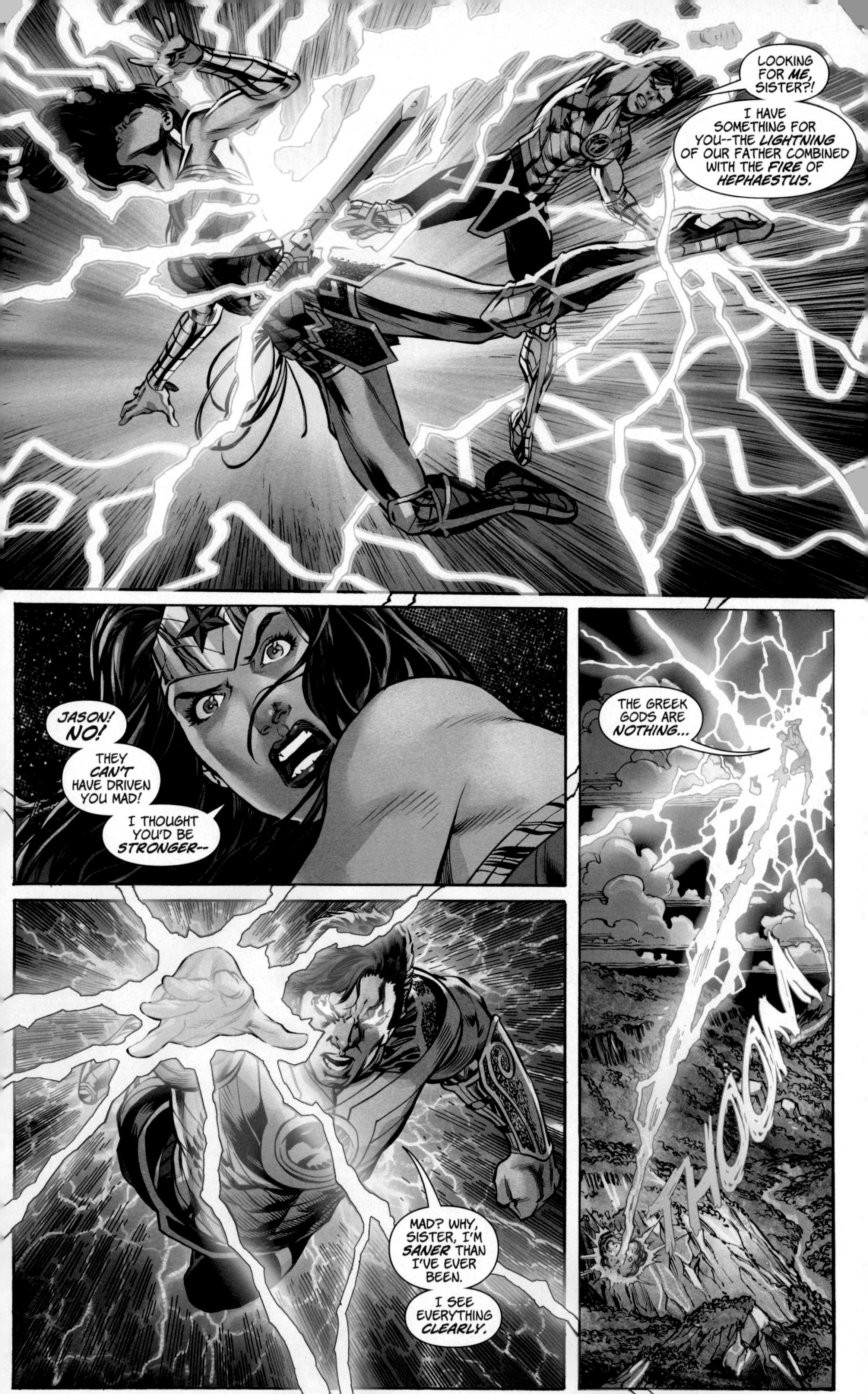

LOOKING FOR ME, SISTER?!
I HAVE SOMETHING FOR YOU--THE LIGHTNING OF OUR FATHER COMBINED WITH THE FIRE OF HEPHAESTUS.
JASON! NO!
THEY CAN'T HAVE DRIVEN YOU MAD!
I THOUGHT YOU'D BE STRONGER--
MAD? WHY, SISTER, I'M SANER THAN I'VE EVER BEEN.
I SEE EVERYTHING CLEARLY.
THE GREEK GODS ARE NOTHING...
THOOOM

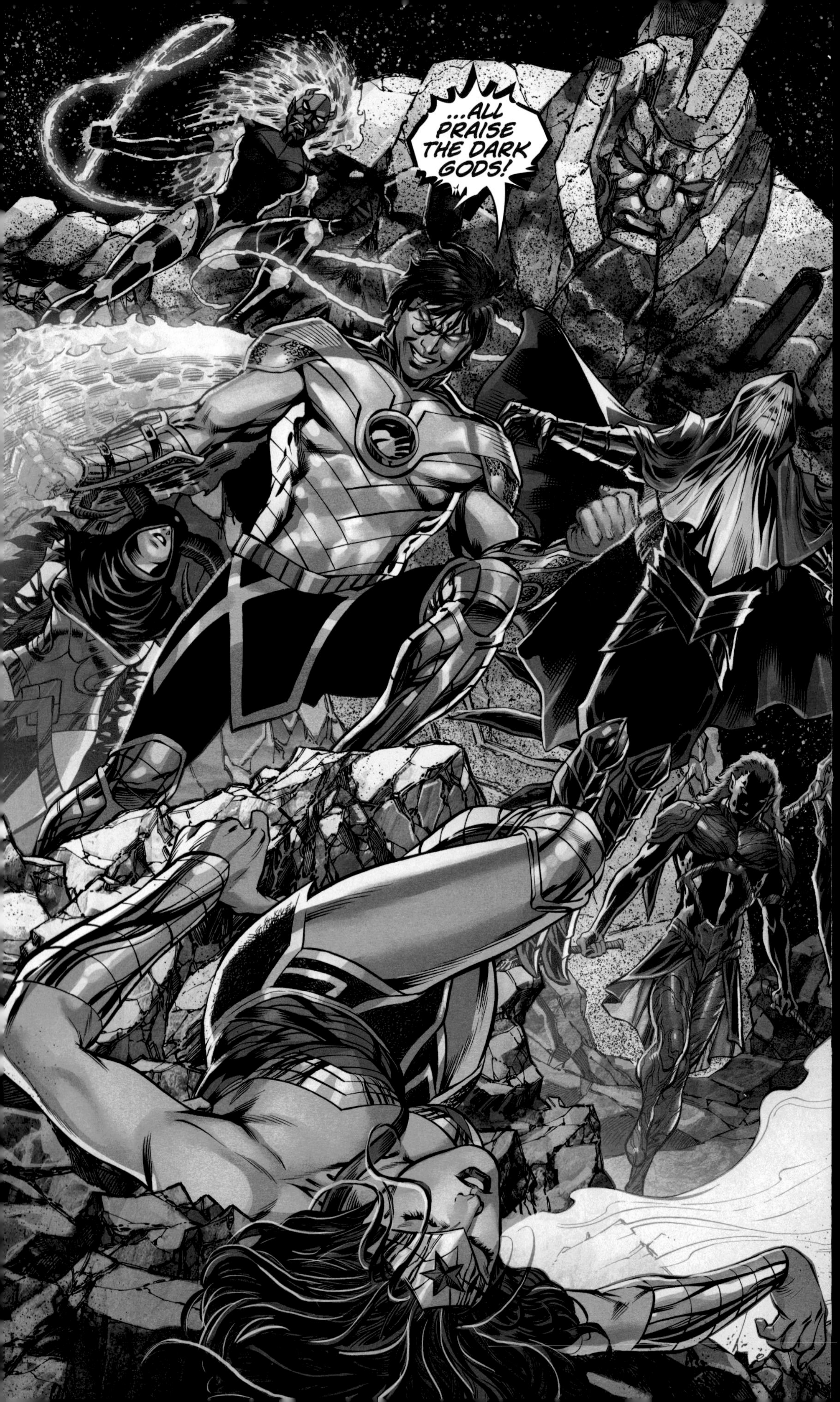
...ALL PRAISE THE DARK GODS!

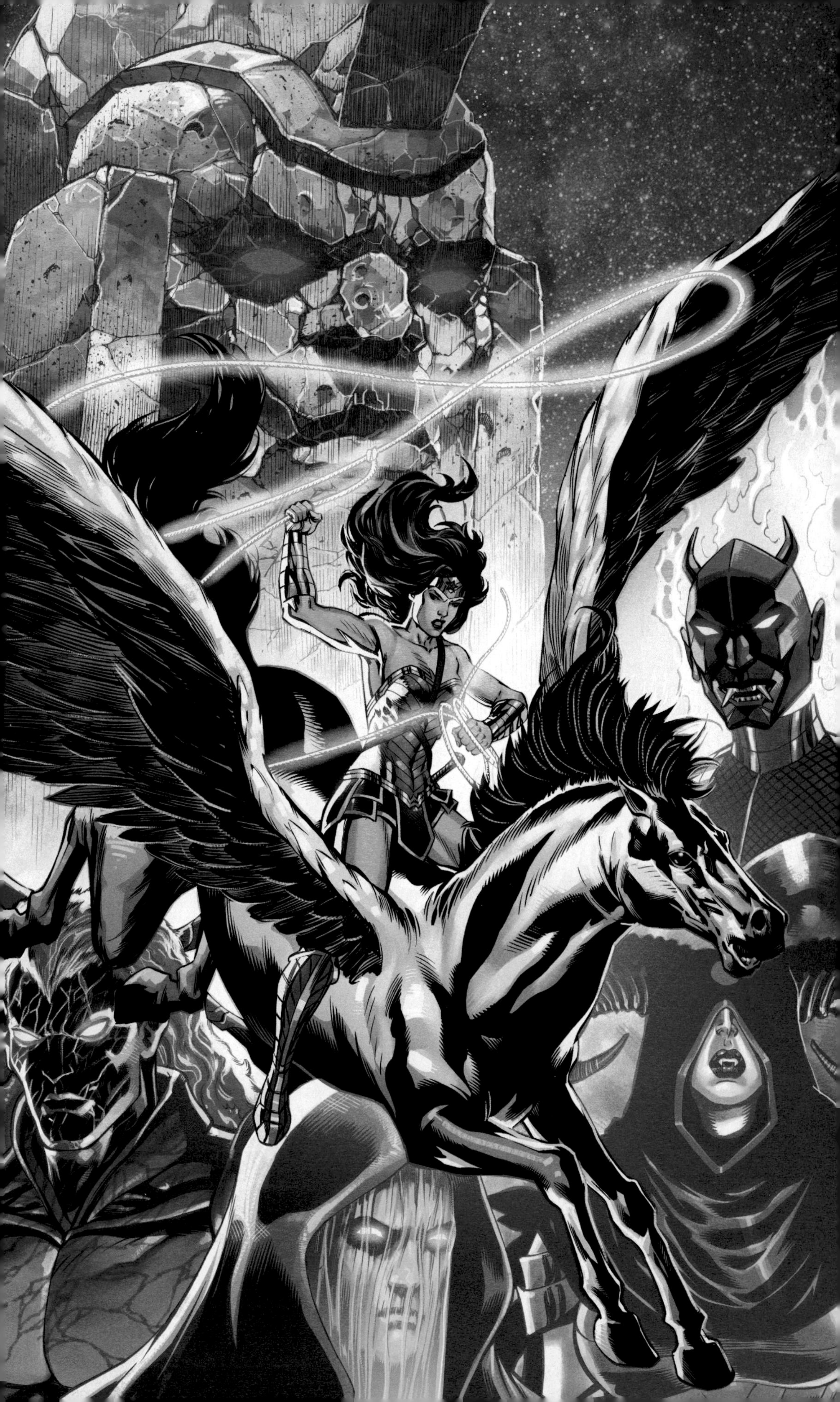

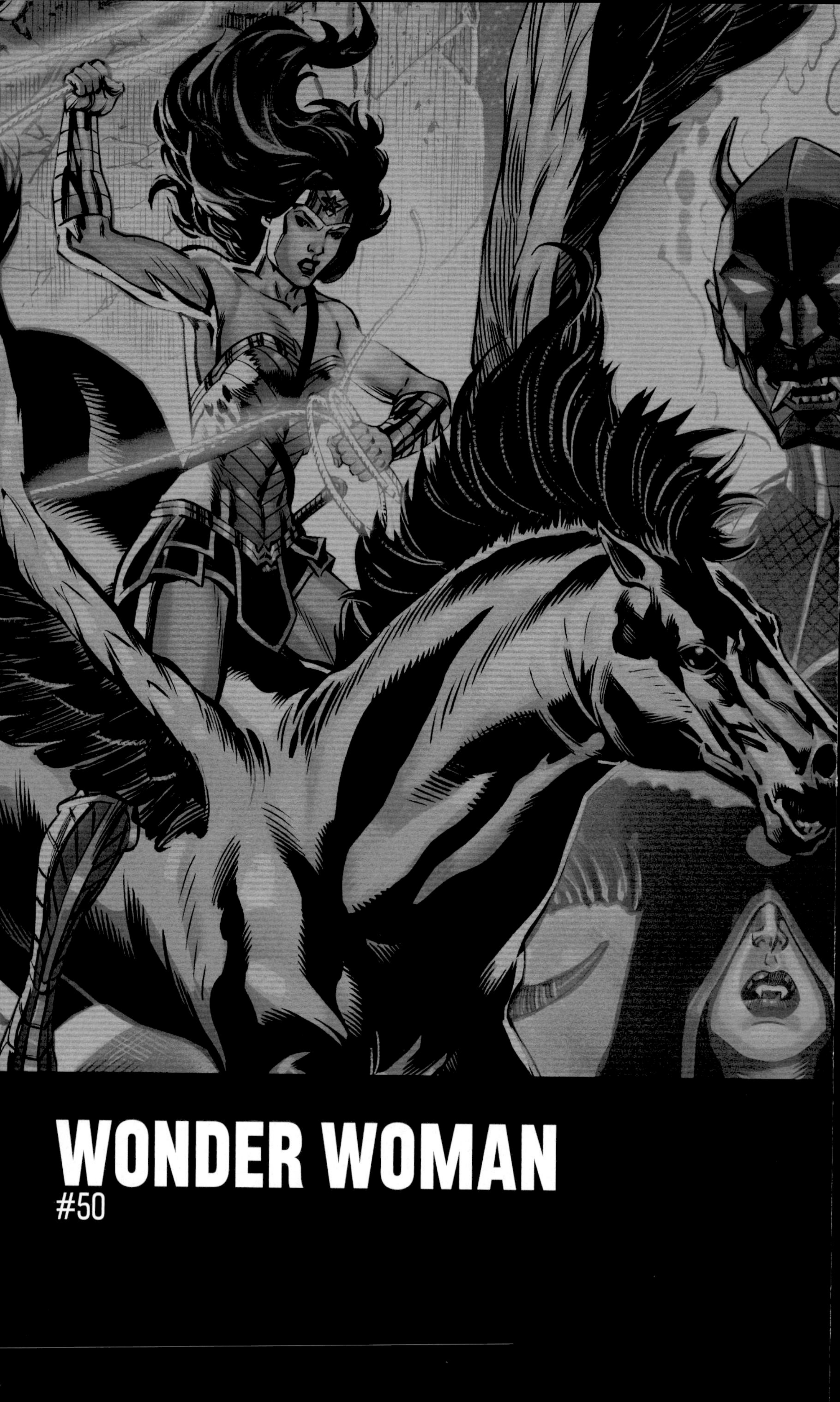

WONDER WOMAN
#50

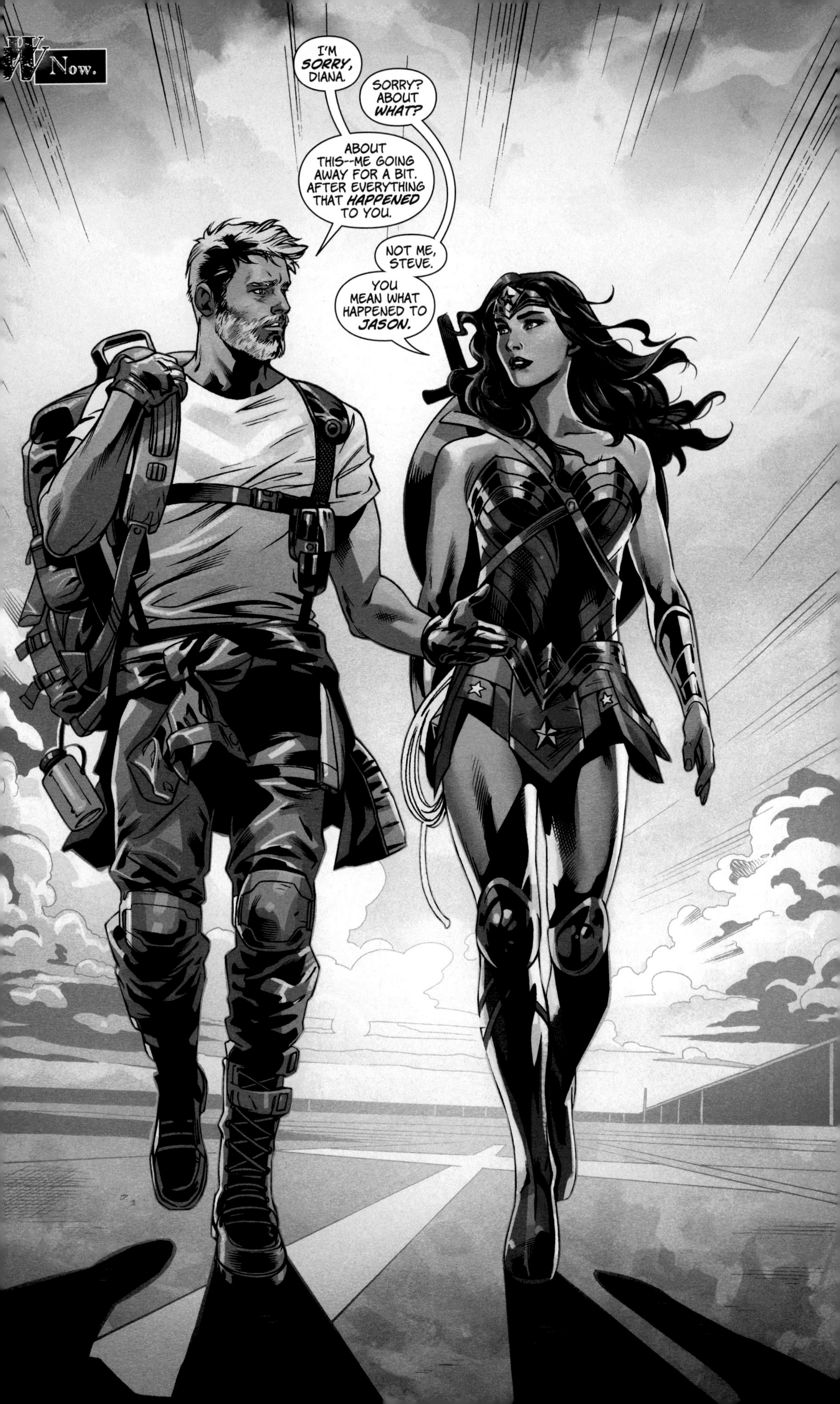
Now.
I'M SORRY, DIANA.
SORRY? ABOUT WHAT?
ABOUT THIS--ME GOING AWAY FOR A BIT. AFTER EVERYTHING THAT HAPPENED TO YOU.
NOT ME, STEVE.
YOU MEAN WHAT HAPPENED TO JASON.

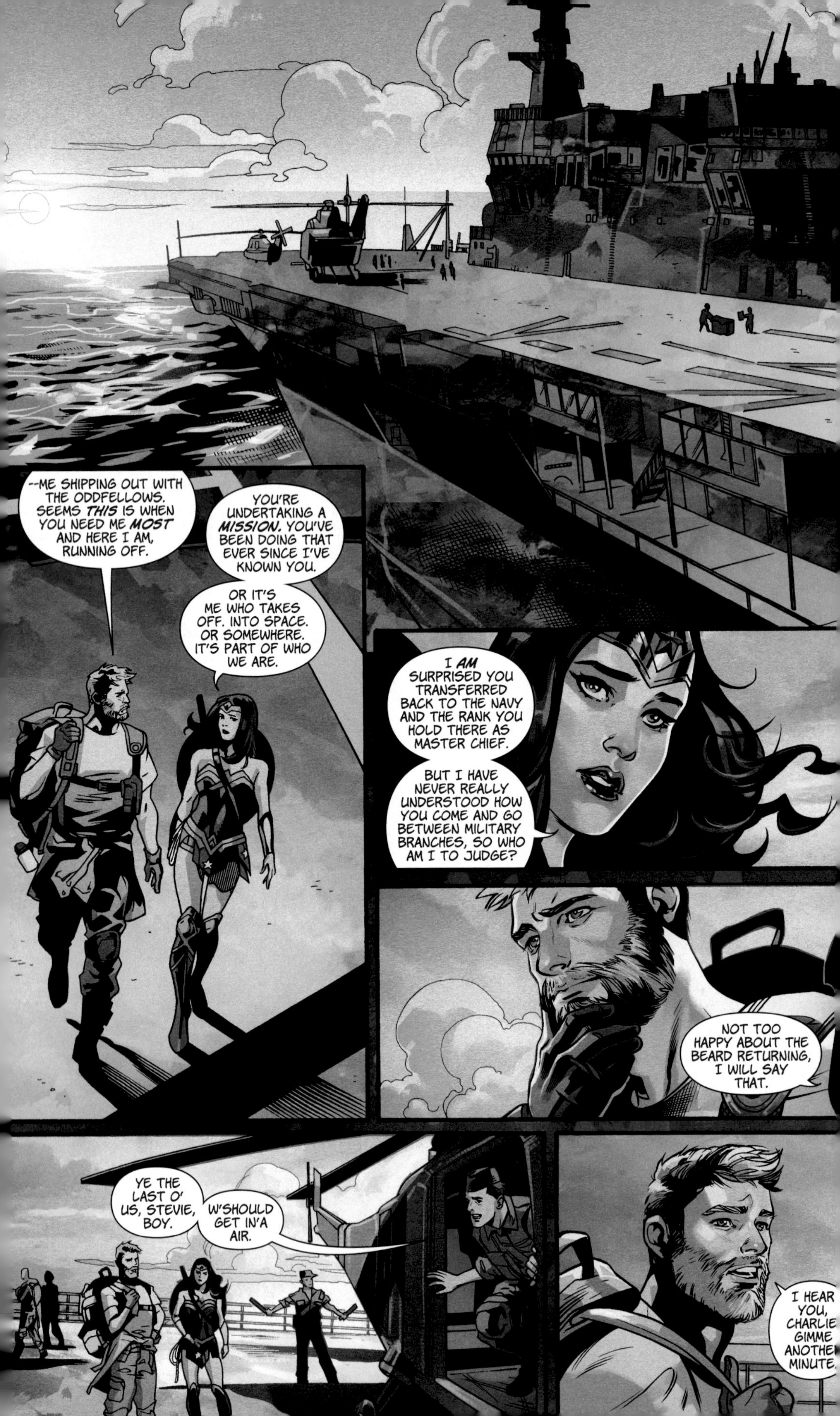
--ME SHIPPING OUT WITH THE ODDFELLOWS. SEEMS *THIS* IS WHEN YOU NEED ME *MOST* AND HERE I AM, RUNNING OFF.
YOU'RE UNDERTAKING A *MISSION.* YOU'VE BEEN DOING THAT EVER SINCE I'VE KNOWN YOU.
OR IT'S ME WHO TAKES OFF. INTO SPACE. OR SOMEWHERE. IT'S PART OF WHO WE ARE.
I *AM* SURPRISED YOU TRANSFERRED BACK TO THE NAVY AND THE RANK YOU HOLD THERE AS MASTER CHIEF.
BUT I HAVE NEVER REALLY UNDERSTOOD HOW YOU COME AND GO BETWEEN MILITARY BRANCHES, SO WHO AM I TO JUDGE?
NOT TOO HAPPY ABOUT THE BEARD RETURNING, I WILL SAY THAT.
YE THE LAST O' US, STEVIE, BOY.
W'SHOULD GET IN'A AIR.
I HEAR YOU, CHARLIE GIMME ANOTHE MINUTE

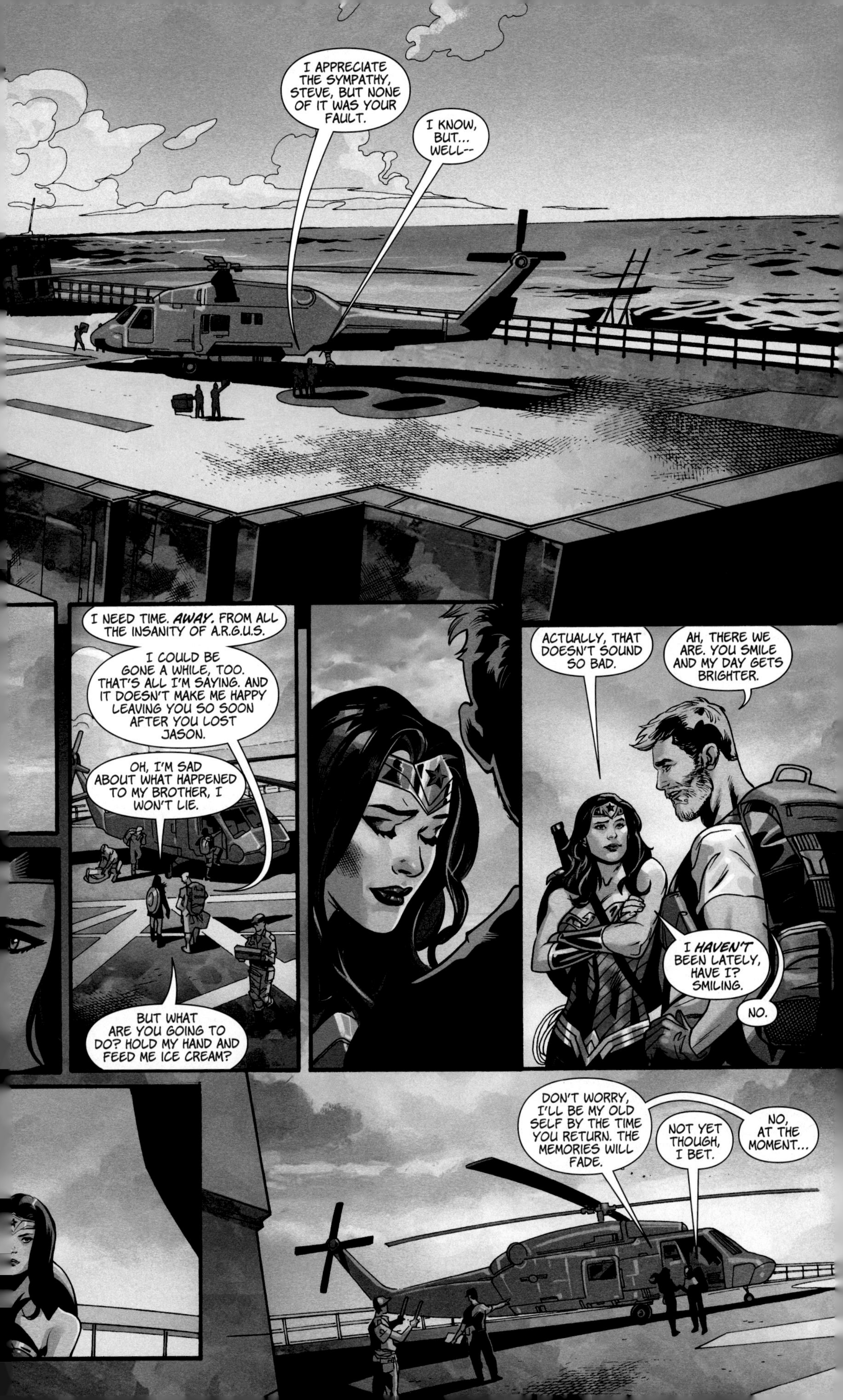
I APPRECIATE THE SYMPATHY, STEVE, BUT NONE OF IT WAS YOUR FAULT.
I KNOW, BUT... WELL--
I NEED TIME. AWAY. FROM ALL THE INSANITY OF A.R.G.U.S.
I COULD BE GONE A WHILE, TOO. THAT'S ALL I'M SAYING. AND IT DOESN'T MAKE ME HAPPY LEAVING YOU SO SOON AFTER YOU LOST JASON.
OH, I'M SAD ABOUT WHAT HAPPENED TO MY BROTHER, I WON'T LIE.
BUT WHAT ARE YOU GOING TO DO? HOLD MY HAND AND FEED ME ICE CREAM?
ACTUALLY, THAT DOESN'T SOUND SO BAD.
AH, THERE WE ARE. YOU SMILE AND MY DAY GETS BRIGHTER.
I HAVEN'T BEEN LATELY, HAVE I? SMILING.
NO.
DON'T WORRY, I'LL BE MY OLD SELF BY THE TIME YOU RETURN. THE MEMORIES WILL FADE.
NOT YET THOUGH, I BET.
NO, AT THE MOMENT...

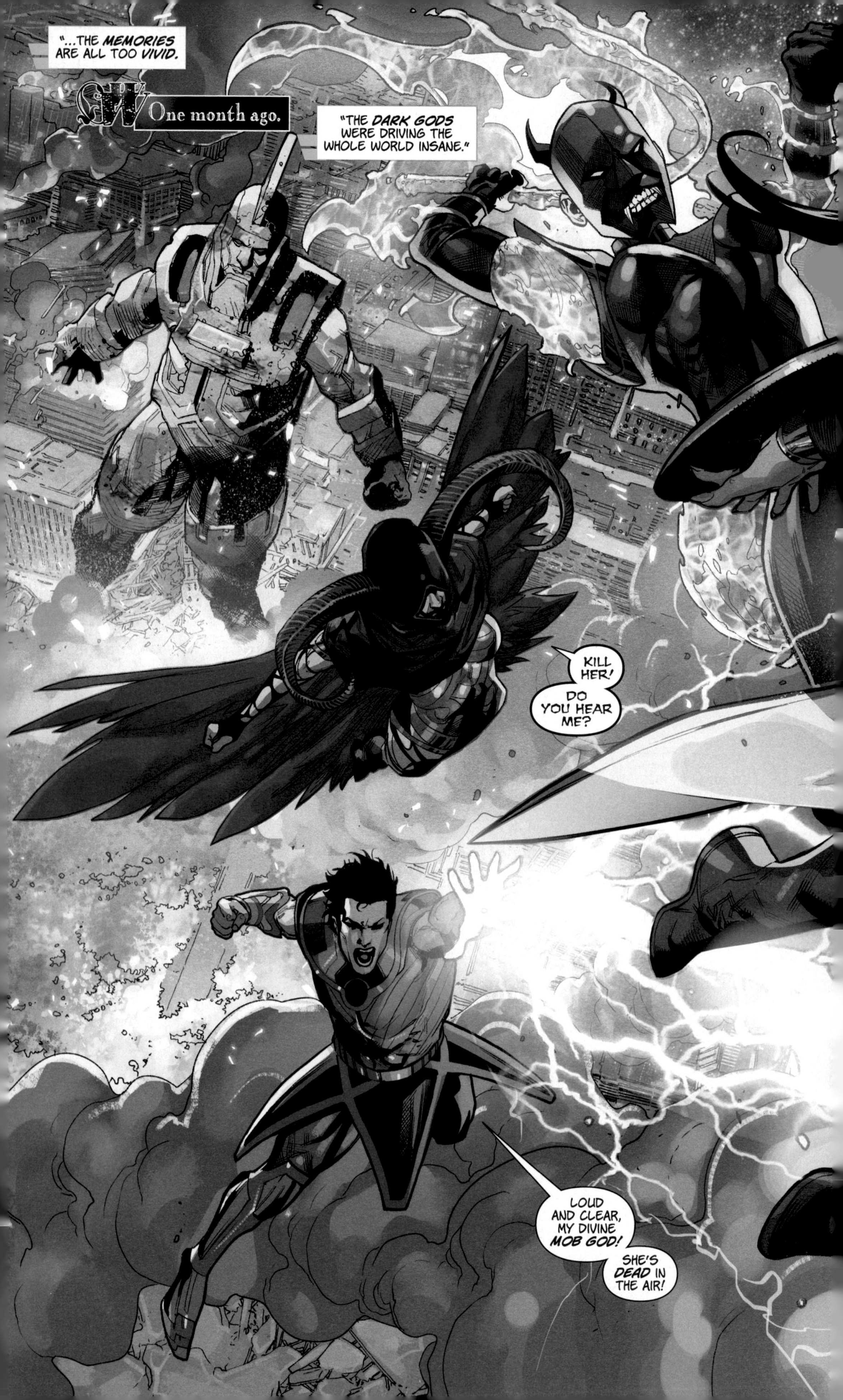
"...THE MEMORIES ARE ALL TOO VIVID.
One month ago.
"THE DARK GODS WERE DRIVING THE WHOLE WORLD INSANE."
KILL HER!
DO YOU HEAR ME?
LOUD AND CLEAR, MY DIVINE MOB GOD!
SHE'S DEAD IN THE AIR!

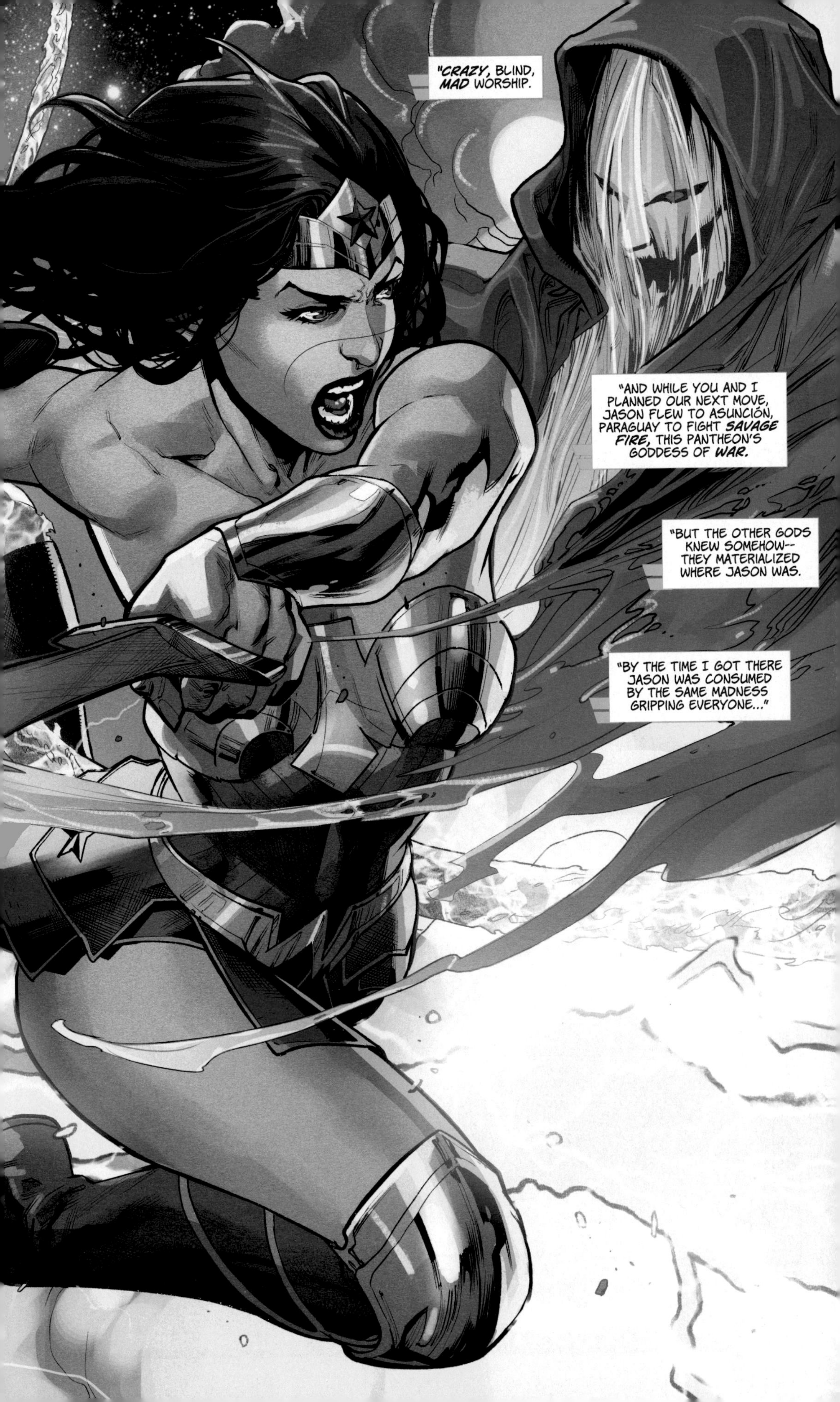
"CRAZY, BLIND, MAD WORSHIP.
"AND WHILE YOU AND I PLANNED OUR NEXT MOVE, JASON FLEW TO ASUNCIÓN, PARAGUAY TO FIGHT SAVAGE FIRE, THIS PANTHEON'S GODDESS OF WAR.
"BUT THE OTHER GODS KNEW SOMEHOW--THEY MATERIALIZED WHERE JASON WAS.
"BY THE TIME I GOT THERE JASON WAS CONSUMED BY THE SAME MADNESS GRIPPING EVERYONE..."

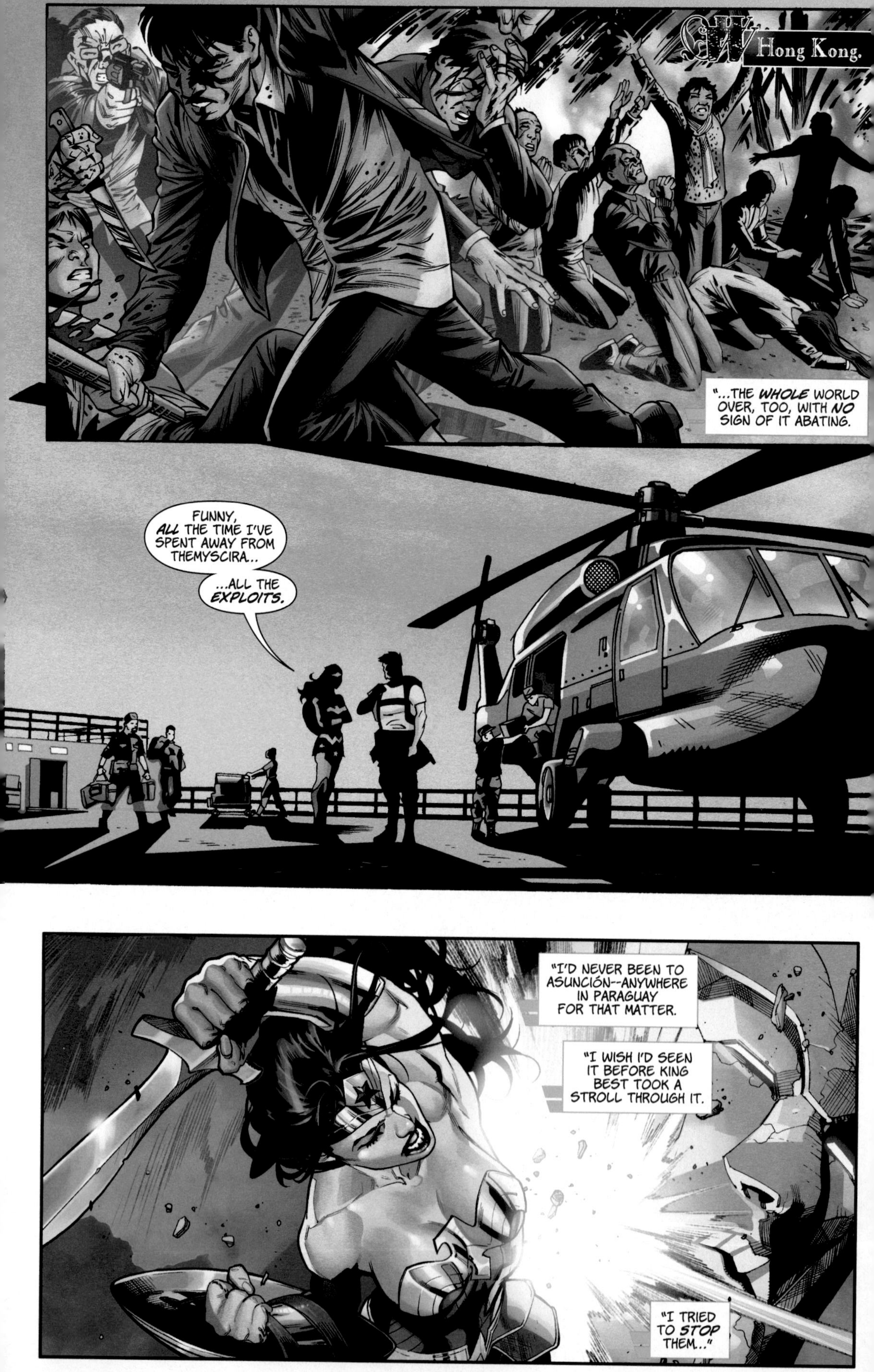
Hong Kong.
"...THE WHOLE WORLD OVER, TOO, WITH NO SIGN OF IT ABATING.
FUNNY, ALL THE TIME I'VE SPENT AWAY FROM THEMYSCIRA...
...ALL THE EXPLOITS.
"I'D NEVER BEEN TO ASUNCIÓN--ANYWHERE IN PARAGUAY FOR THAT MATTER.
"I WISH I'D SEEN IT BEFORE KING BEST TOOK A STROLL THROUGH IT.
"I TRIED TO STOP THEM..."

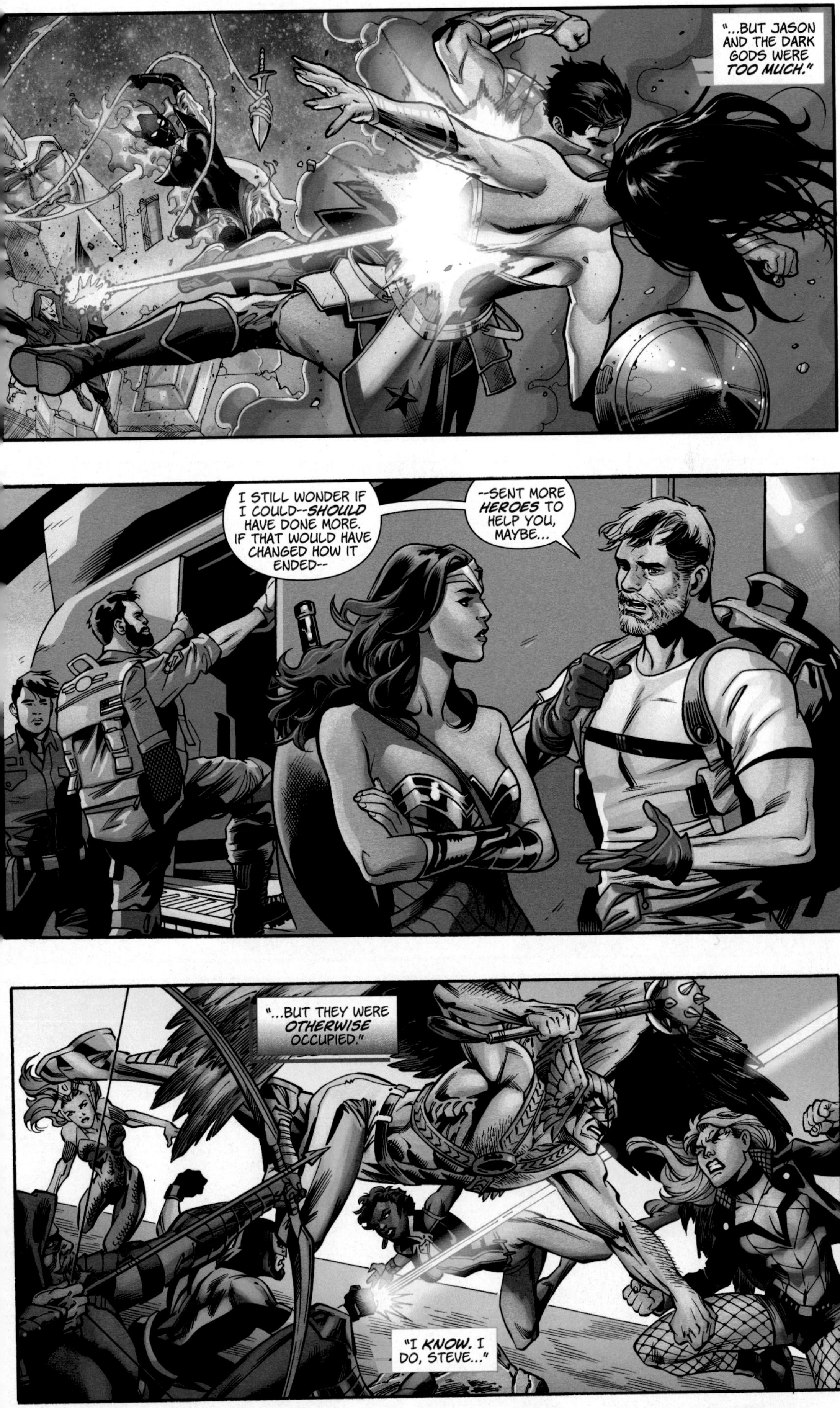

"...BUT JASON AND THE DARK GODS WERE *TOO MUCH*."
I STILL WONDER IF I COULD--***SHOULD*** HAVE DONE MORE. IF THAT WOULD HAVE CHANGED HOW IT ENDED--
--SENT MORE ***HEROES*** TO HELP YOU, MAYBE...
"...BUT THEY WERE ***OTHERWISE*** OCCUPIED."
"I ***KNOW***. I DO, STEVE..."

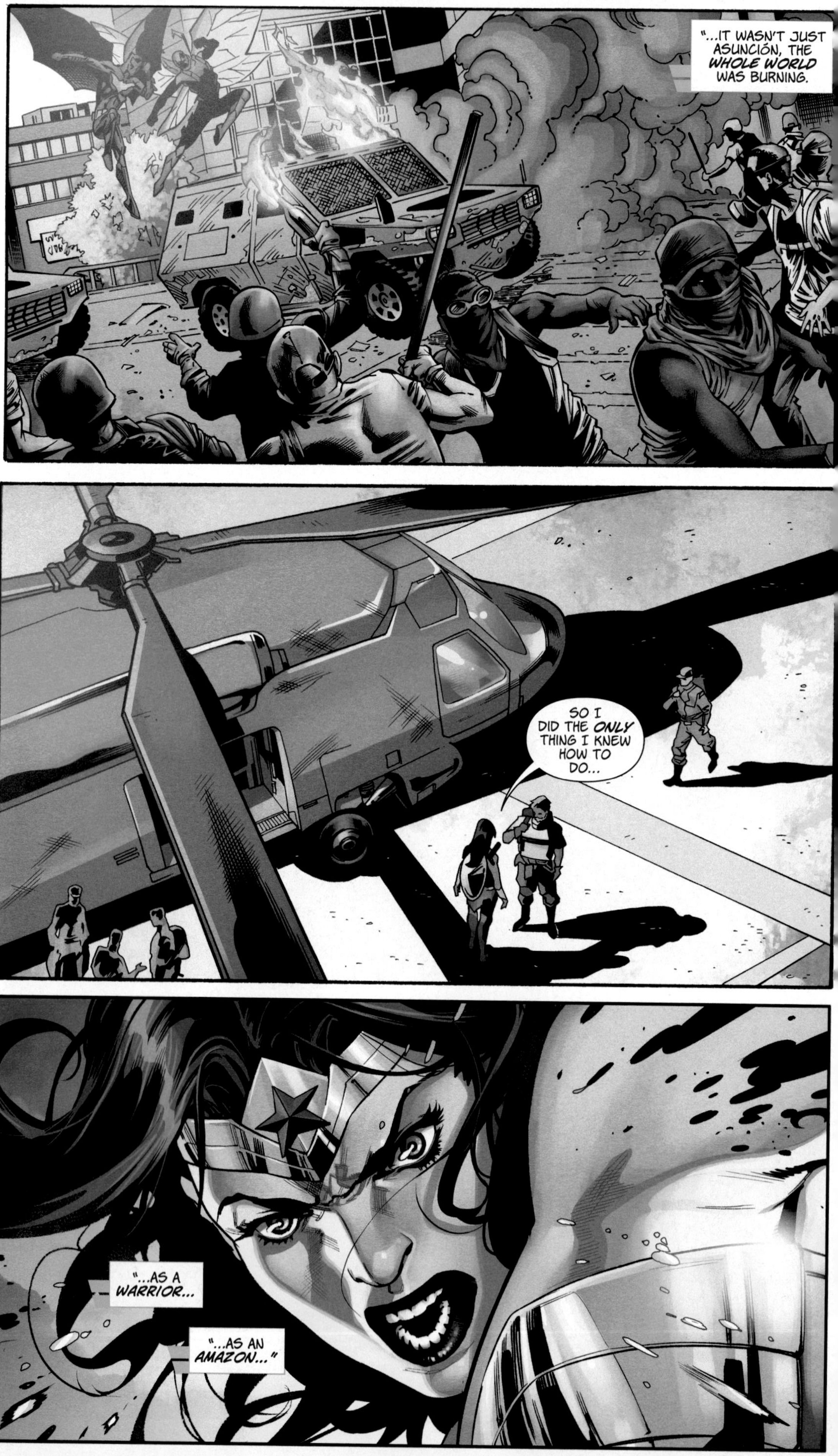
"...IT WASN'T JUST ASUNCIÓN, THE WHOLE WORLD WAS BURNING.
SO I DID THE ONLY THING I KNEW HOW TO DO...
"...AS A WARRIOR...
"...AS AN AMAZON..."

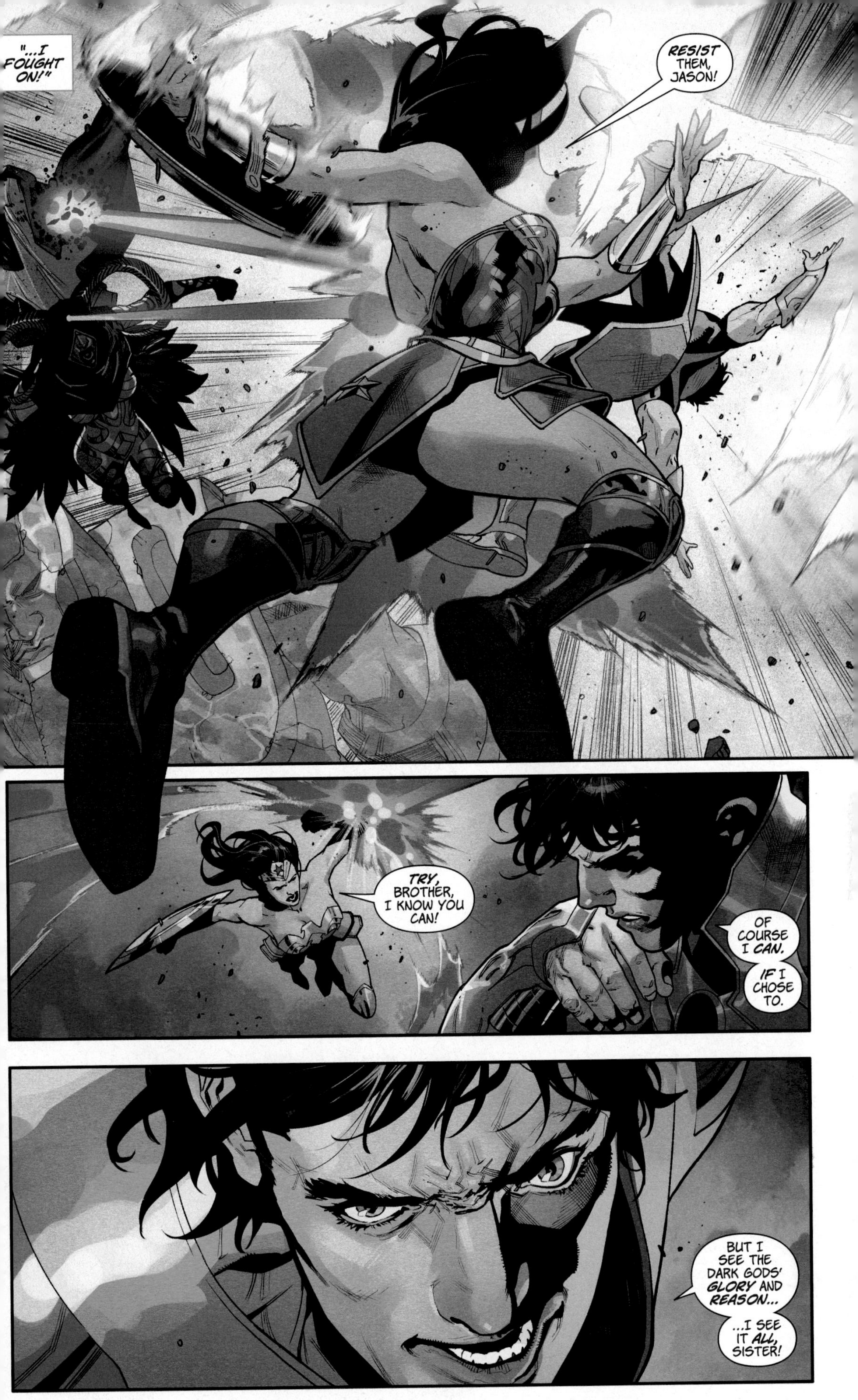

"...I FOUGHT ON!"
RESIST THEM, JASON!
TRY, BROTHER, I KNOW YOU CAN!
OF COURSE I CAN.
IF I CHOSE TO.
BUT I SEE THE DARK GODS' GLORY AND REASON...
...I SEE IT ALL, SISTER!

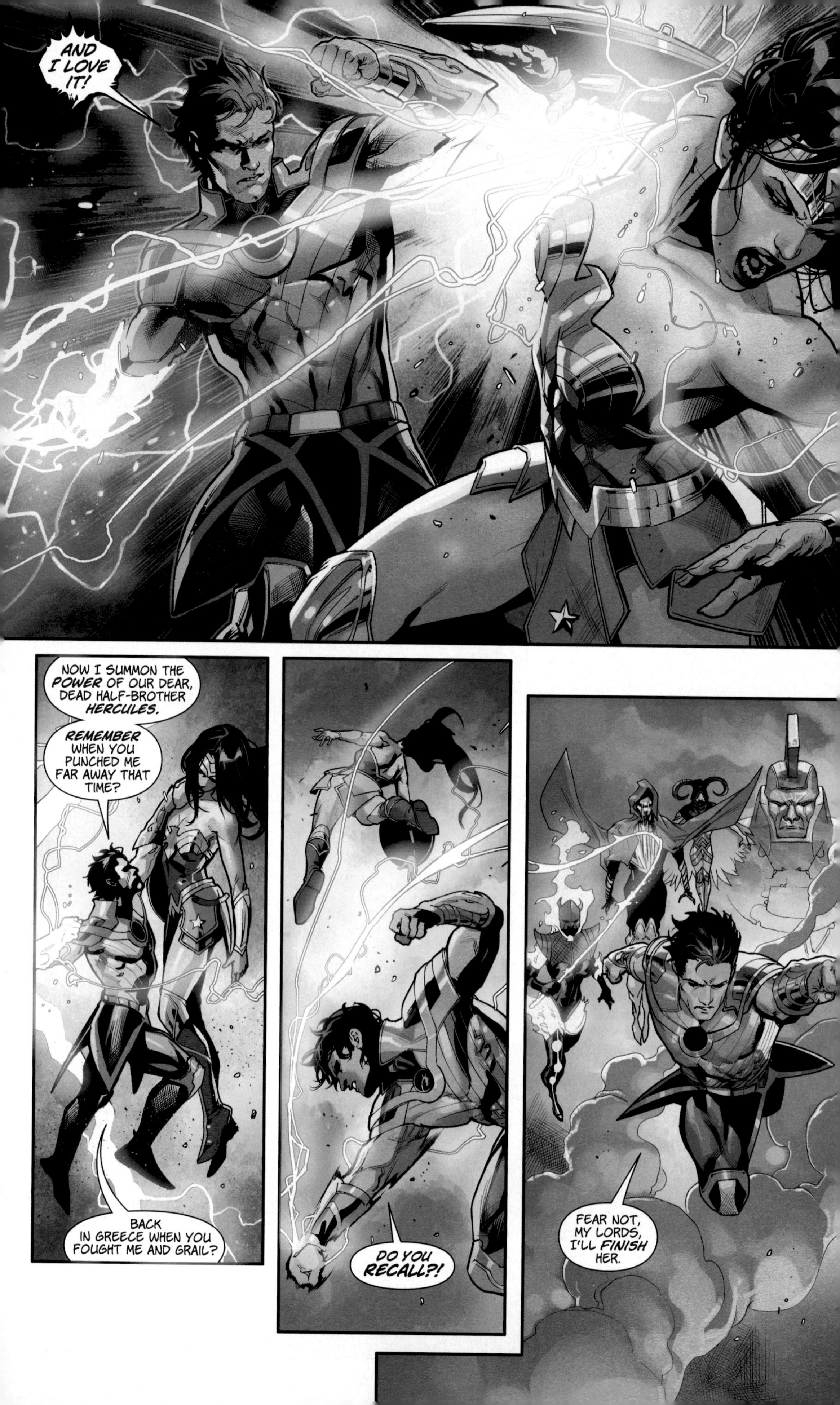
AND I LOVE IT!
NOW I SUMMON THE POWER OF OUR DEAR, DEAD HALF-BROTHER HERCULES.
REMEMBER WHEN YOU PUNCHED ME FAR AWAY THAT TIME?
BACK IN GREECE WHEN YOU FOUGHT ME AND GRAIL?
DO YOU RECALL?!
FEAR NOT, MY LORDS, I'LL FINISH HER.

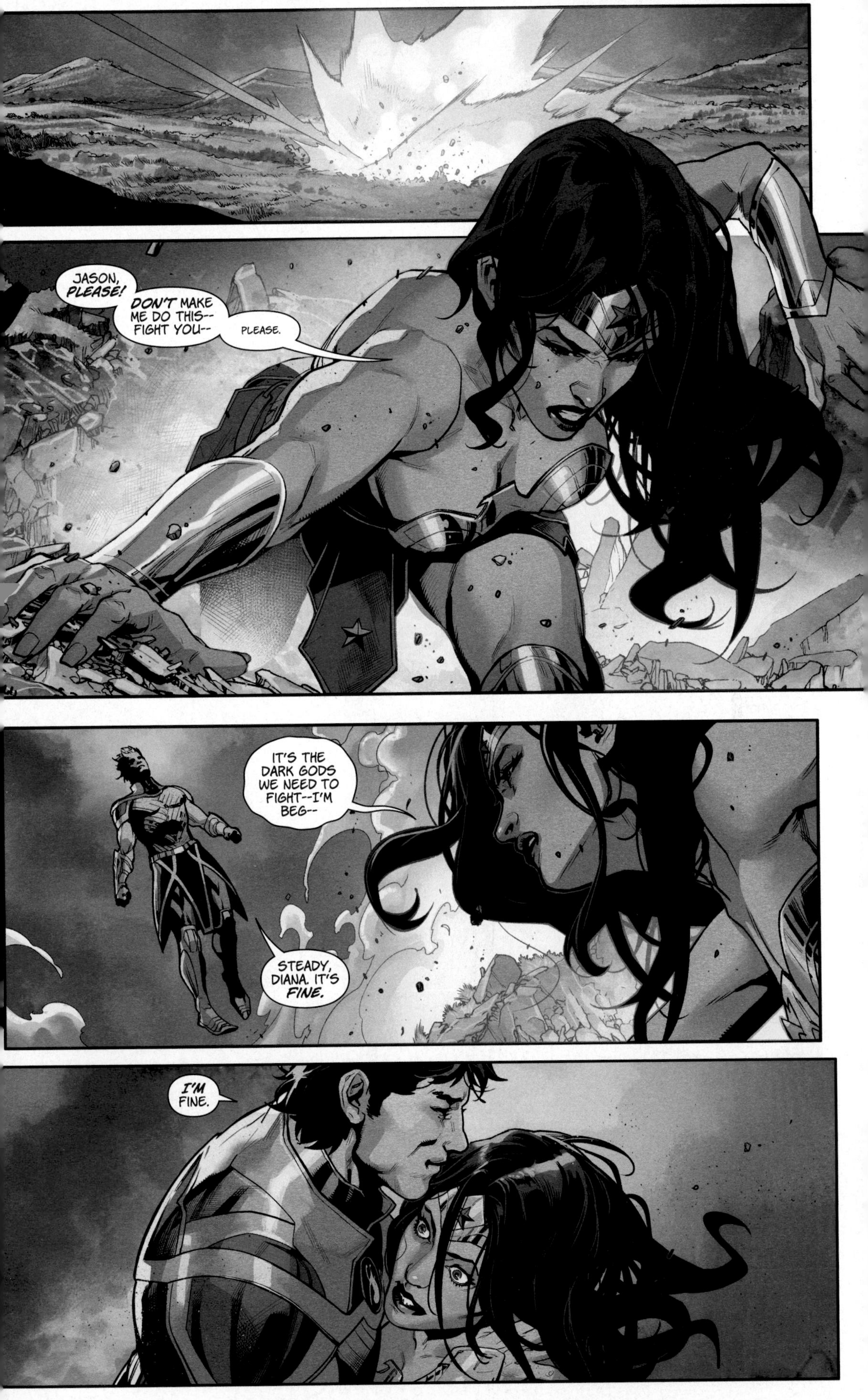

JASON, *PLEASE!*
DON'T MAKE ME DO THIS--FIGHT YOU--
PLEASE.
IT'S THE DARK GODS WE NEED TO FIGHT--I'M BEG--
STEADY, DIANA. IT'S *FINE.*
I'M FINE.

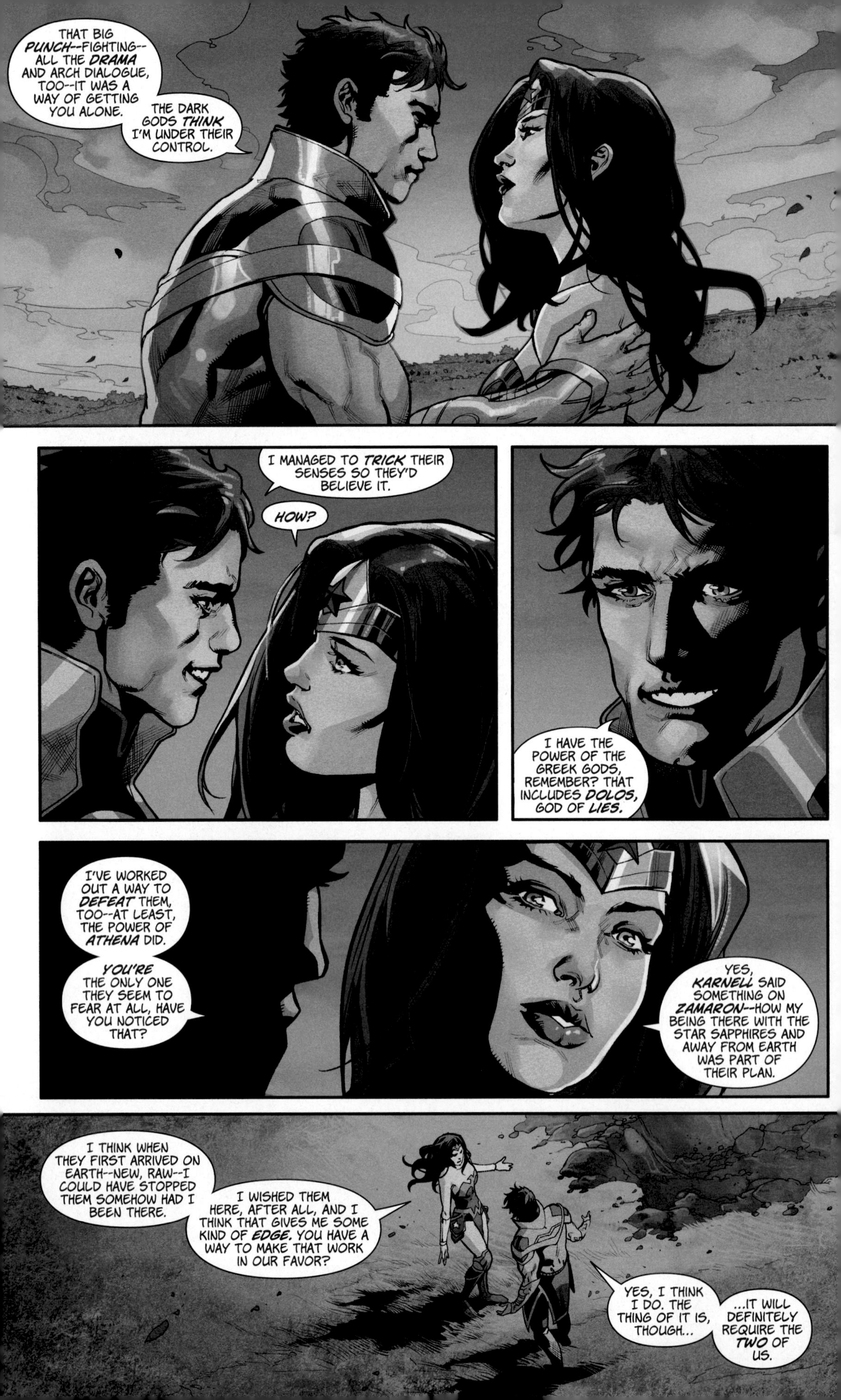
THAT BIG PUNCH--FIGHTING--ALL THE DRAMA AND ARCH DIALOGUE, TOO--IT WAS A WAY OF GETTING YOU ALONE.
THE DARK GODS THINK I'M UNDER THEIR CONTROL.
I MANAGED TO TRICK THEIR SENSES SO THEY'D BELIEVE IT.
HOW?
I HAVE THE POWER OF THE GREEK GODS, REMEMBER? THAT INCLUDES DOLOS, GOD OF LIES.
I'VE WORKED OUT A WAY TO DEFEAT THEM, TOO--AT LEAST, THE POWER OF ATHENA DID.
YOU'RE THE ONLY ONE THEY SEEM TO FEAR AT ALL, HAVE YOU NOTICED THAT?
YES, KARNELL SAID SOMETHING ON ZAMARON--HOW MY BEING THERE WITH THE STAR SAPPHIRES AND AWAY FROM EARTH WAS PART OF THEIR PLAN.
I THINK WHEN THEY FIRST ARRIVED ON EARTH--NEW, RAW--I COULD HAVE STOPPED THEM SOMEHOW HAD I BEEN THERE.
I WISHED THEM HERE, AFTER ALL, AND I THINK THAT GIVES ME SOME KIND OF EDGE. YOU HAVE A WAY TO MAKE THAT WORK IN OUR FAVOR?
YES, I THINK I DO. THE THING OF IT IS, THOUGH...
...IT WILL DEFINITELY REQUIRE THE TWO OF US.

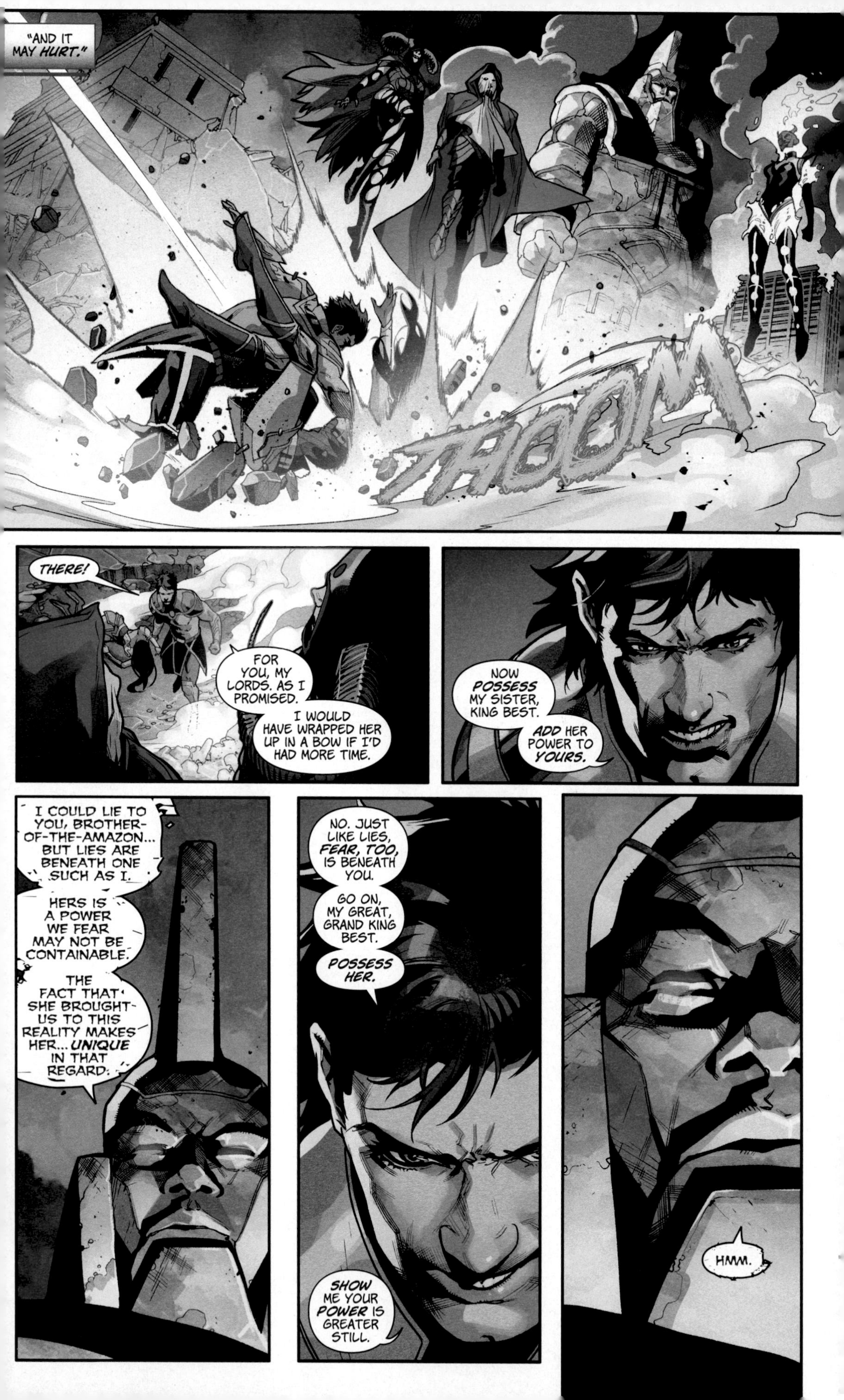
"AND IT MAY HURT."
THOOM
THERE!
FOR YOU, MY LORDS. AS I PROMISED.
I WOULD HAVE WRAPPED HER UP IN A BOW IF I'D HAD MORE TIME.
NOW POSSESS MY SISTER, KING BEST.
ADD HER POWER TO YOURS.
I COULD LIE TO YOU, BROTHER-OF-THE-AMAZON... BUT LIES ARE BENEATH ONE SUCH AS I.
HERS IS A POWER WE FEAR MAY NOT BE CONTAINABLE.
THE FACT THAT SHE BROUGHT US TO THIS REALITY MAKES HER... UNIQUE IN THAT REGARD.
NO. JUST LIKE LIES, FEAR, TOO, IS BENEATH YOU.
GO ON, MY GREAT, GRAND KING BEST.
POSSESS HER.
SHOW ME YOUR POWER IS GREATER STILL.
HMM.

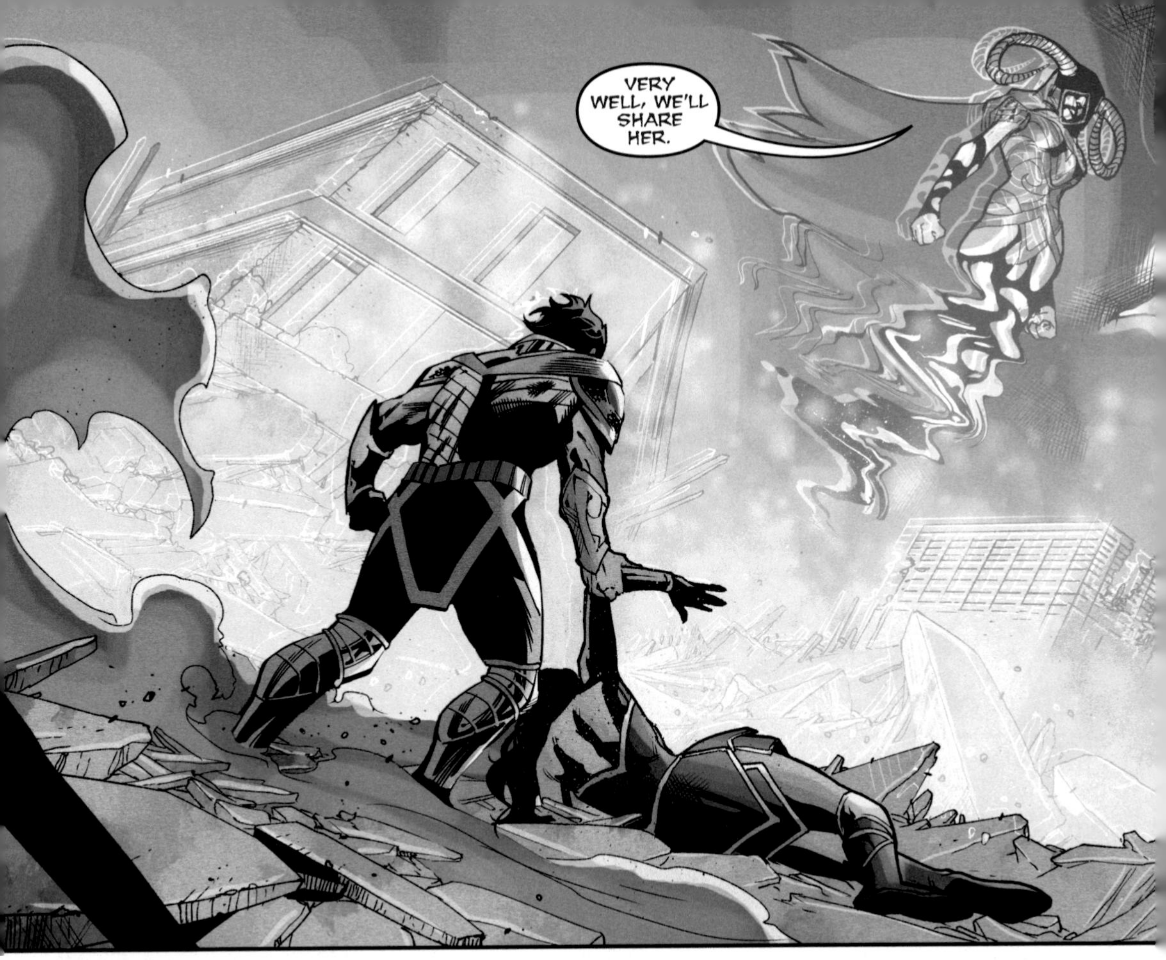
VERY WELL, WE'LL SHARE HER.

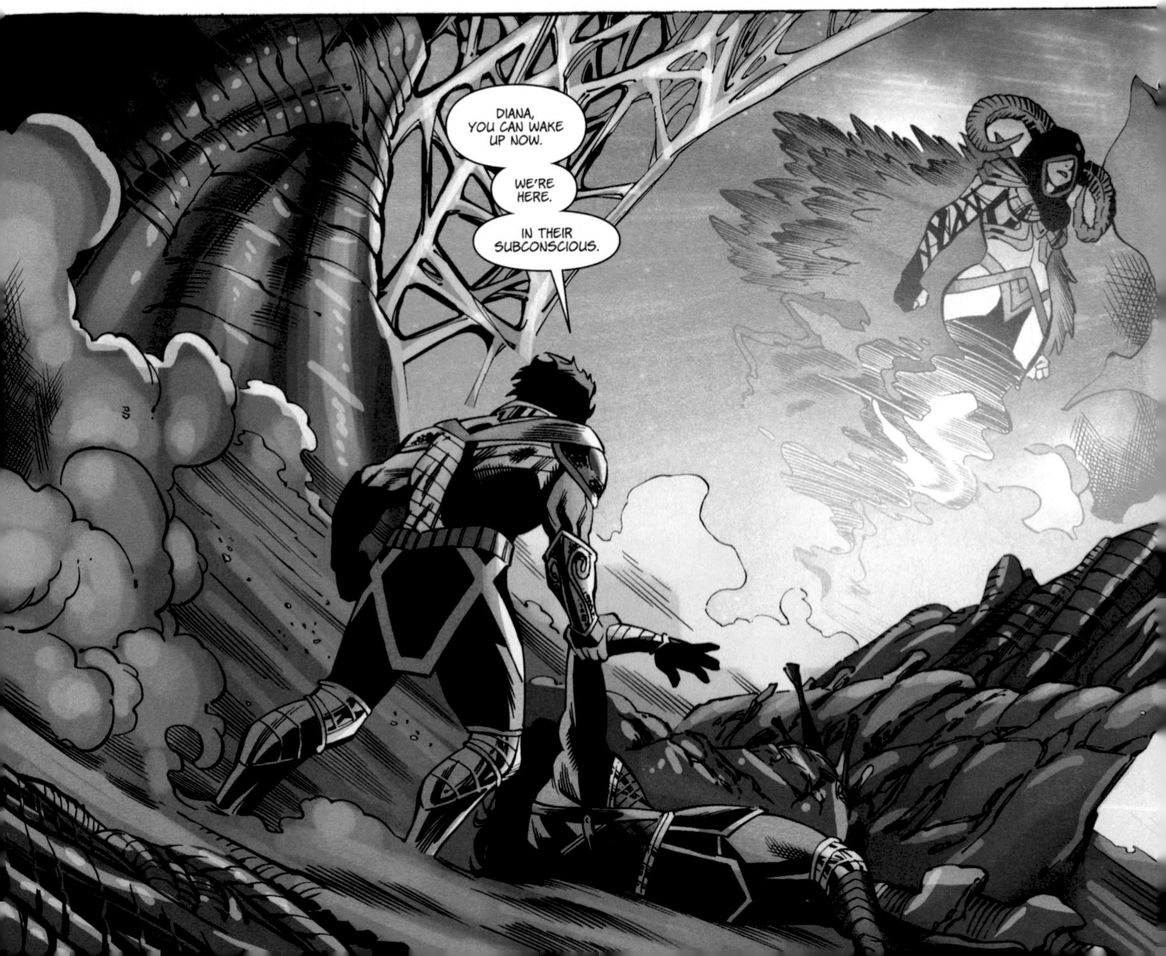
DIANA, YOU CAN WAKE UP NOW.
WE'RE HERE.
IN THEIR SUBCONSCIOUS.

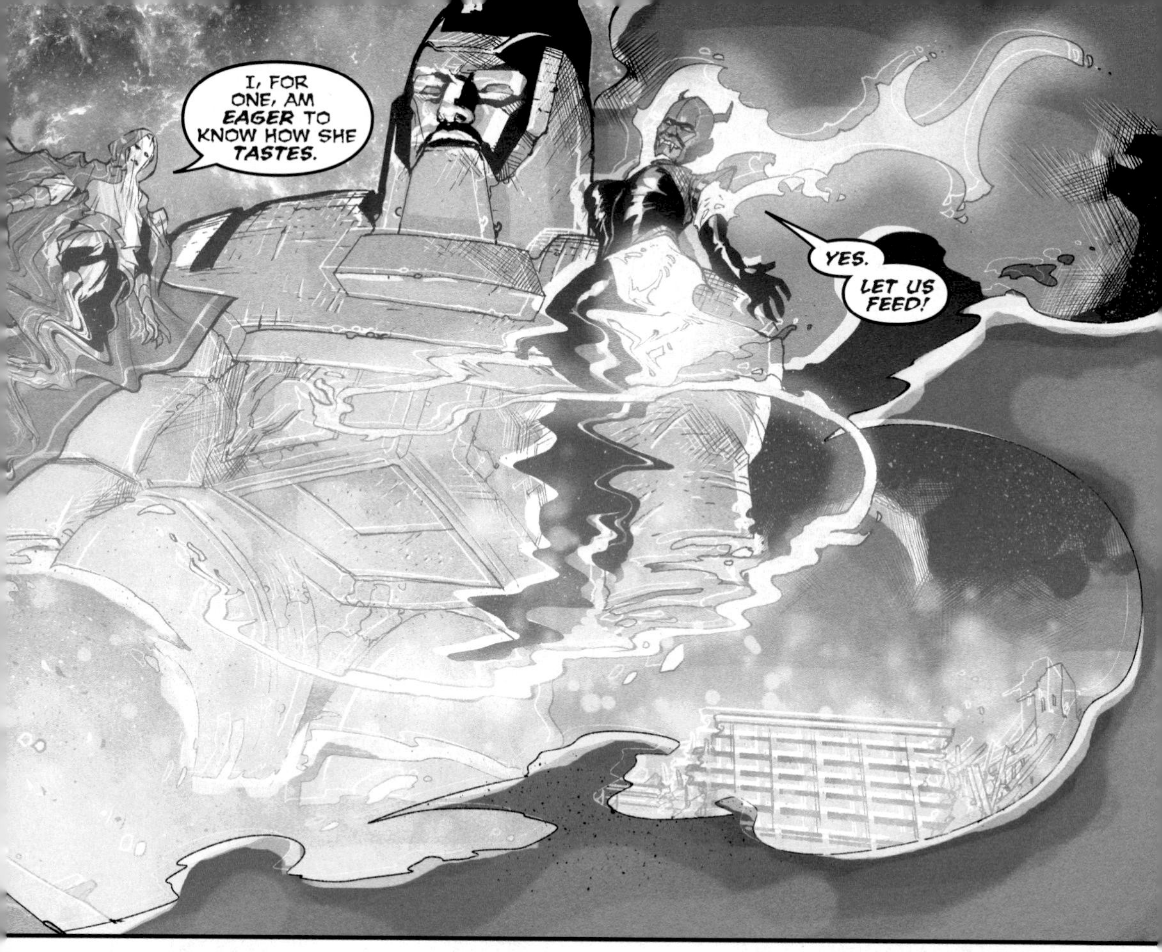
I, FOR ONE, AM EAGER TO KNOW HOW SHE TASTES.
YES. LET US FEED!

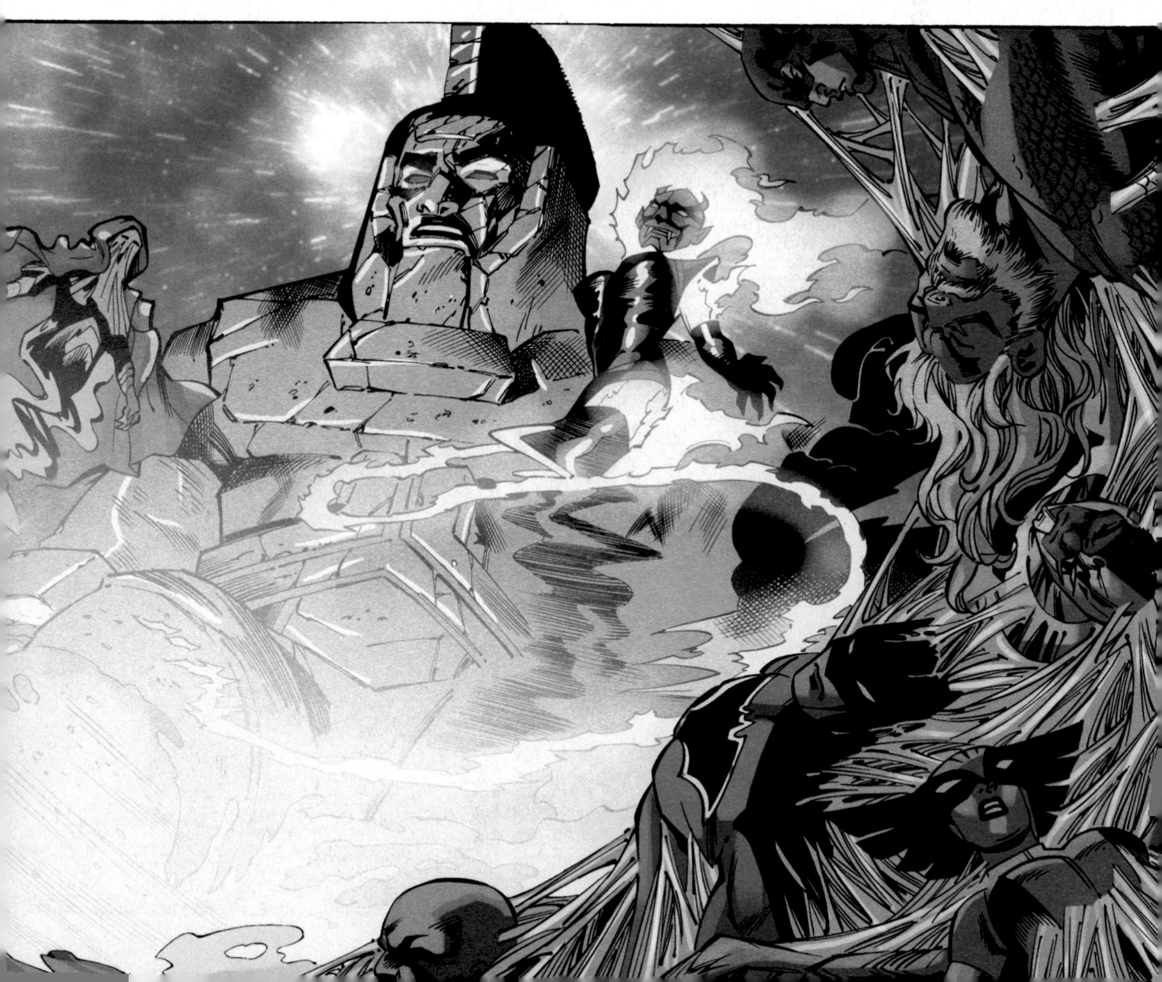

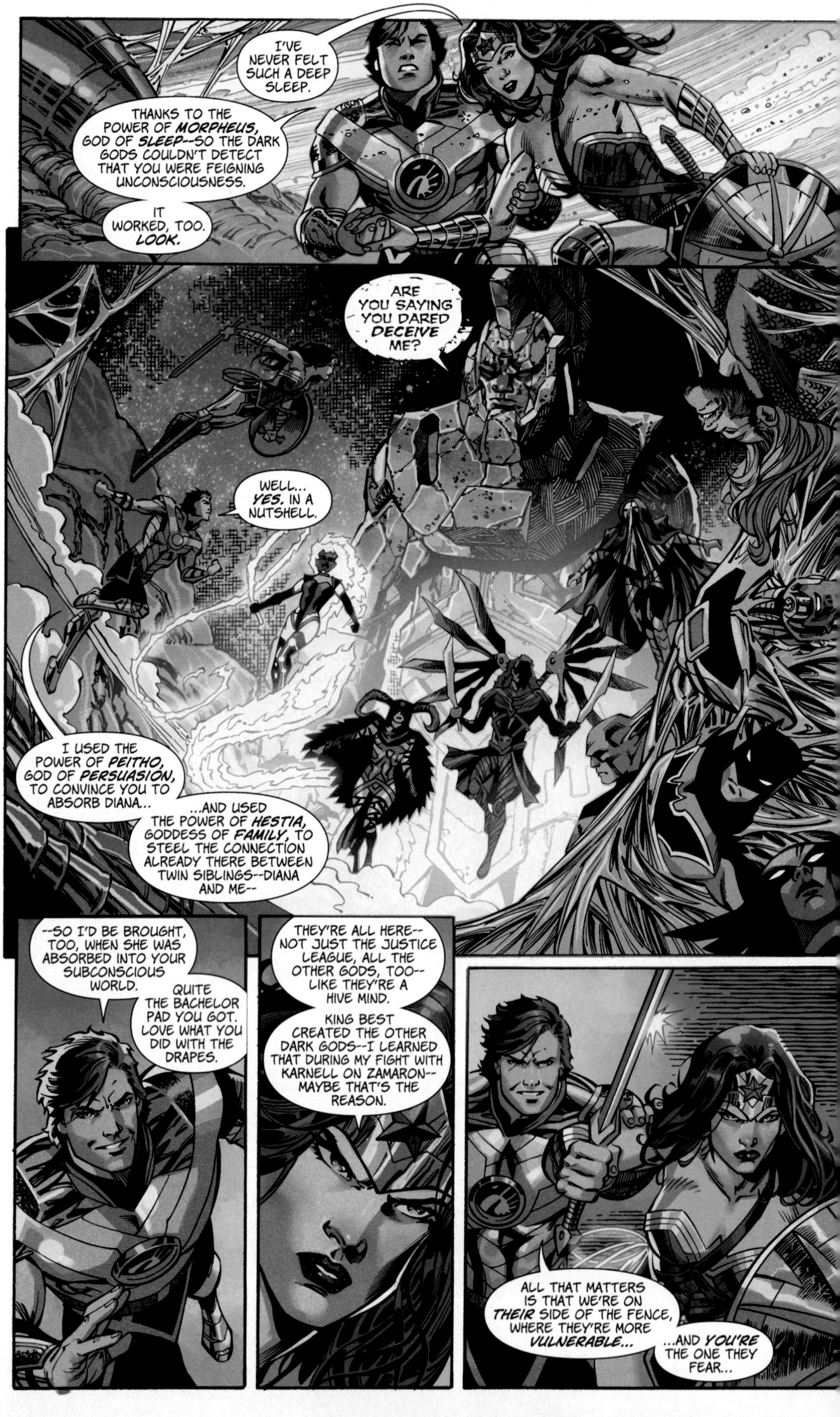
I'VE NEVER FELT SUCH A DEEP SLEEP.
THANKS TO THE POWER OF MORPHEUS, GOD OF SLEEP--SO THE DARK GODS COULDN'T DETECT THAT YOU WERE FEIGNING UNCONSCIOUSNESS.
IT WORKED, TOO. LOOK.
ARE YOU SAYING YOU DARED DECEIVE ME?
WELL... YES. IN A NUTSHELL.
I USED THE POWER OF PEITHO, GOD OF PERSUASION, TO CONVINCE YOU TO ABSORB DIANA...
...AND USED THE POWER OF HESTIA, GODDESS OF FAMILY, TO STEEL THE CONNECTION ALREADY THERE BETWEEN TWIN SIBLINGS--DIANA AND ME--
--SO I'D BE BROUGHT, TOO, WHEN SHE WAS ABSORBED INTO YOUR SUBCONSCIOUS WORLD.
QUITE THE BACHELOR PAD YOU GOT. LOVE WHAT YOU DID WITH THE DRAPES.
THEY'RE ALL HERE-- NOT JUST THE JUSTICE LEAGUE, ALL THE OTHER GODS, TOO-- LIKE THEY'RE A HIVE MIND.
KING BEST CREATED THE OTHER DARK GODS--I LEARNED THAT DURING MY FIGHT WITH KARNELL ON ZAMARON-- MAYBE THAT'S THE REASON.
ALL THAT MATTERS IS THAT WE'RE ON THEIR SIDE OF THE FENCE, WHERE THEY'RE MORE VULNERABLE...
...AND YOU'RE THE ONE THEY FEAR...

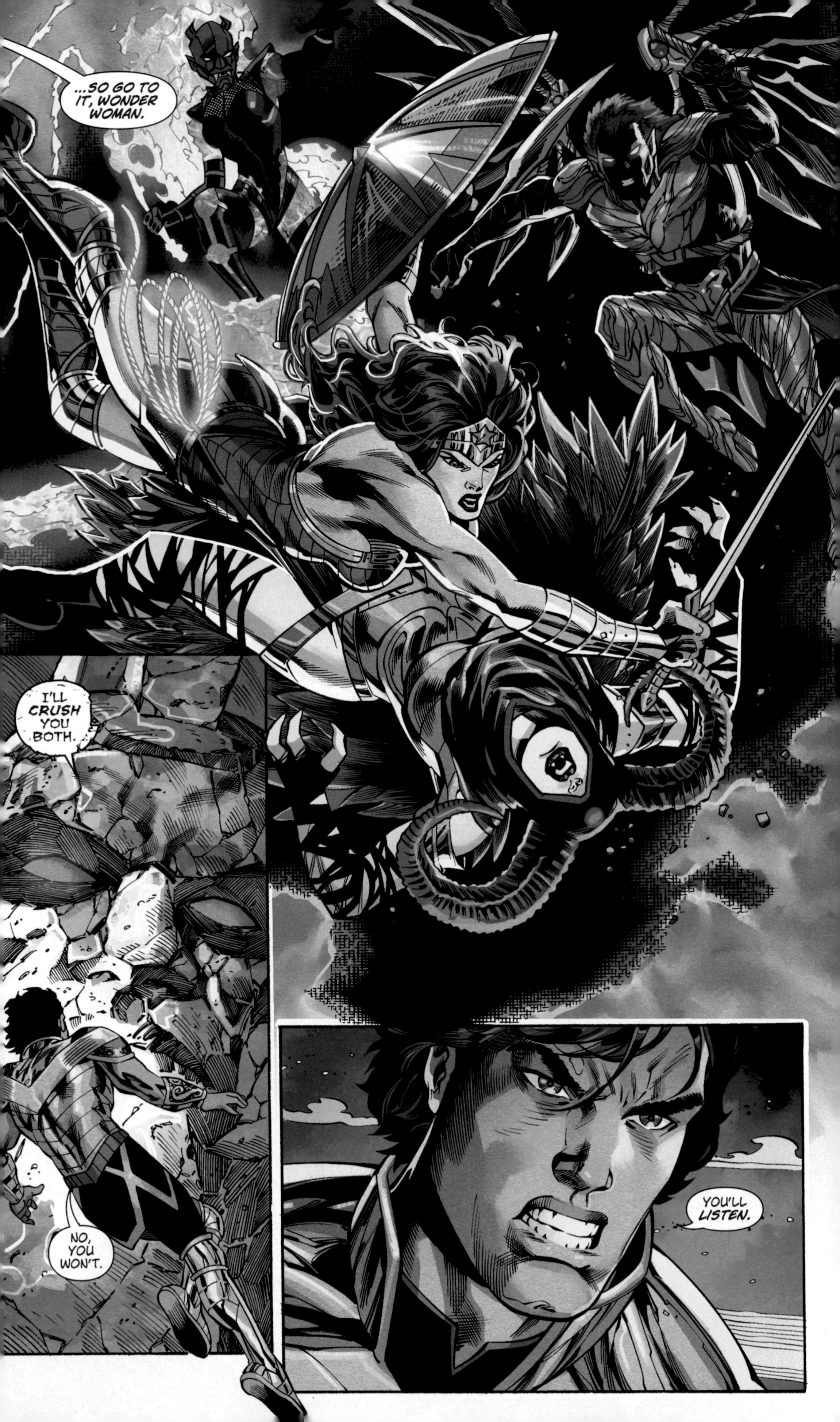
...SO GO TO IT, WONDER WOMAN.
I'LL CRUSH YOU BOTH.
NO, YOU WON'T.
YOU'LL LISTEN.

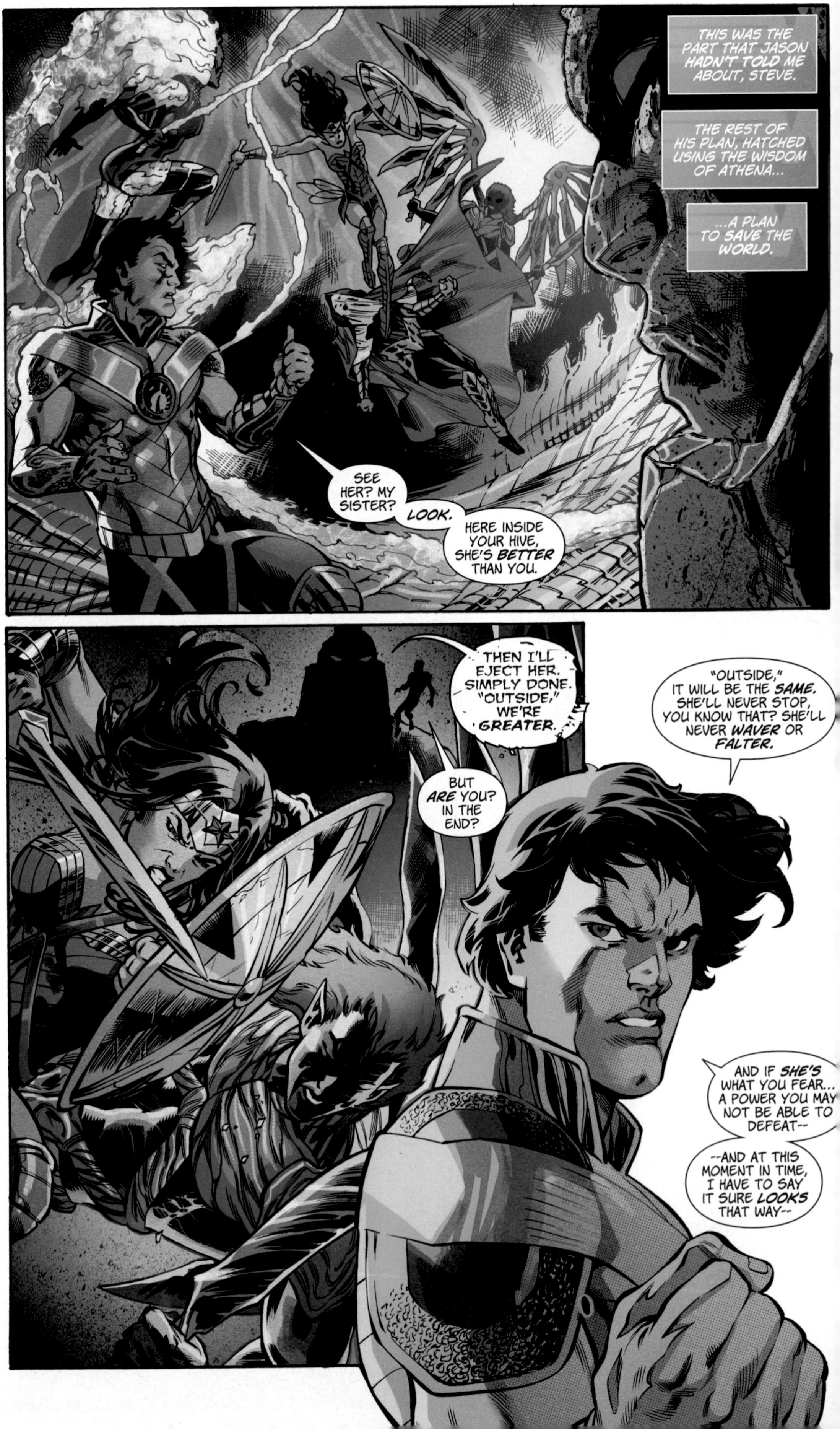
THIS WAS THE PART THAT JASON HADN'T TOLD ME ABOUT, STEVE.
THE REST OF HIS PLAN, HATCHED USING THE WISDOM OF ATHENA...
...A PLAN TO SAVE THE WORLD.
SEE HER? MY SISTER? LOOK.
HERE INSIDE YOUR HIVE, SHE'S BETTER THAN YOU.
THEN I'LL EJECT HER. SIMPLY DONE. "OUTSIDE," WE'RE GREATER.
BUT ARE YOU? IN THE END?
"OUTSIDE," IT WILL BE THE SAME. SHE'LL NEVER STOP, YOU KNOW THAT? SHE'LL NEVER WAVER OR FALTER.
AND IF SHE'S WHAT YOU FEAR... A POWER YOU MAY NOT BE ABLE TO DEFEAT--
--AND AT THIS MOMENT IN TIME, I HAVE TO SAY IT SURE LOOKS THAT WAY--

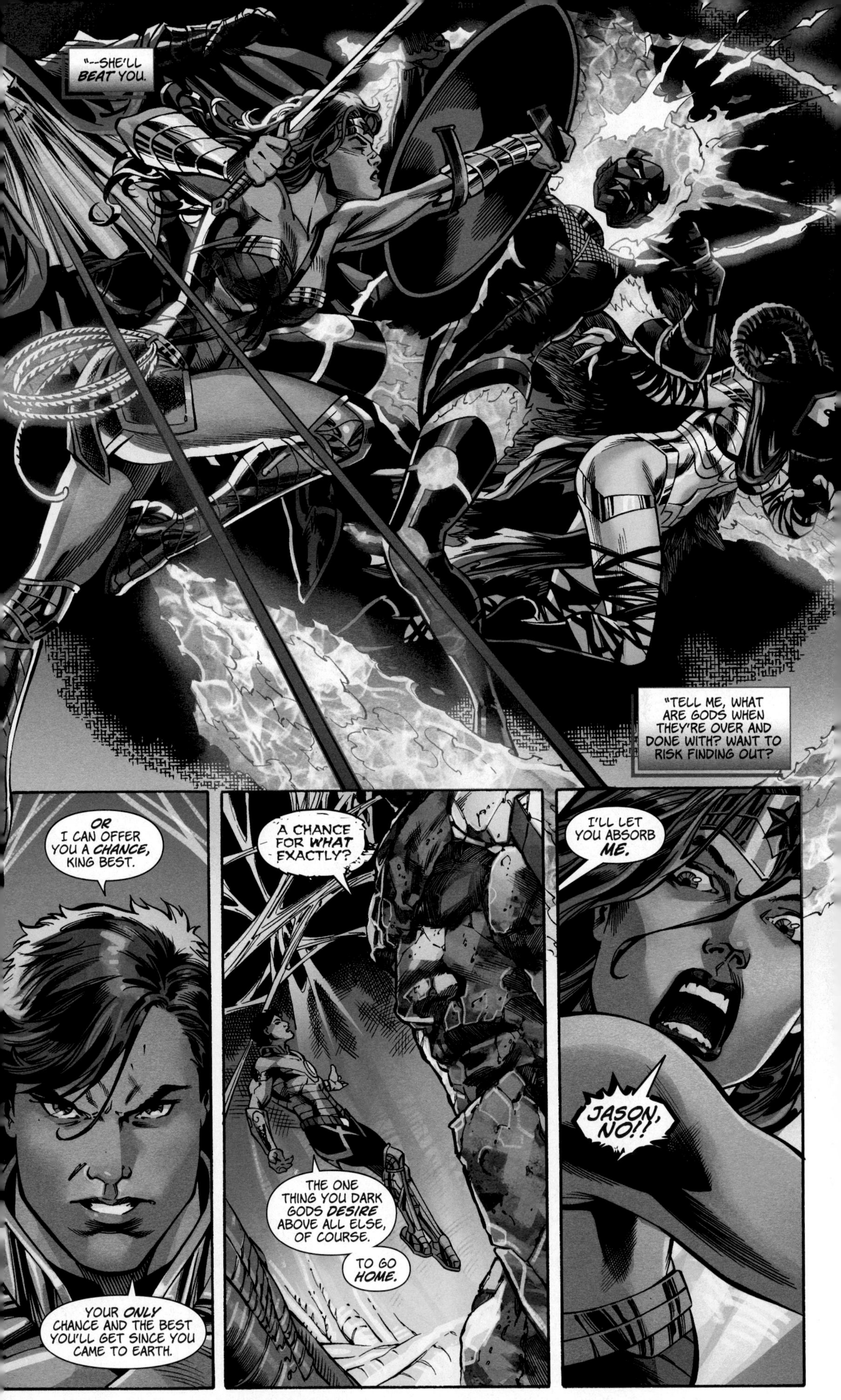
"--SHE'LL BEAT YOU.
"TELL ME, WHAT ARE GODS WHEN THEY'RE OVER AND DONE WITH? WANT TO RISK FINDING OUT?
OR I CAN OFFER YOU A CHANCE, KING BEST.
YOUR ONLY CHANCE AND THE BEST YOU'LL GET SINCE YOU CAME TO EARTH.
A CHANCE FOR WHAT EXACTLY?
THE ONE THING YOU DARK GODS DESIRE ABOVE ALL ELSE, OF COURSE.
TO GO HOME.
I'LL LET YOU ABSORB ME.
JASON, NO!!

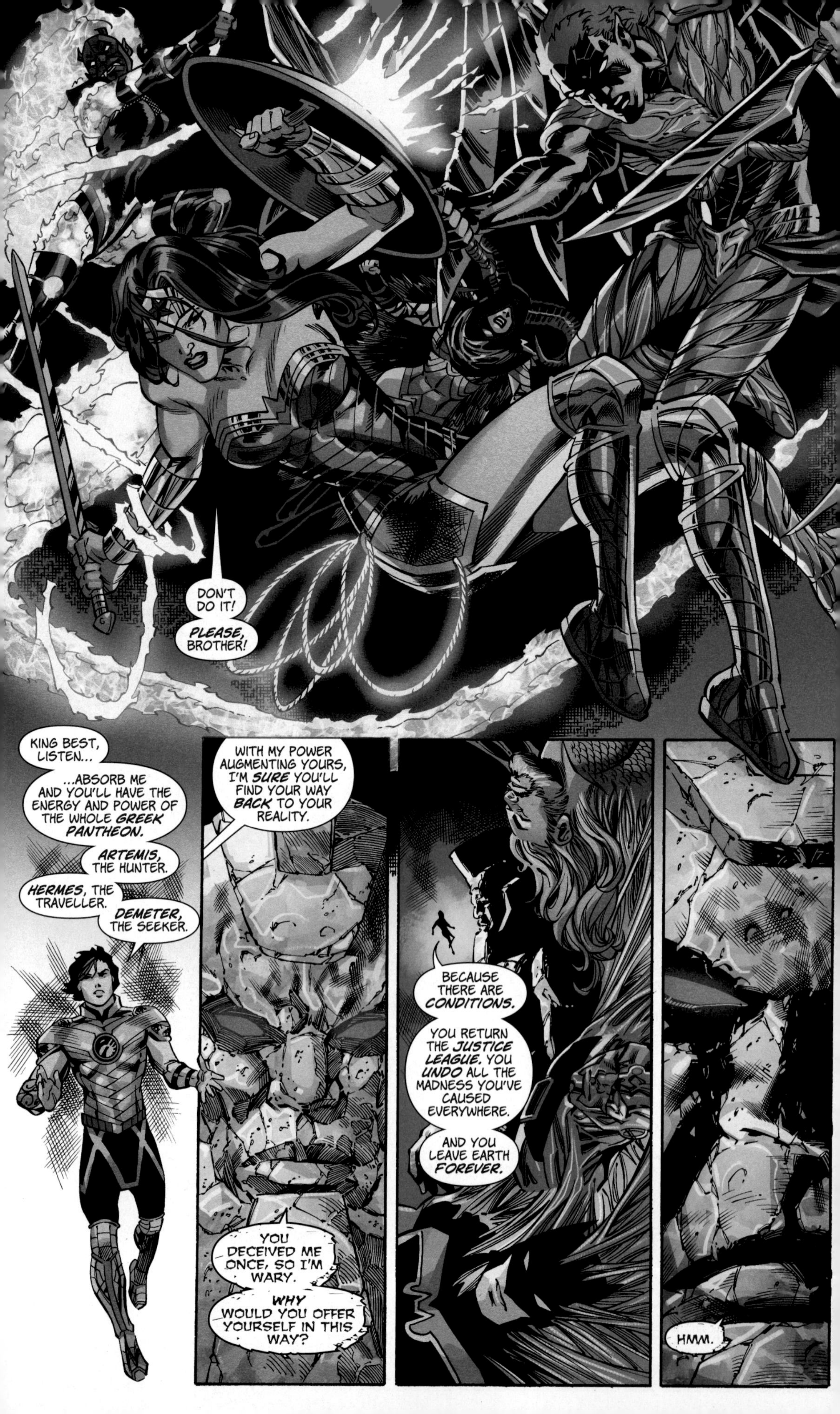
DON'T DO IT! PLEASE, BROTHER!
KING BEST, LISTEN...
...ABSORB ME AND YOU'LL HAVE THE ENERGY AND POWER OF THE WHOLE GREEK PANTHEON.
ARTEMIS, THE HUNTER.
HERMES, THE TRAVELLER.
DEMETER, THE SEEKER.
WITH MY POWER AUGMENTING YOURS, I'M SURE YOU'LL FIND YOUR WAY BACK TO YOUR REALITY.
YOU DECEIVED ME ONCE, SO I'M WARY.
WHY WOULD YOU OFFER YOURSELF IN THIS WAY?
BECAUSE THERE ARE CONDITIONS.
YOU RETURN THE JUSTICE LEAGUE. YOU UNDO ALL THE MADNESS YOU'VE CAUSED EVERYWHERE.
AND YOU LEAVE EARTH FOREVER.
HMM.

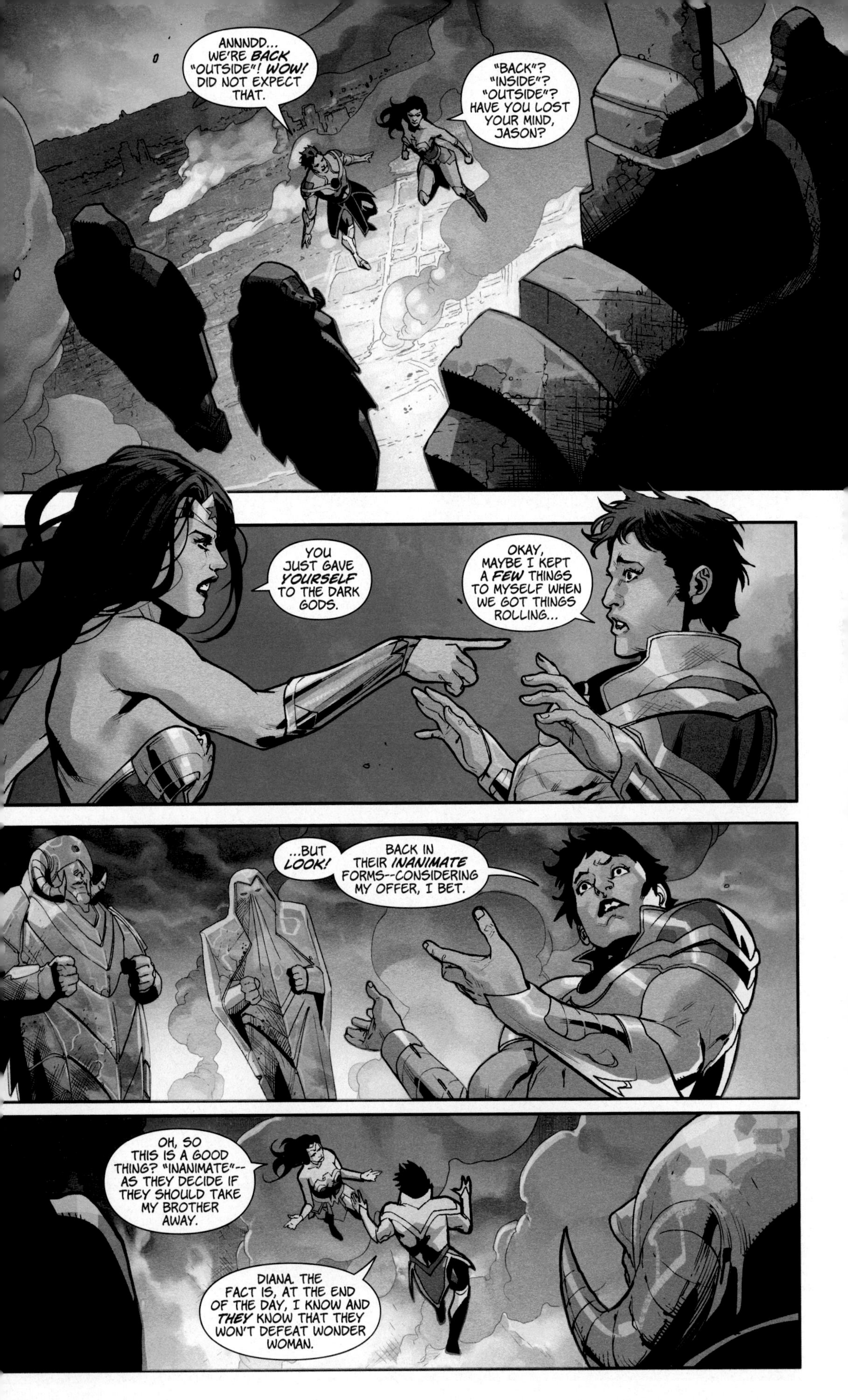
ANNNDD... WE'RE BACK "OUTSIDE"! WOW! DID NOT EXPECT THAT.
"BACK"? "INSIDE"? "OUTSIDE"? HAVE YOU LOST YOUR MIND, JASON?
YOU JUST GAVE YOURSELF TO THE DARK GODS.
OKAY, MAYBE I KEPT A FEW THINGS TO MYSELF WHEN WE GOT THINGS ROLLING...
...BUT LOOK!
BACK IN THEIR INANIMATE FORMS--CONSIDERING MY OFFER, I BET.
OH, SO THIS IS A GOOD THING? "INANIMATE"--AS THEY DECIDE IF THEY SHOULD TAKE MY BROTHER AWAY.
DIANA. THE FACT IS, AT THE END OF THE DAY, I KNOW AND THEY KNOW THAT THEY WON'T DEFEAT WONDER WOMAN.

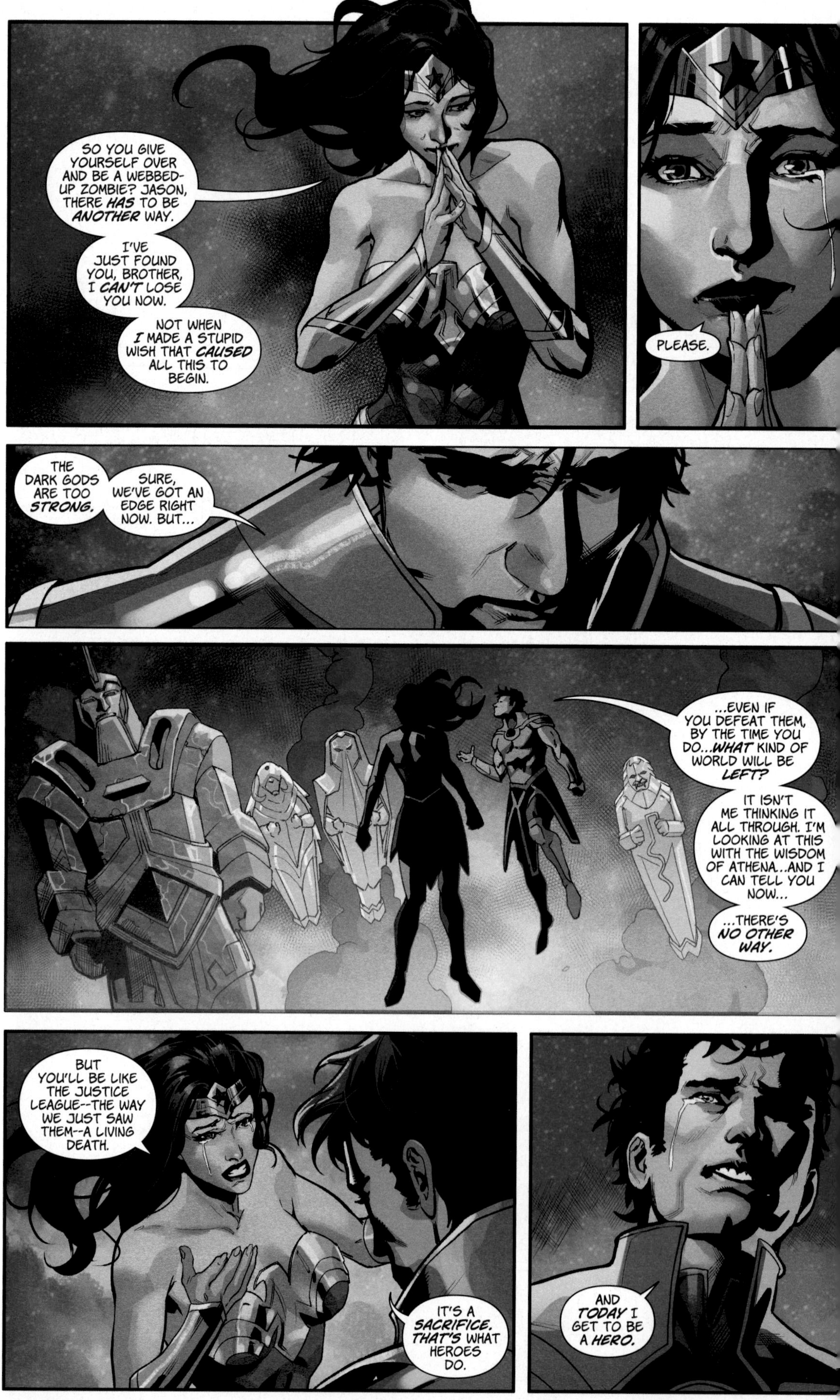

SO YOU GIVE YOURSELF OVER AND BE A WEBBED-UP ZOMBIE? JASON, THERE HAS TO BE ANOTHER WAY.
I'VE JUST FOUND YOU, BROTHER, I CAN'T LOSE YOU NOW.
NOT WHEN I MADE A STUPID WISH THAT CAUSED ALL THIS TO BEGIN.
PLEASE.
THE DARK GODS ARE TOO STRONG.
SURE, WE'VE GOT AN EDGE RIGHT NOW. BUT...
...EVEN IF YOU DEFEAT THEM, BY THE TIME YOU DO...WHAT KIND OF WORLD WILL BE LEFT?
IT ISN'T ME THINKING IT ALL THROUGH. I'M LOOKING AT THIS WITH THE WISDOM OF ATHENA...AND I CAN TELL YOU NOW...
...THERE'S NO OTHER WAY.
BUT YOU'LL BE LIKE THE JUSTICE LEAGUE--THE WAY WE JUST SAW THEM--A LIVING DEATH.
IT'S A SACRIFICE. THAT'S WHAT HEROES DO.
AND TODAY I GET TO BE A HERO.

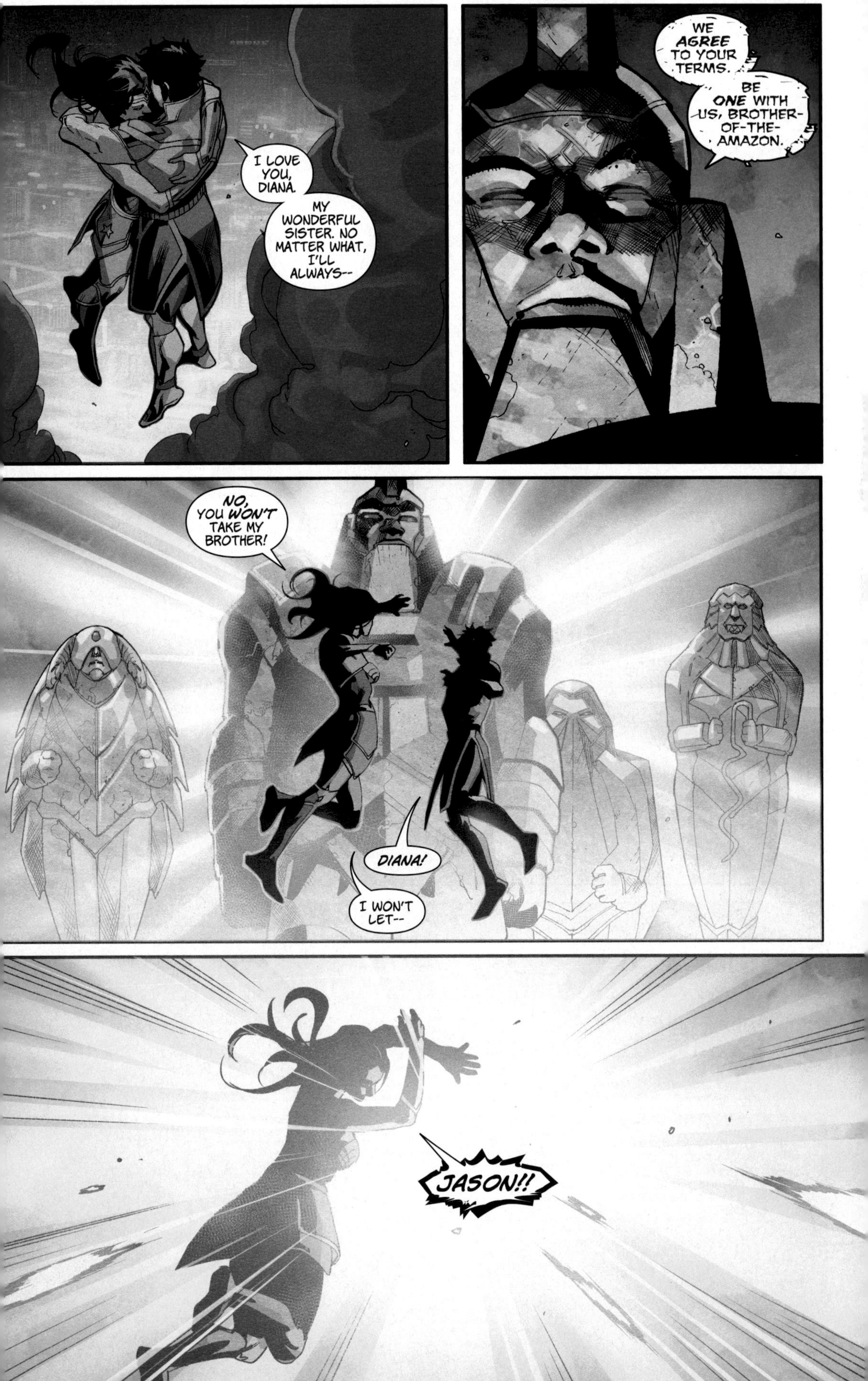
I LOVE YOU, DIANA.
MY WONDERFUL SISTER. NO MATTER WHAT, I'LL ALWAYS--
WE AGREE TO YOUR TERMS.
BE ONE WITH US, BROTHER-OF-THE-AMAZON.
NO, YOU WON'T TAKE MY BROTHER!
DIANA!
I WON'T LET--
JASON!!

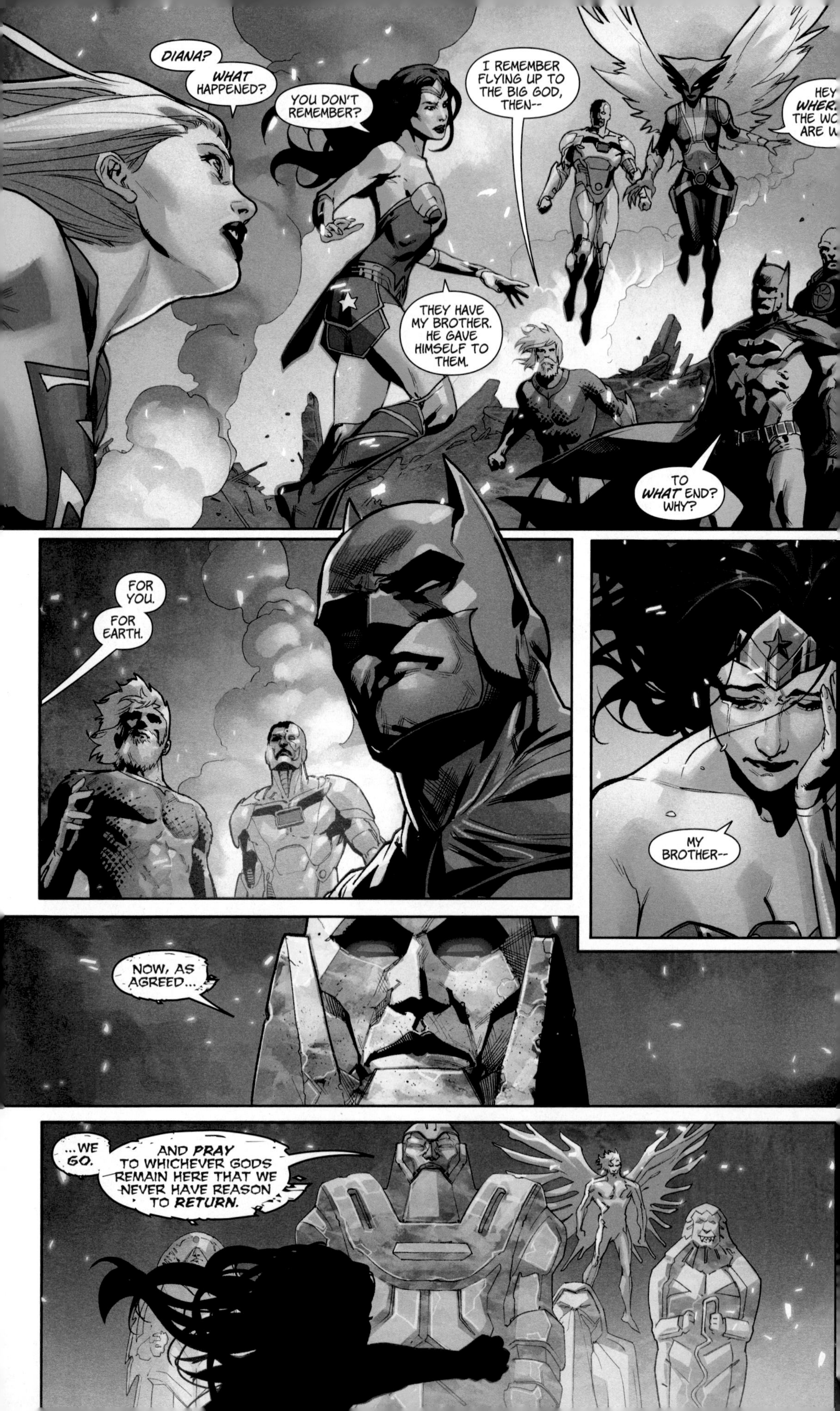

DIANA? WHAT HAPPENED?
YOU DON'T REMEMBER?
I REMEMBER FLYING UP TO THE BIG GOD, THEN--
HEY WHER THE WO ARE W
THEY HAVE MY BROTHER. HE GAVE HIMSELF TO THEM.
TO WHAT END? WHY?
FOR YOU.
FOR EARTH.
MY BROTHER--
NOW, AS AGREED...
...WE GO.
AND PRAY TO WHICHEVER GODS REMAIN HERE THAT WE NEVER HAVE REASON TO RETURN.

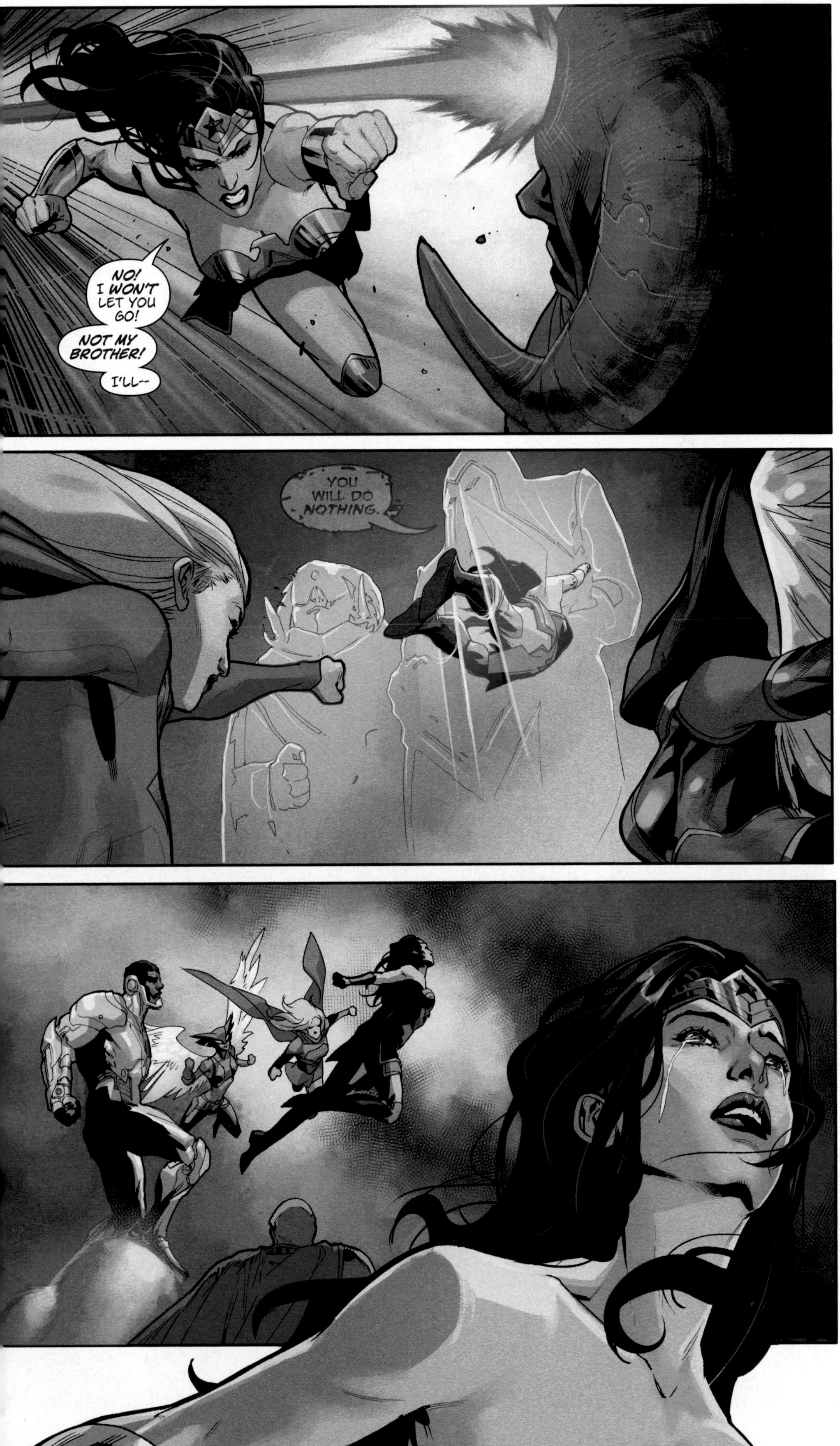
NO! I WON'T LET YOU GO!
NOT MY BROTHER!
I'LL--
YOU WILL DO NOTHING.

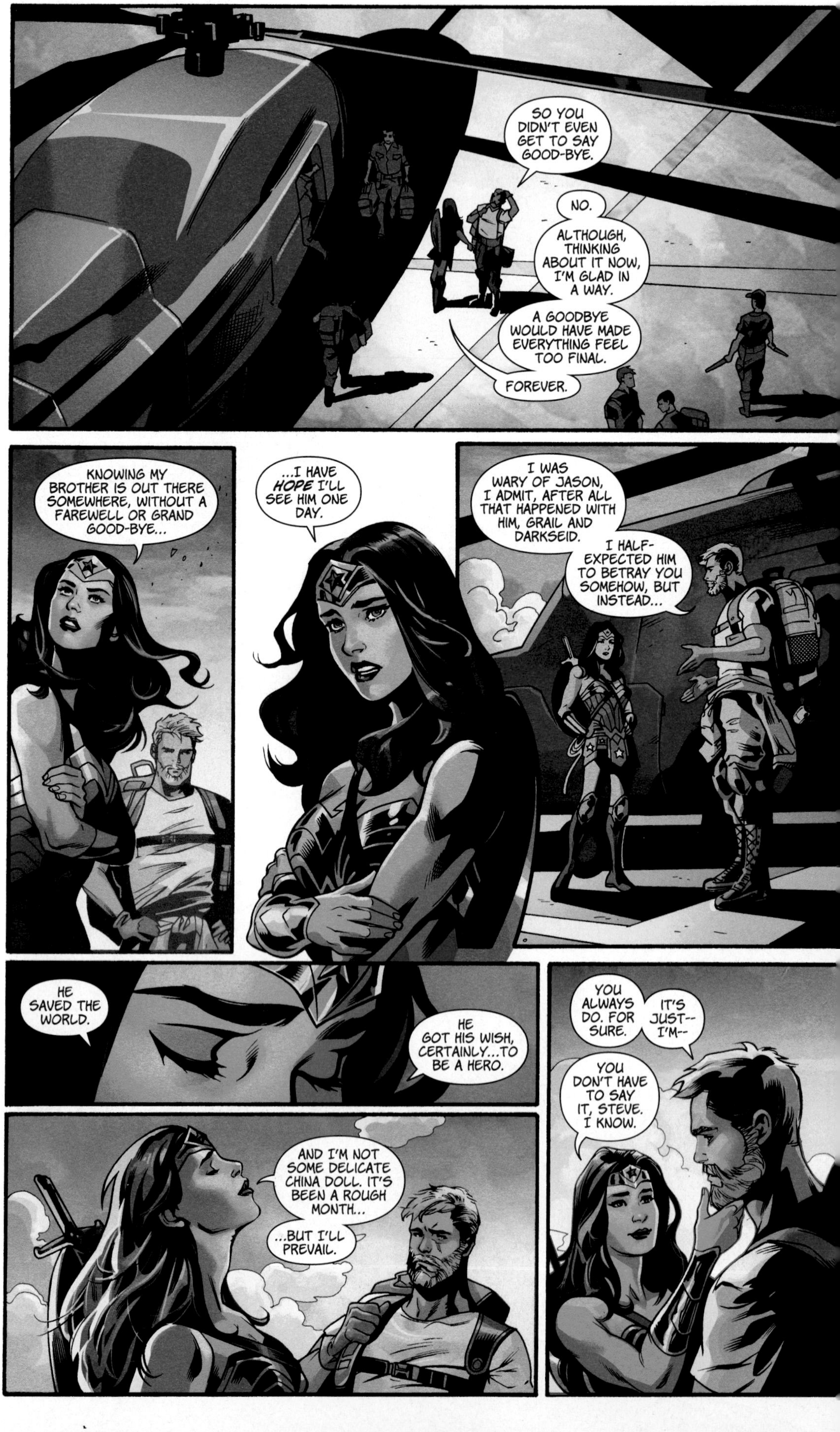
SO YOU DIDN'T EVEN GET TO SAY GOOD-BYE.
NO.
ALTHOUGH, THINKING ABOUT IT NOW, I'M GLAD IN A WAY.
A GOODBYE WOULD HAVE MADE EVERYTHING FEEL TOO FINAL.
FOREVER.
KNOWING MY BROTHER IS OUT THERE SOMEWHERE, WITHOUT A FAREWELL OR GRAND GOOD-BYE...
...I HAVE HOPE I'LL SEE HIM ONE DAY.
I WAS WARY OF JASON, I ADMIT, AFTER ALL THAT HAPPENED WITH HIM, GRAIL AND DARKSEID.
I HALF-EXPECTED HIM TO BETRAY YOU SOMEHOW, BUT INSTEAD...
HE SAVED THE WORLD.
HE GOT HIS WISH, CERTAINLY...TO BE A HERO.
AND I'M NOT SOME DELICATE CHINA DOLL. IT'S BEEN A ROUGH MONTH...
...BUT I'LL PREVAIL.
YOU ALWAYS DO. FOR SURE.
IT'S JUST-- I'M--
YOU DON'T HAVE TO SAY IT, STEVE. I KNOW.

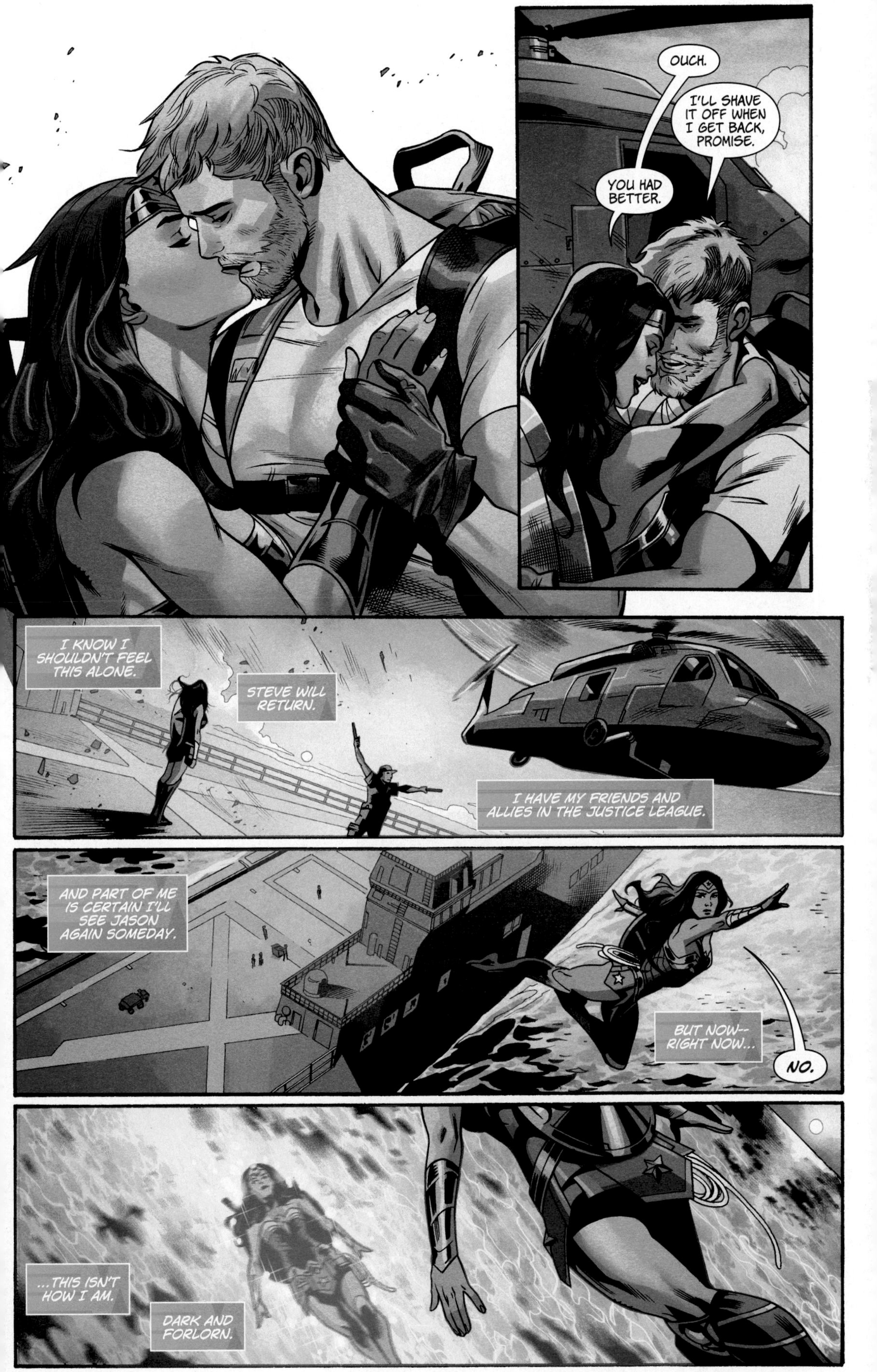
OUCH.
I'LL SHAVE IT OFF WHEN I GET BACK, PROMISE.
YOU HAD BETTER.
I KNOW I SHOULDN'T FEEL THIS ALONE.
STEVE WILL RETURN.
I HAVE MY FRIENDS AND ALLIES IN THE JUSTICE LEAGUE.
AND PART OF ME IS CERTAIN I'LL SEE JASON AGAIN SOMEDAY.
BUT NOW--RIGHT NOW...
NO.
...THIS ISN'T HOW I AM.
DARK AND FORLORN.

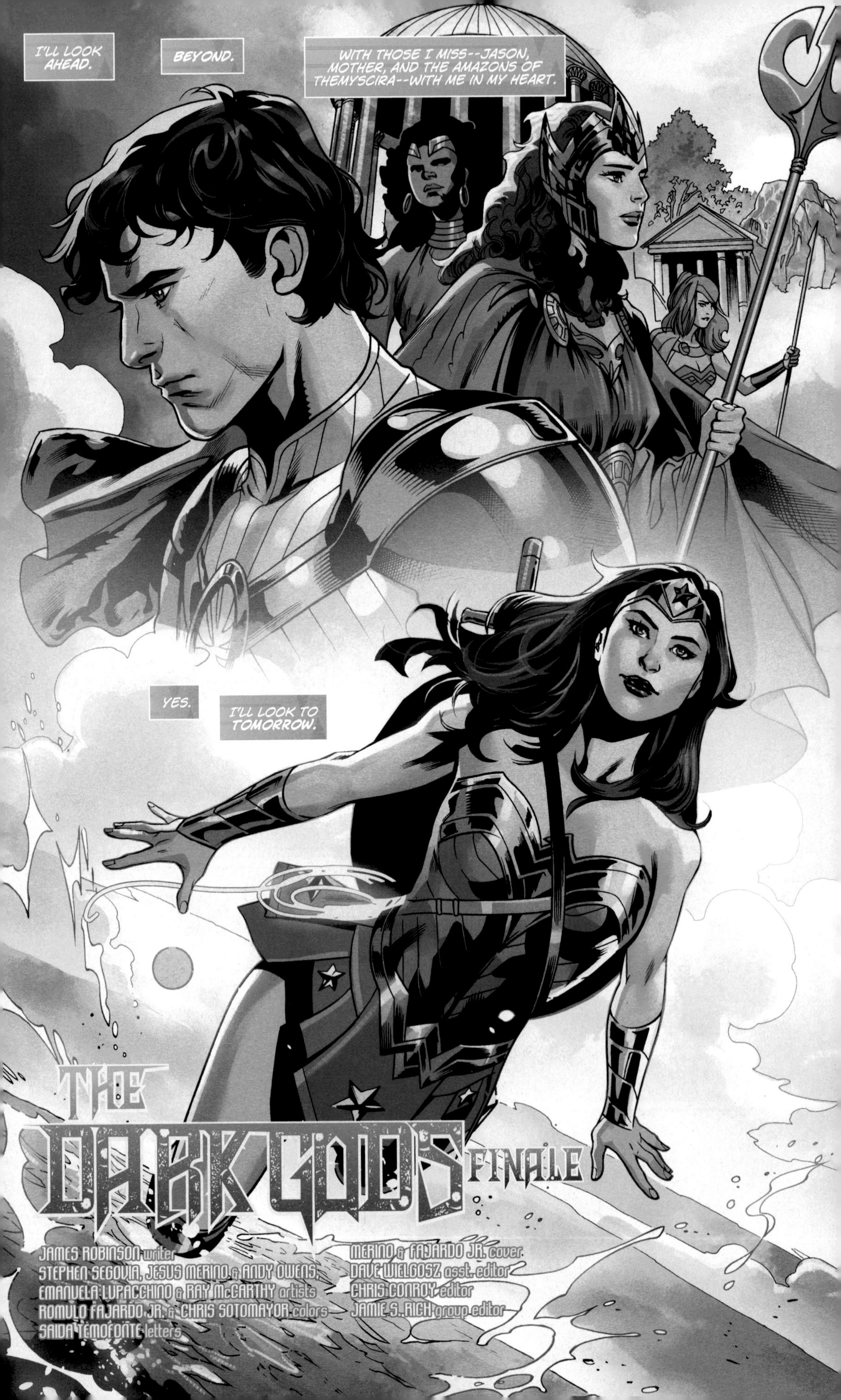

I'LL LOOK AHEAD.
BEYOND.
WITH THOSE I MISS--JASON, MOTHER, AND THE AMAZONS OF THEMYSCIRA--WITH ME IN MY HEART.
YES.
I'LL LOOK TO TOMORROW.
THE DARK GODS FINALE
JAMES ROBINSON writer
STEPHEN SEGOVIA, JESUS MERINO & ANDY OWENS, EMANUELA LUPACCHINO & RAY McCARTHY artists
ROMULO FAJARDO JR. & CHRIS SOTOMAYOR colors
SAIDA TEMOFONTE letters
MERINO & FAJARDO JR. cover
DAVE WIELGOSZ asst. editor
CHRIS CONROY editor
JAMIE S. RICH group editor

WONDER WOMAN #46 variant cover
by JENNY FRISON

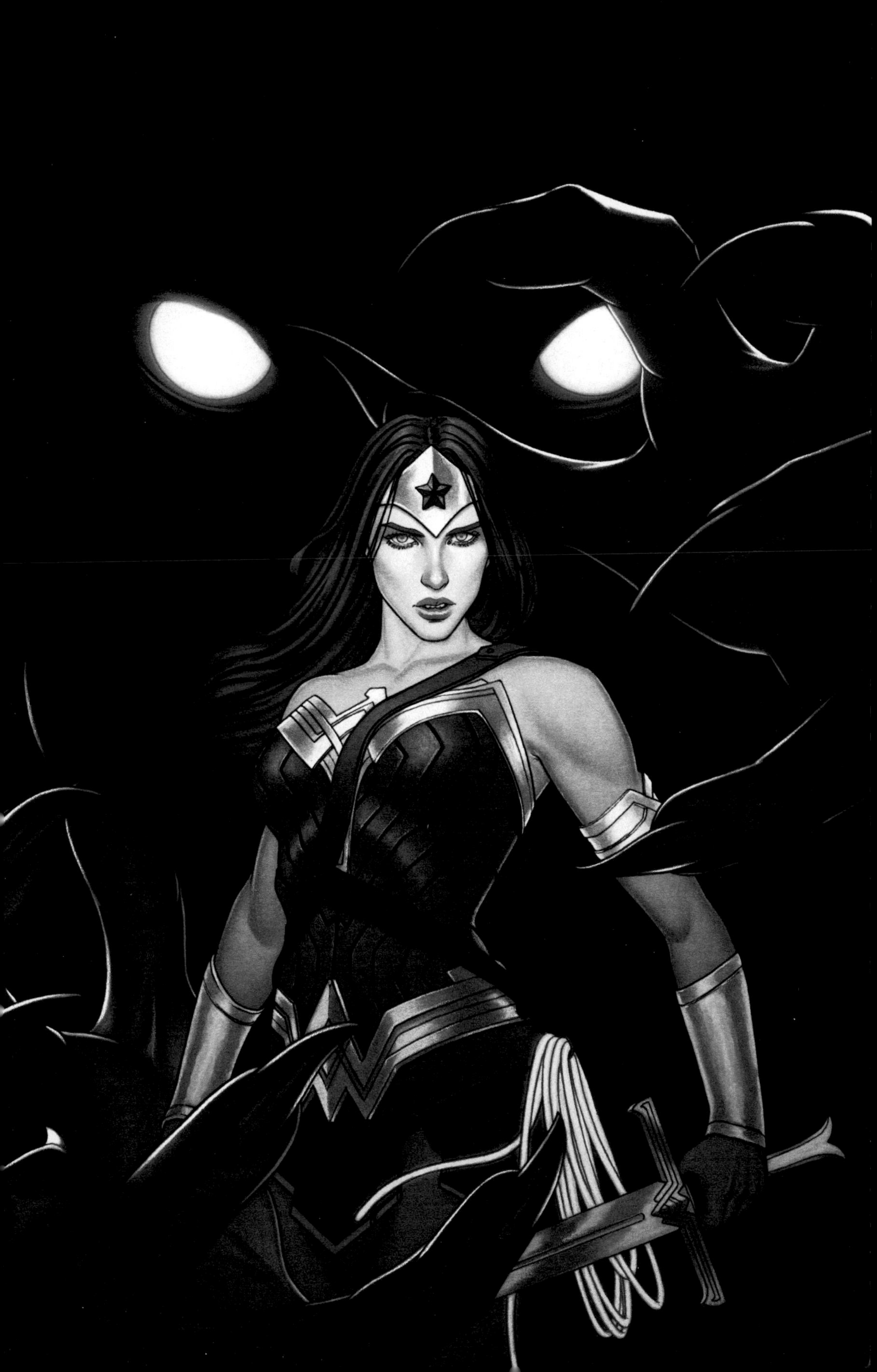

WONDER WOMAN #47 variant cover
by JENNY FRISON

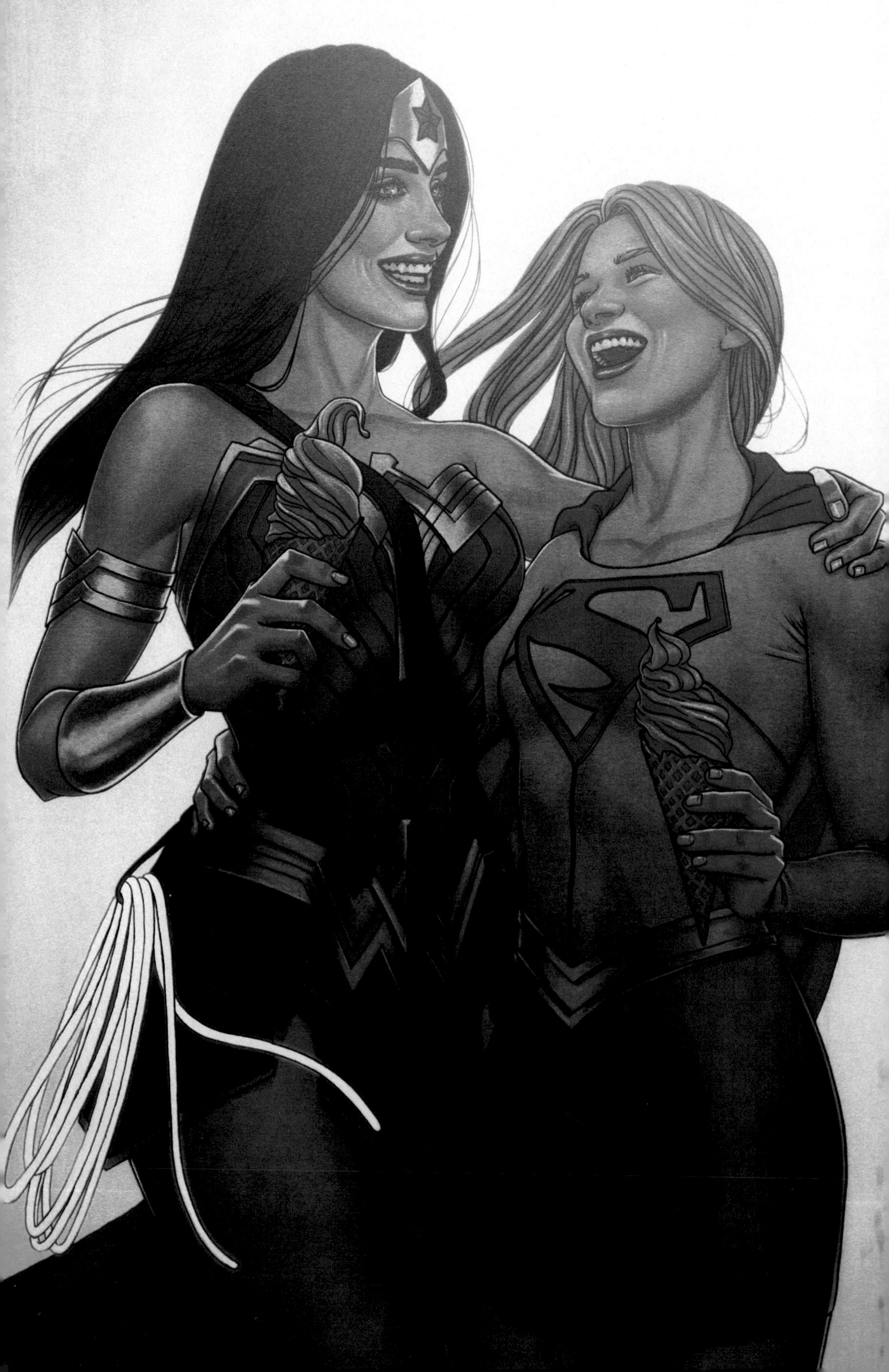

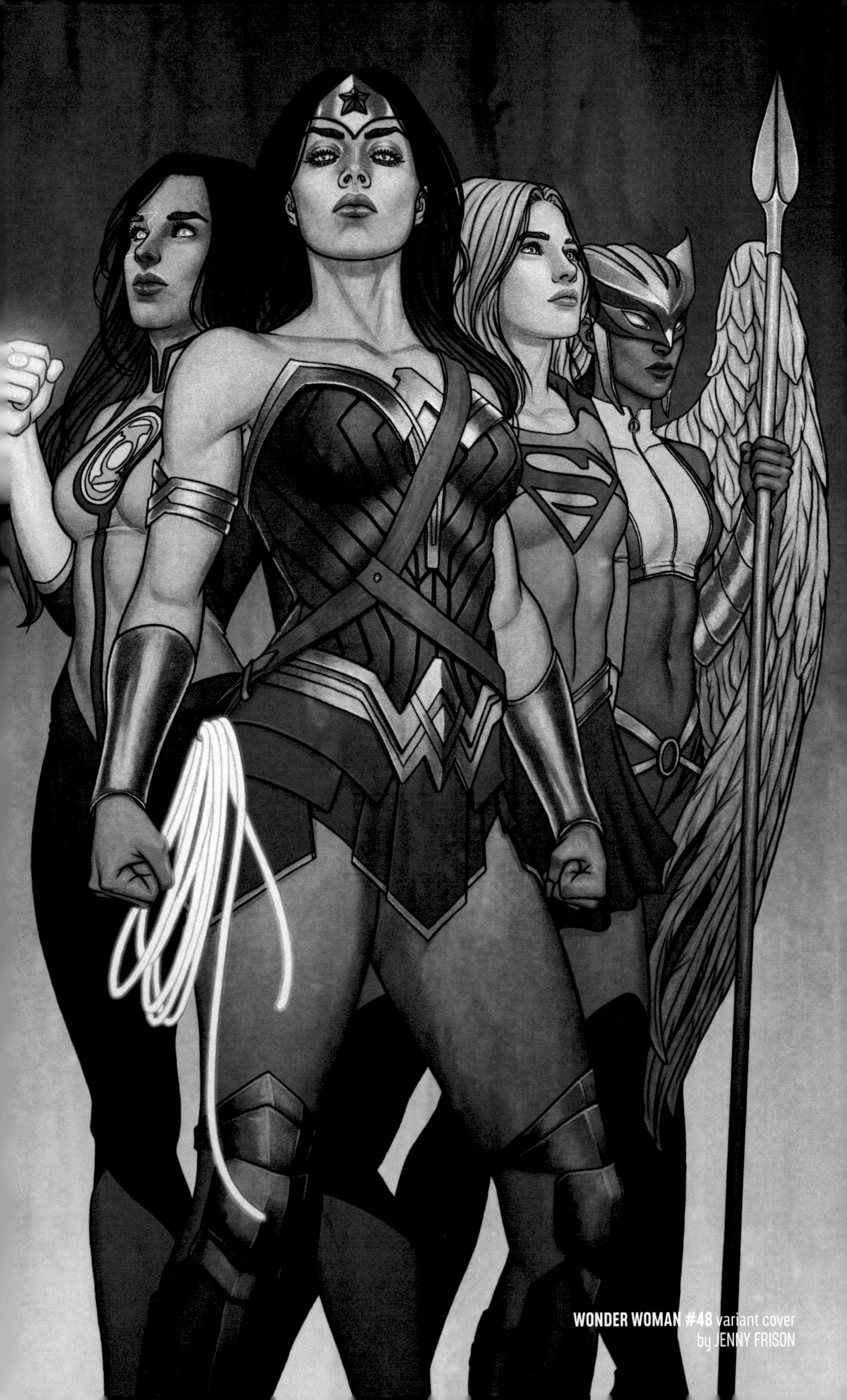

WONDER WOMAN #48 variant cover
by JENNY FRISON

WONDER WOMAN #49 variant cover
by JENNY FRISON

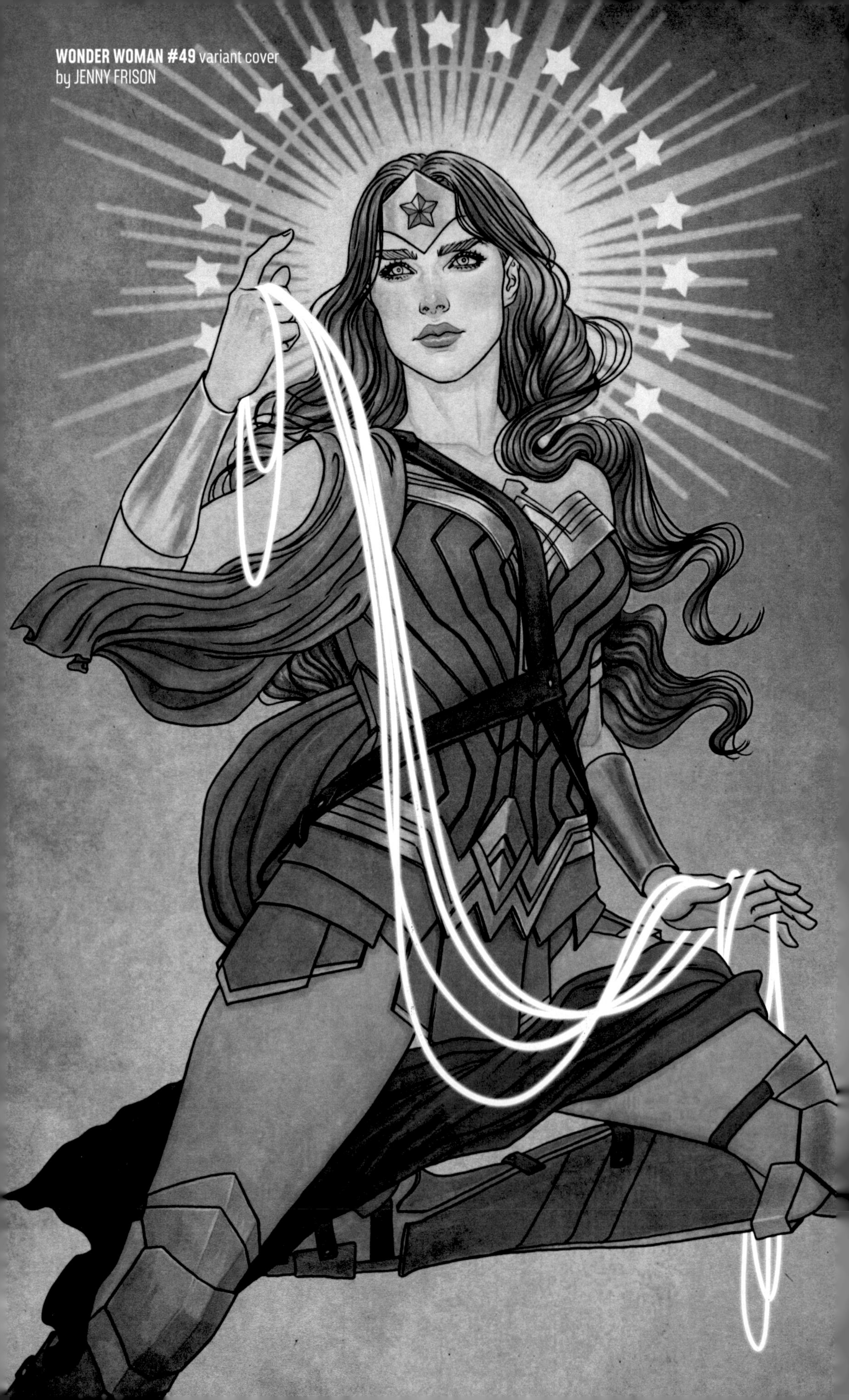

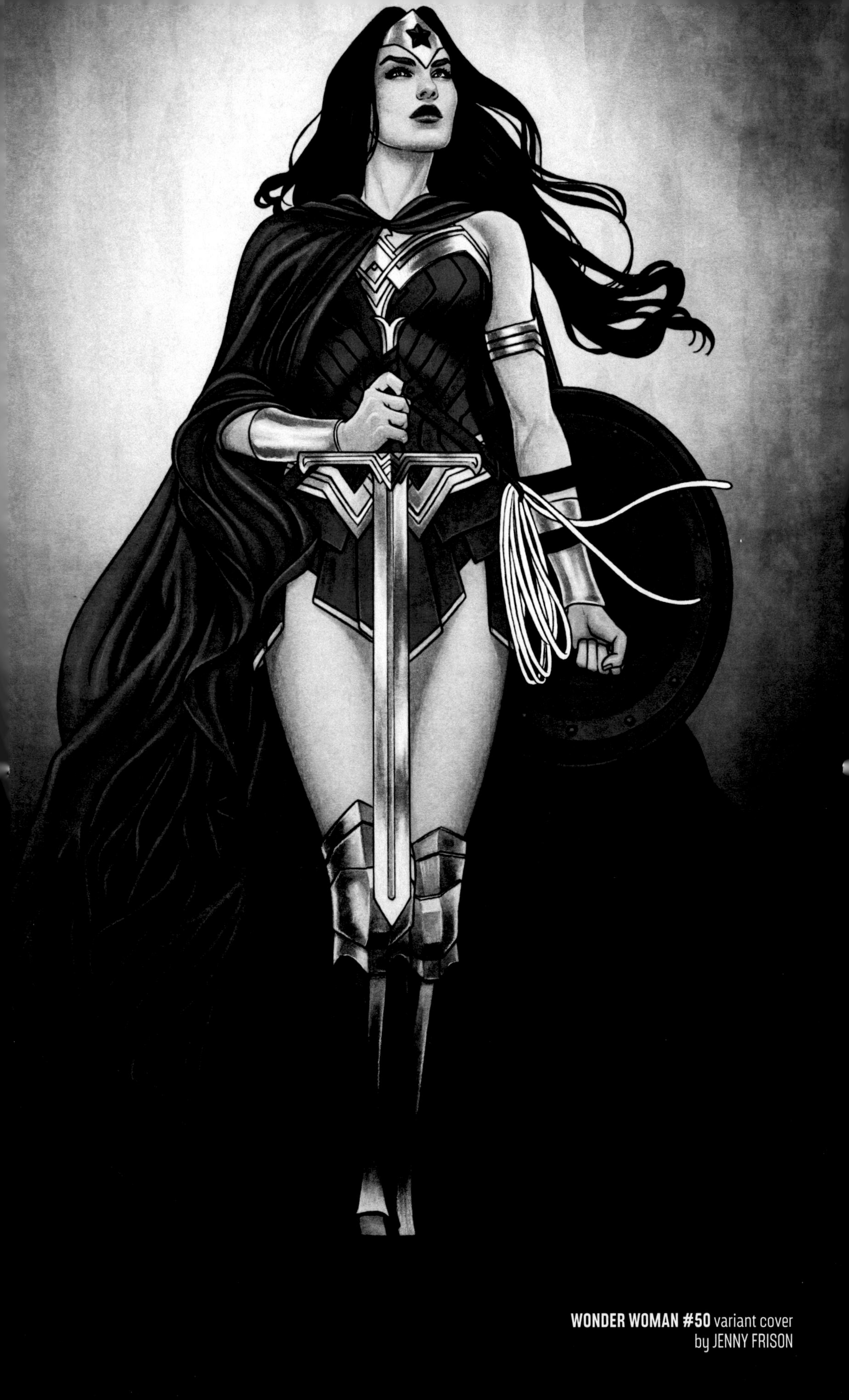

WONDER WOMAN #50 variant cover
by JENNY FRISON

"Greg Rucka and company have created a compelling narrative for fans of the Amazing Amazon."– **NERDIST**

"(A) heartfelt and genuine take on Diana's origin."– **NEWSARAMA**

DC UNIVERSE REBIRTH

WONDER WOMAN

VOL. 1: THE LIES
GREG RUCKA
with LIAM SHARP

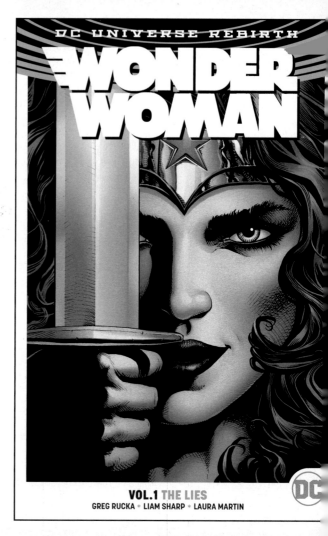

VOL.1 THE LIES
GREG RUCKA • LIAM SHARP • LAURA MARTIN

JUSTICE LEAGUE VOL. 1: THE EXTINCTION MACHINES

SUPERGIRL VOL. 1: REIGN OF THE SUPERMEN

BATGIRL VOL. 1: BEYOND BURNSIDE